FEDERALISM
IN
AFRICA

FEDERALISM IN AFRICA

Volume I:

FRAMING THE NATIONAL QUESTION

AARON T. GANA AND SAMUEL G. EGWU
(EDITORS)

A PUBLICATION OF
THE AFRICAN CENTRE FOR DEMOCRATIC GOVERNANCE

Africa World Press, Inc.

P.O. Box 1892
Trenton, NJ 08607

P.O. Box 48
Asmara, ERITREA

Africa World Press, Inc.

P.O. Box 1892
Trenton, NJ 08607

P.O. Box 48
Asmara, ERITREA

Book Design: 'Damola Ifaturoti
Cover Design: Ashraful Haque

Library of Congress Cataloging-in-Publication Data

Federalism in Africa / edited by Aaron T. Gana and Samuel G. Egwu.
p. cm
Includes bibliographical references and index.
ISBN 0-86543-977-X (v. 1) -- ISBN 0-86543-978-8 (v. 1 : pbk.)
1. Federal government--Nigeria. 2. Federal government--Africa. 3. Federal government--Case studies. 4. Comparative government. I. Gana, Aaron Tsado. II. Egwu, Samuel G.

JQ3086.S8 F48 2002
320.4669'049--dc21

2002151485

CONTENTS

Section IV: Federalism in Comparative Perspective

DEDICATION

This book is dedicated to the Memory of Professor Bade Onimode, late Professor of Economics and Deputy Vice-Chancellor University of Ibadan, Nigeria and Professor Neelan Tiruchelvam, late Director of the International Centre for Ethnic Studies, Colombo, Sri Lanka, both contributors to this two-volume series and scholar-activists who died in the cause of federalism and democracy in their troubled lands.

ABBREVIATIONS

AG	Action Group
Afrigov	African Centre for Democratic Governance
EPLF	Ethiopian Peoples Liberation Front
EPRDF	Eritrean Peoples Revolutionary Defence Force
GNPP	Great Nigerian People's Party
INEC	Independent National Electoral Commission
JACON	Joint Action Committee on Nigeria
NCF	National Consultative Forum
NCNC	National Council of Nigerian Citizens (originally of Nigeria and Cameroons)
NEC	National Electoral Commission
NEF	Northern Elders Forum
NEPU	Northern Elements Progressive Union
NGF	Nigerian Guild of Editors
NNDC	Northern Nigeria Development Company
NNPC	Nigerian National Petroleum Company
NPC	Northern Peoples' Congress
NPC	Nigerian Press Council
NPN	National Party of Nigeria
NPP	Nigerian Peoples' Party
NRB	Newspaper Registration Board
NTA	Nigerian Television Authority
NYSC	National Youth Service Corps
SPLA	Sudan Peoples' Liberation Army
SPLM	Sudan Peoples' Liberation Movement
UMBC	United Middle Belt Congress
UNO/UN	United Nations Organization
UNESCO	United nations Educational Scientific and Cultural Organization
UPN	Unity Party of Nigeria

ACKNOWLEDGMENTS

The idea of this book came in a flash in the serene environment of the Center for International Affairs, Harvard University whose vibrant intellectual atmosphere inspired the project during a seminar organized by the then Chair of African Studies Committee, late Professor Leroi Vail in March 1994. His insistence that 'tribalism' (read 'ethnicity') was the creation of European imperialism in Africa which was the theme of his own scholarship on Africa, generated heated debates amongst Africanists at Harvard, from which the project was incubated. The opportunity for such interaction was provided by the Rockefeller Foundation's Reflections Program managed by its Nairobi Office, under Dr. David Court, and the Council for the Development of Social Science Research in Africa (CODESRIA). David Court's interjections during the presentation of the final reports in Nairobi in September 1994, propelled a further 'reflection' on the ethnic question and the political framework for addressing it in Africa. This was made possible by another grant by the New York Office of the Rockefeller Foundation which facilitated a one month stay at their Bellagio Centre to refine the report. It was from this that the proposal for a conference on *Federalism and the National Question in Africa* emerged, following a discussion with Professor Julius Ihonvbere, the ebullient scholar-activist in charge of Ford Foundation's Governance Program and whose deep commitment to the resolution of the ethnic question in Africa assured us of the Foundation's support. To these lovers of Africa we express our profound appreciation.

Wole Soyinka, Africa's irrepressible member of the global club of literary genius bent over backwards to honor our invitation to deliver the keynote address at the conference. He did make the day for the organizers, judging from the caliber of participants at the conference and the quality of the debate throughout the conference, which caught the attention of many, not the least the Nobel Laureate himself. To him we express our gratitude. Without the papers we would have had a dull conference, if we had the conference at all. And so our gratitude goes to all who not only responded to our invitation but presented thoroughly researched papers, evidenced by the fact that most of them passed through the peer review process, forcing the publisher to issue the book in two volumes. To the authors and the anonymous reviewers we express appreciation. We would not reach this final stage of getting the manuscript roll off the press but for the indefatigable commitment of three Secretaries who worked under extreme pressure to produce the manuscript: Bimbo Daramola, Femi Owolabi, and Imoh Orok.

But all efforts recorded above would have come to naught but for two critical components of this long list: our wives—Mrs. Joanah E. Gana and Mrs. Egwu, who bore the burden of lonely nights often with apprehension and feelings of neglect—and the Almighty God, who in His mercy gave us not only the intellect but the health and the loving wives that stood by us in all the travails of translating conference papers into an edited book. To God Almighty, and to our wives we will remain eternally grateful. All of us—the human components—share both the strengths and weaknesses of the product of this collective labor.

Aaron T. Gana and Samuel G. Egwu
September 2002

FOREWORD

Federalism in Africa Volume I: Framing the National Question has attempted to bring together in one volume, and from a multidisciplinary focus, serious and refreshing reflections on one of the most pressing and fundamentally enduring public policy problems in Africa. This problem, which has acquired even more critical dimension and compelling relevance with the end of the Cold War, the emergence of *Neo-Liberalism* as the new global ideological hegemony, the current democratic transitions in Africa and the turn of the New Millennium, pertains to the appropriate political arrangement for resolving or containing what is generally referred to as the *national question*.

By this is meant welding the various ethno-religious and other social groups in the African state, under a form of constitutional government, character-ized by the rule of law and by participatory democratic politics which in practice recognizes and accommodates not only the civil and political rights but also the cultural, economic and social rights of the various nationality or ethnic groups.

To say this is to locate the importance, indeed intellectual significance of *Federalism and the National Question in Africa* within historiographical and para-digmatic shifts in the last thirty years in the comparative study of political systems and social change and of their underlying philosophical assumptions.

These intellectual shifts which, in the case of comparative politics, have seen alternation between what David Apter recently described as *institutional-ism, developmentalism and neo-institutionalism,* brought renewed interest in the en-during *ethno-cultural pluralism or diversity* of the modern state and in the prob-lem this particular form of pluralism or diversity, as opposed to, say, *social pluralism* or *diversity* poses, for the interrelated questions of *nationality and citi-zenship*.

To take one aspect of the larger problem of the national question: what has become clear, as a result, is the fact that ethnicity, as a manipulatable and mobilizational resource in competitive politics and ethnic politics, is as problematic for the developed, mainly European world as it is for the developing, largely non-European world.

At the heart of these shifts and the analyses they have engendered is *the question of the character and role of the state, as the central contested terrain in economic, political and socio-cultural processes and exchanges.* In other words, more important in understanding these shifts is the fact that they reflect, and attempt to grapple at the level of theoretical and empirical analyses with the reality that the state has become or has always been, as a result of manipulation by the hegemonic (class, religious, ethno-cultural, occupational, etc) groups in society, an important protagonist in, and the central locus of, communal and other forms of socioeconomic and political conflicts.

It is within this broader canvass that *Federalism and the National Question in Africa* must be read. If the political salience of ethnicity or more generally of the national question is not unique to Africa, then what are its *specificities* in the African context? What is it about the political economy of Africa that has contributed to *the national question* being so much of a dysfunctional and disequilibrating force on the continent?

What combinations of exogenous and endogenous forces and of idiosyncratic factors account for this state of affairs in Africa? Need ethnicity or the national question be so disruptive and negative in its impact on the nation-building processes in Africa? What does the experience elsewhere tell us? For example, is there some kind of relationship between the national question or ethnicity and forms of government? If so, is there any theoretical and/or empirico-historical reason for assuming that a federal solution is more preferable or better than any other solution (e.g. unitary or confederal ones) to contain the centrifugal pull of ethnicity in the multi-national or multi-ethnic state?

The on-going democratic transitions in Africa provide a fascinating opportunity for African intellectuals and policymakers to revisit the inherent contradictions *between liberalism and socialism on the one hand, and the national question and other group identities on the other hand.*

The liberal emphasis on individual rights and its underlying, if tacit, denial of *group* rights has been at the heart of political conflict generated by the failure of the liberal state to respond imaginatively and proactively to demands by marginalized groups, such as ethnic minorities, women, students and workers, among other groups, for inclusion, for broadened political participation and access to the state.

The *centralizing or totalizing* imperatives of the socialist state, on the other hand, have had much the same effect in precipitating and aggravating the national or ethnic question, as the demise of the commandist state in the former Soviet Union and Eastern Europe so graphically demonstrated.

The institutionalized monopoly of access to the state by hegemonic or dominant ethno-cultural groups, creating in effect a virtual situation of internal colonialism, has raised in Africa but no less so in other multi-ethnic parts of the world the strategic policy issue of the permissible level and scope of ethno-cultural and other diversities and how best to design institutions and structures to recognize or to accommodate the diversities and, simultaneously, to reconcile them with national unity, national identity and the imperative of loyalty to the state. Neither the cohesion of the liberal or socialist state nor the loyalty of marginalized groups to the liberal or socialist state can or should be taken for granted.

The new post-Cold War global context has further eroded the sovereignty on which the state has always rested, fuelling international interests in the collective rights of ethnic and other communal groups and subjecting national policies in this area to international searchlight and accountability to supranational institutions and an emergent international law in this and related areas.

Federalism in Africa: Framing the National Question, in addressing these problematic issues, offers rich, stimulating and empirically grounded theoretical and comparative historical perspectives on the relationship between state formation or the nation-building process and the multi-ethnic or multi-national state in Africa. Drawing on data from Africa (Democratic Republic of the Congo, Ethiopia, Nigeria, South Africa and the Sudan), Brazil, Canada, India, Sri Lanka and Yugoslavia, the various contributions examine a complex range of topical policy and constitutional issues which are divided into eight useful and well-organized sections. The result is a veritable vein of knowledge, which both the scholar and the policymaker should be able to mine profitably.

What *Federalism in Africa: Framing the National Question* has done, extremely well, in my view, is to bring on the policy agenda the relevance of the federal solution to the national question in Africa. This is indeed timeous, given the opportunity provided by what has been described as the third wave of African independence to reconstitute the multi-national African state on a constitutional basis that guarantees and entrenches ethnic or nationality rights by granting such groups limited autonomy or home-rule.

The demise of the African one-party state, with its centralizing ideology, has shown that the *national question or ethno-cultural pluralism* cannot be wished away but must be positively accommodated through some form of *power-sharing or consociational* institutional arrangements. The African dislike for the federal solution, a relic of the African nationalist disdain for the colonial policy of divide and rule and opposition to the colonialist attempt to impose it in Central and Southern Africa, among other parts of the continent, remains a powerful obstacle which has to be assuaged by showing that there is no *pure* or *true* form of federalism; that what exists is a *federal spectrum, along which there are variations, characterized by some devolution of power.*

The African Centre for Democratic Governance must be congratulated for bringing together leading scholars in the humanities and the social sciences to discuss a critical policy issue which confronts Africa and scholars with an abiding interest in peace and development in Africa, as we enter the new millennium and seek to resolve the enduring challenge of nation-building, of finding solutions to the ageless oxymoronic problem of *unity in diversity or diversity in unity.*

L. Adele Jinadu
Vice-President
International Political Science Association (IPSA)

The Crisis of the Nation-State in Africa and the Challenge of Federalism

Aaron T. Gana and Samuel G. Egwu

The collapse of the nation-state project in many African countries in the 1980s and the 1990s has been a recurring theme in the massive return of "Afro-pessimism." Where actual state collapse has not occurred as in Nigeria or Kenya, the enthusiasm to build new nations initially ignited in the wake of the anti-colonial movement considerably waned. For a number of reasons, nation-building amounted to a high political stake. To begin with, the desire to attain nationhood in which the various socio-cultural aggregates transfer their primordial loyalties to the ecumenical level of the state was a major goal that undergirded the anti-colonial movement. The quest for development, democracy and justice against the background of the negation represented by colonialism were the other components. All these were united in the quest for modernization.

The experience of Africa and the African people in the quest for the two most stressful, and elusive goals—nation-building and development—has received adequate attention in the literature. Although the degree of ethno-cultural pluralism vary from one country to another, the 'transition to neo-colonial dependence', to some extent, appeared to have accepted, as an article of faith, the commitment to liberal democracy and the expression of pluralism. Hence, open and competitive elections in most cases based on multiparty system flowered at the early post-independence period, providing initial hopes, as in the case of Nigeria, that democratic form of politics may survive and take a firm root.

However, this was not to be. The reification of the ideology of development (Gana, 1987) and the preoccupation of state elite with survival precipitated the erosion of the political landscape. The consequence of this in most African states was the abandonment of the 'social contract' that in the first place made the attainment of sovereignty realizable. Thus, the beginning of the crisis of the African state was laid: the emergence of one-party rule, personalized rule, life presidents and military dictators, with over-arching powers. These trends were well entrenched in many African states, supported by multi-lateral financial and development agencies, and justified in the name of development (Ake, 1978:66).

One tendency is to explain the crisis in terms of the problem of diversity. Attributing the incidence of state collapse in the African continent to problems related to the management of diversity and the plurality of competing ethnic identities without factoring in the more enduring issues of the African political economy will be an unproductive enterprise. It must take into account the neo-colonial economies anchored on narrow frameworks of accumulation: heavy foreign domination, absence of a coherent and well-conceived industrialization strategies, and the export of agricultural crops and extracted minerals. State collapse was also a result of a combination of several other factors which include the absence of popular participation and the exclusion of opposition and minority groups from the process of governance, the waning legitimacy of the state in the face of growing incapacity to provide social needs, and the accompanying bureaucratic inefficiency.

All these ripples of what Rene Dumont (1969) has described as the "false start" in Africa came to a head coinciding with the dramatic collapse of "actually existing socialisms" and the "command economies" of the former Soviet Union and Eastern Europe. The crisis of socialist development resulting from the internal contradictions of the system and the ascendancy of the forces of globalization as well as the triumph of the free market ideology led to a detour in policies in the economic and political spheres with devastating effects on the African continent. Among others, it led to the discrediting of the state-led approach to capitalist modernization and the very notion of the developmental state. But even more crucial, it delegitimized the claims of the African ruling elite who, hiding behind the stone wall of ideology of development eroded the democratic culture and indulged in gross human rights abuses. The Africanist critique of the post-colonial state, though largely overstated, draw attention to these problems.

Nevertheless, the inability to develop appropriate political frameworks and arrangements for the management of ethnic, regional and religious diversities led to political tensions and contradictions, which undermined the nation-state project. The evidence across the continent provides indications regarding the debilitating impact of the exploitation of these diversities by political elites and ethnic entrepreneurs whose interests are defined in opposition to the nation-state project. Liberia and Somalia demonstrate the human tragedy that accompanies state collapse and the disintegration of central authorities. Similarly, the redrawing of the political map of Ethiopia with the emergence of Eritrea as a sovereign state after decades of fratricidal war sent out a very strong signal that there may be nothing sacrosanct after all, about the artificial boundaries of the new states drawn in Berlin unless some creative form of political architecture as well as statecraft are brought to bear on the process of governance. This is precisely the sense in which federal political arrangements provide credible alternatives to African countries that share elements of deeply divided societies.

Nigeria for now stands as the only country where the idea of a federal polity has been adopted in the management of ethnic, regional and religious diversities. Despite the strains and stresses which Nigeria's federal experiment has undergone, especially since decades of military rule eroded the constitutional basis of federalism, the consensus among the political elites, both civilian and military, on the relevance of the federal principle, has secured the corporate survival of Nigeria. Although the explanation partly derives from the inherently pluralistic character of the Nigerian state, the deliberate choice of a federalist ideology reflected in the country's constitutional development accounts for the survival of the Nigerian polity, despite repeated threats of disintegration as in the civil war between 1967 and 1970, and the return to hard regionalist feelings and positions in the dark years of the Abacha military junta.

This isolated experience does provide a strong basis for the increasing appeal of federalism as a mechanism for dealing with the problem of pluralism and territorially distributed differences. For, in addition to the tragic experiences of Liberia, Somalia, Ethiopia and the intractable civil war in the Sudan over the question of distribution of power between the north and the south, the possibility of adopting a federal approach as a solution to the problem of diversity in South Africa was raised in the political debates on the post-apartheid era. The contributions in this book try to examine the manifold dimensions of the nation-state project in Africa, and explore the relevance of federalism to very obvious cases, or the need for adjustments in the practice of federalism in cases such as Nigeria where at least, federal practice exists nominally.

Four questions should be identified from the onset. What can scholars and political actors pre-occupied with governance and the management of diversity in contemporary African states learn from the plethora of writings on the origins, evolution and the historical, economic and political contexts of the emergence of federations? What practical lessons can be deciphered from the experiences of older and 'mature' federations such as those of the United States of America, Canada, Australia and Switzerland? What are the specific expressions of diversity that proved somehow insurmountable and intractable to the few examples of federal experiments in Africa, especially that of Nigeria that require adjustment? What is the potential of federalism for countries which in general terms can be said to possess "federal qualities"?

Attempts to provide answers to these questions will not be made here. Nevertheless, it is useful to give indications as to how attempts have been made to meet the tasks set forth by these set of questions. For instance, it requires drawing heavily from the diverse contributions in the field of comparative federalism, both in terms of the theories of federalism and comparative experience. It is even more so desirable that we return to the theoretical and philosophical underpinnings of federalism considering that the crisis of the nation-state project in the African continent is occurring in the twilight of the forces unleashed by the processes of globalization, market reforms and democratization. These forces are not restricted to the 'rational' elements of the market, but also the 'irrational' expressions of primordial identities and cleavages, which have to be accommodated through constitutional designs in the forms of democracy, federalism and consociational measures.

The universalities and complexities of ethnic, religious and other forms of territorial diversities have been re-emphasized in a number of contributions that draw from theoretical and comparative research on federalism. Aaron Gana (chapter 2) draws attention to the limits and possibilities of the national question in the framing of a federal polity, while Bishnu Mohapatra (chapter 20) deals with how the desire to institutionalize democratic governance in India's diverse setting has structured the country's federal arrangement. Where centralization of power undermines desire for group autonomy as in the case of the Tamils in Sri Lanka, Tiruchevlam Neelan (chapter 14) points to the tendency to accentuate secessionist demands by disaffected ethnic and sub-national groups.

The reflections of Wole Soyinka (volume I: chapter 1) which is based on the Nigerian and other African experiences demonstrate in bold relief, the danger of over-centralization of power, which ignores the desire of subgroups for relative autonomy. In dealing with the management of diversity through the federalist principle, Soyinka sees the matter beyond the problem of ideology; rather, it is a choice between centralization on the one hand, and a structured dispersal of both social and economic power bases on the other, so as to guarantee both productive initiatives at all levels as well as a sense of participation in the very decisions that affect daily life. The problem of centralization, described as "Nigerian version and parody of sovietized economy military-collectivism" allows for resources to flow only in the direction of the center. The violence in the Niger Delta over resource control and the creation of economically unviable states are evident of the "cracked model" represented by Nigeria's federal arrangement.

Leo Dare (volume I: chapter 5) uses the Canadian example to show how over time, the practice of federalism has provided a solution to the problem of centralization of power which is at the core of the political crisis in most federations. He suggests that 'deconcentration' has been used to manage rather than resolve conflicts by striking a balance between various components. His conclusion which amounts to a critique of the Nigerian experience is that, federalism and constitutional change are processes that grow and evolve, ensuring that changing solutions are found for changing problems.

While there is little disagreement concerning the reality of territorial diversities in the framing of a federal polity, Aaron Gana (volume I: chapter 2) interrogates the very nature of ethnic demands, which are problematized in the form of the national question. He demonstrates with the Nigerian example that ethnicity is not just a natural expression of ethnic diversity, but a deliberate construction by the political elites which has historical basis in capitalist modernization. The post-colonial elites, building on the colonial legacy, have been the driving force behind the political expressions of ethnic demands that have been the source of strains and stresses in Nigeria's federal experiment. Jibrin Ibrahim's contribution (volume I: chapter 6) which tries to draw lessons for Nigeria in terms of ethno-religious limits to the construction of federalism in the former Yugoslavia, emphasize the inability of the elite to accede to power sharing, and when they do so, emphasize ethnic and religious differences.

At the core of the problematic of comparative studies on federalism is the issue of revenue allocation and the formal division of fiscal powers between the various levels and layers of government. The controversy generated by both vertical and horizontal revenue allocation is not limited to emergent federations; 'mature' federal polities such as the United States, Canada and Switzerland have continued to face challenges with the task of assigning fiscal powers and sources of revenue for various levels of government in ways that enhance their capacity to fulfill their constitutional expectations. In no other federation is the thorny nature of fiscal federalism dramatized as in Nigeria. The resurgence of ethnic nationalism among the oil producing communities in the Niger Delta and the clamor for resource control provides one strong evidence of the furore generated by the politics of revenue allocation. Expectedly, the manifold dimensions of the economics of federalism has received considerable attention in the contributions of Bade Onimode (volume I: chapter 8), Adebayo Olukoshi (volume I: chapter 7) and Olutade Okediji (volume I: chapter 9).

Onimode for example, deals with the problem of Nigeria's fiscal federalism against the background of what he describes as "fiscal unitarism". Military incursion into politics in 1966 is identified as the key factor in the demise of constitutional federalism and the abandonment of the principle of derivation in favor of "federal character", ethnicity and related criteria. Against this highly centrist background, the increasing demand for democracy, human rights, community autonomy and greater space for political pluralism ought to force a return to derivation. Onimode's account of how the unified command structure of the military was brought to bear on all aspects of governance, including the centralization of fiscal relations is complimented by Ekeng Anam-Ndu (volume I: chapter 3).

However, Olukoshi (volume I: chapter 7) and Okediji (volume I: chapter 9) deal with the more general economic issues and nuances in ways that are mutually reinforcing. Olukoshi for example, challenges the inherent neo-liberal assumption that political liberalization is a prerequisite for the establishment of a free market without recognizing the top-heavy centralizing logic of a kleptomaniac neo-colonial state. His point seems to be that beyond the ideology of market-driven accumulation, there is urgent need to redress problems of regional inequalities as well as promoting decentralization and devolution of decision-making for socio-cultural and administrative autonomy. Without this, addressing the problem of class inequality may not be as meaningful. Okediji's comparative analysis of economic development between Brazil and Nigeria in the context of federal arrangement concludes that despite the commonality of problems of ethnic and cultural diversity to the two countries, the former has done better in terms of economic development. What is instructive about this contribution is the demonstration that non-economic (or non-quantifiable) variables such as ethnicity, religion and culture are susceptible to positive response to an economic development policy rooted in a visionary and purposeful leadership.

Some contributions take us beyond the traditional pre-occupation with federalism either as a mechanism for coping with the problem of territorial distribution of power and constitutional factors such as separation of powers (especially between the center and the constituent units) and the role of an independent judiciary, which we find in Leo Dare (volume I: chapter 5), Ekang Anam-Ndu (volume I: chapter 3), and Onje Gye-Wado (volume II: chapter 4). Bishnu Mohapatra (volume II: chapter 6), while not discounting these factors with respect to the Indian experience, draws attention to other factors. One of these is the romanticism and statecraft of Nehru, the Indian nationalist, whose desire for "a nation of multiplicity of nations" provided some kind of ideological consensus on which successive leaders built. This perhaps, explains, despite periodic tensions, the ability of the Indian nation to exist and look into the future with over 2,000 linguistic groups, 15 major religions, 20,000 castes, and 2,800 ethnic communities.

Yet, two additional issues raised in this volume take the debates on federalism beyond orthodox concerns. One re-emphasizes the relevance of Arendt Lijphart's original contribution about the need to build into formal constitutional designs of federalism and democracy consociational measures that take into account the notions of grand coalition, the principle of proportionality and some degree of autonomy (Lijphart, 1969, 1977). Two contributions on India (volume II: chapter 6 and volume I: chapter 13) by Bishnu Mohapatra and R. Jain respectively, draw attention to the need to undertake constitutional reforms to promote the protection of rights of ethnic, linguistic and cultural minorities through establishment of special commissions with mechanisms to ensure accountability. The import of this stems from the prospects of bringing marginalized groups into the mainstream of the nation's socio-economic and political life. Pita Agbese (volume II: chapter 12) raises the prospect of using some of these measures to deal with die increasingly volatile minority question in Nigeria's context.

The other dimension, even more crucial, interrogates the obsession of classical discourses on federalism, which narrows the scope of diversity to territorially and spatially distributed differences. Both Charmaine Parreira (volume II: chapter 14) and Pat Williams (volume II: chapter 13) represent original contributions in their strident call for 'engendering' our conception of federalism. The point they make, which set their contributions apart, is not to dismiss the relevance or concern for promoting equality or proportionality, or to whittle down spatial dimension of differences, but to factor in disadvantaged social groups, especially women into the policy-making process. Both, but Parreira with more vigor, trace the marginalization of women to factors such as ethno-religious chauvinism, widespread conflict and most importantly, prolonged military rule whose over-centralization ensured the complete patriachalization of governance. The dilemma of women in Nigeria who are involved in marriages across state boundaries bring out in bold relief the way in which 'territoriality' pits states against citizens in a way that is fundamentally gendered. This issue, which is already the focus of feminist struggles in Nigeria, is cross-cutting as it re-echoes in Samuel Egwu's discussion on citizen's rights in federal states (chapter 16).

Closely related to this is the way citizens' rights have been defined in relation to claims based on "indigeneity" in many African countries, and the tendency for this to be used as the basis of exclusion of people from participating in the social and political life of their communities. Whereas in most countries, especially those with federal political arrangements, residency is the basis for defining access to citizenship rights, the situation in most African countries differ because the notion of "indigeneship" which is defined in biological terms, creates obstacles to the realization of such rights for those who are not "indigenes". The political crisis in Zambia following attempts by the ruling party to exclude the former President, Kenneth Kaunda, and in Cote d' Ivoire, as a response to attempts to exclude the former Prime Minister, Allassane Quattarra on the ground that they are not citizens may be slightly different, but they bring to the fore the deep-seated nature of the problem of citizenship in Africa.

Mahmood Mamdani (volume II: chapter 1) discusses the crisis of citizenship in the Kivu region of the Democratic Republic of Congo, which is at the vortex of the recent tension, and instability in the country. While he discusses the problem in terms of the partial and incomplete reform of the colonial state at independence, the point that the root is in the bifurcated nature of the colonial state which made a distinction between urban and rural governance regimes return us to the important issue of how colonialism framed the national question in contemporary Africa. The Nigerian situation discussed by Samuel Egwu (volume II: chapter 2) appears to be worse because of the frequent re-drawing of internal administrative boundaries as a result of persistent demand for new states. Since demand for new states are fueled by ethnic-related pressures in the first place, people who reside in states other than the ones in which they can authenticate their status as "indigenes" suffer exclusion and all kinds of deprivations.

The various forms of distortions imposed on the practice of federalism appear to be a key cross-cutting issue in virtually all the contributions in this book. This should not be surprising given the consensus that is being built across civil society, the political class and even some elements within the military itself that the Nigerian military poses a fundamental challenge to the survival of constitutional democracy. Beyond staying in power for much of the post-independence period, the pervasive impact of its rule is manifested in the militarization of society and civic consciousness, the centralization of power and resources, and the erosion of the constitutional basis of Nigeria's federalism, Ekeng Anam-Ndu (volume I: chapter 3) and Bade Onimode (volume I: chapter 8), for example. Oyesina Alli (volume I: chapter 4) shows in a graphic manner the consequence of military rule for the progressive weakening of the constitutional framework of Nigeria's federalism which historically evolved from a unitarist structure in the pre-second world war period to a highly decentralized and regionalized structure between 1954 and 1966 prior to the implosion of the military into political governance. The negative impact on the local government comes out clearly in Alex Gboyega's contribution in volume II: chapter 3.

However, two contributions on the military are quite specific on drawing our attention to the immediate task of strengthening democratic governance and constitutional rule. Kayode Fayemi (volume II: chapter 7) raises the problem of entrenched military interests considering the pervasive influence peddled by the military oligarchs who are increasingly translating their economic power into political influence.

The control of other security apparatuses such as the police is yet another matter of controversy, heightened by the strong desire expressed by some sections to establish a state police. For anyone familiar with the history of police performance in Nigeria, especially in the second Republic when the force became an instrument of political repression and control by the ruling party at the center, National Party of Nigeria (NPN), the clamor for a regional or state police force, is not misplaced. Etannibi Alemika (volume II: chapter 8) takes up the issue of managing the police in Nigeria's federal system against the background of public disaffection with police performance since independence. Despite the attraction for a state police, he draws attention to the danger of abuse when control is localized, as was the experience with the Native Authority police in the erstwhile Northern Nigeria. What needs to be done is to strengthen existing mechanisms of control, which, as provided for in the 1999 Constitution, as in those of 1960 and 1963, assigns the responsibility to a Police Council on which state governors are represented.

One dynamic aspect of federal polities has to do with inter-governmental relations, especially the way in which the relationship between the federal government and the constituent units are subject to frequent reconstitution. This relationship is never fixed or static, nor can it be determined *a priori*. What determines the form and the content of the relationship is the ever changing contexts of power and resources. The only contribution that focuses on this dimension is Alex Gboyega (volume II: chapter 3) which takes up the issue of the historical evolution of the local government system in Nigeria. Equally since the 1976 reforms the local government system, christened as "grassroots" administration has become an autonomous tier of administration with clearly defined constitutional responsibilities. He shows that over the years the pendulum of control has swung between the federal government and the states with the former enjoying pre-eminence. The highest point of central control occurred under the military dictatorship of General Ibrahim Babangida when among others, the presidential system of government was introduced at the local level and local elections subject to the control of the national electoral body, the National Electoral Commission (NEC). What is suggested is that contestations for the control of this level of governance will remain a feature of Nigeria's federal experience.

The domain of foreign policy is often a domain of contestations and contradictory claims between the federal authority at the center on the one hand, and the constituent units on the other. Rafiu Akindele (chapter 19) provides useful insights to the conduct of foreign policy in Nigeria's federal system in the first and second Republics. He shows that the explicit provisions in the 1979 Constitution which defines foreign policy as the exclusive domain of the federal government attenuated considerably, the level of conflicts and contradictions that were witnessed in the first Republic between the federal government and the regional authorities.

Without doubt, federal political arrangement is not about the elimination of conflicts and differences; rather, it is about the creative management of such conflicts and differences. This comes out in the numerous contributions ranging from the experiences of "older" federations and the emergent ones, especially the Nigerian case. It is however, the Nigerian experience, which until recently and for all practical purposes, has been the only federal experiment on the African continent that is paradigmatic of the African crisis. The relevance of the Nigerian example largely stems from the fact that the inherently plural and diverse nature of the social formation has always been recognized by both the military and civilian factions of the ruling class, despite the presence of centralizing trends. It is the logic of this pluralism that has enabled various groups to challenge authoritarian rule at different points, and to keep the hope of sustaining the territorial integrity of the country alive.

As noted earlier, despite the odds and challenges which federalism has encountered in Nigeria, it has been able to avoid fragmentation and total state collapse as witnessed in Liberia, Somalia and Sierra-Leone, or the complete re-drawing of the geo-political map, as in Ethiopia. This appears to provide a strong case in recommending the federal option to other countries in Africa such as the Democratic Republic of Congo, Kenya, Cote d' Ivoire, Zambia and South Africa to mention just a few examples. The recent Ethiopian constitution which begins by recognizing the rights and autonomy of the various ethnic nationalities discussed by Asnale Kefale (chapter 12) provides one recent example to explore the federal alternative in the management of diversity. Sudan at best represents a half-hearted attempt in the application of a federalist solution to the management of ethnic and religious differences as the analysis of Awad Al-Karsami (chapter 11) has shown.

It is against this background that Eghosa Osaghae's contribution (volume I: chapter 10)which explores the suitability of the federal logic to South Africa's fledgling democracy is instructive. His contention is that despite attempts to openly reject the attraction which federalism offers, it is an issue which re-echoes in the debates on post-apartheid South Africa. The strong "federal flavor" in South Africa derives largely from the fact that it is a deeply divided society, which requires through a federal arrangement, a mechanism to reduce the effects of division and inequality without sacrificing strong attachments to primary groups and identities.

A recurrent theme in the debate on democratization in Africa which may as well be the key to the sustenance of the current initiatives is the civil society. The role of the civil society, both potential and actual, in pushing democratic and constitutional reforms required for the promotion of diversity, inclusivity and legitimacy has not been ignored in the contributions in this book. In a discussion that challenges orthodox formulations on federalism, Abubakar Momoh (volume II: chapter 9) points to the ways in which the intervention of various civil society groups represent attempts to retrieve or redirect discourses away from the mainstream tendency which equate the demand for true federalism with re-dressing ethnic and regional grievances. The import of civil society's contribution, especially those involved in the struggle for human rights and democracy, is that the real issue to address is social, rather than ethnic justice.

In a more profound sense, Julius Ihonvbere (volume II: chapter 10) takes the issue to a much deeper level starting from the premise that the Nigerian state as presently constituted and the class character of the ruling cabal are the obstacles to the realization of democracy and true federalism. What stands out in this contribution to the Nigerian debate which has much relevance to other African states is that, civil society has a crucial role to play in the emergent trends which favor process-led (as opposed to state-led) constitutional reforms. This then provides the immediate agenda for civil society in reforming the 1999 Constitution which "is anything but federal". This contribution appears to set the agenda for civil society groups in initiating a process-led, people-oriented constitutional designs and reforms.

Above all these considerations and nuances, the construction of federal polities, if it is to meet the challenges of governance and the management of pluralism, must pay attention to the question of a federal culture, built on a spirit of dialogue, trade-off, negotiation and consensus-building. As Mohapatra's contribution (volume II: chapter 6) on India highlights, where this is lacking, the survival of the nation-state through a federal arrangement becomes an impossible enterprise. Despite the numerous disagreements and threats emanating from different religious, social and cultural groups, the Indian federation has weathered the storm through the enthronement of "federal discourse" which has become the basis of the country's 'dialogic' democracy. Nigeria and Africa, most certainly, can benefit from the Indian experience.

Certainly, the foregoing cannot be said to represent a detailed review of the numerous contributions to this volume, nor a satisfactory summary of the arguments put forward by the contributors. It is however, no matter how sketchy, an attempt to provide some insight into the trends, forces and factors that have, in post-colonial Africa, shaped the character of the nation – state project, the crises that have attended the construction of both political order and nation-hood, and how policy-makers, political actors and the civil society at large can best respond to the challenges set forth.

What seems to emerge as the consensus is the attraction, which the 'federal logic' appears to offer, in the management of political pluralism expressed in ethnic, religious, racial and spatial terms. While not ignoring the disruptive potentials represented by the political mobilization of these identities, accommodation rather than repression, inclusion rather than exclusion, recognition rather than denial and tolerance for and opposition to the demands put forward by these identities offer a more creative response to the crises of the nation-state in Africa. In other words, providing accommodation for such identities that have undergone tremendous explosion in the context of globalization through constitutional safeguards and measures may not be incompatible with the desire for large domestic markets which a federal pact guarantees as a part of the requirement for the competitiveness of domestic economies that is part and parcel of the challenges of globalization.

The numerous African nations that have experienced in varying forms, the stresses and pressures of competing ethnicities and irreconcilable religious differences among their populations do have opportunities in the options and choices which federalism and associated consociational measures offer. The Sudan, Cameroon and South Africa for example, may need to draw lessons from the experiences of 'older' federations such as the United States, Switzerland and Australia as well as the 'newer' federations such as India and the novel experiment begun under the new Ethiopian constitution. This however, should not ignore the different historical experiences, including the history of inter-group relations and the changes they have undergone over time in the options and choices they have to make.

In a similar manner, Nigeria will have to face the challenge of adjustment in her federal arrangement in order to meet the new and emergent challenges and opportunities. Interestingly, a key issue in the current debate regarding her political future has centered on the federal structure arising largely from the distortions imposed by decades of military dictatorships and the over centralization of power and resources. Indeed, for Nigeria and many other African countries, the creative deployment of federal principles is inevitable in the management of the peculiar challenges of ethnic-religious and cultural pluralism.

However, as useful and problem-solving as the federal solution may be, two crucial issues will determine how African nations will fare in the 21st century: restructuring of domestic economies and the challenge of democratization and the consolidation of democratic governance. This prognostication arises from the recognition that they impact, negatively or positively, on identity and the national question depending on how they are responded to. The fact remains, however, that federalism both as a principle and form of governance offers societies deeply divided by race, ethnicity and religion the more democratic route to the resolution of the national question.

ENDNOTES

1. Among the earliest works to bemoan the derailment of Africa's development are Walter Rodney's *How Europe Underdeveloped Africa,* (Dar es Salam, Tanzanian Publishing House, 1972); and Franz Fanon's *Wretched of the Earth* (New York, Grove Press).
2. Dumont's critique of agricultural policies in Africa at the time of his writing applies to virtually all spheres of public policy primarily because of the character of the neo-colonial state. (Rene Dumont, *False Start in Africa,* New York, Praeger, 1969).

REFERENCES

Ake, C. 1978. *Revolutionary Pressures in Africa* London: Zed Press Ltd.

Dumont, R. 1969. *False Start in Africa.* New York: Praeger.

Fanon, F. 1966. *The Wretched of the Earth.* New York: Grove Press.

Gana, A. T. 1987. "Development as Ideology" in Stephen Olugbemi, ed. *Alternative Political Futures for Nigeria.* Lagos: Nigerian Political Science Association.

Lijphant, A. 1977. *Democracy in Plural Societies.* New Haven: Yale University Press.

_____ 1969. "Constitutional Democracy in World Politics 21 pp. 207-225

Rodney, W. 1972. *How Europe Underdeveloped Africa.* London and Dar es Salaam: L'Ouverture Publications and Tanzanian Publishing House.

SECTION I:
THEORETICAL CONSIDERATIONS

CHAPTER ONE

The Federal Quest

Wole Soyinka

The most massively centralized government in the history of the world finally imploded during the last decade. It had been held together by the union of violence and remove the euphoria of its coming-in-being from the dead-end of a feudal order held together by great vision of universal brotherhood, by the solidarity that comes from a people under external threat, by war and its emotive patriotism and the binding machinery of mobilization, by crafted images of the internal ideal contrasted with the disorder and inhumanities of the external world, by the spell-binding rhetoric that was often short on logic but long on mass psychology, by a succession of powerful personality cults, by savage repression, intolerance of dissent, by vast population shifts, involuntary mass deportations that raptured organic, nationalist centers of resistance but reinforced the schematic tidiness of a centralized order, by the "us or them" paranoia of the cold war, but again let this be always conceded by a seductively utopian, transcendental vision that held some hopes for humanity, until its betrayal from within.

As some of these factors receded into the obscurity of time, losing their immediacy, significance, terror or romance for new generations in addition to gradual penetration of the once impregnable Iron Curtain by alternative social realities, the primacy of nationalities inserted itself into the vacated spaces of the ideological mortar of the supranational edifice. In short, that edifice began to crack, even from within.

Mind you, the signs were never completely absent. The "nationalities question" engaged the attention of Lenin, Engels, Trosky and Stalin in numerous essays and lectures, sometimes objective and analytical, often simply vitriolic and intolerant. Even Josef Stalin himself found it necessary, from time to time, to adopt policies that conceded measures of autonomy to nationalities, both in economic and in cultural policies. But the foundation of the super-state carried inherent weaknesses, and could not stand the aggressive onslaught of world capitalism. Nothing underscores for us the structural deficiencies of the centralized system of the Soviet Union more than the astonishing pace of collapse of its internal economy. Without a doubt, one contributory factor to that collapse was that of a productive system that simply did not allow for minimum level of productive and economic self-sufficiency among its member units. When the crunch came, a lack of productive and entrepreneurial initiative even at state level took its toll. Today, that vacuum appears to have been filled by nothing less than Mafia power, making the Soviet Union, within a short time, one of the most violent scenes of organized crime in the business world.

If we turn our faces inwards for a change of environment, that is, into Nigeria, we encounter disturbing parallels. Nigeria has not disintegrated, and certainly Nigeria has never even pretended to espouse any ideology capitalist, socialist or liberal welfarist. But, since the first coup of January 1966, that nation has attempted to make of centralized governance a "progressive" virtue. Never mind that it was principally this project—at least it has been thus prominently cited it was this unitarist project that produced the second military coup, provoked gruesome massacres of a section of the nation, resulted in the secession of a violated people and eventually a civil war. Despite this reality, regime after regime has gone after the unitary option like some millennial gospel of salvation. The result? A blatant sectarianism of power masquerading as national, complemented by a decency syndrome, and without even any accompanying centralized productive systems to complement, in the instance, the mono industry of petroleum. Initiative became either comatose or frustrated; government became the sole business of an ideal, proliferating class where preferment and profit without labor were guaranteed by access or proximity to a single source of power. Initiative and enterprise, wherever they dared raise their heads were stifled by a centralized resource dispensation operating through hi-faulting policies such as "import license scheme", "counter trade" and of course what we should dub the Nigerian version and parody of Sovietized economy-military collectivism—where resource accumulation headed in only one direction centrally but little outward redistribution; not even in terms of public services or creation of public welfare ever took placed. The monetary policies of an imposed centralized system have ensured that genuinely needy and deserving enterprises are starved of basic funds for the procurement of machinery or other basic requirements. Even state governors have been reduced to traipsing - first to Dodan Barracks, and next to Aso Rock to plead for what is to be statutory allocations, in order to run their governments and service even government projects.

Or is it to Zaire that we turn for another shining example of centralism? Or Ethiopia under Mariam Mengistu? We see by these related failures that the issue is not strictly ideology but one of the governance options, a choice between monolithic centralism and the federalist principle, a structured dispersal of both social and economic power bases that would guarantee both productive initiatives at all levels, and a sense of participation in the very decisions that affects daily existence. And let no one think that the unitary tendency has been limited only to our military experience. Permit me to recall the instances of our centralist genius, President Shehu Shagari, whose government undertook a universal low-cost housing scheme in all the various states against all sense and well-argued protestations. Which administrative levels, let us ask ourselves in all objectivity, is better positioned to assess and undertake the housing needs of its people: is it the center, or is it the state in partnership with local governments? But land was forcibly acquired and houses mostly without relation to urban demographic distribution or labor requirement in industrialized centers. What is left of these houses today are mostly tenanted by antelopes, snakes and rodents. I tend to roam in the bush for relaxation and that is where I made acquaintance with several units of the NPN populist charade called low-cost housing scheme. But of course Shagari was merely extending the lessons of private profitability from military precedents. We must not forget the grand spectacle we made of the nation through the massive cement armada that was supposed to provide the material for earlier vainglorious schemes, a prodigal venture that clogged up the harbors for years and ate up the national treasury in demurrage. Or the rice importation scheme, again centrally conceived and centrally manipulated ... but why go on?

Suffice it to remind ourselves that the civilian regime, and others before it, including those that bore the qualification "Military", insisted on flaunting the title "Federal Government of Nigeria". Even a new organization on federalism, based in Canada, is still obliged to list Nigeria as one of the Contemporary Federations of the world, in company with Germany, India, South Africa, Switzerland, Russia, Comoros, Venezuela, the United States, Ethiopia, plus some other two dozen members of the United Nations. Well, in the process of this conference, I can only hope that we shall uncover just what Nigeria has in common, in that aspect, with South Africa or the Federation of Czechoslovakia. Of course we know that the understanding of some past dictators about the nature of federalism has been, very simplistically, the creation of more states. You increase the number of states within a nation, and you persuade yourself that you have thereby expanded the concept and the practice of federalism, never mind if one state or two were created as a birthday present for your importuning spouse. Or as a bribe for the then going price of loyalty to one constituency or another, and even with diabolical calculation, to set one section of the nation against another through disputes over boundaries and assets. Non-viable state entities have been created which simply underline the contradictions inherent within a so-called federal system they are kept alive only by sporadic blood infusions from the center. Those states were never meant to be self-sufficient entities, and do not exist beyond the establishment of another bottomless pit of a parasitic bureaucracy.

The setting for this conference, Nigeria, serves therefore as a prime example of the failed federation, but perhaps failure is the wrong word, for it implies that an attempt has been made in the first place, one that unfortunately ended in failure. The truth is that beyond the first four years of Nigeria's independence, the federal principle was simply thrown overboard. A deliberate subversion of the rational relations of the states to the center was embarked upon, upsetting the balance between federal authority, the state, and even local government. We need to study the Nigerian cracked model very carefully in order to appreciate the distance between promise and performance, and the tragic choices that has been made. I use the word "tragic" deliberately, and not even because it took us through a civil war, though we must not be permitted to forget that. Following the massacres of 1966 and the atmosphere of deepened mutual distrust between the component nationalities within Nigeria, an effort was made to re-establish the federal principle and to go even further I refer to the Aburi conference where a short-lived attempt was made to restructure the nation on a less claustrophobic basis. "Confederation" was a word that surfaced repeatedly, and indeed the Aburi agreements virtually enshrined the practicalities of such internal relations as the guarantee for the continuation of Nigeria as one entity. Thereafter, of course, there came second thoughts and before long, those agreements were repudiated and "confederation" even became a dirty word. To breathe it at all was to be regarded as reactionary, as a tribal jingoist and even possibly a CIA agent.

Today, fortunately, we have learnt that words do not even necessarily mean how they sound, much less what they say. We have learnt that "federal" can survive for decades as the handle for a government without the nation it describes being anything but federal in conduct. This conference has assembled experts who are thoroughly equipped to assist us in sifting the grain from the chaff, and they will roam the world, I am confident, in meticulous detail to present viable models that will enable us to forget the emotive connotations of mere categories and confront actualities, their positive and negative effects on the lives of people. For we must never forget that systems of governments do not exist in the abstract, but in their consequences on peoples both in the present and in succeeding generations. Let me offer you one speculative proposition: do we dare reject, with absolute confidence, the suggestion that if Nigeria had been faithful to its truly federal beginnings, had pursued the creation of states, not as administrative arteries and internal neo-colonies, but as genuine entities within a federated union, we could have avoided the Ogoni tragedy, and the Delta would not be in a state of conflagration? It is worth considering. But the oil-producing regions have been treated as vassals to a remote, indifference and avaricious center, and today we are looking at consequences that involve, not simply a confrontation between a region and that center, but murderous confrontations along the length and breadth of the region, a rupture of former harmonious relationships, a desperation and intransigence beyond anything that has been witnessed in the nation since the Biafran civil war.

When we consider all these factors of our short history, it would appear that Nigeria does indeed offer a unique specimen for serious laboratory study in our quest for a system of equitable government. Well, our experts will obviously throw up our rivals. India has much to offer in this respect, a large post-colonial democracy where the principle of federalism has survived serious internal upheavals both from religious and secular causes, not to forget the exercise of a part and the continuing border disputes that have placed that democracy virtually in a state of undeclared war. There are others too, whose vicissitudes and triumphs illustrate the strength and weakness of a system under scrutiny, and its viability for a continent undergoing various degrees of convulsion. It does not require a prophet to predict, however, that Nigeria will preoccupy most minds at this conference, and this is only partially because of the political events of the past years that have created a timely and relevant background to our gathering and the very nature of our concerns. What happens here, in this country, in the immediate future that is, within the next one, two or three years matters, and it matters not only to us, but to the West African sub-region. It matters ultimately to the entire continent, and to the so-called international community. It matters desperately even to the external kites that are already hovering over the pickings to be had from a luscious and productive slice of real estate that they already determined as being probably ready to emerge from a prolonged period of drought. There will always be birds of prey hovering over this space; this we have learnt to live with. It is when the shadows that they cast become indistinguishable from those of crows and vultures that we shall acknowledge, once again, that a nation's nightmare has never absolutely departed its horizons.

I shall be honest with you: there are moments when I do wish that I had been born somewhere else on the continent, in one of those tiny or resource-starved, desolate slabs of earth that no one wants, nobody cares about, offers no strategic prospect that any powers would covet. It becomes exhausting to belong to a nation from which, not only is so much expected, but from which, you objectively admit to yourself, even much more should be demanded. One of my most chastening encounters took place shortly after the annulment of the results of Nigeria's June 12, 1993 presidential election. I visited the Horn of Africa in fulfillment of a long-standing invitation to a conference, the theme of which was: "From Conflict to Concord: The Horn of Africa". I have made various references to that meeting, which was attended by the political, intellectual and technocratic cream of Africa's leadership. It was non-governmental, even though it was attended by a handful of both past and serving ministers, including a former head of state or two. I am not too certain now that I have the exact wording of the conference theme correctly and perhaps, it is better thus. That title is one that now holds only ironic, even mocking resonance for us all, and rebukes my recollections of that optimistic gathering.

Optimistic, yes, even euphoric, but not without an overcast of foreboding. And the reason for that pall was that the most looked-up-to nation on that continent, Nigeria, had just reversed what appeared to be a definitive step in the direction of its long-awaited goal-democratization and, as a corollary, comparative stability through a structure of participation, accountability, and a foundation in human rights. My invitation had been sent long before our elections, and my participation should have been, for me, a triumphal presence. I had accepted that invitation confidently, convinced, as millions of Nigerians were, that we were about to link up with South Africa, and with the Horn of Africa in a sweeping resolve to embark on a new, progressive direction for the continent. I nourished the secretive pleasure of being an unaccredited emissary of good tidings.

I had planned to take with me a clutch of invitations to a conference with quite a similar orientation to this one—and what better assemblage the meeting in Addis, was, from which to select participants: historians, pan-Africanists, economists, political scientists, liberation fighters, etc.—whose contributions would be invaluable during the continent-wide Forum for Democracy that my association, the African Democratic League was then organizing for January 1994, that is, after what would have been the successful conclusion of the Nigerian democratic election and the installation of a representative system of government. The timing and purpose of that meeting approximates, as you can see, to this one following immediately after elections and concerned with the nature of democratic governance. This meeting at least has taken off, and within Nigeria, and the peculiar feeling that I have is one of being at a parallel conference that is taking place five years late.

Preparations for that other conference were already under full steam, scheduled for Cotonou in the Republic of Benin, with the full blessing and logistical support of her then President, Nicophore Soglo. Our motivations were however somewhat different: once we had taken the first step towards democracy, we felt that the next step was to assist others in taking theirs and, in the process of course, consolidate our own. So, that projected conference was not altogether altruistic: we all know that no one democracy can stand alone and, after several years of subjection to military rule, it seemed only sensible to create vital links with existing democracies, with opposition groups whose nations were still undergoing the travails of dictatorship and of course with political activists whose democracies were only so in name. Our catchment area included the Caribbean. I recall that we paid special attention to the opposition groups in Haiti, to whose exiled President, Aristide, a special invitation was issued. It was, as you see, an ambitious project, but of course, haven't we all discovered at various times that more was annulled in June 1993 beyond our elections, and that those consequences reached beyond our national borders? Perhaps we should begin to think of resurrecting whatever is still viable from the many casualties of that annulment and the four-year reign of terror that it spawned.

After the annulment, needless to say, I did not really feel like traveling to Addis Ababa. I appeared to carry a stigma of personal disqualification, rather like one of those political contestants whom our former dictators so much took pleasure in disqualifying for one reason or the other. But I truly felt disqualified. It seemed to me that I no longer belonged at a gathering that was clearly intended to celebrate, but also to critically examine within the context of the continent and its other on-going problems, the lesson to be drawn from the resolution of the wasteful, destructive conflict that had resulted in the overthrow of the leftist butcher—Mariam Mengistu—and then, most crucially, set an example for others through the amicable dissolution of an uneasy empire. What did I now have to contribute? We had all been invited to learn from the example of the Horn but, again, at the time that I accepted the invitation, I had felt a certain sense of political advantage; I would be able to proffer Nigeria as an even more salutary example - because peaceful - of political transformation. After decades of sustaining itself on the life-blood of the Nigerian nation, military dictatorship was in its death-throes, but even though it was not quite stone dead, we felt obliged to plan for its then seemingly inevitable demise.

Then came June 12, and the crude annulment of the presidential election. I arrived in Addis Ababa with my tail between my legs. And just as well. From the moment of my arrival, I was attacked by delegates from every corner of the continent and from every walk of life. *"Why have you people done this to us? Do you know what you've done, what example you've set? Do you realize how much we had all looked to citing your example, holding you up as the model, instructing our own people how it should be done?"*

In vain I tried to extricate myself from guilt, to remind them that I was in fact embattled, with others, in the effort to reverse the hand of this backwards moving clock, to retrieve a nation's estimation in the eyes of her sister nations and set her feet back on the path of her potential greatness. In vain I reminded my inquisitors that all this was none of my personal doing: I mean, I was not the one who annulled the elections and in any case I had risked my life participating in the protest movements against this assault of the nation. A waste of time. No one was in the mood to grant me a personal exemption. I was a Nigerian and therefore guilty! I had let down the continent in my own person. We had no right to do this to our sister nations on the continent. We had no right to fall below their expectations and, in that regard, we were all guilty, each and every single Nigerian. Since I was available at the time, I was obliged to bear the full brunt of condemnation.

It is difficult for anyone not present at that conference, one that took place so soon after the June 12 annulment, to appreciate the full depth of pain, of the sense of betrayal that was expressed by our colleagues from everywhere on the continent. And, paradoxically, I found myself both uplifted and demoralized at the same time: uplifted because it was clear that so many fellow Africans were passionately involved in the fate of Nigeria, and that were motivated by nothing less than pride and conviction in our potential to move the continent in a progressive direction; and then of course I was simultaneously demoralized because I felt that we had let others down, and must be held morally responsible for that betrayal of just expectations.

Present at that conference were, needless to say, both Ethiopians and Eritreans, all basking in the rational resolve of their decades-old conflict under contrasting regimes, feudal as well as Marxist. Eritreans and Ethiopians alone had undergone unspeakable agonies under both ideologies, the people had been repressed and enslaved by representatives of two totally irreconcilable social projects which though the latter—the Marxist regime—would have indignantly denied it shared common grounds in which they luxuriated, those grounds being the self-proliferating space of alienated power. And so, in Addis Ababa, while internationally I squirmed under the censure of my peers, I outwardly celebrated the end of a decade-old nightmare, the end of a senseless conflict by two sides that were enslaved to an elitism of power whose legitimation was based on notions and practices that were intolerant of the fundamental worth of the humanity that alone creates society.

In addition, let this be remembered: the leadership of the Horn, and Ethiopia in particular, was then occupied with arbitration in the problems of Somalia. I held discussions with Ethiopian leadership, including her Prime Minister, and was impressed by their commitment and realistic assessment of the demands of that disintegrating society. I learnt much. I left with enormous respect for the seriousness with which, so soon after their own baptism of fire, these men appeared to have accepted that they had nowhere to turn for solutions except inwards, utilizing their intimate knowledge of that region's politics and history to arbitrate the tensions and rivalries that had sent the United States scuttling from that region, leaving the natives to fend for themselves.

Today, what lessons can we claim that the Horn is impacting to the African continent? "Like play, like play", as we say in my part of West Africa, the Horn, from tiny spurts and negligible smoldering, has suddenly exploded. A region that we had seized upon as a redeeming contrast to the dismal example of Somalia and Sudan, and presented to the rest of the world as an example of African common sense and maturity, of her ability to resolve seemingly intractable issues, once left to themselves, has eventually elected to flaunt themselves to the entire world as being yet another zone of mindless belligerence. "Like play, like play", what we considered as inconsequential "teething problems" have deepened into septic abscesses which now threaten erstwhile conflict mediators with becoming, yet again, candidates for global medication.

Today, it is probably to Nigeria that the world is preparing to turn once again, in desperate hope, for such lost images of self-redemption and authoritative mediation. Nigeria remains the worse luck for its nationals, not any other nation space. Willy-nilly, she has a strategic function that cannot be wished away, and it is this perception, this yet unfulfilled destiny that defines for outsiders, as well as for many thinking citizens of Nigeria, the full meaning of that frustrating nation space.

But not to all, alas! Do we need to contrast with the foregoing what Nigeria meant to Abacha and his accomplices, with the incorrigible among them who probably even now, are calculating how soon they can safely strike to take their turn at the roulette of power? For this, the definition of Nigeria is simply direct access to the Central Bank of the nation, to royalties accruing from oil exports, sometimes given the elegant name of Dedicated Accounts, but in reality vast sums that are self-dedicated, dispensed without the necessity of accounting through the Ministry of Finance or being permitted to complicate the fiscal routine of the Central Bank of Nigeria.

With the passage of such deviants of power and responsibility, does it mean that we have effectively eliminated this aberrant reading of the Nigerian nation? Alas, no! There exist allied readings that stem from the same fabric of alienation. The nation is also misread by a minority group of an atavistic order, for whom Nigeria simply represents, even right till this moment, power and domination. The elements that we speak of regard economics as consisting of neither more nor less than government business. That is, they do not understand a nation's economy as a dynamic process of productivity, of labor and other means of life enhancement. For them, Government means business, and whoever controls government, controls business. Thus, they evince no interest in developmental pre-requisites such as education and training; no, it is enough that they control government. For this, they are prepared to go to inordinate lengths, including the infiltration and domination of the nation's military, so that when they civic route to power appears to be blocked, they resort to the military. Complacency therefore remains the gravest danger to the Nigerian polity. The snake may appear motionless from the buffeting of these past years, but the head is not yet scotched. It is not yet time to lower our guard.

So here we are in Abuja, the seat and engine room of past horrors. I used to wonder from time to time when next I was likely to see this shifted sepulcher, speculate about the route to its purification, for that day of reckoning was inevitable, sooner or later, and from whatever direction. So one was left to wonder if the only route to its salvation lay only in its being blasted out of existence, pulverized in entirety and sent back to the pristine undergrowth from where it has sprung in the flush of a unifying ideal turned tragic, a mockery of its original designs. Seeing that I am here however, and Abuja is still standing, let me use these very grounds of alienation to comment on its recent past, and to pass a message to our neighbors, both near and far. After all, it was from this very station that Sani Abacha's killer squads operated, it was from the confidence of its seeming impregnability that they took off in the presidential jet, carried out their gory business, and returned to regale their boss with the results of their dastardly exploits.

Oh yes, let us never forget that it was on these very grounds that three hundred odd Nigerians gathered together to fashion out for Nigeria a new constitution that no one had requested, one third of them nominees of the incumbent tyrant but all of them knowing fully well that they had been brought together, not for any meaningful mission, but to bury beneath the deepest layers of concrete - like the nuclear time-bomb of the Chernobyl reactor— the expressed electoral will of the Nigerian people. It was among that same assembly that exceptions such as the late Shehu Yar'Adua committed the ultimate sin that guaranteed his eventual murder, that sin being his dare in activating his political machinery on behalf of a menaced democratic future so that, even before settling down to the alleged business that brought them together, the assembly voted a departure date for the ambitious dictator. It was of course from within that same assembly that its whinnying chairman groveled before the dictator and rushed to engineer a reversal of that decision, declaring that the assembly had gone beyond its brief. Let me yield voice here to a perceptive commentator on that most abominable waste of Nigerian funds and the formal inauguration of Abacha's self-perpetuation machinery. Professor Eskor Toyo wrote in The Guardian:

> *Those who assembled at Abuja to make the 1995 draft were very much like Abacha. They saw Nigeria simply as a giant national cake to be shared by exercising arbitrary and greedy power. We have seen how the cake sharers around Abacha's presidency handled the national revenue. They pleased themselves with billions of naira or dollars while the working masses starved and while hospitals, schools, and all that the people need in every town or village decayed. Nigeria is a country to be built and a hope for the Nigerian people and Black Africa to be fulfilled. It is not for some of us a cake to be shared.*

Yes, it was indeed in this same Abuja that these men and women of destiny, having been alternately bribed and whipped into orderly conformity by their paranoid puppet master, operating through the headmasterly autocracy of the *bowler-hatted* ringmaster who was allegedly but unbelievably a former justice of the courts, here it was that they evolved their masterpiece of the presidential zoning principle, which, in that same article, was lucidly and exhaustively reduced to its infantile proportions by Eskor Toyo as it has been by several commentators. But of course all but a handful of them knew, and had accepted that, even if they had produced the sublime constitutional model for any inhabited portion of this earth, the occupant of the top slot was already reserved for the devil. The handful who knew but did not accept such a diabolical attribution would later be subjected to intense physical and/ or economic terrorism, often extended to their families and any recognizable associates. Others would land in Sani Abacha's dungeons, framed on fabricated coup attempts and undergo horrendous torture. A number would not emerge alive.

And yes, this assembly's peaceful air that harbors our civilized exchanges once rang out with the cries of the tortured and the groans of the dying. We screamed out to the world that there were crimes being committed within this fortified hell that would make the devil himself cringe with fear! Every new revelation instructs us today that we have yet to fully fathom the depths of man's capacity for depravity. Let us never forget that it was from within this space that a decision was taken to hand Ken Saro-Wiwa and his eight companions, and that even as we speak here, today, their remains have yet to be returned to their kinsfolk.

The guilt of the defenders and apologists of what happened here is however no less gross and unforgivable than the crimes of the actual perpetrators. I would ignore them, for theirs are names that should not be permitted to desecrate our lips, but some of them persist in aggravating our sensibilities, our extreme tolerance level by daring to open their loot—encrusted

13

mouths and insisting that they have no apologies for the role they played during the assault on our nationhood. Some have even begun to ingratiate themselves into this hard won democratic dispensation by declaring themselves sponsors or supporters of one contestant or the other. Their language is liberal with pledges - monetary and "delivery". Which means, in plain language that they pledge their undiscriminating support for the likely top dog, no matter the means of his ascendancy or his conduct in power, and promise to "deliver" their constituency but always into servitude. They attempt to rehabilitate their putrid careers by lavishly donating to campaign funds and pontificating on a process that they had spent years of shameless collaboration in frustrating, building up, in the process huge financial bases for their bootlicking, unprincipled existence. We must constantly remind ourselves of their careers in order to ensure that amnesia, that debilitating disease of mass will, does not encourage them to revise a history that has traumatized the majority of our people.

In this very Abuja it was, for instance, that the factories of lies were established, where Task Forces were set up for physical liquidation and sustained campaigns of calumny against democratic leaders, operated it would sometimes appear, by black descendants of Josef Goebells. For some of these agents and mercenaries of the most obscene concoctions, this has become such a way of life that they seem unaware, even today, that their paymaster is dead. Or perhaps that is not strictly true, perhaps the satanic engine of that era is still manned, is still maintained in active service, which means of course that portions of that agenda are very much alive. Abacha suited a handful of causes in this nation, so let us not be complacent.

It was from this all-perceiving observatory that several of the opposition, including this author, were discovered sneaking into the country, planting bombs among the innocent and slipping out swiftly again, as repeatedly announced by one former village tailor, then designated Minister for Special Duties. "What a noise!" I believe, was the title that the press bestowed on him. It was from here, that that tailor with the all-penetrating eye of a needle perhaps spied on this very author as he held meetings with all the dissidents of the nation-students, workers, market women, etc.—and planned how to overthrow his master's regime with violence. It was a sister hotel, a stone's throw from here, that ministered to one Minister at all hours, servicing the famous thirst of the unctuous servitor as he gathered his retinue together for his next mission to some new corner of the world, there to present, contrary to his own conceited assessment of his performances, the worst side of the regime. He constituted himself in many instances into the best propaganda machine that the democratic movement could ever have invented. Heads of states, ministers, legislators, television interviewers took one look at, and listened to his permanently inebriated lump of lard, oozing with borrowed authority and the insolence of the uncouth, and they decided that the democratic opposition could not be all bad if such was the image of authority against which they had declared war. Don't take my word for it. Speak to diplomats and anyone with whom the Chief Tomfoolery of the nation ever came in contact during the days of his ministerial affliction, and you find that they all come up with one single opinion that never in their experience had they ever encountered a more noxious bag of flatulence that attempted to pass for a foreign spokesman.

Let us not forget also that this was the take-off spot for the Aerial Bank of Nigeria; same initials, by coincidence, as those of the moribund Association for Better Nigeria. The Aerial Bank of Nigeria flew our nation's largesse to other African heads of states, in return for Public Relations services at international gatherings. This was an activity that was proclaimed from the roof top. It is all now being revealed in all its nauseating details, how African Heads of States were bought, as well as their foreign ministers. But there is the consolation, the obverse side of this high-placed venality. I must use this occasion, and this erstwhile seat of perfidy, to proclaim and publicly applaud the nobility of others who withstood Abacha's bullying and blackmailing gambits. Malawi, several Caribbean nations, Canada, the Scandinavian countries, New Zealand, the European Union as a body, not however as individual sovereignties etc. We must never forget all those leaders and peoples who stood by their brothers and sisters of this nation. And so, even as we have a responsibility to pursue the exposure of the venal collaborators of the Abacha regime during our darkest days, we must also compile an honor list of all those who placed humanity and justice before dollars, petroleum and technical aid, beyond royal receptions and all expenses paid tours of Nigeria's fleshpots, beyond business opportunities and corrupt deals, be they African, Asian or European, and irrespective of religious or ideological alibis. We must recall the Human Rights organization, UNESCO, congressmen and women such as Maxine Walters, Donald Payne and other activities such as Randall Robinson, Flora MacDonald, the Congressional Black Caucus of the U.S. legislators and a host of others. For it is only when we bleed, when we mourn and are confronted with the bleak immensity of a future that we remember that tyranny knows neither color nor race. It is thanks to many, no matter in what modest measures, that we are assembled here today, of our own will, and resolved to seize our destiny by the throat.

This conference must, therefore, not be conceived of as taking place in a vacuum, but at a potential watershed in this nation's history - that much, but no more, we dare acknowledge - the potentiality of even this hugely flawed, improbable but recurrent Nigerian moment. The horizons of the initiators of our meeting are modest enough. We know that deliberations will not result in the philosopher stone that dissolves all internal contradictions of the continent. Nevertheless, a blueprint, or several, may emerge that answer one or more categories of the search for an equitable order within the multiple roads that confront the democratic quest. And that will be a lot more than the power custodians of this continent, with their record of expensive, abysmal and sanguinary failures will dare pretend is irrelevant and consign yet again to the musty shelves of utopian dreams.

It only remains for me to thank the landlords of our meeting place for accommodating us within this precincts especially, as the world knows, this space known as Aso Rock, was recently put up for rent, and it has duly gone to the highest bidder. Let us therefore acknowledge the real victors of the recent contest for occupancy: Candidates cashflow, military machine, and pandemic prostitution. The loser of course, as if you did not know, was Democracy. Let us however take consolation in a Yoruba proverb: 'B'a o ba r'adan, aa fi oode s'ebo'—the translation, in this context would read, "if we cannot yet speak democracy, let us at least address 'federalism.'"

CHAPTER 2

Federalism and the National Question In Nigeria: A Theoretical Exploration*

Aaron T. Gana

*The author acknowledges the financial support of the Rockefeller Foundation, through CODESRIA, as well as the Management of its Bellagio Center in Italy, for providing the conducive intellectual environment for the writing of the original version of this chapter. The chapter has also benefited immensely from the critical comments of Georges Nzongola-Ntalaja and other anonymous reviewers. Together we share the readers' judgement!!

Introduction

The year 1954 remains a watershed in Nigeria's evolution into statehood. For, whichever way the current crisis of legitimacy of the Nigerian state is resolved, reference cannot but be made to the year when both the colonial state functionaries and the "nationalists" reached a consensus that federalism was the best form of power sharing for the nation - in the making. On the part of the British, it was the formula that assures their friends - the northern oligarchy - of progress at their own pace. On the part of the other anti-colonial agitators from the south, it facilitated the consummation of a dream - the termination of British rule and the consequent realization of sovereign statehood. In the euphoria of the moment, little attention was paid to the dynamics of inter-ethnic competition for scarce state resources that was soon to be unleashed to undermine the process of national integration as the new republic crawled off. Of course, a full appreciation of 1954 must begin with 1914, the year Lord Lugard, then Governor-General, in a lightening move, decided to unite the administrations of the two hitherto separately-administered protectorates. But the picture of the process of Nigeria's march into the "federalist revolution" (Elazar, 1979:2) will not be complete without reference to another imperial act of administrative expediency. In 1939, the southern protectorate was split into East and West, completing the process of constructing the tripod federal structure that was consummated in the 1954 constitution. The choice of the federal formula was informed, not so much by the intrinsic qualities of federalism as a mode of exercising sovereign authority while simultaneously accommodating irredentist claims to cultural autonomy, as by the realization, especially within the ranks of the southern segment of the anti-colonial movement, that it was the best deal they had for wresting independent statehood from the British.

Dudley (1966: 17) had argued that the 'nationalists'[2] fell for the federal formula because they saw it as fitting in with the sociological realities confronting them. According to him, the change from unitarism (which was the modus operandi of the colonial state) to federalism in 1954 can be explained neither by reference to the sociological complexity of the country - i.e., its ethnic and geographic diversity - nor by the often cited disagreement between the southern and northern fractions of the emerging political elite over the date for self-government.

Rather, the explanation lies in the attraction of the Nigerian leaders to "a particular kind of federal structure" - the Wheare model —which they saw as fitting the sociological reality confronting them, in a way in which the Canadian, Australian and Indian federal experience did not. Their choice was thus not based on an abstract model, but on what they frequently referred to in their debates on the issue, as "real" or "true" federalism. The other reason Dudley adduced for his contention was the prospect for fiscal self suffi- ciency, which the Korean war boom dangled before aspiring regional pre- miers. This had the prospect of juridical autonomy with a wide range of discretionary powers and functions for the regions. As evidence for this position, Dudley noted that the regions where the demand for the Wheare formula was strongest (East and West) were also the regions with the highest increases in revenues between 1953 and 1960; recording increases of 214 percent and 247 percent respectively as against 94.4 percent for the North and 74.4 percent for the Central Government.

If this explanation is sustained—and empirical evidence since the adop- tion of the federal solution to the nagging problem of political development in the context of differential incorporation of the various regions into the British imperial economy would seem to confirm it - then it sheds light on the subject of our investigation. For what it suggests is that national integration was never in the agenda of the Nigerian successors to the state apparatus of power or if it was, they did not appreciate the enormity of the challenge and that the federal formula was adopted merely as an expedient strategy for terminating colonial rule. It can therefore be hypothesized that the national question was hardly posed until the Biafran crisis. I will explore this thesis in subsequent sections of this chapter, but first a review of the relevant literature.

Conventional Wisdom on Nigerian Politics

Conventional explanations of the crisis of development in Africa in general, and Nigeria in particular, are anchored on the plural character of African/ Nigerian societies. The modernization paradigm, once discredited by radical scholarship for its ahistoricity, has rebounded back into mainstream social science in the wake of the collapse of the Soviet experiment in social engineering (Sklar: 1993: 83). The thrust of the various strands in this paradigm is the location of ethnic conflict at the level of exchange, i.e., the question of who gets what when and how. Thus Lasswell's conception of politics is central to the explanation of politics in these ethnically plural societies. The logic is that ethnic pluralism is a drag on development. Although scholars have differed in the way this theme is articulated within a particular variant of the paradigm, as when Post and Vickers (1973) focused on the particular reward system to underline the sources of ethnic conflict, the conclusion remains the same: the incompatible ethnic claims on the state, and the attendant crisis of its legitimacy. The impression is unmistakable that these ethnic groups were, prior to colonial intervention, in a state of permanent hostility. Perhaps no account underlines this image better than that provided by O'Connell (1979: 634-5) quoting G. I. Jones:

> *The whole (Eastern) region was, and to a large extent still is, divided up between a very large number of small local communities each virtually independent and autonomous. You can call these communities "villages" in the case of the Ijo and Ibibio, village-group in the case of Ibo ... The Ibibio villages were joined together into larger groups which you can call "tribes" (government reports refer to them as "clans"), so were Ibo villages in some areas - notably in the East. But except in the case of the smaller ones, these tribes were held together by ritual and cultural ties, rather than by any unifying political system. Each of these villages or towns was in a state of opposition to, if not of armed neutrality with, its neighbours and unless you were related to neighbouring towns or had a guide who was, it was extremely hazardous to travel any distance from your home. You risked losing your head or falling into an ambush. But this was not a condition of ordered anarchy or anything like it. It was more like the relationship between European nations in the eighteenth and nineteenth centuries but on a smaller scale. There was a system of law which covered relations between different communities and it was supported by economic sanc-*

tions. As in the European case, a community had the choice of enforcing its rights by resort either to law or by the use of force (war). It usually preferred the former because, unlike Western Nigeria, a war was hardly ever decisive, the communities (except in the Ogoja Province) were too evenly matched.

It is anthropological accounts such as this that provide the "empirical" grounding for the modernization theories as applied to culturally heterogeneous societies such as Nigeria. In what remains paradigmatic of discussions of Nigerian politics, Melson and Wolpe (1971) analyzed the Nigerian conflict that culminated in the three-year civil war through the analytical prism of communalism.

Anyone familiar with the Nigeria about which Melson and Wolpe organized their twenty-five chapter book will, on reading the theoretical chapter, realize the proximate encounter by the authors with the events that shaped their perspective. This knowledge brings into sharp relief the debate over the validity of observations and conclusions arrived at in the heat of the events about which the scholar theorizes. The immediate background to that study was the Nigerian civil war which lasted from July 1967 to January 1970. The war was the culmination of the distrust generated by the cycle of violence unleashed in the wake of the inconclusive federal elections of 1964 and the Western regional elections of 1965. The Balewa government had, by December 31, 1965, finalized arrangements for the deployment of the military to the Western region to quell the disturbances that were increasingly undermining the legitimacy of the state. According to Muffet (1982: 12) the operation - code named "Operation No Mercy" - was to be led by Brigadier Zakariya Maimalari, but had to be delayed because of the conference of the commonwealth Heads of States summoned by Nigeria over the Rhodesian crisis. When on January 15, 1966, Major Chukwuma Nzeogu "Kaduna" and his co-mutineers struck, Nigerians from all parts of the country - including the North - heaved a sigh of relief, having watched with anxiety the drift of the country since the general elections of 1964. But this was short-lived, as the character of the putsch soon betrayed the motive of the mutineers and from then on the crisis assumed a logic of its own that culminated in the thirty-month civil war. It was the struggle for power that preceded military intervention and the civil war which followed it that provided the empirical foundation for *Modernization and the Politics of Communalism* (Nelson and Wolpe, 1971). The thrust of the authors' argument is that it is neither poverty nor cultural diversity that accounts for the "politics of communalism" as some accounts suggest. Rather, the Nigerian case, they insist, "is a particularly appropriate illustration of the relationship between communal conflict and modernization, in that on most social and economic indices, Nigeria showed signs of relatively rapid growth in comparison to other developing nations subject to comparable ecological and historical conditions." In other words, communal conflict is an inevitable accompaniment of modernization. The authors make bold the universality of this theoretical "discovery" by asserting that the Nigerian case "is by no means unique," and proceed to identify other instances of communal identity with its potential for conflict in the race for competitive modernization. These include the Nagas of India, the Chinese and Javanese in Indonesia, the French Canadians and the Black Americans who have all refused to "melt" into their respective wider societies. "In each of these cases," the authors declare, "the contemporary pattern of communal formation and conflict may be seen as an immediate by-product of the modernization process" (1971: 2).

As indicated above, anyone who has a superficial acquaintance with Nigeria's post-independence history and politics will be struck by the extent to which the propositions which guided the study approximate developments in the first five years of Nigeria's independence. Take for example, the first proposition which asserts that in culturally plural societies, competition for scarce resources takes place within a communal framework. This perception is not unconnected with the ethnic content of the political process (Gana, 1983). In spite of Nnamdi Azikiwe's spirited efforts to establish a "national" infrastructure for political competition, later arrivals such as Obafemi Awolowo and Ahmadu Bello had to resort to cultural idioms in order to challenge his grip on the political space created by the colonial state. But this development succeeded in derailing Nigerian nationalism only because the colonizers engaged in a deliberate strategy of dividing the 'colonized' in order to ensure their control and ultimately frustrate attempts to build a united nation (Isichie: 1985: 5; Nnoli: 1980:23). One cannot but agree with Nnoli (1980: 25) that "ethnicity in Africa emerged and persisted either as a mechanism for adaptation to the imperialist system or as an instrument for ensuring a facile and more effective domination and exploitation of the colonized. In most cases it served the reactionary purpose of the system: the degradation of the African in order to better and more easily exploit him."

While one cannot deny the functional utility of ethnicity in the competition for the scarce values in society, it is a mystification of the social reality to cast every demand on the state in communal terms as the modernization perspective does. The distortion becomes more glaring when one encounters thousands of Nigerians (including this author) who reached the peak of their careers without resort to communal identity. The fundamental pitfall of the modernization model is its subsumption of every citizen of the society under consideration as belonging to either one or the other of the ethnic groups in conflict rather than recognizing that (a) it is individuals seeking to advance their personal life chances in a competitive context in which their achievements do not entitle them to the position/status/resource(s) they aspire to appropriate that, by and large, resort to the exploitation of ethnic identity; (b) that more often than not it is members of the hegemonic ethnic blocs that engage in this short-cut approach to success, and (c) for every citizen that resorts to such primordial criteria for advancement, there are literally thousands of others who pursue their individual aspirations without recourse to ethnicity. Therein lies the severe limitation to the explanatory power of the modernization perspective.

The Marxist Paradigm Revisited

In response to this weakness of the communal framework for analyzing plural societies, Marxism offers a refreshing perspective, due primarily to its methodological procedure, a procedure which insists on the dynamic interrelation of matter. Thus, what the modernization model throws up as the substance of politics in these societies, Marxism treats as the shadow. For instance, Melson and Wolpe acknowledge the role scarcity of values play in generating anxiety amongst citizens whose aspirations have been expanded as they become available for mobilization in a modernizing economy. "They come to want, and demand, more - more goods, more recognition, more power" (1971: 5). Men (and women), they rightly conclude, enter into conflict not because they are different but because they are the same. Thus it is by making men "more alike" through the generation of similar or identical wants that modernization promote conflict. If we substitute "modernization" with "capitalism" we arrive at the same conclusion. For the Marxists, it is not modernization per se that generates conflict, but the particular form it takes under capitalism. Since capitalism is anchored on the private appropriation of surplus it enthrones crass individualism which festers alienation and antagonism. Ethnicity becomes a ready tool for the advancement of personal interest disguised as communal interest. In its application to the Nigerian crisis, Nnoli (1980) shows how the colonial urban setting provided the cradle for ethnicity, while scarcity conditions resort to ethnicity. Of the latter, he surmises:

> *Scarcity was pervasive of the colonial order. It was evident in the economic, social and political spheres of life. It affected employment, education, political participation and the provision of social services to the population. Under these circumstances the competition for the limited resources and opportunities could only be intense and destructive. Individuals had to rely on various useful devices to gain access to the scarce goods and services. One*

of these is alignment with other members of the individual's communal groups, including the most inclusive of them, the ethnic group. <u>Under conditions of low-class conscious-ness and the manipulation of communal sentiments by the privileged classes as well as the colonialist, such an alignment was inevitable</u> (1980: 87).
(Emphasis added).

The underlined sentence reflects the frustration with Marxism's inability to account for the potency of the primordial, a point to which we shall return later in this chapter. For now, it is pertinent to draw attention to the continu-ing saliency of ethnicity in Nigeria. Indeed, it can by hypothesized that the potency of ethnic identity in Nigeria positively correlates to the level of ma-terial and social advancement.

Egwu (1993) provides empirical support for the thesis that communal identity remains a potent instrument for material advancement in Nigeria. He shows how the new patterns of accumulation, especially the transformation of the agrarian based state into a rentier state, following the oil boom of the seventies, has accentuated the struggle for ethnic ascendance, geo-political advantage, personal accumulation and class consolidation. Add to these the violent clashes engendered by land hunger wearing ethnic togas and a sce-nario described by O'Connell (1967) as the 'inevitability of instability' is en-acted in the tradition of classical Marxist analysis. There are substantial em-pirical evidence for the view that the intense debate and struggle over state creation, revenue allocation and the Nigerian version of affirmative action - the federal character and quota principles - are all ploys by the ruling class to divide the popular masses in order to continue their exploitation.

The saliency of the "ethnic" question otherwise known as the "nationality question" remains an unsettled theoretical issue in Marxism. The classical position - from Marx to Stalin - has been that the national question or nation-alism is a ruse for bourgeois domination of society. A study of the strategy and tactics of African ruling classes since independence seems to buttress this position. As Ake (1978, 1993: 32) and Gana (1987) pointed out, African ruling cliques since independence, have employed the idiom of unity and national integration not only to demobilize the masses but to make the case for the primacy of development over personal freedom, insisting that this requires not only unity of purpose but unanimity of method. In the blind pursuit of such self-interested goals, they proceeded to justify "the criminalization of political dissent and the inexorable march to political monolithism." Marxists scholars have been quick to point to the self-serving character of the drive for development and national integration, insisting that the national question, while posing a threat to African states, remains but a secondary contradiction, the primary contradiction being the class question

(Nnoli, 1980, 1989; Ake, 1981, 1993). However, theoretical combats on the subject continue to generate more heat than light as the combatants line up behind classicism and revisionism. The classicists insist that the national question was eternally settled by Lenin who, advancing the legacy left behind by Marx and Engels (1976: 503), opted for the principle of national self determination. But it must be stated, without equivocation that if there is any consistency in the Marxist theory of nationalism, it is its inconsistency. For while Lenin is credited with the more accommodating view of the nation as a historical reality, Munck (1986) points to the blurry distinction between Lenin's and Stalin's, which has come down memory lane as the definitive Marxist treatise on the national question. Of course the pedigree of Marxist thought on the national question must be traced back to the founding fathers of Marxism - Karl Marx and Frederick Engels.

As with the state, they left only fragmentary impressions that have obfuscated more than clarify. While appearing to defend the right of nationalities to self determination, they, in fidelity to their vision of a future communist society, insisted that this is only a transient stage in the evolution of the human community. This ambivalence makes it possible for Ollman (1976: 22) to posit that Marx's vision of the post-revolutionary status of nations and nationalism is such that "the divisions we are accustomed to seeing in the human species along the lines of nation, race, religion, geographical section (town dwellers and country dwellers), occupation, and class have all ceased to exist" in the communist society they (Marx and Engels) foresaw. But the same vision leads Bloom (1967: 22) to insist that "what the author (of the Manifesto) foresaw was not the complete disappearance of all natural distinctions whatever, but specifically the abolition of sharp economic and social difference, economic isolation, invidious distinction, political rivalries, wars, and exploitation of one nation by another. Both interpretations remain at the level of vision, awaiting national and international conjunctures to translate them into social realities.

Karl Kautsy hypothesized the disappearance of colonial oppression with the emergence of industrial capitalism. This was not to happen, however, as inter-imperialist rivalries collapsed the Second International into its national components (Munck: 1984: 3). Otto *Bauer's The Nationalist Question and Social Democracy* (1907) was regarded by some (Kolakowski, 1978: 225) as the "best treatise on nationality problems to be found in Marxist literature and one of the most significant products of Marxist theory in general." Yet, Lenin discarded it as advocating merely a policy of "cultural autonomy." All through, from the revisionist Eduard Bernstein to Rosa Luxembourg, for whom the national question is subordinate to the class struggle, and Kautsky who insisted on the assimilation of small nationalities into larger ones because of the language problem, we see an ambiguity rooted in the desire to avoid the disintegration of what Engels called 'historic nations' (i.e. the more established nationalities) and the necessity to advance the socialist cause.

Although this position was to change in the face of the traumatic experience of 1917 - 1920, especially in nationalist uprisings in Belorussia, Transcaucasia and the Ukraine, forcing the Bolsheviks to adopt *the federal principle* which Lenin had repudiated in 1913 when he categorically stated that "Marxists will never, under any circumstances, advocate either the federal principle or decentralization" (Lenin, 1920:46), the fundamental thrust of Marxist position on the national question remains unaltered: *that the nation is a transient phenomenon and natural sentiments a dependent reactionary rather than an autonomous force*. Marx and Engels had declared in the *Communists Manifesto* that, "National difference and antagonisms between peoples are daily more and more vanishing... The supremacy of the proletariat will cause them to vanish still further," And Engels (1976:6) had gone further to idealize the internationalist credentials of the working class by declaring, at the festival of nations held in London in 1845, that:

> *The great mass of proletarians are by their very nature free from national prejudices... Only the proletarians can destroy nationality, only the awakening proletariat can bring about the fraternization between the different nations.*

This idealization of the proletariat is understandable if one recognizes the centrality of the ideological in social analysis - whether in Marxism or liberalism. For Marxism, class is the central analytical category while class struggle is the motor force of historical evolution. Thus class is to Marxism what market is to liberalism. And because historically the formation of nation-states was a product of capitalist expansion, Marxist analysis of the national question, as of many other social issues, has focused more on the economic, precisely capital accumulation, than on the accompanying physical and political consolidation of territory, its analysis concentrating "exclusively on economics as the sole determinant of social classes, and these classes as the sole engine of human history" (Munck: 1984: 1). This accounts for the poverty of Marxism in explicating the national question, leading Poulantzas (1980: 93) to conclude that "we have to recognize that there is no Marxist theory of the nation, and despite the passionate debates that have taken place within the workers' movement, it would be far too evasive to say that Marxism has underestimated the reality of the nation."

Federalism and the National Question in Nigeria

The central contention of this chapter is that on reflection, the Nigerian "nationalists"[1] who delivered Nigeria from British colonial rule were less concerned with forging a Nigerian identity than with carving out a geographical base for their personal material advancement. That legacy continues to haunt Nigerians as a people till date (1999). The current political and constitutional stalemate is the clearest testimony to this assertion. In the preface to his study of Nigerian federalism, Eleazu (1979: 9) wondered:

> The 'founding fathers' of Nigeria adopted federalism as a pragmatic instrument for holding together the entity called Nigeria... They thought that through federalism they will maintain unity in diversity; that within the federal structure the diverse ethnic groups can be welded into a modern nation. They were full of hope for this country and I am inclined to believe that they all meant well. But by 1966, the hope was blighted by the very same leaders who espoused it. _What had happened? Why did it happen? Where did the ship of state start steering away from its course? How can future pilots or captains of the ship of state ensure that they keep on course?_ (Emphasis added).

These are the very questions we seek answers to in this chapter. To the first question, we say what happened was the logical consequence of the very basis of Nigerian federalism, not as he ascribed to the founding fathers, a constitutional framework within which a Nigerian national identity was to evolve, but a political expedient to facilitate the material advancement of the key players in the negotiations that produced the 1954 federal constitution. Once this point is grasped, the two subsequent questions become superfluous. The real question to which we can then address ourselves is: how can a repeat of 1967 - 70 be avoided? At the risk of being considered a prophet of doom rather than a social _scientist_ [3] there is sufficient evidence that all the trappings of 1967 have been unfolding since 1993 and may soon assume a logic of their own (if they have not already) from which we may never recover as a corporate entity. To provide both theoretical and empirical validity to this conclusion, it is necessary to examine the literature on federalism and match the prescriptions therein with the Nigerian reality.

The Wheare Doctrine and Nigerian Federalism

We had made reference to the Wheare thesis on federalism at the onset of this chapter. There is neither the need nor the space to rehash the elements of this paradigm, except to note that the one thing that constitutional theorists have

26

had to admit is that there is always a gap between the theory of government - not just federal government and its practice. This is why Ostrom (1988:14) argues, in respect of the United Kingdom that:

> *Using the definition of federalism offered by Alexander Hamilton, an "impartial" coder might reasonably classify Great Britain or France as being more federal than the Soviet Union. Units of local government in Great Britain and France probably exercise more autonomy than the constituent "republics" or units of local government in the Soviet Union. Failure to cope with the "Irish Problem" and the rise of Scottish nationalism, however, may indicate serious weakness in the British constitution, which might be remedied by greater recourse to federal structures in organizing a system of government of the British peoples.*

The point Ostrom is at pains to make is that one can hardly deduce actual practice from constitutions, which though providing the legal framework for a particular form of power sharing between levels of institutions, remains, in essence, statements of intentions. Thus Nigeria has been described as a military federalism (Elaigwu: 1979: 177), which, to all intents and purposes, is a contradiction in terms. What has happened is simply the transformation of federalizing intentions into a unitary command structure under military rule. The reality is that a unitary constitution may in practice produce a federal form of governance, while a federal constitution may operate as if it decrees a unitary structure. Thus, with respect to theoretical formulations, Sawer's (1969: 117 - 30) distinction between dual, cooperative and organist federalism, Livingston's spectrum of federal societies (1967; 39-42) or Riker's federal spectrum (1975: 103) are no more than attempts to reconcile the existential reality of dynamic political processes with static formulations.

Notwithstanding what Jinadu (1979:43) would rather classify as an epistemological issue, events since 1954 would tend to lend credibility to Watts' (1966: 6) conclusion that the "federal solution" was adopted by the parties - the British and the pro-independence agitators we have called "nationalist" for lack of a more economizing expression - as "an ad hoc expedient to be applied where particular circumstances allowed no alternative."

For, the structure of the federation from the onset vitiated a primary requirement of functional federalism, i.e. "that there should not be any one state so much more powerful than the rest as to be capable of vying in strength with many of them combined. If there be such a one, and only one, it will insist on being master of the joint deliberations" (Mill: 1948: 367-8). Efforts to ensure a more balanced structure were resisted both by the colonial power and the northern fraction of the successor elite (Osuntokun: 1979:10, Oyovbaire: 1986:37).[2] Second, and more importantly, however, is the fact that the Nigerian political class was not only devoid of a vision of Eleazu's "historical identity" but even an elementary conception of nation-building which was what the receding colonial power claimed they were embarking on and the literature on "modernizing elites" confirmed was their historic role. With these disabilities, it is a miracle or fortuitous flow of events that the experiment has lasted for as long as it has, because as Jennings (1953: 40) observed, the choice before the parties to the independence contract was not between good, effective and efficient government and bad ineffective and inefficient one, but between having a government at all or not having one. The fragility of the arrangement was reflected in the events that followed the downing of the British flag and the hoisting of the flag of the new entity known as Nigeria, which contrary to Eleazu's assertion (1977: 25) that in 1960, Nigeria had "emerged as a state and thus the process of state-building was complete", was still in the process of being built (Elaigwu: 1979: 170), except if we limit the notion of "state" to juridical status rather than a socio-political reality.

From the census controversy of 1963 through the federal elections of 1964, the western regional elections of 1965, the military intervention and the consequent transformation of the federal arrangement into a unitary state through military rule to the civilian interregnum of 1979 - 83 and the emergence of military presidentialism under General Babangida; from the Interim National Government to Abacha's plutocratic absurdity, the cord that connects the chain of events to give them coherence is the consuming desire of the actors to actualize their pet dream of 'president' over their local empires with absolute powers to distribute the largesse to relations, friends and cronies. Thus, one cannot but ask scholars who present this kaleidoscope as the pangs and pains of nation-building (Eleazu: 1977 - 25 - 26) what historical precedence they rely on for their teleological projections regarding such "conglomerates of related ethnic groups" as Nigeria. The distinction between "wish" - the "ought" - and reality, the "is" - can hardly be more blurred!

If nation-building is "the process of politically socializing the people into becoming good citizens of the political order and making the citizens feel they have a stake in the community worth fighting for", certainly we are yet to witness the essence of the process in Nigeria. And if nation-building in federal states is a process "whereby the associative" type of relationship (Weber: 1964: 136) implied in the conscious creation of a federal state, is transformed into the "communal type" in which orientation to social action is based on a feeling that everyone in the federal state belongs together, then events since June 23, 1993, suggest that we are yet to unleash that process. While it may be plausible that groups of people in a state may desire a federation "only if there are social-cultural conditions which make a unitary system unacceptable and independent existence unviable, making federalism a residual means for harmonizing similarities and accommodating differences", it is not clear that this pre-condition impelled the Nigerian elite to submit to the federal formula. Of the conventional pre-conditions for federalizing – (i) a sense of military insecurity and of the consequent need for common defense; (ii) a desire for independence of foreign powers; (iii) a realization that only through union could independence be secured; (iv) a hope of economic advantage for the union; (v) some prior political association; (vi) a similarity of political institution and (vii) geographic contiguity (Wheare 1964:37-38), only (ii), (iii) and (vii), can be argued to have had a decisive impact on the decision by the founding fathers of Nigerian federalism to submit to the federal option. Carl J. Friedrich (1963: 6) defines a federation as:

> *A union of group selves, united by one or more common objectives but retaining their distinctive group being for other purposes. Federation is, on the inter-group level, what association is on the inter-personal level. It unites without destroying the selves that are uniting, and it is meant to strengthen them in their mutual relations* (emphasis added).

The Nigerian federal state has been transformed into a political monster-thanks to the oil economy - that is poised to consume the "selves" that federated, in an inferno of nihilistic plutocracy. If Karl Deutsch (1966) is correct in theorizing nation-building as a five stage process of transition from "tribe to nation" and Wheare's expectations of the outcome of the federal formula are valid (Wheare: 1964), Nigeria, at this point in time, should have arrived at stage four - the point in which the state can count on the people's "unsupervised compliance in most situations and on their active support in case of need." This is the stage of integration, a stage at which regional, religious and ethnic walls collapse and a pan-Nigerian identity is on the verge of consolidation. It can be argued that Nigerians did arrive at that stage on June 12, 1993, not because of what their leaders did but *in spite* of what they had done. However, true to their character, they suddenly realized their vulnerability to the ultimate status to which their performance condemns them and fought back with a ferocity that turned the clock of the integrationist agenda back full circle. This is in reference to what happened on June 12, 1993, when for the first time since 1914, Nigerians escaped from their "tribal", sectional and religious cocoons to assume a new historical identity by electing Moshood Abiola as President of the Federal Republic of Nigeria. An examination of the epochal feat shows that Abiola made history in a double sense: in breaking through the thick sectional walls in both the East and the North, but much more importantly in exploding the myth of the political invisibility of local or regional political chieftains. For never in the history of electoral politics in Nigeria was a local political hero crushed in his state, as Tofa, his opponent was. The sweetness of the victory for Abiola lies in the crushing defeat Tofa suffered in his local government in Kano! As the tables in Appendices 1 and 2 show, whereas Shagari's electoral spread in the 1979 elections was a function of the exploitation of the ethnic, religious and predatory incline of his party, the NPN, Abiola's reflected a determination by Nigerians to move beyond the communal enclave. This suggests that Nigerians had arrived at Deutsch's fifth stage in the process of nation-building - the stage of assimilation- in which Nigerians have "learned to communicate with each other and to understand each other well beyond the mere interchange of goods and services" (Deutsch: 1966: 91). But this was to be reversed by an act that calls to mind Gowon's infamous "no basis for unity" statement in 1966, when he assumed the leadership of a fractionalized army and a virtually collapsed state. For on June 23, 1993, Babangida, acting at the behest of the northern "oligarchy," sent an unsigned statement to the press, annulling the presidential election. With no tenable reason adduced for the action, the only interpretation that the circumstance imposed on the action was that it was taken to forestall a 'southerner' from acceding to the highest office of state. Thus began the reverse process of de-nationalizing the state. By the first anniversary of the historic June 12, the once - promising "giant in the sun" was at the precipice of another civil war.

In answering the question - why did 1967 and now 1993 happen, we may need to reflect on "how Nigeria was governed into federation" (Eleazu: 1977: 72). Specifically, we concur with the view that part of the problem was the manner in which the British vacillated in their commitment to the "making of a (Nigerian) nation," which, as we mentioned earlier, they had announced to the world was the end product of their mission in Africa and Asia.[3] According to Flint (1969: 255), the British, either because of lack of imagination or indecisiveness, failed to seize a golden opportunity to lay a more solid foundation for national integration in 1914:

> There was scarcely any discussion in London concerning the fundamental significance of amalgamation. Even in 1912, imaginative men might have seen the union of north and south as a great advance in Britain's Nigerian Mission, as the first step towards a new nation. But British officials never seriously discussed how conflicting policies in the two Nigeria's might be harmonized, how the rapidly growing individualism of the South with its cash crops, its rapidly expanding mission schools, its growing wage-earning and clerical class, its African entrepreneurs and petty capitalists, could be blended with northern feudal conservatism, Muslim law and self-sufficiency.

While this judgment may be valid, the fact remains that there is no guarantee that if the British officials had been sincere in their claim regarding the new entity they were creating, we would have witnessed a more cohesive state. The crux of the matter is that nations have historically been forged by a combination of force and appeasement. But, as the Indian case demonstrates so eloquently, leadership is the critical ingredient. Nigerians once snubbed anything Indian, having inherited British racial prejudices and images of the filth on the streets of Calcutta. Today no one can deny that India is truly "giant" in the Asian sun. Yet Indian society is no less heterogeneous or plural than Nigeria. Indeed, it can be argued that India is a macrocosm of the Nigerian cultural mosaic. Historical animosities are more deep-seated in India than in Nigeria for, as Ganguly (1999:222) notes, India is "the largest concentration of human diversity within a fixed geographic space." Haggi (1979: 143) describes the Indian cultural mosaic thus:

> *India has been the melting pot of races and religions but with an unenviable record of feuds, cleavages and prejudices which are exploited by narrow-minded and/or parochial leaders for short-term sectarian aims and ambitions. The social divisions have been both horizontal and vertical, inhibiting cultural homogeneity and social mobility; often accentuating differences and social divisions. India has been characterized as one of the largest geographical museums in the world, where several centuries jostle together, where population expands faster than production, where political behaviour is strongly coloured by consideration of communal identification, and where there is a lack of integration among elite and masses because of the absence of a unified communication system.*

India shares the same historical humiliation in the hands of British colonizers as Nigeria, separated by only thirteen years in the attainment of flag independence. Yet it is not only the largest democracy on earth, it has produced the first post-colonial historic identity that enables it to export not only material goods, but material culture - in the form of music and cuisines. How did it happen? In answering this question, Marx' dictum is relevant here. "Men" Marx insisted "make their own history, but they do not make it in a vacuum but in circumstances transmitted from the past". This posits the great philosophical debate on the tension between voluntarism and determinism in the development process. Assuming that the British were insincere or unimaginative in laying the foundation for Nigerian unity, how sincere or creative have been the successors to state power? The verdict of history on their performance is certainly harsh. In a rather prophetic statement, Fanon (1966: 72) had concluded that the African political class - the national bourgeoisie - is neither national nor bourgeois, but mere transmission belt for the transfer of national capital abroad. The Indian bourgeoisie, much to the shame of their

31

Nigerian counterpart which used to snob them, has been transformed into a national bourgeoisie in the mould of the middle classes in Europe and North America that have been associated with the consolidation of the national state. Of this Rath (1984: 90) observes:

> *The national consciousness that was developed in the course of the struggle for the independence had to be put in a national mould by creating a political union. This was done haphazardly by the Government of India Act of 1935. But it was accomplished fully and astutely by the Constitution of 1930. The leadership proved wise enough to gauge the national mood for union <u>by recognizing diversities and giving each region its due place in the federal structure.</u>* (Emphasis added).

What a contrast to the leadership in Nigeria. A rare historic opportunity presented itself on June 12, 1993, for Nigerian leaders to make their own history in the fashion of the Gandhis of India but this was blown away on the altar of personal, sectional and class interest. Babangida, in the course of his ego trip, had claimed he was inaugurating the dawn of a new socio-political order. "We now have a clean slate," he announced with fanfare at the launching of his two political parties on October 7, 1989, "and new political parties which can provide the turn around for all Nigerians, rich or poor, irrespective of their individual loyalties or geo-political location. In this new grassroot mass party experiment, we are all equal ' founders' and 'joiners.' I am confident that none of us will let this opportunity to dramatically change our political system for the better slip away again" (1989: 23). Four years later, on June 23, 1993, he was the first to "let the opportunity" for a new Nigerian identity "slip away" at least for now. This was the regime about which Oyovbaire and Olagunju (1989:2) had written with unmitigated passion:

> *The IBB era is a radical departure from the state of the nation during the first two and a half decades of independence. Without mincing words and at the risk of being uncharitable to past post-independence administrations and leadership of the country, the IBB administration is the only administration, which has proceeded on the basis of well thought out philosophy and programs of national redefinition and reconstruction. The essential philosophical elements here are those of economic recovery, social justice and self-reliance. The commitment of the administration is to what it believes to be the proper path to true independence unity and progress of the country, and it has, despite the vagaries, turbulence and contradictions of the nation, adhered doggedly to this commitment. <u>We can perceive and feel some primary recession of the old order and the main blocks and filaments of the new order.</u>* (My emphasis).[4]

It would be interesting to know what the authors of these sycophantic lines think six years later as they watched a country which produced June 12, 1993, totter on the brink of disintegration, because of the actions of a man supposedly committed "to true independence, unity and progress of the country!" It is the greater tragedy of using their intellects to ideologize the subversion of democracy that reinforces Joseph's characterization of Nigerian politics as prebendal. Prebendalism was institutionalized by the regime of Shehu Shagari, but was elected to a principle of state management under Babangida. The concept of prebendalism as an explanatory framework for understanding Nigerian politics was popularized by Richard Joseph (1991) in a scintillating analysis of Shagari's regime. It provides a refreshing and perceptive explanation of the failure of the Nigerian federalist experiment, specifically its failure to forge a Nigerian national identity. The failure, he insists, is rooted in the character of the post-colonial state in Nigeria. The state, he posits, "has increasingly become a magnet for all facets of political and economic life, consuming the attention of traders, contractors, builders, farmers, traditional rulers, teachers as much as that of politicians or politically motivated individuals". In the process the colonial state was transformed into the prebendal state, which is

> *not only one in which the offices of state are allocated and then exploited as benefices by the office-holders, but also as one where such practice is legitimately by a set of political norms according to which the appropriation of such offices is not just an act of individual greed or ambition but concurrently the satisfaction of the short-term objectives of a subset of the general population (Joseph, 1987:67).*

This, to a large extent, explains the annulment of June 12 and the institution of the contraption called *Interim National Government*, just as it explains the Abacha phenomenon and the grand deception that was his transition phantom. [5] Above all, it explains why intelligent Nigerians become so gullible to the tantalizing deceptions of armed pen-robbers encased in palatial state mansions as presidents or heads of state. But it also explains the continual truncation of the state to carve out prebendal space for unruly agitators even as it explains the Aburi agreement of 1967 (Elaigwu: 1979: 165) whose primary concern was the sharing of state offices. Finally, it accounts for why the revenue sharing formula remains the most contentious and divisive of all constitutional issues since independence (Oyovbaire: 1985: 162-97). Elazar (1979:39) postulate that Nigeria is "the one African nation where federalism has survived past the first few years of independence, that appears to do well even under less than democratic conditions."

Certainly for staying together, however tenuously, for forty years, is itself an achievement. If that can be passed for doing well, especially for surviving a grueling civil war, certainly Nigeria has done well. But if we are to measure the Nigerian performance against the ends with which federalism has been historically identified, especially in the "new nations" of Asia and Africa; if, as Elazar himself (1979:42) argues, the purpose of federalism is "to achieve (the) linking of the real and the ideal or the prosaic details of who does what and get what on a daily basis with the messianic aspirations for justice," if this effort to require humans constantly to grapple with both the prosaic and the messianic in relation to one another, never allowing the human pursuit of ideal states to bring people to ignore the hard realities of politics, and never allowing people's concern for the hard reality of politics to give them an excuse for ignoring considerations of justice, then the Nigerian experiment has been a disaster. For forty years after its institution the "politics of communalism" so well caricatured by Melson and Wolpe has been "born again" in the aftermath of June 23,1993, thanks to the character of the Nigerian ruling class.

Not only have the various factions of the class contributed in varying degrees to the near-collapse of the state (which is what the current impasse represents), they have returned Nigerians to a stage in the evolution of nationalism Alfred Cobban (1969: 17) calls "the stage of state-breaking." For what is it other than the collapse of the federal state when elected representatives, such as state governors, threaten secession should the results of an election adjudged to be the cleanest in the nation 's history be respected? [6] How else can one interpret the resort to ethno-religious revivalism to justify the annulment of June 12 and the inauguration of a fresh transition agenda. It is all, we contend, to prevent the passage of power from a section of the country - the North - that has become habituated to determining "who gets what" in the federation, to another - the Southwest - that has fought so relentlessly in the past but were denied by its leaders' inability to forge cross - cultural alliances so critical to electoral success in a multiglot that Nigeria is (Zakka: 1994: 10 - 17).

All this is not to deny some tentative steps taken by the political class toward advancing the cause of national integration. These include the creation of more states and local governments (the original three-region federal state with fewer than 200 local governments have, by 1995, metamorphosed into a 36 state structure with 774 local governments) to contain ethnic agitations; the institution in 1972 of the National Youth Service Corp, to inculcate and "establish a national psyche" in the Nigerian youths (Usman: 1987:42) and the institutionalization of affirmative action, otherwise known as the federal character in the Nigeria constitution (Ukwu: 1987: Ekeh and Osaghae: 1989). This was extended even to political parties in the 1979 competition for offices (Egwu: 1993: 48) in compliance with the Constitution.[7]

Most crippling of all, this logic was extended to what is, by Weberian prescription, the pillar of the modern state - the state bureaucracy. Habibu Sani captures the tragedy of prebendalism in the Second Republic in which he played a key role as Director of Research for the ruling party - the National Party of Nigeria (NPN).

> *The component units of the federation... saw themselves as competing for key posts of permanent secretaries and other chief executives of the federal boards and corporations at the centre. Every regional government saw to it that it was given a fair share in the distribution of these important posts in very much the same way as it saw to it that the national political cake is equally shared.*

At the sub-national level (Kwara State) where he functioned as a senior bureaucrat, he makes this revealing observation about the extent to which the bureaucracy was prebendalized:

> *The concept of "ethnic balancing" in the appointment and promotion of officers to intermediate and senior posts has been accorded a greater dimension. The various ethnic groups forming the state... clamour for all manner of posts for their respective sons of the soil in the various arms of the public services. Any appointment, promotion, or even dismissal to a new post is seen and judged from the narrow perspective of the effect it has on the unofficial quota of the ethnic group concerned.* (Quoted in Joseph : 1991: 84). (Emphasis added)

This represents the nadir of institutional decay, and shows how efforts ostensibly designed to "produce in citizens a perception of covariance of rewards and punishments with other citizens to convince them they now belong together" (Eleazu: 1977:29) have moved the country further. The ruling elite has thus failed to deploy the great potential inherent in the federalist logic to establish the foundations of an operational national identity.

Conclusion

It is the failure of the federal state in Nigeria (thanks largely to the militarization of governance between January 1966 and May 1999), that has produced the strident calls for the dissolution of the union (Saro-Wiwa: 1992: 13). Explanations for the failure range from the communal frame of mind in multi-ethnic societies (Melson and Wolpe: 1971) to the "irrelevance of the state" to the needs and concerns of the vast majority of the population (Ihonvbere:

1993). Because Nigeria cannot be classified as belonging to what Furnival (1948: 303: 12) called "plural societies" characterized by cultural divergence, the confinement of cross-cultural contacts to economic relations, economic specialization by cultural sectors (a sort of ethnic division of labor) a lack of shared values and the absence of a common will, explanations for the failure of the federal experiment have to be sought outside the institutional incompatibility thesis advanced by Smith (1965: 1969). Marxist analysis of the ethnic question, as we noted above, considers ethnicity as a dependent variable, a form of "false consciousness" in which ethnic consciousness is superimposed on the interest of the masses thereby blurring the objective class question. Yet one cannot but agree with Horrowitz, (1985) that the class question must be complemented with the "psychic" question before a full and valid explanation of the phenomenon can be offered.

Why, we may ask, do the masses of the Igbo, Yoruba or Hausa continue to follow their kinsmen in their struggle for scarce resources that ultimately end up in the construction of palatial mansions in the Ikoyi and Victoria Islands that constitute the oases of affluence in the ocean of unconscionable misery across the country, not to talk of numbered accounts in Swiss Banks, rather than in improved material conditions for the Igbo, Yoruba or Hausa masses? The explanation for this, according to Horrowitz, lies in the fear of ethnic domination. Power, in this context, is not, as the processual theories of politics posit, " a means to and end" i.e. for the authoritative allocation values (Truman: 1951: Key: 1956: Easton: 1953), but an end in itself. Accordingly:

> The fear of ethnic domination and suppression is a motivating force for the acquisition of power as an end. And power is also sought for confirmation of ethnic status. Broad matters of group status regularly have equal or superior standing to the narrow allocative decisions often taken to be the uniform stuff of everyday politics - fundamental issues such as citizenship, electoral systems, designations of official languages and religions, the rights of groups to a "special position" in the polity, rather than merely setting the frameworks for politics, become the recurring subjects of politics. Conflicts over needs and interests are subordinated to conflicts over the rules to govern conflict. (Horrowitz: 1985:187)

The point of this perspective on ethnicity is that once the ethnic leaders succeed in posing the class question as status question, the material conditions of the masses are subordinated to the psychological burden of group status. The situation in Benin Republic illustrates this eloquently, as captured by Dov Ronen (1975: 188): "for one of the three chief political leaders (of regional ethnic groups) not to be in power - mere representation and participation in government do not count - means for his supporters not only to be 'out of power' but also to be ruled by another region or regions which are in power; it means not only to be 'out' but also to be 'under'; it means to be politically over-powered by 'others'. Herein lies the saliency of ethno-religious primordialisms for political competition. Its manipulation (Usman:1987; Jibrin: 1991; Kukah: 1994) assures the primacy of the north in Nigerian Politics, or, more accurately, the sustenance of "a bloodsucking parasitic oligarch" (Usman: 1987: 64). The conclusion that emerges from all this is that even though federalism was consciously cultivated to promote "unity in diversity" the critical ingredient - patriotic leadership - has been missing, leading to the stalemate that eventuated in the historic compromise of January 1999 which produced Obasanjo as the presidential candidate of the People's Democratic Party and Olu Falae (both from the pensive southwest) as the candidate of the Alliance for Democracy. June 23, 1993, was, indeed, a watershed in the transition from state-building to state-breaking. Having confronted the state "not as a public force but as an alien hostile coercive power." (Ake; 1993:32) Nigerians have increasingly resorted to the primordialism of "tribe" which provides "entry points" into the atomized existence of urban life. As Ihonvbere (1993: 55) points out, ethnic unions displaced the state in popular consciousness because they "provide support in cases of unemployment and of ill health. They take care of families in cases of accidents and transport corpses to villages for burial. They run scholarship schemes, serve as sources of information and provide refuge and hope in times of crisis. They also have political functions, since they can be easily mobilized in support of particular political interests or candidates at minimal cost"[8]

With the near collapse of the state on which federalism is anchored in the first instance, the prospects for resolving the national question in Nigeria are dim, unless the strident calls for restructuring the polity, as echoed in Soyinka's introductory chapter, are heeded by those who control the levers of power in the current dispensation. June 23 1993, the date the annulment of the presidential election was announced, has come to make the resolution more remote by elevating the ethnic question to the domain of group psychology, in which fears of perpetual ethnic hegemony have been confirmed by the denial of the fruits of what was clearly a fair game. Olusanya (1986:15) argues that it is the failure to idolize our heroes that accounts, in part, for Nigeria's failure in nation-building. The "problem with the solution" (Ayoade: 1988) suggests, is that like all such prescriptions -state creation, National Youth Service, federal character - for every step taken in the progression to nationhood, our leaders take the equivalent of ten steps backward in a single act, such as the politicization of religion - à la membership of the Organization of Islamic Conference (OIC) or the June 23 1993 annulment of the presidential election. Once a leadership is bankrupt to the point that it does not link its destiny with the destiny of the nation, no prescription provides a lasting solution.

Perhaps Elazar's conclusion that ethnic federations are among the most difficult of all to sustain and least likely to survive is dawning as the Nigerian reality. Ojukwu had suggested in 1967, on the eve of the outbreak of the civil war, that "it is better we move slightly apart and survive (in a confederation?); it is much worse that we move closer and perish in the collision " (Kirk-Greene: 1971 : 335). This may be an unfortunate course to take, but given the character of the present crisis, the options are increasingly becoming fewer. "Ethnic nationalism, Elazar (1993: 194) insists, "is the most egocentric of all nationalisms, and the most difficult basis on which to erect a system of constitutionalized power-sharing; the essence of federalism. Federal theory calls for nationalism on the basis of consent, whatever its democratic content, consent which allows both for the division and sharing of powers. Most of today's nationalisms, on the other hand, emphasize those things which separate people: language, religion, national myths or whatever."

The Christians' holy book- the Bible- puts the Nigerian dilemma in a poignant but instructive perspective: "Where there is no vision," King Solomon, one of Israel's accomplished historic leaders, declared, "the people perish, (Prov. 29: 18)." In secular rendition, and in the Nigerian context, this is a call for re-conceptualizing national integration not as a total unity, but as a process of assimilation through which regional forces, however strong, do not weaken or sacrifice the "nation-in-the-making" but merely want their identity to be reckoned with as a factor in its growth and prosperity. But such a feeling has to be nurtured by visionary leadership. Unless this happens, the choice before Nigerians narrows to, at best, confederation, as advocated by leaders of the Movement for National Reformation (Momoh, 1993:35) or at worst disintegration into ethnic states, as contemplated by Orka (Ibrahim: 1991: 134-5). Should that happen, Nigeria will merely be following in the footsteps of Yugoslavia, Somalia, Ethiopia, Liberia, and most tragic of all, Rwanda, to mention a few of the celebrated cases of state-breaking by the new Jacobinism (Cobban: 1969:17). This would confirm Enloe's thesis that there is nothing sacrosanct about the nation-state, only social scientists make it look so (Enloe: 1973: 12)! The challenge before Nigerians is to design a constitution that would assure 'that some constitutionally guaranteed and entrenched autonomy and collective right to self determination should be granted to states as they are now or in a re-configured structure, something close to Obafemi Awolowo's ethno-linguistic federalism. This may not necessarily remove, entirely, the bogey of irredentism along the trajectory of democratic federal consolidation, but it will make such agitations less appealing to the majority of citizens whose narrower identity and culture would be sheltered in such a re-constituted federal state. If the current political actors can be "forced" *in their own interest* to midwife such a constitution, federalism would have regained its promise as the panacea for deeply divided societies.

* Ethiopia has blazed the trail in this direction.

ENDNOTES

1. I use this label for lack of a more economizing one, given the fact that they were more concerned with winning independence than building a nation. O'Connell is certainly correct to say that, "in multi-national colonial quasi-states, it makes more sense to speak of independence movements than national movements" (See Melson and Wolpe, 1971: 663).

2. That the colonial administrators considered the northern fraction of the "nationalist" movement as friends is evident, not only from the shared aristocratic values, but even more importantly, from the fact that the north became the last colonial outpost, the regional civil service absorbing most of those who were too young to retire but could not be absorbed into the home service. As a result, many of them cherished the special status they enjoyed in the northern civil service, and developed warm personal relationships with the northern leaders. A typical example of this is the strenuous effort one such officer made to "tell the truth" about the 1966 coup. See D. J. M. Muffett, *Let the Truth Be Told* (Zaria, Hudahuda Publishing Company, 1982). See especially the glowing tribute he pays to Ahmadu Bello, p. 12. Similarly, in his independence speech, Prime Minister, Balewa expressed *gratitude* to the British "whom we have known, first as masters, and then leaders, and finally as partners, but *always as friends*" (my emphasis). See *Mr. Prime Minister: A Selection of Speeches Made by Alhaji Abubakar Tafawa Balewa, Prime Minister of the Federal republic of Nigeria* (Lagos, Nigerian national Press, Apapa, 1964). P. 49.

3. The British Government put out a series of pamphlets titled, "The Making of a Nation," for each of the territories it "granted" independence. For Nigeria, it was: "Nigeria: the Making of a Nation".

4. For a critique of that transition program see Aaron T. Gana "The Limits of Political Engineering: A Critique of the Transition Programme," Jos: Covenant Press Ltd. 1990 pp. 22-23.

5. For the various agenda, see *Timesweek,* February 28, 1994, pp. 19-25.

6. *The African Guardian*, October 25, 1993, pp. 19 - 25

7. The constitution provides that "the composition of the Government of the Federation or any of its agencies and the conduct of its affairs, shall be carried out in such manner as to reflect the federal character of Nigeria and *the need to promote national unity,* and also to command national loyalty thereby ensuring that there shall be no predominance of persons from a few states or from a few ethnic or other sectional

groups in that government or in any of its agencies" (Section 14.3 of the 1979 constitution).

8. A former student of mine narrated his bitter experience with representatives of the Nigerian State in New York when he lost his immediate senior brother in a car accident. Asked to assist in getting the corpse to the family in Benin, the Nigerian Consular officials said they could do nothing to assist. It is difficult to imagine anything that is capable of alienating the citizen from the state more than this. If in such circumstances, especially in a foreign land, the state cannot assist the bereaved, it is no wonder that ethnic associations displace the state in the hearts of citizens. In the student's case, of course, the ethnic association in the United States pulled members' resources together and sent the corpse home.

REFERENCES

Ake, C. 1967. "Political Integration and Political Stability," *World Politics*, Vol. XIX, No.3 pp.486-499.

———. 1978. *Revolutionary Pressures in Africa*. London: LED Press.

———. 1981. *A Political Economy of Africa*. London: Longman.

———. 1993. "What is the Problem of Ethnicity in Africa?" *in Transformation, 22.*

Amin, S. 1976. *Unequal Development*, New York: Monthly Review Press.

———. 1978. *The Arab Nation*. London: Zed Press.

——— 1980. *Class and Nation*. New York: Monthly Review Press.

Arikpo, O. 1967. *The Development of Modern Nigeria*. Middlesex, England: Penguin Books.

Awolowo, O. 1947. *Path to Nigeria's Freedom*. London: Faber.

———. 1966. *Thoughts on Nigerian Constitution*. Ibadan: Oxford University Press.

Ayoade, J.O.O. 1988. "Federalism in Nigeria: The Problem with the Solution," mirneo, Faculty of the Social Sciences, University of Ibadan.

Babangida, I.B. 1989. "The Dawn of a New Socio-Political Order: An Address to the Nation." Abuja: MAMSER

Balewa, A.T. 1964. *Mr. Prime Minister*. Lagos: Nigerian National Press.

Blaut, J.M. 1987. *The National Question: Decolonizing the Theory of Nationalism*, London: Zed Press.

Bloom, S. 1967. *The World of Nations: A Study of the National Implications in the Work of Karl Marx*. New York: AMS.

Bose, T.C. ed. *Indian Federalism: Problems and Issues*. Calcutta: K.K. Bagchi.

Bienen, H.L. 1962. *Power and Stability in Nigeria*. New York: Praeger.

Brown, M.E. ed. 1993. *Ethnic Conflict and International Security*. Princeton, N.J: Princeton University Press.

Cobban A. 1969. *The Nation-State and National Self-Determination*. London: Collins.

Coleman, J.S. 1958. *Nigeria: Background to Nationalism*. Berkeley: University of California Press.

Dudley, B.J. 1966. "Federalism and the Balance of Political Power in Nigeria" in *Journal of Commonwealth Political Studies*, 4, pp. 16-29.

Deutsch, K. 1966. *Nationalism and Social Communication: An Inquiry into the Foundation of*

Nationality. Cambridge Mass: MIT Press.

Easton, D. 1953. *The Political System: An Inquiry into the State of Political Science*. New York: Knopf.

Egwu, S.G. 1993. "Ethnicity, Economic Crisis and national Development in Nigeria" in O. Nnoli ed., *Dead-End to Nigeria Development*. Dakar: CODESRIA, pp. 44-78.

Ekeh, P.P. and Osaghae, E.E. eds., 1989, *Federal Character and Federalism in Nigeria*. Ibadan: Heinemann.

Elaigwu, J.I. 1979. "The Military and State Building: Federal-State Relations in Nigeria's Military Federalism, 1966-76," in A.B. Akinyemi, et. al., *Readings on Federalism*. Lagos: Nigerian Institute of International Affairs, pp.155-181.

EIazar, D. 1979. *Federalism and Political Integration*. Ramat Gan: Turtledove Publishing.

————. 1993 "International and Comparative Federalism," in *Political Science and Politics*, Vol. XXVI, No.2.

Eleazu, Uma O. 1977. *Federalism and Nation-building: The Nigerian Experience, 1945-1964*. Devon, UK: Arthur Stockwell.

Enloe, C.H. 1973. *Ethnic Conflict and Political Development*. Boston: Little Brown.

Fanon, F. 1966. *The Wretched of the Earth*. New York: Grove Press.

Flint, J.E. 1969. "Nigeria: The Colonial Experience from 1880-1914, "in L.H. Gann and Peter Duignan eds., *Colonialism in Africa, 1870-1960 Vol. 1: The History and Politics of Colonialism, 1870-1914*. Cambridge: Cambridge University Press.

Friedrich, C.J. 1963. *Federalism: National and International*. London: Oxford University Press.

Furnivall, J.S. 1948. *Colonial Policy and Practice*. London: Cambridge University Press.

Gana, A.T. 1983. "Politics and the Development Process in Nigeria", *Journal of African Marxists*, Vol. 4, pp. 63-78.

————.1985. "The State in Africa: Yesterday, Today and Tomorrow", *International Political Science Review* Vol. 6, No. 1, pp. 115-132.

————.1987. "The Politics and Economics of State Creation in Nigeria," Nigerian Journal of Policy and Strategy, Vol. 2, No. 1, pp. 12-23.

————.1990. *The Limits of Political Engineering: A Critique of the Transition Programme*: Jos: Covenant Press Ltd. 33 pp.

————. 2000. "Civil Society and the Consolidation of Democracy in Nigeria," in I.A. Ayua et al., *Nigeria: Issues in the 1999 Constitution*. Lagos: Nigerian Institute of Advanced Legal Studies.

Haggi, S.A.H. 1979. "Nation-Building in India: Problems and prospects, "in *Indian Journal of Politics*, Vol. XIII, No. 1 & 2.

Hardgrave, R.L., Jr. 1993. "India: The Dilemmas of Diversity, "in *Journal of Democracy*, Vol.4, No.4. pp. 54-68.

Horrowitz, D.L.E. 1985. *Ethnic Groups in Conflict*. Berkeley: University of California Press.

Ibrahim, Jibrin. 1991. "Religion and Political Turbulence in Nigeria," in *Journal of Modern African Studies*, Vol.29, No. l, pp. 115-136.

Ihonvbere, J.O. 1994. "The irrelevant state: Ethnicity and the Question of Nationhood in Africa, "in *Ethnic and Racial Studies*, Vol. 17, No. 1, January 1994, pp. 42-60.

Isichie, E. 1983. *A History of Nigeria*. London: Longman.

Jennings, I. 1966. "Some Characteristics of the Indian Constitution", in R.L. Watts, *New Federations: Experiments in the Commonwealth*. London: Oxford University Press.

Jinadu, L.A. 1979. "Federalism and Democracy: Debate and Its Lessons, "in S.E. Oyovbaire *Democratic Experiment in Nigeria*. Benin: Omega Publishers, pp. 40-64.

Joseph, R.A. 1991. *Democracy and Prebendal Politics in Nigeria: The rise and fall of the Second Republic*. Ibadan: Spectrum Books.

Kedourie, E. 1961. *Nationalism*. New York: Fredrick Praeger

Key, V.O. 1956. *Politics and Pressure Groups*, 3rd ed. New York: Crowell.

Kirk-Green, A.M.H. 1971. *Crisis and Conflict in Nigeria: A Documentary Source Book*, (2 Vols.), London: Cambridge University Press.

Kolakowski, L. 1978. *Main Currents of Marxion*. Vol. II. Oxford: Oxford University Press.

Kukah, M.H. 1993. *Religion Politics and Power in Northern Nigeria*. Ibadan: Spectrum Books.

Kuper, L. and Smith, M.G., 1969, *Pluralism in Africa*, Berkeley: University of California Press.

Lenin, V.I. 1964. *Collected Works*, Vol.20 Moscow: Progress Publishers.

Lijphart, 1977. *Democracy in Pluralistic Societies*. New Haven: Yale University Press

Livingston, W. S. 1967. "A Note on the Nature of Federalism," in A. Wildavsky, *American Federalism in Perspective*. Boston: Little Brown.

MacRae, Kenneth D. ed. 1994. *Consociational Democracy: Political Accommodation in Segmented Societies*. Toronto: MacClellan and Stewart

Marx, K. 1963. *The 18th Brumaire of Louis Bonaparte*. New York: International Publishers.

————. and Frederick Engels, 1976, *Collected Works 1945-1948*. London: Lawrence and Wishart.

Melson, R. and Wolpe, H. eds. 1971. *Nigeria: Modernization and the Politics of Communalism*. Ann Arbor: Michigan State University Press.

Mill, J. S. 1948. *Representative Government*. London: Everyman.

Momoh, A. 1999. "The Movement for National Reformation and the Struggle for Democracy in Nigeria" in Oyeleye Oyediran and Adigun A.B. Agbaje eds. *Nigeria: The Politics of Transition and Governance (1986) – 96*. Dakar: Council for the Development of Social Science Research in Africa (CODESRIA).

Munck, R. 1984. *Politics and Dependency in the Third World*. London: ZED Books Ltd.

Muffet, D.J.M. 1982. *Let the Truth Be Told: The Coup d' Etat of 1966*. Zaria: Hudahuda Publishing Company.

Nnoli, O. 1980. *Ethnic Politics in Nigeria*. Enugu: Fourth Dimension Publishers.

————. 1989. *Ethnic Politics in Africa*. Ibadan: Vantage Publishers.

————. 1993. *Dead-end to Development: An Investigation on the Social Economic and Political Crisis in Nigeria*. Dakar: CODESRIA Book Series.

Ollman, B. 1976. *Alienation: Marxist Conception of Man in Capitalist Society*, 2nd edition, Cambridge: Cambridge University Press.

Olusanya, G.O. 1986. *Nation-Building in Nigeria: A Study in the Poverty of Imagination*. Lagos: Nigerian Institute of International Affairs.

Ostrom, Vincent, et al. 1988. *Local Government in the United States*. San Francisco: California: Institute of Contemporary Studies Press.

Oyovbaire, S. E. 1985. *Federalism in Nigeria: A Study in the Development of the Nigerian State*. London: Macmillan.

————. and Olagunju, O. eds. 1989. *Foundations of a New Nigeria*. London: Precision Press.

Post, Kenneth and Michael Vickers. 1973. *Structure and Conflict in Nigeria:1960-1966;* London: Heinemann.

Poulantzas, N. 1980. *State Power and Socialism*. London: Vevso

Riker, N.H. 1975. "Federalism" in Nelson Polsby and Fred Greenstein, eds. *Handbook of Political Science* 8 vols. Reading: Addison – Wesley Publishing Company

Ronan, D. 1975. *Dahomey: Between Tradition and Modernity*. Ithaca Cornell University Press

Saro-Wiwa, K. 1992. *Ogoni Bill of Rights*. Port Harcourt.

Sklar, R.L. 1991. "Democracy in Africa" in Richard L. Sklar and C.J. Whitaker eds. *African Politics and Problems in Development*. Boulder, Colorado: Lynne Rienner.

Truman, David B. 1951. *The Governmental Process*. New York: Crowell.

Usman, B. 1987. *The Manipulation of Religion in Nigeria, 1977-1987*. Kaduna: Vanguard Press .

Watts, R.L. 1966. *New Federations: Experiments in the Commonwealth*. London: Oxford University Press.

Weber, M., ed. 1964. *Theory of Social and Economic Organization*. New York: Free Press.

Wheare, K. C. *Federal Government*, 4th ed.. New York: Oxford University Press.

Young, C. 1994. "Democratization in Africa: The Contradictions of a Political Imperative, "in Jennifer A. Widner. ed., *Economic Change and Political Liberalization in Sub-Saharan Africa*. Baltimore: The John Hopkins University Press.

Zakka, T. 1994. "Leadership: Why the South Always Losses," in *Citizen*, April 4-10, pp. 10-17.

APPENDIX 1

The Annulled June 12, 1993, Presidential Election Unofficial Results

State	Rank by 1991 Census	Rank By Total Votes	Votes Cast SDP	NRC	Total (SDP+NRC)	% of Total SDP	NRC
Lagos	1	2	883,965	149,432	1,033,397	85.54	14.46
Kano	2	22	169,519	154,809	324,328	52.27	47.73
Sokoto	3	12	97,726	372,250	469,976	20.79	79.21
Bauchi	4	4	339,339	524,836	864,175	39.27	60.73
Rivers	5	3	370,678	640,973	1,011,651	36.64	63.36
Kaduna	6	5	389,713	356,880	746,593	52.20	47.80
Ondo	7	1	883,024	162,994	1,046,019	84.42	15.58
Katsina	8	13	171,162	271,077	442,239	38.70	61.30
Oyo	9	7	536,014	105,785	641,799	82.52	16.48
Plateau	10	6	417,565	259,394	676,959	61.68	38.32
Enugu	11	8	263,101	254,050	517,151	50.88	49.12
Jigawa	12	27	138,557	89,636	228,193	60.72	39.28
Benue	13	15	246,830	186,302	433,132	56.99	43.01
Anambra	14	18	212,024	155,029	367,053	57.76	42.24
Borno	15	25	153,490	128,684	282,174	54.40	45.60
Delta	16	11	327,277	146,001	473,278	69.15	30.85
Imo	17	20	159,650	195,836	355,186	44.86	55.14
Niger	18	19	136,350	221,437	357,787	38.11	61.89
Akwalbom	19	16	214,782	159,342	374,124	57.41	42.59
Ogun	20	14	365,266	72,068	437,334	83.52	16.48
Abia	21	26	105,273	151,227	256,500	41.04	58.96
Osun	22	10	425,725	59,246	484,971	87.78	12.22
Edo	23	23	205,407	103,572	308,979	66.48	33.52
Adamawa	24	24	140,875	167,239	308,114	45.72	54.28
Kogi	25	9	22,700	265,732	488,432	45.59	54.41
Kebbi	26	28	70,219	144,808	215,027	32.66	67.34
Cross River	27	21	189,303	153,452	342,755	55.23	44.77
Kwara	28	17	288,270	80,219	368.489	78.23	21.77
Taraba	29	30	101,887	64,001	165,888	51.42	38.58
Yobe	30	29	111,887	64,061	175,948	63.59	36.41
FCT	31	31	19,968	18,313	38,281	52.16	47.84

APPENDIX 2

Ethnic Factors in Nigerian Politics: Results of the 1983 Presidential Elections*

State	Votes Cast	Shagari NPN	Awolowo UPN	Azikiwe NPP	Waziri GNPP	Yusuf PRP	Braithwaite NAP
Anambra	1,158,293	385,297 33. 33.36%	23,859 3.06%	669,348 57.79%	36,165 3.12%	16,103 1.39%	27,511 2.38%
Bauchi	1,782,122	1,507,154 84.57%	98,974 6.55%	55,258 7.66%	37,203 2.09%	54,554 9.05%	18,979 1.07%
Bendel	1,099,851	452,776 41.17%	566,035 51.45%	53,395 4.35%	11,723 1.05%	7,359 2.67%	8,653 0.79%
Benue	652,795	384,045 58.83%	79,699 12.21%	152,209 23.31%	19,897 3.05%	6,381 2.09%	19,573 1.60%
Borno	718,043	348,974 48.6%	120,138 16.73%	26,700 3.76%	170,265 24.96%	96,066 3.76%	15,608 2.10%
Cross River	1,295,710	696,592 54.00%	505,922 39.43%	46,418 3.61%	15,582 1.29%	8,209 0.54%	10,397 0.85%
Congola	735,648	282,820 38.44%	160,720 21.85%	148,255 20.13	25,530 3.47%	81,205 11.04%	37,310 5.27%
Imo	1,588,975	298,453 25.07%	22,649 1.43%	1,054,436 66.99%	52,354 3.29%	19,370 1.16%	32,694 2.04%
Kaduna	2,137,398	1,266,894 59.28%	225,878 10.57%	225,919 10.58%	80,862 3.06%	300,472 14.02%	37,260 1.75%
Kano	1,193,050	383,998 32.19%	48,494 4.06%	274,102 22.98%	35,252 2.95%	436,997 36.63%	14,207 1.19%
Kwara	608,422	299,654 49.25%	275,134 45.22%	16,245 2.66%	7,670 1.26%	3,693 0.61%	6,356 1.00%
Lagos	1,640,381	126,165 7.59%	1,367,807 83.39%	119,455 7.28%	11,748 0.72%	6,570 0.24%	8,636 0.05%
Niger	430,731	274,085 63.17%	15,772 3.66%	112,971 25.23%	12,994 3.01%	8,736 2.03%	8,182 1.90%
Ogun	1,261,061	43,821 3.47%	1,198,033 95.00%	5,022 0.04%	6,874 0.55%	4,559 0.35%	2,862 0.23%
Ondo	1,829,343	355,217 20.03%	1,412,539 77.25%	20,340 1.11%	11,629 0.63%	7,052 0.39%	10,566 0.58%
Oyo	2,351,000	885,125 37.55%	1,396,225 59.39%	34,852 1.48%	15,732 0.57%	9,174 0.39%	9,891 0.42%
Plateau	652,302	292,606 44.86%	38,210 5.86%	292,803 18.05%	18,612 0.85%	11,581 1.77%	10,490 1.61%
Rivers	1,367,715	921,654 67.88%	251,825 18.55%	151,958 11.15%	12,981 0.95%	4,626 0.34%	15,051 1.11%
Sokoto	2,837,786	2,605,985 91.38%	75,428 2.66%	63,238 2.23%	46,752 1.65%	24,280 0.65%	22,152 0.75%
Abuja FCT	135,351	127,372	1,102	2,156	1,103	641	977
Total	**25,454,166**	**12,47,648**	**7,885,434**	**3,534,633**	**142,128**	**1,037,481**	**308,842**

Source: Samuel G. Egwu, "Ethnicity, Economic Crisis and National Development in Nigeria," in Okwudiba Nnoli ed. *Dead End to Nigerian Development* (Dakar, Codesria. 1993) p. 52.

*The second figure in each column represents percentage of the total votes cast in each state.

CHAPTER 3

Renewing The Federal Paradigm In Nigeria: Contending Issues And Perspectives

Ekeng A. Anam-Ndu

Introduction

The distress and persistent call for restructuring the country, for a sovereign national conference, for regionalization of the army, for radical review of our fiscal federalism, for 'sharia' law as an alternative penal code based on religious particularism, and for the zoning principle to be enshrined in the constitution, are cumulative outcome of a nation under pressure of suffocating unitarism. Besides, the demand by ethno-political groups for a re-negotiation of the basic agreements of the federal union albeit sporadic, is increasingly taking a violent dimension. Referring to themselves as 'nations' or 'race', recent ethnic agitation and restiveness aggregated as resistant movements tend to make plausible the belief that feelings of unity, common citizenship and nationality were more pervasive in the 1960s and 1970s than in the late 1980s and 1990s. Perhaps never before in the history of post-independence Nigeria has ethno-nationalism reached a crescendo of militancy and ungovernability marked by readiness to kill and destroy on a large scale, as now.

Whether these issues are seen as landmines that could explode and disintegrate Nigeria and, therefore, should not be publicly discussed, or are mere extremist positions that arise out of deep seated frustration of a marginalized people, they raise a number of questions that touch on the conceptualization of federalism and, consequently, on the way it is practiced in Nigeria in particular, and in other federal countries of Africa, generally. Unfortunately, there is no theory of federalism or universally acceptable meaning of the term under which we can take refuge and correct misconceptions and misapplications. Kenneth Wheare's (1963:10) conceptualization of federalism as "…the method of dividing powers so that general and regional governments are each, within a sphere, coordinate and independent…"[1] does not help beyond stating as he rightly points out, "…a principle of organization and practice whose ultimate test rests on how each federal system operates."[2]

Despite the variety of contributions made to the study of federalism by latter day scholars,[3] the contrasting reformulations have been undertaken basically within the Anglo-Saxon tradition and provides little or no theoretical handle for dealing with problems of federalism in African countries. Two inter related problems arise from this paradigmatic bias. First, rather than help the conceptual clarity of the term, it confuses it as all sorts of constitutional arrangements designed to meet different circumstances in different societies are dubbed as federalism. Riker has aptly noted that "an initial difficulty in any discussion of federalism is that the meaning of the word has been thoroughly confused by dramatic changes in the institutions to which it refers…. Hence, a word that originally referred to institutions with an emphasis on local self government has come to connote also domination by a gigantic impersonal concentration of force…"[4] Second and, consequently, the practice in non Anglo-Saxon areas of federalism so conceptualized has been impoverished for want of response to the integrative challenges of such areas.

African scholars of federalism have not helped matters either. Rather than relate their conceptual formulations to the challenge of integrated development and participatory democracy, most of their studies have tended to bask under the protection of theoretical formulations of Anglo-Saxon scholars. Yet the need for the development of paradigmatic individualism in African social science remains imperative and urgent.

From the point of view of structure, Nigeria has gone a long way to lay a solid foundation of a federal union but appropriate institutional practices have not been contrived to reflect our plural social setting and political experiences. Such fundamental and thoughtful federal practices cautiously designed by the founding fathers were destroyed in the wake of military rule in 1966. In recent times, the introduction of democracy after prolonged military rule has opened a floodgate of widespread demands, agitations and restiveness by ethnic groups, minority and majority alike. It would be foolhardy to view these developments as temporary outbursts of suppressed feelings that will disappear with time. That these movements are sufficient to liquidate the

Nigerian federation, or at best, impoverish democratic governance, is the more reason they must be urgently addressed.

Without any intention to dampen expectations of a democratic dispensation in 21st century Nigeria, it is argued here that the current experiment in democratic governance is in no way different from the earlier ones which failed for want of congruence between political practice and the popular expectation of the Nigerian people. Provoked by reflections such as these, this chapter confronts the issue of restructuring the Nigerian federalism basically on four fronts. Section 1 deals with the problem of centralized federalism and how to restore democratic health in Nigerian politics and governance. Section 2 examines the character of Nigeria's fiscal federalism which, in practice, is best categorized as fiscal patriarchalism, and argues for an urgent need to federalize inter-governmental fiscal relations. The recurrent challenge of producing democratic leadership in which all the component units of Nigeria simultaneously participate and which is capable of recreating democratic values unique to our plural setting is addressed in Section 3. If leadership is one of the critical problems facing Nigeria, then followership must be part of that problematic. Section 4 analyses this interrelated phenomenon and argues for qualitative rather than mass political participation.

Centralized Federalism

In all modern societies where there are deep ethnic, religious or ideological cleavages, a federal form of government of one type or the other has been used quite successfully to regulate relations among such groups. The degree of 'dividedness', the historical antecedents, or the shared experience within a given federal union, the imperatives of economic development, the political impulses of the various segment of the federal society, have always determined whether or not the center should carry the bulk of legislative and development burden, or, whether such burden should be dispersed to the federating units for a more effective and efficient handling. These challenges account for why each federal society devices its unique federal form congruent with its peculiar socio-economic and political problems and, consequently, why there is a wide spectrum of federal forms of government.

In this country, strong ethnic and religious cleavages are real. This notwithstanding, they are epiphenomenally relevant politically. In other words, they assume problematic political relevance in response to public policies and observable political practices that offend the cherished and civilized values of equality, freedom and justice. However, among States, sharp differences in the social structure, in their level of social development and in natural resource endowment are also real. These differences provide the necessary infrastructure that not only calls for a federal form of government, but also the basis for its success.

The recognition of these givens influenced the founding fathers not only to choose a federal form of government as a settled imperative, but also to approach the organization of governance cautiously and heuristically. It cannot be argued that the approach was guided by nothing national in their vision hence their fear of coming together and, consequently, their approach to national unity through separateness as it were. To date, their foresight remains, in my estimation, one of the veritable heritage that we must come to grips with sooner or later. But unfortunately, that visionary development of federalism specifically from 1954 to 1965 abruptly ended with the gunshots of that early harmattan morning of January 15, 1966, which not only eliminated some of the founding fathers of federalism in Nigeria, but also killed the essence of federalism itself.

The federal form which survived that military onslaught and on the basis of which the country precariously persisted as an entity, has never since regained its true essence. Two interrelated developments accounted for that demise. First, the coup and the eventual threat to the unity of the country following secession and the Civil War, were traumatic events that called for centralized authority capable of pulling things back into one fold. Second, there was, and still has always been the professional practice of unified command with which soldiers are familiar. Ever since, successive military regimes - eight of them in thirty-three years (1966-1999) - have perfected the menace of centralization. To date, the concentration at the center, of a formidable array of legislative and other responsibilities remains one of the disruptive heritage of military rule in our country. One would have thought that the series of constitutional reviews undertaken after the Civil War would have restored the true essence of federalism but rather, the orgy of centralization was in each case, perfected and constitutionalized

The first constitution-making after the civil war was in 1979. That Constitution was made largely under the pressure of haunting fear and, consequently, with an intellectual background that the federating units should be made as weak as they could possibly be. The centralization of power designed and perfected in a single constitution for the Federal and the 19 State governments at that time, aimed at forging national unity but it was short of the vision that such unity was best promoted through conscious provision for diversity. Three decades after the Civil War, it has become clear that the secession pretence of one Region had left a permanent fear even among soldier statesmen of harmless worms mistaken for deadly serpents.

For whatever purpose it was meant to serve, another constitution making exercise was undertaken in 1989. Nigerians involved in that exercise worsened matters as they were largely "new-breed", inexperienced and unemployed recruited to alienate and displace the experienced politicians of the First and Second Republics, most of whom were banned from political participation. Although the 1989 Constitution eventually came to nothing, the unfortunate outcome of both exercises was the placement of over 67 items under the legislative jurisdiction of the Federal Government while leaving jurisdiction on only 12 items with States in the Concurrent List.

In spite of its reformist posture, the 1995 constitution succumbed to these paranoiac posture particularly on issues involving devolution of power. The setting up of a Committee on Devolution of Power after the dissolution of the National Constitutional Conference gave hope, but it was forlorn as the Committee, desperately working to actualize General Abacha's self-succession bid, desecrated all the sensitive provisions in the Draft Constitution, which addressed some of the suppressed issues of federalism in Nigeria.

Rather than start from where the 1995 Draft Constitution ended, General Abubakar's administration not only reverted to 1979 Constitution, but concentrated more powers at the center than before. Thus, the so-called 1999 Constitution has 68 items on the Exclusive List and 30 minor ones on the Concurrent List. Decisively, the 1999 Constitution is a blueprint of unitarism in a country that is supposed to be a federal union of states. It is, therefore, at best meant to consolidate power in an hegemonic coalition of major ethnic groups and thereby impose the hegemony of one ethnic group on the rest of the country under the cloak of multipartism. It has not reflected the lessons from Nigeria's political crises since independence, nor insured the future against a repeat of such crises.

Amidst intense pressure of centrifugal forces markedly pointing in the direction of state autonomy, the Obasanjo administration called for memoranda from the public to review the Constitution. Given the enormity of the problem and the regional impulse of the National Assembly on issues relating to power sharing, it is doubtful whether the National Assembly can effect the restoration of the missing links in the development of federalism in Nigeria. As it affects the legislative functions of government, such links missing are highlighted below.

It is common knowledge that most states in Nigeria are feeble particularly in their extractive capability and, consequently, can hardly perform as federating units. Some commentators have employed this argument to justify the deprivation of powers from states to the center. In the same vein, some have proposed the abolition of the state structure in preference to regions corresponding to the six geo-political zones in the country. It needs be emphasized here that states are feeble not because they lack the resources and manpower that would make them strong economically and administratively, but because the fiscal and legislative relationships between them and the Federal Government render them feeble. Centralization kills initiative. In a fragile federal setting as ours, it suffocates the federating units thereby providing basis for potential territorial dissent. Decentralization not deconcentration stimulates competition, development and efficient service delivery. The achievement of these objectives does not lie in creating monstrous geo-political units to replace the state structure as has been suggested, but in energizing the states as they are without rendering the center impotent. So structured, states would be challenged into taking initiative and learn.

To build this institutional capacity, states must have their own Constitutions through which they can reflect their interests and set their priorities within the overall framework of the Nigerian nation. Such provisions would enable them, for instance, to

a) determine the size of their legislative assemblies, the qualification for membership, their pay based on their unique circumstances;
b) fix salaries and perquisites for their public servants provided the minimum wage rate set by the Federal Government is not contravened;
c) organize governance to reflect their unique capabilities, priorities and cherished traditions.

In order to give meaning to the foregoing, power must be devolved to the States. With due consideration to such imperatives as national unity, social diversity and national development with a diversified economic base, the following items are proposed for the Exclusive List:

1. Defense
2. Citizenship, naturalization and aliens
3. Currency, coinage and legal tender
4. Custom and Excise
5. Foreign relation including international commerce
6. Census
7. Extradition
8. Exchange control
9. Immigration and emigration
10. Interstate highways
11. Implementation of Treatise
12. Banking and Insurance
13. Post and Telegraphs
14. Drugs and Poisons

15. Prisons
16. Passport and Visas
17. Mines and Minerals
18. Maritime shipping, Navigation etc.
19. Copyright
20. Railways
21. Public Debt of the Federation
22. Meteorology
23. Interstate Relations
24. Museums
25. Agricultural establishments owned by the Federal Government
26. Education (Federal Universities and other institutions owned by the Federal Government)
27. Federal Public Service
28. Nuclear Energy
29. Patents, trade marks (etc.)
30. Any matter incidental or supplementary to any of the items listed above.

All other items in the Exclusive and Concurrent Lists in the 1979 and 1995 Constitutions should be under the Concurrent List. With the above division of legislative functions, and the corresponding change in inter-governmental fiscal relations which we shall discuss presently, it is hoped that States would be energized to assume the political and economic responsibilities expected of them.

Restoration of Fiscal Federalism

The financial stress increasingly being encountered in the states either through honest development burden, or through fraud, have, during the past decade or so, generated a renewed concern with the problem of inter-governmental fiscal relations. Just as the states have been immobilized by over-concentration of power and responsibilities at the center, our national economy has suffered equal suffocation and near collapse arising from:

(a) dependence on oil as the only main source of national revenue, and
(b) enfeeblement of states resulting from the patriarchal relationship between them and the federal government on one hand, and imposition of uniformity and, therefore, weakness in the extractive capability of states, on the other.

Prior to the coup of 1966, our fiscal federalism took full cognizance of the need for diversification. The vision that the regions should develop their economic potentials accounted for the diversified economic base of those years: groundnut in the Northern, palm produce in the Eastern and cocoa in the Western regions. The phenomenal infrastructural development in those Regions in the relatively short period of their existence, lends credence to the importance of diversification. Besides, regional autonomy had the salutary effect of imposing responsible economic management on the regions.

The discovery of oil in the late 1950s and the phenomenal impact of its earnings on the national economy coincided with the high tide of military rule, the civil war and, consequently, unified command in the administration of the country. By the provisions of the 1963 Constitution (Chapter IX), fifty per cent of the proceeds of any royalty or mining rents were paid to the region from where the mineral, including oil, was extracted. But the military government which followed the coup of January 15, 1966 suspended the Constitution and centralized the administration of every facet of our public life. Even after the civil war, inter-governmental fiscal relations reminiscent of a federal society were not restored. Power at the center was merely deconcentrated to the states not even as semi-autonomous level of government, but as an extension by delegation, of federal authority. The creation of states and the convulsive upsurge of statism undermined the 'regional' base of the diversified economy and with the enormous oil revenue at its disposal, the Federal Government was able to fund the administration of the states without recourse to their ability to absorb part of the fiscal responsibilities. Thus, the oil strength of the Federal Government was made perfect in the weakness of states so long as the former was resilient enough to pick up the monthly bills and determine the strength, priority and pace of the latter's development.

For over two decades now, this patriarchal relationship has been a major source of stress for both federal and state governments. For most of this period, most state governments have found it difficult to meet their monthly financial obligations. While the federal government has tended to blame them for not giving enough attention to their internal revenue generation, state governments have argued that the monthly allocations given them are grossly inadequate to meet the fundamental obligations of state administration.

The phenomenal growth in the public services of the states following state creation exercises particularly between 1975 and 1996 (24 states created in a period of 21 years), and the dependence of states on the Federal Government - these have overstretched the absorbtive capacity of the later. Consequently, for the past one and a half decades, there has been minimal, and in some states with large and old bureaucratic machinery, zero investment in infrastructural development owing to lack of funds. Existing public utilities such as roads, educational and health facilities have either collapsed or decayed following poor or no maintenance inputs. These aside, the financial recklessness of most state administrations have resulted in the current situation in the country in which some state governments are unable to pay salaries of civil servants for months. This is, to say the least, unhealthy and does not make for internal stability needed for smooth transition to, or sustenance of, lasting democracy.

The inability of state governments to pay salaries and other recurrent obligations or undertake any meaningful development projects has serious implications which cannot be overlooked. First, there is currently very poor attendance at work places, low morale and general atrophy in most states' public service. Second, it shows that the structure of our fiscal federalism is faulty and needs serious adjustment. Carried as it has been to civilian administration, this trend is obviously a false start to, and a sure sign of imminent collapse of, a stable civil government.

It is a negation of federal principle to fix uniform pay packages for public servants in the states marked by critical variations in the cost of living, level of social development, administrative capacity, and the challenge of development. In circumstances such as this, why would one expect Katsina state, for instance, to pay the same salary scales and other perquisites to its public servants as Lagos or Rivers state? Constitutionally, however, states are equal one with another. Equal treatment of equals is a value in any federal society. Even development of the federating units is a wish not an attainable goal in any federalism and, therefore, equals are never in the long run, and in practical economic terms, treated equally. The desire for even development and the reality of variations in resource endowment, executive capacity, level of social development, constitute an unresolved tension in federal societies.[5] The resolution of this conflict does not lie in destroying one for the other, but in choosing which of the two to promote, when and why.

Ipso facto I submit, that given the ever deepening economic crisis in our nation, and so that states can develop their economic potentials and achieve some autonomy, our fiscal federalism should be geared more towards stimulating divergent economic growth than in pursuing welfarist policies in revenue allocation. States must be encouraged, in fact coerced through appropriate fiscal measures, to develop their extractive capacity, executive confidence and pursue their development choices and preferences based on the resources available to them. The challenge of sustainable economic growth as a basis for viable democracy, calls for an urgent need to restructure our fiscal federalism anchored in the diverse strengths and weaknesses of our federating units. And the sure guiding principle to bring this desired outcome is derivation.

Contrary to fears expressed in some conservative quarters, derivation will strengthen rather than weaken the roots of our national unity, quicken the pace of social development in each state based on its capacity and unique challenges, check fissiparous demand for creation of states and local governments and, re-channel attention away from the federal to the states and local government areas as strong centers for institution-building and development. Within the states, derivation will broaden the base of economic activity and, consequently, promote healthy revenue generation. The current desperate drive for revenue in the states contracted out to non-governmental organizations destroys our nurture capitalism because of insensitive tax bites resulting from baseless or faulty tax assessments. Healthy revenue generation managed by effective and modernized internal revenue departments is best promoted through diversified economic activities, and hardly from incentive destroying practices currently employed in the states.

In working out the modality for revenue allocation with a bias for derivation, and, based on the suggested roles for both federal and state governments, care should be taken to ensure that the adjustable formula used is capable of creating a dynamic balance at two levels simultaneously. These are: at the federal level, relative *capacity* and relative *need* to discharge its obligation as a Federal Government, and at the state level, relative capacity of a state to perform under a federal system and based on that capacity, its relative *need* within the overall framework of revenue allocation.

So that the needs of states are monitored and transformed overtime to capacity, the Presidential Commission for revenue allocation should be given additional responsibilities in the area of revenue generation and renamed Revenue Generation and Allocation Commission. Equally necessary as a means of ensuring horizontal equity, (i.e. equal treatment of equals in the long run) a special grant called Capitalization Grant should be set up to help needy states develop or increase the productive capacity of their economic institutions and activities such as agricultural production, processing and marketing, exploration and production in large-scale industries with locally based raw materials. The use of such grants by needy states should be strictly monitored to ensure that only the states which are indeed needy benefit and that such grants are applied to the purposes for which they are meant.

So far, we have argued in favor of financial independence of states as federating units in Nigeria. It is a popular argument that local governments should also be autonomous since they are a tier of government. Obviously, such argument is one of the outcomes of the bias people have for the practice in advanced democracies. Unfortunately, the argument fails to reflect the historical antecedents in those countries, and the experiences in financial management at the local government level in Nigeria.

Based on our experiences, it would be most unwise to grant autonomy to local government. Several reasons support this position. There is the problem of accountability. Because of the low caliber of personnel resulting in low institutional performance, any checks and balances neatly written to guide public conduct at that level, easily gives way to corruption and sycophantic support. Besides, institutional weakness resulting from poor personnel means poor executive capacity manifesting in poor problem perception and solution proposals. These are factors that have always led to wastage of public funds.

All through the years of local government autonomy in Nigeria, the absence of effective monitoring of their activities has always left the entire local government system in a wild state of financial recklessness and chaos. We cannot leave the destiny of Nigerians in the rural areas to an institutional situation totally incapable of protecting their interest. This is why it is here proposed that local government should not, for now, be autonomous; their operation should be carefully monitored and controlled by state administration. Federal grants to local governments should be channeled through their respective states serving as their supervisory authority for, and on behalf of, the Federal Government. Disbursement of such grants should be based strictly on approved projects and monitored implementation. However, as a check against abuse, local governments should have the constitutional right to defend their perceived interests abused by state governments. There is no doubt that a prolonged period of tutelage is necessary for institution-building and attitude change at the local government level. It is only after such a phase that responsible, high profile and public-spirited individuals can be attracted to serve in local governments.

A possible criticism of this position is that all the tiers of government in a federal system should be autonomous. Without over-stretching this argument, it should by now be clear that, given the inchoate process of institution-building, including the development of a civic culture in Nigeria, we cannot unreflectively borrow structures and principles under the guise that such structures and principles constitute 'ideal models'. This is because there are no such ideal models anywhere in the world of nations. What we have in nations are structures adapted to respond to the challenges of their experiences, their aspirations and stages of institutional development. Ours should not be an exception.

In sum, the restoration of fiscal federalism in Nigeria must be based on pragmatic adjustment of fiscal relations based, not on any abstract theory or principles, but on the lived political experiences over the past four decades of our nationhood. The enormous resources expended on, and our commitment to, the establishment of an enduring democracy will come to nothing unless adequate, open-ended and institutionalized attention is given to the economic foundation of our federalism. Kenneth Wheare (1963: 117) has correctly summarized the approach to this problem:

> *There is and can be no final solution to the allocation of financial resources in a federal system. There can only be adjustments and re-allocations in the light of changing conditions. What a federal government needs, therefore, is machinery adequate to make these adjustment and to make them also in such a way that the financial independence of the general and regional governments is preserved as far as possible.*

The Failure of Patriarchal, Hegemonic Leadership

Bad leadership as argued elsewhere, is the commonest diagnosis of the Nigerian sickness. Yet like the study of leadership or executives, very little academic interest has been shown in this critical aspect of Nigerian politics and government. A number of reasons account for this paucity but probably the most important may well be that political scientists take for granted that leadership or executive models conventionally practiced in the Western democracies can be and are applicable to our situation. The resultant complacency among theorists and political practitioners have always provided two fixed options for African countries: parliamentary and presidential models. In Nigeria, the familiar problems that always beset the smooth operation of these models are usually exploited by soldiers as the basis for coups. And when they take over, as they have always done, the leadership put in place has never been different from the patriarchal hegemonic coalition model of their civilian counterparts, the details of which are sketched below.

This is a coalition of major ethnic groups seeking to establish hegemony over other groups in the country mainly for the purpose of capturing and perpetuating itself in power to the exclusion of other group members except in so far as such members qualify as agents. Thus, the model emphasizes political alliances, institutions and policies that aim at promoting acquiescence. This, it does by building a formidable network of patriarchal relationship serviced by corruption and patronage largesse. In civilian setting, emphasis on executive recruitment is always placed on federal character principle. As experience has shown, such recruitment has always served the personal needs of those recruited rather than the needs of the states or community from where they are recruited.

To give a semblance of democracy in action, multipartism is always the choice of patriarchal hegemonic leadership. That such a choice is a liberal trap to install one party that serves as the political machine of the hegemonic coalition is demonstratively evidenced by three interrelated practices. First, the provision for multipartism is never enriched with the corresponding provision for proportionality in cabinet representation. Second, all through the history of party politics in Nigeria, multipartism has always resulted in one party dominance. And third, the dominant party has always been the property of one hegemonic ethnic group in precarious coalition with another ethnic group while others serve as satellite vote enclaves.

The origin of this problem is traceable to colonial times when Nigerian nationalism became regionalized following the hegemonic struggle for power among the three major ethnic groups in the country. By independence in 1960, the struggle has produced a precarious hegemonic coalition with each group in the coalition struggling to use the federal bureaucracy and the coercive apparatus of the state to consolidate its position. The untidy process of competitive consolidation produced outcomes that invited the military in 1966. Its firm hold on power ever since marked by massive capital accumulation, domination of the oil, finance and shipping sectors including the control of the national political machine, has to date, resulted in the consolidation of the military, including retired generals, as a political class superimposed upon ethnic lines. The future of democracy in Nigeria unencumbered by the military factor particularly in a situation such as sketched, remains a permanent source of anxiety.

Over the years, however, the curious interaction of ethnic and class factors have produced legitimacy crises of many dimensions:

(a) nationally unacceptable leadership and orderly leadership succession.
(b) life and death struggle for leadership positions motivated not by the sobering decision to serve the people, but mostly by the craze for access to the public treasury;
(c) internal colonial relationship among geo-political zones and states,
(d) weakness and in some instances, outright destruction of democratic institutions and values;
(e) declaratory elections and enthronement of dictatorial rule;
(f) performance failure of many a government.

The Corporate Leadership Paradigm

It is in consideration of these recurrent problems that this paper proposes a corporate leadership paradigm that:

(i) provides for simultaneous participation of representatives from all the geo-political areas identified without in any way weakening, but has the capacity of strengthening and recreating democratic values congruent with the imperatives of our national political life;

(ii) is based on two mutually re-enforcing democratic ingredients of competition and consensus;

(iii) has a built-in mechanism and coherent resilience for absorbing shocks and the capacity to build confidence, institutionalize power, ensure orderly and stable leadership succession without necessarily destroying the basis of, or compromising the need for, democratic dissent;

(iv) facilitates governability i.e. it must maximize the ability of government to give effective direction to our economy, politics and society.

A half-way house between federal and consociational[6] arrangements based on the state structure and the six zones which have come to be used as the basis for distribution of values, the model has among others, two important and interrelated defining characteristics which have been discussed in a number of works. Two of these are:[7]

(a) a grand coalition of rotational office holders; and
(b) minority veto power

Let us examine these carefully:

Grand Coalition:

It is a common behavioral trait among Nigerian politicians to always want to belong to the winning party. It is, therefore, not uncommon for party founders to abandon their parties mid-air for the winning party. This trait aside, there is need to discourage the winner takes all electoral practice by proportionally recruiting the executive from the parties which win not less than 10%, for instance, of the total number of seats in the National Assembly.

In order to ensure that the six geo-political zones in the country are represented in the apex of government at any given time, six posts namely: President, Vice President, Senate President and the Vice, Speaker in the House of Representatives and his Deputy should rotate among the six zones. These, along with members of the executive council should form an organ to be called *President-in-Council*. It will serve as a consultative, advisory, proposing, and consenting organ. Besides, it is a forum where members articulate their zonal feelings, re-assess government policies and evaluate frankly, the overall performance of government.

Minority Veto

As a means of ensuring that the principle of proportionality is not a mere gesture of concern, members of the *President-in-Council* are protected with minority veto power against possible tyranny of the majority. That is, suppose a bill comes to the *President-in-Council* for assent or there is a policy proposal that any rotational office-holder feels strongly against, any member of the *President-in-Council* could veto the bill or the policy proposal provided the power to do so is obtained for that particular purpose through single majority vote in an electoral college of:

(a) all the Governors and their Deputies from the states making up his zone;

(b) all the Speakers in the state Houses of Assembly and their Minority Leaders within his zone

(c) state Chairmen of political parties in the zone, and

(d) majority of members of the National Assembly from that zone.

Minority veto is meant to ensure among other things, that any legislation or policy decision taken or ratified in the *President-in-Council* enjoys as much as possible, the consensus of the largest segment of the society through their representatives. Besides, it ensures that members of the *President-in-Council* use their position to the benefit of their constituencies and not as personal estates as is currently the practice. The stringent condition necessary for the exercise of the veto power is meant to check recklessness and reduce the possibility of using it as a tool of corruption. However, the President has an overriding veto power which he could use to forestall a deadlock or take a decision which he believes is in the national interest although not so perceived by some members of his Council.

With Ministers and rotational office-holders drawn from different political parties, it becomes imperative that collective responsibility must be the guiding principle in the executive arm including the *President-in-Council*. Minority veto ensures a healthy development of that principle.

By arming all the rotational office holders with the power of self protection, the possible temptation among them to constitute their areas of authority into zonal estates is removed. However, a possible danger with the minority veto is that it could slow down the legislative or executive decision process. This needs not be so. If the model is operated by experienced, knowledgeable politicians with national rather than ethnic or zonal orientation, the frequency in which the veto is actually used would be very low indeed. The stringent process of obtaining the power to veto from the zone aside, no serious minded member of the *President-in-Council* would want to pursue an issue that he knows could be traded off with his zonal interest in future. By giving every zone the power to veto, there is virtually a balance of mutually beneficial interest, or should any zone decide to stalemate the collective interest of the coalition pursued by other members of the *President-in-Council,* there is equally a balance of terror and, therefore, a definite possibility that the interest of that zone could in turn be stalemated. This possibility is yet another reason the veto power would rarely be used.

Minority veto encourages the zone to pursue interests that are national rather than ethnic or zonal and even when it is necessary for any zone to pursue its exclusive zonal interest, the veto ensures it of self protection. Thus, the danger of unrestrained use of the veto that could cause a deadlock in a decision process is, therefore, not as serious as it may appear.

An obvious criticism of the zoning concept is that it is not democratic enough in so far as zones are specified for specific posts prior to election. Critics believe such a practice limits the democratic right of individuals to pursue whatever political ambitions they might have. Secondly, specifying zones for specific rotational posts eliminates opposition and, therefore, opportunities for alternative choice of leadership.

Basic as this may seem, these criticisms are obvious outcomes of bias and commitment to Anglo-American democratic ideal which, in large part, does not respond to the integrative challenges of our society. The bringing together of zonal office holders from different parties in a grand coalition regulated as we have proposed, provides for non-formal opposition necessitated by the character of our society. I have argued elsewhere,[8] that the presence and use of opposition is maximized to the extent that the stability of the government and the survival of the country allow it. After all, there can be no democratic rights of individuals to pursue their political ambition if the possibility of democratic government and survival of the country are basically at stake.

Towards a 'Distemper' of Mass Political Participation

No less an important factor in democratic health and stability, is the character of political participation used here in a narrow sense to mean voting. Quite often, little or no attention is given to this potentially useful and potentially stressful phenomenon in post-colonial societies. Ever since the end of the civil war, money and the entrenched interest of 'power custodians' and power seekers have had tremendous influence on the political process including the formation of political parties and who eventually emerges in the so-called elections. Contrary to elections in pre-civil war years, elections in post-civil war Nigeria have been marked by pitiably low voter turn-out and large-scale electoral fraud. They have basically been declaratory elections in which the usually jumbo votes are allocated to the favored party and individuals. This unfortunate practice has always and logically led to crisis of legitimacy of the government formed.

The quality of political participation can affect the quality of political leadership recruited. Much as the force of ethnicity is, quite often, a factor in political recruitment in segmented societies, it is less likely to be a factor where the electorate is politically aware of what it could lose or gain by a wrong choice of candidate. Consequently, an electorate of predominantly poor, illiterate voters is more likely to vote for a less qualified candidate who is able to pay for votes. Conversely, an electorate of educated and politically aware voters is more likely to vote for a qualified candidate without ability to buy votes, than sell their votes to a less qualified candidate with an ability to pay. An electorate where the majority of voters not only are educated, but also belong to occupational and associational groups would seem to be more institutionalized in its electoral behavior than one characterized by uncoordinated mass of voters. Thus, mass political participation within a multi-party framework, in an electorate characterized by low level of institutionalization, would likely be more prone to corruption and poor leadership recruitment, than controlled political participation.

Samuel Huntington (1976: 55) has observed that high level of social mobilization through education, media exposure, urbanization etc. in a situation where the absorbtive capacity of the economy is low is likely to result in increased political participation. This has been the case in this country almost since independence. As argued elsewhere, for instance, that slow economic growth and lack of diversified economic base accounted for the economy's inability to absorb graduates from our tertiary institutions. The government was unmindful of this trend against an unprecedented expansion in educational institutions during the 1980s. Today, and increasingly, the mass of our political activists in our cities and villages are unemployed graduates. Among this category of activists, mass political participation means mass-want formation which government is unable to satisfy. The result has been stress on the part of the government, and frustration among this critical segment of the ruled. Thus, in what looks like Huntington's formulation, a curious process of interaction of the variables in our country has produced a situation in which:

(i) increased social mobilization in a situation of painfully slow economic growth leads to social frustration;
(ii) increased social frustration in a situation of few opportunities for upward mobility leads to riotous political participation;
(iii) increased political participation within multi-party framework in an elec-

torate characterized by low level of institutionalization leads to corruption and poor leadership recruitment.

Before suggesting measures that could help to liberate leadership recruitment from the damaging influence of money and mass participation highlighted above, let us see whether there are insights that history can offer.

In so far as it affects political participation, mass democracy as we know it today in Western Europe including the United States, is a creation of the past 80-90 years, and radically different from the democracy of the 19th century when West European countries were faced with similar nation-building pressures as most Third World countries today. For instance, until the Reform Bill of 1832 which added only some 217,000 voters, there were only 435,000 voters against a population of 14 million in Britain. At the time the Second Reform Bill of 1867 further increased the number of voters by 400,000, not only 5 out of 6 adult males were voteless, but the greater part of the working class remained without the right to vote. Full suffrage was not extended to women until 1928. Before 1830 in France, property qualification limited the franchise to less than 100,000 votes out of 7 million adult males. Between 1831 and 1848, French electorate was confined to some 200,000 voters out of a population of approximately 30 million. In Sweden, electoral inequalities were abolished in 1921. In the United States, full suffrage was granted to women in 1920.[9]

I have brought historical data back in here not to extol the electoral inequalities that existed in European countries until relatively recently, not to assert that what happened in Western Europe must inevitably happen here, but to raise an alarm: 'This is what there is in history! Can we short circuit it?' If we can and must, is it possible in a multi-party situation in an ethnically divided society without creating a riotous environment in which democracy is left with no alternative than to commit suicide?

These reflections bring into sharp focus whether in a nurture democracy as ours, qualitative electorate should not be preferred to mass electorate which was rational during the populist anti-colonial era of our national struggle.

Given a consociational-oriented leadership model proposed in the preceding section, I hasten to urge that mass electorate should be restricted to local government elections while state and National Assembly elections including the election of the President should be conducted in large electoral colleges of knowledgeable and politically aware citizens. If such electoral colleges are carefully constituted with open ballot system, the approach could have the advantage of producing high profile politicians and reducing electoral malpractice and the influence of money in the electoral process.

It might seem paradoxical that rather than argue for the empowerment of the masses, we are arguing for their exclusion in the all important matter of choosing who should represent them. This apart, there is the possible argument that modern representative governments always strive to secure and not to diminish maximum consensus of maximum number of voters in any given electorate. The theoretical veracity of these arguments notwithstanding, we should be reminded that in a rudimentarily evolutionary stage as ours, what have come to be seen as ideal structures and processes within the democratic praxis of the Anglo-American tradition, must be adapted to suit our prevailing circumstances. Given the large scale electoral fraud resulting in fake election results in most instances, the choice is between continuing with our self-deception that we are democratizing, or devising a means no matter how unpopular, to lay a solid democratic foundation that could extol and recreate democratic ideals based on the popular will of the electorate. Thus, the arguments cannot be sustained as the possible harm done to the health and stability of democracy is more than the expected gains derived from unreflective adherence to time and place bound processes. The principle of so called maximum consensus is only on theory; it has never been possible in practice even in the advanced democracies of the West. If it is so dictated by the realities of our political situation as it is, it would seem only wise to devise alternative process to negate this growing vice.

Conclusion

The burden of this paper was to identify some of the critical issues that impoverish Nigerian federalism leading in recent times, to an upsurge of militant ethno-nationalism, violence and institutional weakness. Ever since the coup of 1966, the military mindset characterized by unified command has cumulatively impacted on the organization and administration of the country. The conflictual circumstances which surrounded the creation of states and which later led to the civil war, eclipsed the original philosophy behind state creation namely: equality of access to power resources. As a result of this lapse, the state structure has achieved little beyond mere structural differentiation as it has been encumbered with crippling centralization. In spite of chains of sporadic constitutional experimentation between 1970 and 1999, the essence of federalism and democracy reminiscent of a multi-ethnic society like Nigeria has never been recaptured. By the closing years of 1990s, the grammar of liberation politics among the marginalized groups has changed from the demand for states, to demand for power sharing.

Rather than wait for such change to chart its obviously unstructured course, I prescribe ways in which Nigerian federation, inter-governmental fiscal relations, leadership and political participation could be re-organized for maximum democratic output based on the imperatives of autonomy and disciplined pragmatism. It cautions that the current euphoria about civilian administration mistaken as democracy is false consciousness. It might well be the beginning of new banalities unless our future is boldly designed and constructed to give meaning to every segment of our national population most of which are either marginalized or missing in the national scheme of things.

ENDNOTES

1. Kenneth C. Wheare, *Federal Government* London: Oxford University Press, Fourth Edition, 1963, p. 10.
2. Ibid., p.33.
3. For some of the formulations see: A. W. Mac Mahon, "The Problem of Federalism: A Survey" in A. W. MacMahon (ed). *Federalism, Mature and Emergent.* Garden City: Doubleday, 1955; W.H. Riker, *Federalism: Origin, Operation, Significance.* Boston: Little Brown & Co. 1964; William S. Livingston, *Federalism and Constitutional Change,* Oxford: Oxford Univ. Press, 1956; Ronald L. Watts, *New Federations: Experiments in the Commonwealth.* Oxford: Oxford Univ. Press, 1966; Geoffrey J. Sawer, *Modern Federalism:* London: Watts, 1969; Daniel J. Elazar, "The Ends of Federalism: Notes Towards a Theory of Federal Political Arrangements" in Max Frenkel (ed). *Partnership in Federalism.* Bern: Peter Lang, 1977. Earle Valeri (ed.) *Federalism: Infinite Variety in Theory and Practice.* Itasca, Ill.: *Peacock,* 1968; Carl J. Friedrich, *Trends of Federalism in Theory and Practice.* New York: Praeger, 1968.
4. William H. Riker "Federalism", in Nelson Polsby and Fred Greenstein (eds). *Handbook of Political Science,* 8 Vols. (Reading Addison-Wesley Publishing Company 1975), 5: p.93.
5. Intergovernmental fiscal relations in federal system is examined in Wallace E. Oates, *Fiscal Federalism* (New York: Harcourt Brace Jovanovic, Inc. 1972).
6. Consociational democratic model as could be applied in Nigeria is a subject of investigation in Ekeng Anam-Ndu, *Consociational Democracy in Nigeria: Agenda for the 1990s and Beyond.* (Lagos: Geo-Ken Associates Ltd. 1990). See also P. Ekeh and E. Osaghae (eds.), *Federal Character and Federalism In Nigeria.* (Ibadan: Heinemann. 1989)
7. The idea of grand coalition and minority veto is borrowed from Arend Lijphart, *Democracy In Plural Societies: A Comparative Exploration* (New Haven: Yale University Press, 1977) Chapter 2.
8. Ekeng A. Anam-Ndu, "Perspectives On Educational Crisis", *ThisDay,* vol. 3 No. 843 August 12, 1997, p.6.
9. Geoffrey Barraclough, *An Introduction to Contemporary History* (New York: Penguin Books, 1978 Chap. V See also Stein Rokhan with Augus Campbell, Per Torsvic, and Henry Valen, *Citizens Elections Parties: Approaches to the Comparative Study of the Process of Development* (New York: David Mckay Company Inc. 1970).

REFERENCES

Anam-Ndu E. 1990. *Consociational Democracy in Nigeria: Agenda for the 1990s and Beyond.* Lagos: Geoken Associates Ltd.

———- 1997. "Perspectives on Educational Crisis" *This Day*, August 12.

Barraclough G. 1978. *An Introduction to Contemporary History.* New York: Penguin Books.

Elazar D.J. 1977. "The Ends of Federalism: Notes Towards a Theory of Federal Political Arrangements" in M. Frennel.ed. *Partnership in Federalism.* Bern: Peter Lang.

Ekeh P. and Osagha E. eds. 1989. *Federal Character and Federalism in Nigeria*, Ibadan: Heinemann.

Freidrich C.J. 1968. *Trend in Federalism in Theory and Practice.* New York: Praeger.

Huntington S.P. 1976. *Political Order in Changing Societies.* New Haven: Yale University Press.

Lijphart A. 1977. *Democracy in Plural Societies: A Comparative Exploration.* New Haven: Yale University Press.

Livingston W. S. 1956. *Federalism and Constitutional Change.* Oxford University Press.

Mac Mahon A.W. 1955. "The problem of Federalism: A survey" in A.W. Mac Mahon ed. *Federalism, Mature and Emergent.* Garden City: Double Day.

Oates W. E. 1972. Fiscal Federalism. New York: Harcout Brace Jovanovich Inc.

Riker W. H. 1964. *Federalism: Origin, Operation, Significance.* Boston: Little Brown & Co.

———- 1975. "Federalism" in N. Polsby and F. Greenstein eds. *Handbook of Political Science*, 8 vol.. Reading: Addisan: Wesley Publishing Company.

Rokham S., et. al eds. 1970. *Citizens, Elections, Parties: Approaches to the Comparative Study of the Process of Development,* New York: David Mekay Company.

Sawer G.J. 1969. *Modern Federalism.* London: Watts

Valeri E. ed. 1968. *Federalism: Infinite Variety in Theory and Practice.* Ithaca, Ill: Peacock.

Wheare K.C. 1963. *Federal Government.* London: Oxford University Press.

SECTION II:
MANAGING DIVERSITY IN FEDERAL POLITIES

CHAPTER 4

The Development Of Federalism In Nigeria: A Historical Perspective

W. O. Alli

Introduction

Federalism and its specific configuration in Nigeria was the result of intense philosophical and political debate about the best politico-administrative system that suits the interests of the dominant forces. The resultant constitutional engineering was the outcome of a struggle between conservative colonial officials led by Lord Lugard, who saw in centralized administrative structure, the key to the preservation of British control of this vast and enormously endowed land and the nationalists, who saw in federalism the guarantor of the survival of this complex multinational and multiethnic nation as one entity.

In this struggle, the nationalists won, but the ambition of the British survived. Chief Awolowo was to observe that the federalism imposed by the British was "paradoxical" and British legacy "abominable, disrupting and divisive" (Awolowo 1968:69)

The dream of the British and their ambition was translated to life eventually by the military rulers who imposed themselves on the nation since 1966. As noted by Dotun Philips (1991:103), federalism died in Nigeria on January 15, 1966 when the Military struck.

Before amalgamation in 1914, several officials, among them Mr. E. D. Morel, editor of *the African Mail*, Governor Hasket Bell and Charles Temple, a Lieutenant-Governor, among others, argued for a federal system for the country because they believed it was appropriate for a country like Nigeria and because they thought it would enhance unity. But Lord Lugard had in mind his preferred form of centralized system, which guaranteed the continued separation of the South from the North. Even then, as noted by Nwabughuogu (1996:239), "at the end of the amalgamation in 1914, the colonial authorities still faced the dilemma of finding the structural direction to which the Nigeria state would evolve".

Changing socio-economic and political development particularly, the dynamics of the nationalist struggles made the eventual constitutional adoption of federalism inevitable. This has been the part of federalism in the various forms in which it has been practiced over the centuries, its form being determined by changing dynamics of political development in any given country.

This contribution attempts to trace the development of the peculiar nature of Nigerian federalism through the several national constitutions that have been adopted in Nigeria, for as noted by Ramphal (1979, xii) Federal government is a dynamic application of constitutionalism to the process of nation building. In doing this, we shall be focusing on the administrative structure and the relationship between the center and the units of the Nigerian federation.

Defining Federalism

If we define federalism as an administrative and political system "in which several states unite but keep control over their own internal affairs," then we could appreciate the functional benefits derivable from a federal system. One other quality of federalism is what Wheare described as its method of dividing powers so that central and regional governments are each within a sphere coordinate and independent (Wheare 1963:10a) of the component units with regards to their powers and functions in relation to each other and the central authorities. From this derives a major aspect of federalism - participatory governance of all component units and all levels of government.

This aspect, however, was never appreciated and later the post-colonial rulers of Nigeria, in particular, the military rulers, abandoned it. These and other qualities of federalism recommended it to complex societies like the United States of America, Brazil, India Yugoslavia and the former Soviet Union, and no doubt must be a guiding theoretical framework for the architects of a United Europe. In this regard, each federal arrangement has been put together "the world over with creativity and constant innovation and always on the anvil of political reality. The practical necessities of a miscellany of national circumstances, not the symmetry of academic reasoning have given it its form. It has emerged as a particular kind of functional arrangement between states or more accurately between communities for living and working together nationally while preserving a measure of separate identity. It is a methodology of limited union directed to the production of limited unity" (Ramphal, 1979:xiv).

Another significant aspect of the approaches to federalism is the dichotomy between the constitutional approach, which is much acclaimed and favored by Wheare (1963) and the functional element, which suggests broad cooperation across the levels of governance.

Federalist ideology in Nigeria, however takes as its point of departure, the liberal theory of limited government. But it also reflects an attempt to regulate ethnic politics in an integrative and positive way and therefore the deconcentration of constitutional authority in such a way as to create levels of government with substantial autonomy in their respective spheres (Olagunju et al, 1993: 31). The character of Nigerian Federalism has however been molded by several critical factors, namely the class character and configuration of class forces of the Nigerian state, and the dominant capitalist mode of production and multinational, multiethnic and multi religious nature of the Nigerian society.

Federalism and Constitutional Development, 1922-45

Sir Hugh Clifford was appointed in 1919 to replace Lord Lugard as Governor-General of Nigeria. Sir Clifford was critical of the amalgamation and what it achieved for Nigeria. As an expression of his opinion on amalgamation, he proposed to the colonial office the proper amalgamation of the Northern and Southern protectorates, and the creation of central administrative organs that would truly unite Nigeria. But the colonial office in London turned down his proposals.

In reaction, Sir Clifford turned in the opposite direction, averring that "every homogenous community or any emirate was to be encouraged to be an autonomous nation" (Nwabughuogu, 1996: 46). This is why the 1922 constitution was to pay scant attention to administrative structure. In Crowthers view, there was a significant attack on the idea that there could be a Nigerian nation. (Crowther, 1973:256) Sir Clifford was of the opinion that if "this collection of self-contained and mutually independent native states, separated from one another as many of them are by history, tradition and by ethnological, racial, tribal and political, social and religious barriers were indeed capable of being welded into a single homogenous nation, it would be a deadly blow to the root of national self government in Nigeria, which secures to each separate people the right to maintain its identity, its individuality, its own chosen form of government and the peculiar political and social institutions which have been evolved for it by wisdom and by the accumulated experience of generations of its forebears" (Crowther, 1973:25).

This apprehension was not resolved by the Clifford constitution, which nonetheless created a legislative Council that included only national non-official elements elected from Lagos and Calabar. Successive Governors after Sir Clifford, namely, Gram Thompson, Herbert R. Palmer, Donald Cameron were all apostles of unitary system, with a great belief in the indirect rule system. Sir Cameron however tried to chart a new course for British policy in Nigeria, a policy that recognizes the future goal of a united Nigeria. He also appreciated in Nwabughuogu's view, the obstacles to the achievement of this goal, one of which was the resistance of northern Nigerian political officers.

Cameron moved the nation energetically towards real unification, having won the approval of the Colonial Officer for his ideas. His departure in 1935 and replacement by Sir Bernard Bourdillon retarded the pace of unification which the northern administration opposed. Under the new governor, general federal system of administration came into greater focus. In his memorandum on the future political development of Nigeria, he submitted proposals intimating of the appropriateness and functional benefits of a federal system for Nigeria. As a first step, the Clifford Constitution which had been in use since 1922 was discarded. He created the eastern and western provinces out of the protectorate of southern Nigeria. But the north was left intact.

Foundation of Nigeria Federalism

The foundation for federalism laid by Bourdillon was to be given full expression by Sir Arthur Richards who succeeded him, in the 1946 Constitution. According to Crowther (1973:273), one key element in this Constitution, which took effect from 1st January, 1947, was the recognition of two twin problems confronting Nigeria at that time. These were:

(i) the need to promote the unity of nation; and
(ii) the need to provide adequately within that unity for the diverse elements which makes up the country.

These two factors were indeed strong blueprints for a federal arrangement and Richards Constitution fully prescribed federalism, changing the units designated by Bourdillon as provinces to regions. Each region was to have Regional Council, a House of Assembly and a House of Chiefs. The Constitution also provided some measure of fiscal responsibility to the regional governments (Phillips, 1996:146).

Part of this new development was the inclusion for the first time, of the north in the Central Legislature. This development serves as foundation for Nigeria Federalism. The constitution was however met with several criticisms. Crowther noted that Dike was to write "undoubtedly, the Richards Constitution was a dividing line in Nigerian constitutional development. Before it, the keynote in Nigerian politics was unification towards a centralized state and the realization of a common nationality. But with the Richards Constitution, the tendency towards unification was on the whole arrested (Crowther 1973:273). Other criticisms trailed the constitution. Nationalists were to argue that the constitution was imposed on the country with little consultation with the people (Coleman, 1958:277). Osuntokun (1979:98) observed that Sir Richards expressed "in constitutional form the reality of Nigerian politics of divide and rule which the British did everything to foster". Despite these misgivings, the federal idea was generally accepted by all the political associations. It was a welcome development for the northern officials. It was found attractive by Dr. A. Azikiwe and Chief O. Awolowo who had both canvassed federalism. Obviously at that point in time, there were several directions into which Nigeria could have developed. It was possible to have had three countries made up of northern eastern and western regions. It was possible also to have had the north form a country, while the south also would have formed another. But no doubt for reasons of convenience for the colonial power, it was decided that Nigeria should be kept together as one, while the component units were to be granted some degree of autonomy within the emerging federal structure.

But emerging administrative structure in the 1946 Constitution was defective because a component unit, the northern region, was allowed to be twice as big as the other two units combined. Overall, the Richards Constitution was hastened by the appointment of a new Governor-General in the person of Sir John McPherson in 1948. He was so enthusiastic about introducing a new constitution that just after a few months in the country, he set in motion the machinery for the introduction of a new constitution in the country.

Unlike Sir Richards, Sir McPherson consulted widely for a period of two years. These consultations took place in a politically charged atmosphere in which ethnic socio-political organizations wearing the garb of cultural associations determined the direction of public discourse. Principal among these associations were the Ibibio State Union, the Pan Ibo Federal Union, and the National Council for Nigeria and the Camerouns (NCNC), formed in 1944, the Pan-Yoruba Egbe Omo Oduduwa, formed in 1948 which later transformed into the Action Group party (A.G.). In 1949 the Jamiar Mutanen Arewa was formed. In 1951 this group transformed into the Northern Peoples Congress (NPC). Earlier in 1950, Malam Aminu Kano had led the formation of the Northern Elements Progressive Union (NEPU) from within the fold of the group.

But there were national bodies and movements like the Zikist movement and the Nigerian Youth Movement which preached nationalism and unification. It was therefore clear why the political ideologies were defined and informed primarily by the broader issue of content and structure of associational life among the numerous ethnic groups. It was during this period that ethnic identity and consciousness and ethnic goals became well established, defined and promoted. It was a period that Crowther characterized as being dominated by "tribal nationalism" Crowther (1973:279). The NPC was championing northern interests, the NCNC eastern interests, and the AG western interests.

One great part, however, needs to be stressed. And that is the point that despite the intensity of the debate over the nature of political and administrative structure, and despite the passion for the promotion of ethnic identity and goals, none of the groups considered at that point to opt out of the emerging Nigerian nation. Rather, the major political associations, including the NCNC, saw the future of their communities in a federal arrangement that allows for active participation of all component communities.

As part of the consultations over the new constitution, divisional, provincial meeting and regional constitutional conferences were held in Enugu, Ibadan and Kaduna. The constitution that was adopted reflected the goals of most of the nationalist leaders in that the center was strong but not too strong, while the regions had considerable powers but not enough to undermine the workings of the federal system of government which the McPherson constitution prescribed. The north was to have equal representation with the south in the Federal Legislative Council.

The constitution was generally well received by the political leaders. Awolowo saw it as "a prominent landmark in the nation's political development" (Awolowo 1968:6). The eventual collapse of the McPherson Constitution was blamed on several factors. Some argued that the inability of Azikwe to occupy a seat in the central Legislative led to series of developments that ignited the end of the constitution. It was equally noted that the bill introduced by Anthony Enahoro, an Action Group member, asking for self-government in 1956 caused so much disruption and tension that eventually led to riots and dozens of officially announced deaths and several hundred wounded.

As a result of these developments, the Northern House of Chiefs and Northern House of Assembly passed an eight-point resolution calling for the dissolution of the Federal Government and the formation in its place of a confederation. The reaction of the Colonial Authorities was the preparation of yet another Constitution that would address the grievances that have been brought to the fore. The 1953 constitutional conference took place in London.

There were two main opinions on the constitution. The NPC, still unhappy with the effects and uncomplimentary remarks of many of the southern politicians about its ideas, was prepared to accept only a loose federation. The Action Group and the NCNC, in some form of political cooperation were prepared to demand the creation of a federation of east and west. In effect, according to Nwabughuogu (1966:54), Federalism appealed to the sectional security interests of the political parties that have become convinced of its benefits. The demand of the leaders was thus for a federal system, but one with strong federating units" (Kumo,1994:260). Despite this seeming wide gap in expectations, the London conference was able to adopt, once again, a federal system for Nigeria.

This new federal constitution, which became known as the Lyttleton Constitution granted much more powers to the central government, while at the same time transferring certain residual powers to the regions. According to Falola (1988:56), this was a "loose federation". The thorny issue of self-government was diplomatically resolved with an offer of self-government to regions that wanted it in 1956. Another problem that divided the delegations was the status of Lagos. But eventually through the arbitration of the Colonial Secretary, Lagos was retained as a Federal Capital Territory despite the opposition of the Action Group that saw Lagos as being part of the Western Region.

The second leg of the Constitutional Conference which took place in January 1954 confronted the major problem of fiscal policy (revenue allocation policy) for the nation and the problems of civil service and the judiciary. To a large extent, it could be argued that the principle of derivation was delicately applied in the design of a fiscal policy for the federation. For example income tax was to be collected federally just like mining taxes and was to be distributed on the basis of derivation. The regions were given full control of marketing Boards. The judiciary and the civil service were to be controlled by the regions.

Thus, towards the end of the 50s, the Nigerian nation was increasingly being perfected, with a well-defined peculiarly Nigerian federal system of government. This Nigerian federation had three component units known as regions, a Federal Capital Territory of Lagos and a quasi-federal territory of Southern Camerouns. The North was to have half the legislative seats in a 184 member House of Representatives.

National revenue was to be managed by the national government on principles that approximated derivation. The civil service and the judiciary were regionalized. At a meeting of the three Premiers at Ikorodu in 1957, they prepared an agenda and harmonized their positions for the proposed London Conference. The meeting produced a set of proposals which the three leaders were prepared to table on London.

The Independence Constitution

It could be argued that by 1957, all the parties and their leaders were convinced of the functional benefits of a federal system. However, there were still many unresolved issues. These include the problem of the unevenness of the component units and the unresolved grievances of the minorities in the three regions. These minority groups demanded the creation of more states for an effective federal structure. The agitation of the minority groups led to the formation of many political associations. These include the Benin and Delta Peoples Party (BDPP) formed in 1953, followed by the formation of Midwest State Movement in 1956. The Movement became an ally of the NCNC. The Calabar-Ogoja Rivers State Movement (also known as the COR State Movement) was formed in 1954 to press home the demand for the creation of the COR state from the Eastern Region. In the north, the minority groups were to come together under the umbrella of the United Middle Belt Congress (UMBC) for the creation of a Middle Belt State. It became affiliated with the NCNC while the Borno Youth Movement (BYM) a Kanuri Political Association became affiliated with the NEPU.

However, the 1957 constitutional conference did not resolve the problem of the minorities. Rather it passed it on to the Minorities Commission headed by Sir Henry Willinks. The Commission, while accepting that there were indeed bases for fears of the minorities was, nonetheless, opposed to the idea of the creation of new states at the time. Instead it proposed the creation of special councils for the Calabar and Midwest areas to oversee the activities of regional governments. For the North, the Commission proposed a plebiscite over the fate of Ilorin and Kabba Provinces.

The parties at the 1958 Conference accepted all these points in the Minorities Report. In their struggle and rush for independence, none of the parties wanted to create any obstacle that might delay the attainment of independence. However, the conference added some new elements. A bi-cameral legislature was introduced while the judiciary was granted more powers. Substantially, the 1958 constitution "transformed the Regions into foci of power" (Falola, 1988:50).

Notwithstanding these developments, a member of the Minorities Commission observed that "the hopes of the continued unity of Nigeria and justice for the individuals must rest initially on the grounds that none of these three major parties could dominate the others and that any party seeking to get such domination within the present political structure must seek support outside its regional stronghold and therefore among the minority groups of other regions" (Crowther, 1973:298).

It was with this understanding that the delegates unanimously demanded independence in 1960. On August 8 , 1957, the Eastern and Western regions became self-governing. Shortly thereafter a national government was formed with Alhaji Tafawa Balewa as Head of Government. He was to bring into the national government the NCNC and AG members.

Generally, the Independence Constitution did not differ much from the 1954 Lyttelton Constitution. The imbalance in size of units that was very obvious to all was not addressed. It was to remain one of the major obstacles to Nigerian Federalism. In all these we must recognize the socio-economic and political developments that were taking place in the country. The dynamics of these economic and political changes influenced the direction of the emerging federal system. It was instructive that all political parties appreciated the functional value of staying together in one big country. Besides, each of the regions was contributing and benefiting from available national resources. The pre-independence years saw a remarkable growth in the interaction among the various regions due to economic activities. These developments informed the politics of the immediate post independence period and to a large extent directed the focus of the political parties in dealing with each other and in working out cooperative arrangements.

Perfecting Imperfect Liaisons

Despite the seeming understanding among the major political parties that they had to work together to sustain a stable development, they could not help trying to compete with each other. After independence the opposition parties particularly the AG, embarked on campaigns for the restructuring of the federation, a task that the Willinks Commission had passed on to the incoming administration.

However, the NCNC through its leader Azikiwe, agreed on going into alliance with the NPC after the 1959 Elections. It also pursued the creation of the Midwest Region (Clark, 1991, 406). It was thus an NCNC member that moved a motion for the creation of the Midwest Region. The amendment which the AG proposed to the motion to the effect that the exercise be carried out in all the regions was defeated. Consequently it was only in the Western Region that a new region, and thus a new federal unit was created.

This adjustment of the federal structure from a three-component to a four-component structure did not significantly perfect the imperfect federal arrangement. The adoption of a Republican Constitution in 1963 did not also add any substantial new strength to the federal structure. Rather in the opinion of Graf, "it only substitutes an indigenous Head of State for a British Monarch and established a governing structure whose origins and development lay outside the Nigerian socio-historic experience," (Graf, 1988:27). Significantly, from the point of view of constitutional engineering regionalism became the guiding principle of Nigerian federalism" (Ibid:29). However, the division of functions and powers between the Federal and Regional Governments were carefully defined" (Ijalaye, 1979:142). Almost suddenly, there was a change in the economic and political value of the center to the regions and the consequent desire and intensity to control the center (Falola, 1988:61). This struggle for supremacy at the center took its toll on the body politic and eroded the political focus and ultimately the legitimacy of the ruling class that was self-destructive, and resulted in endless and vicious intra-class squabbles.

The First Military Interregnum

When the Military seized power in Nigeria on 15th January, 1966, the character of the Nigerian federalism was to be fundamentally damaged. The ascendancy of the Military in national politics signaled the total loss of legitimacy by the political class.

General Aguiyi Ironsi, who became the new Head of State, in the aftermath of the failed coup d'etat began a process that was to transform the relatively loose regionalized federal arrangement of Nigeria into one with a strong center. He took the first wrong step when he promulgated the rather radical Decree No. 34 of May 1966 otherwise known as the Unification Decree, which abolished the regions and federalism, and introduced a unitary form of government. Earlier, the Armed Forces had granted themselves political authority by promulgating the constitution (suspension and modification) Decree No. 1 of 1966.

No doubt Decree 34 challenged the delicate federal arrangement which had been nurtured for the whole of the previous two decades. Decree 34 was to lead to the downfall of Ironsi. The decree was, however, reversed by the constitution (suspension and modification) Decree No. 9 of 1966 which reinstated federalism . Its promulgation attracted demonstrations in the north, and as argued by Falola, the fall of Ironsi demonstrated the weakness, at that point, of the center (1988: 64).

Col. O. Ojukwu challenged the new leadership under Gowon. To solve this problem, peace meeting and Ad Hoc Constitutional Conference were held in September 1966. As part of a peace effort negotiated between Gowon and Ojukwu in Aburi, Ghana, Decree No. 8, of May 1967 was promulgated. The decree was considered a confederal decree because it rendered the center weak as demonstrated by the provision that the Head of State needed the concurrence of all the Military Governors of the four regions to operate the Decree. The Decree also gave the regions even more powers than the

Independence Constitution. Notwithstanding this, several other measures were to modify the relationship between the center and the component units that made up the federation as well as the administrative structure of the nation. The almost easy access of the Military to power in the ensuing decades reflected not so much the power of the Military but rather the weakness and lack of confidence of the politicians in their legitimacy and the quality of governance and leadership which they had provided.

The rapidly changing political situation provided Gowon the opportunity to resolve a major obstacle to Nigerian federalism. In May 1967, Gowon announced a new 12 State Federal structure. This was a watershed in the development of Nigerian federalism but it also brought to fore other problems of the inadequacies of the arrangement with regards to the process of governance.

The contradictions between the Federal Government and the Eastern Region led by Col. O. Ojukwu degenerated into a civil war. This war (1967-70) was fought not so much for federalism but for power. That fact was reflected in the outcome in that a certain status quo, built around a strong center, emerged. The center became very attractive (Falola, 1988:61) and this attraction was to define and determine the context of political struggle and the design and future engineering of Nigerian federalism.

This appreciation was to be redefined by the idealism of the Murtala-Obasanjo regime (1975-79) which saw in the two elements of federalism the constitutional and the procedural the key to a stable Nigerian polity. This new focus determined the political engineering efforts of the regime. In the first place, the administrative structure was altered with the creation in 1976 of seven new states bringing the total to 19. But the creation of new states only strengthened the federal might and weakened the component units. Secondly, the 1979 Constitution was to prescribe a presidential system, which significantly affected the procedural aspects of Nigerian federalism. It also called for national, as opposed to, sectional or regional parties.

When these policies are taken together with the introduction of the National Youth Service Corp by the Gowon regime, the direction of political engineering under the first military interregnum became clear; the consolidation of Nigerian federalism through the weakening of regional and sub-national patriotism and loyalty. In this assumption, the sub-nationalism of the major groups was to be curtailed, but the grievances of the minorities were yet to be adequately addressed nor their fears allayed; instead their grievances were suppressed by Federal hegemony.

In preparation for the second Republic, the Obasanjo regime set up a Constitution Drafting Committee (CDC). One of its terms of reference was to decentralize power. Despite the elaborate preparations made by the

Constituent Assembly, to guarantee loyalty to the federal ideal in the 1979 Obasanjo Constitution, the same Federal authorities undermined loyalties through policy decisions and were "relentlessly centralist both in spirit and substance" (Graf,1988:47). The 1979 constitution was a well-crafted and progressive document. It did take into consideration the desire of the people for unity and a stable polity. The constitution was very ambitious and audacious in its declarations. It declared new principles including constitutionalism, separation of powers, presidentialism (Article 122), federal character (Article 14) and the three-tier principle.

Thus, the first military interregnum ended in 1979 with a redefinition of Nigerian Federalism according to which the center is very strong, actually much stronger than at the beginning of the interregnum. The creation of a National Council of States (NCS) which was subjected to the Supreme Military Council (SMC) in 1975 and the subjection of the Federal Executive Council (FEC), also under the SMC were all indicators of the power of the center at the expense of component federal units already weakened by successive state creation exercises.

The Second Republic

The much engineered Second Republic raised much hope of political stability and economic prosperity. The Murtala-Obasanjo regime invested much creativity in the design of the Second Republic. There was the presidential system of Government, and the consolidation of the state structure. The new revenue allocation formula, and the review of the indegenization decree all contributed to the robust expectation of a stable and enduring civil democratic federal rule during the Second Republic.

The civilian leadership of the Second Republic did not have the idealism, ideological rigor and the capacity to sustain the political agenda very well scripted in the 1979 constitution. Within a short period, the NPN Government of Alhaji Shehu Shagari squandered all the domestic and international goodwill by its excesses demonstrated by massive corruption, mismanagement and plundering of the nation's resources, violating, in the process, the letter and the spirit of the 1979 constitution.

One of the problems of the Second Republic was its failure to temper the centralizing legacies of military rule which it inherited. Graf (1988:129) had noted that the de-militarized constitutional order was essentially a rationalization of existing power relationships a kind of balance-sheet of the socio-economic status quo. There was therefore the need to re-organize power after the exit of the military because of liberal democracy and federalism which serve the critical normative yardstick for the evaluation of regime performance. This suffered a great setback, and there were serious lapses in the practice of both between 1979 and 1983 (Olagunju, et al. 1993:59). In temperament and practice the political leadership of the Second Republic was too pre-occupied with primitive accumulation to advance the course of federalism or democratic governance. The Second Republic failed therefore because of the inadequacies of the political leadership. The federal cause suffered greatly with the overthrow of the civilian government of the Second Republic on the 31st December, 1983 just four years after it came into power.

The Second Military Interregnum

The military regime of General M. Buhari succeeded the administration of Shehu Shagari. The military interregnum that it heralded had four significant phases characterized by changing leadership. These were the General M. Buhari phase, the General I. B. Babangida phase, the General Sani Abacha phase, and the General Abdulsalami Abubakar phase which terminated the interregnum. Each of these phases further consolidated the centralizing tendencies begun during the first military interregnum. These tendencies confuse, weaken and in fact as demonstrated under the Abacha era, endangered Nigerian federalism.

All the four regimes were right wing regimes. Despite the initial broad acceptance of the Buhari regime, it soon alienated all social groups by the end of its first year in office because of its extremism. Buhari's contribution to the development of Nigeria's federalism was to further consolidate federal control.

The General I.B. Babangida regime which succeeded the overthrown General Buhari regime after a palace coup d'etat in 1985 was in office for eight years. In the early days of the regime a Political Bureau was established. This was a novel approach to social engineering. The political Bureau, made up of eminent scholars and technocrats collated opinions of Nigerians across the land. After analysis the Bureau submitted a Report that among other things registered the support of Nigerians who expressed "strong commitment to the maintenance of the country as a federation" (Political Bureau, 1985:85) and support for the three-tier structure.

A new constitution was introduced in 1989 as a result of the work of the Constitution Review Panel which essentially revisited the 1979 Constitution. The work of the Panel was later reviewed by a Constituent Assembly. The 1989 Constitution adopted the Federal System and the Presidential System. In line with critical observations that were made to the Political Bureau and the Constitution Review Panel, 149 additional local governments were created, bringing the total to 449. A total of eleven new states were created in two dramatic moves bringing the total to 30.

Despite the enthusiasm of General Babangida for innovations in the management of state affairs, his inconsistencies undermined his success. When he again postponed the end of his elaborate transition to civil rule program and actually annulled a free and fair June 12 Presidential Election in 1993, thus aborting the Third Republic, he was virtually pushed out of office in disgrace.

The Interim National Government which he put in place was too weak to survive the high profile intrigue of the military. Within three months, the regime was overthrown, and General Sani Abacha ascended to power, to begin the darkest years in the history of Nigerian federalism.

Abacha's rule was not only the most authoritarian in Nigeria's history, it was the most brutal. Under Abacha's rule, the centralizing tendency in Nigeria federalism was carried to absurd levels. He used the authority at his disposal to run a crony government appropriating and distributing national resources according to his whims and caprices, to his family members and friends, recklessly appropriating national wealth. He also destroyed national institutions undermining national solidarity. At the international level, his style of governance brought the nation to disrepute and isolation. Nigeria became a pariah nation.

During his time, six new states were created, bringing the number to 36. Additional local governments were also created bringing the total to 770. All these did not in any way enhance the quality of governance or the relationship between the different levels of government. It only continued the centralizing tendencies of previous military administrations. The attempt by Abacha to produce a new constitution through a conference in 1995 never saw the light of day as it was reviewed and edited and revised by executive fiat within the Presidency. Eventually the status of the document and its contents became matters of wild speculations.

It can be argued that the second military interregnum with four Military rulers has significantly weakened the fabric of Nigerian federalism. Olagunju had argued that "the important dimension of the evolution and development of Nigerian federalism has been its periodic strategic construction and re-construction to prevent the monopolization and the consequent abuse and misuse of political power by one ethnic group or a combination of ethnic groups (Olagunju et al. 1993:32). All the regimes, with the possible exception of the General Abdulsalami regime have considerably eroded the ideals of Nigerian federalism beyond just the goal of containment. This occurred largely due to the overbearing nature and over-centralization of decision making of legislative and executive power under military rule. Ogban-Iyam (1998:166) has observed as positive elements, the facts that some non-centralization maintaining elements like constitutionally guaranteed differences in laws and representation of the constituent Federal units exist throughout these period under study. We can equally note that constitutional guarantee was no protector of the federal principle, when the interests of the dominant forces are at stake as we have noted above.

Conclusion

In a study of the requisites for successful Federalism scholars of the New York University concluded that the people of the federation should feel federal (Ramphal 1978, p. xix) and have "sufficiently strong and pervasive political commitment to the primary concept or value of the federation itself." We have shown the evolutionary path of defining factors in all the Nigerian constitutions. In all these it has been argued that Nigerians have accepted, since the immediate post-second world war period the idea that federalism, particularly the regionalized type, was functionally beneficial to the Nigerian state.

The foundation and general outcome of what we have today as Nigerian federalism was laid in the colonial era. The strength of the center and the contradicting tendencies, as well as the hegemony of the Federal might which was already in place during the colonial days was passed on to the post-colonial Nigerian state. The independence constitution, the 1963 Republican constitution, the 1979 constitution, the 1989 Babangida constitution, the 1995 Abacha Draft Constitution and the 1999 Abdulsalami Constitution did not depart from the general tendencies established during colonialism with regards to the centralizing tendencies in content, spirit and structure of Nigerian federalism.

The Republican status of the 1963 Constitution the Presidentialism of the 1979 Constitutions and the pragmatism of the 1989 Babangida Constitution did not in any way strengthen Nigerian federalism. The long period of military rule, and the hierarchical structure and command style of administration combine to frustrate the benefits derivable from the state-creation exercise embarked upon by different regimes to stabilize the Nigerian state.

There is no doubt that the constitution has to play a critical role in the re-definition of Nigerian federalism. But that role would have to be combined with the political clarity of the goal of federalism, which is the creation of a stable and just polity. Federalism, if properly structured and managed should be functionally beneficial to the aspirations of the Nigerian people.

REFERENCES

Adamolekun, Ladipo. 1989 and Ayo S. Bamidele, "The Evolution of the Nigerian

Federal Administration System," *Publius: Journal of Federalism*, Vol. 19, No. 1 (Winter).

Abdullah, Mahdi, Kwanashie, George A., Mohmood, Yakubu 1994. eds. *Nigeria: The State of the National and the Way Forward*. Kaduna: Arewa House.

Adekanye, Bayo. 1981-82. "Military Organisation and Federal Society" *Quarterly Journal of Administration* Vol. 16, pp. 3-25.

Afigbo, A.E. 1991. "Background to Nigerian Federalism: Federal features in Colonial State": *Publics: The Journal of Federalism*, Fall, Vol. 21, No. 4.

Awa, I.O. 1964. *Federal Government in Nigeria, a study of the development of the Nigerian State*. Berkeley: Univ. Of California Press.

Awolowo, O. 1947. *Path to Nigerian Freedom*. London: Faber.

––––––– 1966. *Thoughts on Nigeria Constitutions*. Ibadan: Oxford University Press.

Ayua, Ignatius. 1981. "System of Government" in Abdullahi Mahdi et al, cit. pp. 284-302.

Breth J. *Constitutional Problems of Federalism in Nigeria*. London: Sweet and Maxwell.

Clark, Trevor. 1991. *A Right Honourable Gentleman: The Life and Times of Alhaji Sir Abubakar Tafawa Balewa*. Zaria: Hudahuda Publishing Company.

Coleman, James S. 1996. *Nigeria: Background to Nationalism*, Berkeley: University of California Press.

Elaigwu, J.I. and Uzongwe, G.N. 1996. ed. *Foundations of Nigerian Federalism 1900-1960*, Abuja: NCIR.

Falola, Toyin. 1988. "The Evolution and Changes in Nigerian Federalism". In Olaniyan R.A., ed. *Federalism in a Changing World*. Lagos: The Presidency, pp. 50-72.

Graf, William D. 1988. *The Nigerian State: Political Economy, State, Class and Political System in the Post-Colonial Era*, London: James Currey.

Ijalaiye, D.A. "The Civil War and Nigerian Federalism" in Akinyemi, Bolaji et al., op.cit., pp. 141-154.

Nnoli, O. 1978. *Ethnic Politics in Nigeria*. Enugu: Fourth Dimension Publishers.

Nwabughuogu, A.I. "Unitarism versus Federalism: a British Dilemma 1914-1954," in Elaigwu J.J and Uzogwe G.N. ed. op. cit. pp. 39-59.

Ogban-Iyam 1988. "Federalism in Nigeria: The Journey So Far and the Way Forward", Nnamdi Azikiwe *Journal of Political Science*, Vol. 1, No. 1.

Olagunju, Tunji, Jinadu, Adele, Oyovbaire, Sam. (1993) *Transition to Democracy in Nigeria 1985-1993*. Ibadan: Safare Books.

Olusanya, G.O. 1990. Constitutional Developments in Nigeria 1861-1960 in Obaro Ikime ed. *Groundwork of Nigerian History*. Ibadan: Heinemann.

Osaghae, Eghosa E. 1998. "Managing Minority Problems in a Developing Society: The Nigerian Experience": *The Journal of Modern African Studies*, Vol. 36, No. 1.

Osuntokun, Jide, "The Historical Background of Nigerian Federalism," in Bolaji Akinyemi et al. Readings on Federalism. Lagos: Nigerian Institute of International Affairs pp.

Oyovbaire, S. 1985. *Federalism in Nigeria in Nigeria*. London: Macmillan Press.

Phillips, A.O. 1991. "Managing Issues of Fiscal Federalism: Revenue Allocation in Nigeria" *Publius: Journal of Federalism*, Vol. 21, No 4.

Report of the Constitutional Conference Containing the Draft Constitution, 1995. Vol. 1

Abuja.

Report of the Political Bureau. 1987. Abuja, Mamser.

The Constitution of the Federal Republic of Nigeria 1979. Daily Times, Lagos.

CHAPTER 5

Federalist Deconcentration and Group Rights in Canada: Some Lessons for Nigeria

Leo Dare

General Introduction

C anada and Nigeria share many common qualities. Both are multicultural states struggling to forge national unity on the basis of a federal constitution. Canada adopted a federal system following extensive negotiations among the provinces from 1864 to 1867. As a result of the agreements reached, some of the provinces joined together while others waited for some time before deciding to enter confederation. The Western provinces were admitted into the Canadian union at different times after the initial signing of the British North America Act, which became the Canadian Constitution. As of today, three northern territories are evolving toward provincial status.

In Nigeria, the three original regions that had evolved during the colonial era negotiated the Nigerian independence agreement of 1960. Shortly after, Southern Cameroon voted to merge with the Cameroon Republic, and thus stayed out of Nigeria, while Northern Cameroon voted in favor of a merger with Nigeria, and became Sardauna Province in Northern Nigeria. However, we must note a curious aspect of the Nigerian federal experiment, which centers on the subdivision of the units in terms of creating additional states. From the three original regions of 1960, Nigeria today has thirty-six states. State-creation exercises were carried out in 1963, 1967, 1976, 1987, 1991 and 1996, while the geographical boundaries remain unchanged. The development impacted on the relationship between the center and the component units, but did not alter the essence of federalism. Nigeria remains committed to federalism as a system of governance.

Federalism commits Canada and Nigeria to constitutional respect for the component units and evolving group formations. The nature of the Canadian society continues to change due to the arrival of new immigrants who are unaffiliated with the original groups who joined at confederation. The pressure from the new ethnic groups forced the adoption of multi-culturalism as the official policy. In addition, more respect and recognition is accorded the Aboriginal populations in terms of self-government and political autonomy. For Nigeria and Canada, the problems of integration remain. In both countries, there are vibrant groups and communities seeking further constitutional recognition for themselves, or agitating for constitutional reforms. Since Confederation in 1867, Canadian leaders appear committed to the idea of a perpetual dialogue on federalism. They have used many Royal Commissions, Conferences, federal/provincial negotiations and different levels of citizen participation to discuss confederation and national unity. Within the past thirty years, Canadian leaders have taken the approach we shall classify as **deconcentration** to resolve the problems of federalism. To a considerable extent, the strategy seems to be working, and has pre-empted the type of violence, which Nigeria has been witnessing of late. Though one is mindful of the dangers in transposing solutions from one political system to another, the Nigerian and Canadian problems are sufficiently similar that Nigerian leaders may benefit from looking at these tried and tested federal experiments. Nigerian leaders seem unable to comprehend the fact that federalism and constitutional change are processes that grow and evolve, and for which changing solutions must be found for changing problems. They will be better off looking outside Nigeria at similar situations for lasting solutions.

The term **federal** denotes some form of covenant or compact among the component states, and among the citizens of the various states to establish a common civil order. This is why in federations a citizen is simultaneously under two levels of government. The process of establishing a federal system may take place through the integration of previously autonomous units, or through the disaggregation of a former empire. At the time of the compact, the component units agree to certain terms. These conditions which are usually in form of a written constitution place limits on the powers exercised by both the component units and by the center. The various levels of government share power, and the right to exit for each level is not dependent on the convenience of the other. Consequently, each level of government can trace its rights, duties and obligations to the original compact. Ideally, these conditions must exist in some form before a political system can be classified as federal.

As long as multi-ethnic societies find themselves trapped under the same political system, or as long as several small societies aspire to live together within the same state, sharing sovereignty, so long will the theory and relevance of federalism remain on the front burner of political analysis. A federal constitution is a complex constitutional machinery adopted simply because there are no viable alternatives short of outright separation. In other words, federalism is necessitated by the contradictory pull for both unity and diversity. The desire for unity may be dictated by economic, defense and military considerations. The desire for diversity or self-preservation may be dictated by linguistic, cultural or religious concerns. Whatever may be the motivating factors for the adoption of federalism, the goal is to accommodate special interests, ethnic, geographical or cultural concerns while forging enough unity for the political system to move ahead. The constitutional allocation of powers to the different levels of government is made to reflect the balance of forces at the time the constitution is drafted. This allocation of responsibilities is based on the understanding that the component units will have the capability collectively and individually to operate and shoulder the responsibilities conferred on them.

The major appeal of federalism is that it places emphasis on pluralism, and seeks constitutional recognition for the rights of the component units. This it does through a matrix of constituent institutions that together share power, not through a single center but in a multi-centered, or non-centralized way. Through federal constitutional arrangements, the constituent units have the constitutionally endowed right to existence, together with the right to an area of legislative competence and administrative autonomy. Thus, in the words of Daniel Elazar (1987: 12), "the very essence of federation as a particular form of union is **self rule plus shared rule**".

Those who favor the federal solution like David Nice (1987: 13), are quick to highlight its advantages. These they list as including decentralized management and efficiency, flexibility in adapting to regional differences, encouragement of healthy competition among the component units, prevention of the abuse of power and encouraging innovation while sharing the benefits of the enlarged market.

Just as some see federalism as a solution to many problems of multi-cultural societies, the opponents complain that it is a very difficult system of government to operate. Critics claim federalism is legalistic, complex, conservative and rigid. They allege that the need for constant balancing, negotiation and compromise makes federalism immobile as a system of government in a dynamic world. They criticize federalism as being too expensive in that there must be a multiplication of governmental structures of decision-making. Each level of government and each component unit must establish the machinery for governance. Offices must be provided and manned, and political institutions to take care of the responsibilities of the level of government must also be paid for. Consequently, under any real federal arrangement, there are many centers of government, and the levels of government may duplicate services at considerable expense and overlap.

Given the fact that federal constitutions have rigid amendment procedures, the constitution is not easily changed to meet changing political and economic situations. Fundamental constitutional conflicts that are endemic to federations are often referred to the judicial branch for resolution. Critics of federalism complain that the judiciary exercises too much power in determining conflicts in federal political systems. It should however be noted that an arrangement which is based on negotiation and bargain which eventually resulted in a written document which participants regard as treaties, must be legalistic, and treated as such. For this reason, the judiciary must of necessity play a central role in federations where it can adjudicate conflicts.

Finally, critics of federalism claim that the written and rigid constitution entrenches articulated differences at a particular point in time. Federalism is thus accused of stabilizing conflict or institutionalizing those differences that were present at the time the constitution was drafted. Participants are usually reluctant to relinquish concessions granted them even when circumstances change. Federalism shares authority, and seems to abhor authoritarianism. For these reasons, political leaders who have a disposition toward authoritarian centralization of power find the decentralizing tendencies of federalism inconvenient. They question the ability of federalism to create lasting unity, or to confront the dynamics of economic development in a rapidly changing world. Such leaders equate federalism with balkanization, and argue in favor of centralization. In other words, the checks and balances of federalism create jurisdictional conflicts, which may slow down the pace of mobilization. The costs of federalism include the problems of coordinating programs of various units, inequality of services and resources among the components, inter-jurisdictional conflicts, local bias, the dispersal of responsibilities and unresponsiveness to citizens from other units, and so on.

Federalism is noted for its restraints on the concentration of power. Federalism counters the trend towards unrestrained uniformity. Yet, federal constitutions may not be amended fast enough for it to take care of changing political circumstances. It is for this reason that practitioners find ways round the rigidity of the constitution by engaging in inter-governmental consultations. This consultation depends on the willingness of the component units to make federalism work. The mental disposition to give and take, rather than resort to rigid legalism are the cartilage or joints that allow the skeleton of federalism to bend and adapt.

Trends in federalism: Centralization, Decentralization and Deconcentration

Empirical evidence from different parts of the world point to the fact that federal constitutions reflect the pulls and pressures of a particular historical point. The framing of a constitution does not in itself eliminate those contradictory pressures, which make federalism a political necessity. With time, the pulls may lead to the disintegration of the federal system through civil wars and secession of some parts. On the other hand, events may move the component units closer together thus removing the necessity for a federal constitution. In such case, the federation may become a unitary state. Both centrifugal and centripetal forces usually operate concurrently, with the effect that the federation may avoid either of the two extremes highlighted above.

Where the federal system does not collapse, it has been argued that there must be a constant effort to find ways to accommodate conflicts and build upon fundamental agreements in the society. Scholars of federalism have identified three possible trends in any existing federation: **Centralization, Decentralization and Deconcentration.** (Francois Rocher & Christian Rouillard, 1997). **Centralization** is represented by policy responsibilities assumed by the central government, and toward contraction of the policy responsibilities assumed by the component units of the federation. Centralization refers to the ability of the central government to exercise its authority in areas defined as provincial or regional, through a transfer from the constituent units to the center or through the implementation of constraining mechanisms of conception, evaluation, orientation and/or control to which the provinces are subordinate (Rocher & Rouillard, 1997: 105).

Decentralization on its part is represented by the tendency toward assigning increased responsibility to the constituent units of the federation. This can be achieved through a formal constitutional amendment, or administrative and fiscal decentralization. Under administrative decentralization, the federal authorities may delegate administrative responsibility for the execution of certain federal functions to the units. Fiscal decentralization may encompass the transfer and withdrawal of federal money to the units, particularly, money for which no conditions are attached.

Deconcentration, however can be seen as a dynamic process of interaction between the federal and state levels of government in such a way that the center brings the units in to participate in the decision-making process without the prerogative of the former being eroded. That is, in the process of deconcentration, the central government maintains its authority intact, contrary to decentralization, which involves a formal transfer of authority to subordinate administrative units. Deconcentration should therefore be seen as an aspect of executive federalism, which allows for change without the necessity of constitutional amendments. Centralization, decentralization or concentration can follow the process of deconcentration. In fact, deconcentration could be a way to share power with the component units without some of the problems associated with decentralization.

Nigerian Federalism in Historical Perspective

While many African countries opted for unitary centralization at the time of their political independence, Nigeria adopted a federal arrangement reflective of the multi-cultural nature of the Nigerian society. The history of the various groups, prior to and during colonialism helped in shaping the differences among the various ethnic groups within the geographical border of Nigeria. At the time of Nigeria's independence in 1960, there were three regions. In each of these, a major ethnic group was dominant, while there were minority groups. In other words, none of the three regions was ethnically homogeneous. With about two hundred ethnic groups each of which occupies an identifiable territory, the only political arrangement that could promote peaceful co-existence and reduce the fear of domination or assimilation is a federal one. It was therefore a matter of political necessity that Nigeria adopted a federal constitution.

Reflective of the prevailing state of inter-ethnic suspicion, the constitutional format of 1960 was one of a weak center and strong regions. The regions had developed on their own during the dying days of colonialism. The leading nationalists, namely Ahmadu Bello, Obafemi Awolowo and Nnamdi Azikiwe had all been premiers of their regions, thus enhancing the legitimacy of the regional administrations. The center was not as established as were the regions. In fact, the central government was created through negotiation by the regions, each attempting to protect regional interests. The premiers were protective of their turf, and only agreed to what would not erode regional powers and interests. All through the early days of Nigerian federalism, the center was therefore weaker than the constituent regions. It was this weakness that set the stage for the political crises of the First Republic, which was then popularly blamed on regionalism.

In terms of the groups operating in Nigeria at the time of independence, it is fair to say that the structure of the federal system was determined by the struggle among the three major ethnic groups in the regions. Minority groups looked across to other regions for political protection from their regional dominant group. The initial fear of domination centered on the major regional group. Hence, the Tiv in the north fearful of domination by the Hausa/Fulani oligarchy and their political organization, the Northern Peoples Congress (NPC), sought the support of and alliance with the western based, Yoruba dominated Action Group (AG). In the same way, the Edo in the Western Region who were apprehensive of Yoruba domination, looked across to the Eastern Region and the NCNC for support. The Ijaw, Ogoja and Calabar minorities in the Eastern Region looked for support from the Action Group of the Western Region.

All over the federation, minority areas were the seats of the political opposition to the ruling parties in the various regions. The minorities demanded for their own separate states or the restructuring of the federation so as to avoid domination by the regional majorities. Given the fact that the advocates for minority rights were usually from opposing regions, those in power in the regions downplayed the legitimacy of the demands, and tended to view the case for the minorities as one of meddling. This perhaps explained why the politicians did not condone the subdivision of their areas, through the creation of separate states for minorities in their regions, while promoting the creation of states for minorities in other regions. It is for this reason that both the NPC and the NCNC supported the creation of the Mid-West Region in 1963. They did this at a time when the Action Group in the Western Region was in disarray, and her political opponents from both the North and the East seized the opportunity to reduce the political strength of the Action Group and the Yoruba in Nigerian affairs.

Military Rule and Centralization of Power

The military intervened in Nigerian politics on January 15, 1966. Since then until the present, military rule was interrupted only from October 1979 to December 1983. Beginning with Decree 1(1966), the Ironsi regime established the Supreme Military Council (SMC) and the Federal Executive Council (FEC) to legislate on matters within federal jurisdiction. Regional Governors could legislate on matters within regional authority as spelt out in the 1963 Constitution. By March 1966, Ironsi had started drifting towards more centralization. On May 24,1966, Ironsi decreed Nigeria a Unitary State (Decree No. 34 (1966). The Federal Military Government was renamed the "National Military Government", while all the civil services in the federation were to be unified. Needless to say, this mis-adventure prompted a northern rebellion and coup, which terminated Ironsi's administration. The in-coming regime of Yakubu Gowon had no choice but to revert to the original federal structure and administrative style.

In view of the brewing crisis following the re-establishment of northern rule and the threat of secession of the Eastern Region, Elaigwu (1986) noted that Gowon pursued centralization through consultative measures rather than by decrees. This culminated in the Aburi Accord of March 1967, which effectively made Nigeria a confederation. The drift continued till the end of May when Ojukwu declared the secession of Biafra from Nigeria. Gowon was forced to take preemptive measures to protect the territorial integrity of Nigeria. He declared a state of emergency, and seized the opportunity to create twelve states thus reducing the political and economic might of the former regions. From this point, the trend toward centralization of power has remained unchecked. This centralization has become so total that analysts claim Nigeria no longer operates a federal system of government. Some of the developments that facilitated this centralization include, the central government's assumption of emergency powers during the civil war, the many decrees that subordinate the states to the absolute authority of the central government, (see for example Decree No. 32 of 1975). Others are the various state creation exercises embarked upon by the various military administrations in 1967, 1976, 1987, 1991 and 1996 respectively. Each state creation exercise has been carried out at the convenience of the central government, further reducing the political and economic relevance of the states. The public was rarely consulted, and the interests of the masses have largely been ignored. Each occasion had been used by the central military authorities to tighten their grip on the state administrations. The states eventually became passive observers in the restructuring of the geo-politics of Nigeria.

On the economic front, the super-imposition of the military structure altered the fate of Nigerian federalism in the direction of further centralization. This was further enhanced by the emergence of oil as the dominant source of foreign exchange earnings. The principle of derivation guided revenue allocation in Nigeria from 1946 to 1965, and each region was virtually autonomous in its financial dealings. Military rule and improved wealth from oil, which the federal government appropriated, made the subordination of the units of the Nigerian federation complete. The center began to encroach on the states, even in jurisdictions that are the exclusive preserve of the state administrations. The period 1975 to 1979 can be classified as the era of assertive centralization in Nigeria. The federal government forcefully appropriated important state functions: Universities, media houses, roads and embarked on projects in the exclusive jurisdiction of the states, such as primary education and local government reform. The unification of the public services of the federation following the recommendations of the (Udoji) commission in 1975 was just the last nail in the coffin of state autonomy.

The shift back to competitive federalism under the civilian administration from 1979 to 1983 was short lived. As soon as the military repossessed power in 1983, the swing was toward unrestrained federal power. Even after Babangida deposed Buhari, Babangida continued with the centralizing tendencies. Minute administrative details were handed down to state administrators for immediate implementation. On many projects such as education and local government finance, the federal government made direct grants to local agencies thus eroding further, the powers of the state governments. Under Abacha, the trend continued. The Federal government went to the extent of directing that traditional rulers must be paid a specific percentage of the budget. As a consequence, Nigerian federalism operated as a highly centralized unitary government. Every important decision was taken at the center.

The Nigerian Groups

As indicated above, the Nigerian federal structure was designed to produce limited unity. The three regions that negotiated independence were conglomerates of groups. The minorities within the regions were vocally apprehensive. The colonial administration had responded to the fears and concerns by establishing the Minorities Commission (1958) chaired by Henry Willink. The Commission recognized the genuineness of the fears and made recommendations for allaying them, notably constitutional guarantee of rights, centralization of the police and the decentralization of governmental functions. According to Akande (1988), these constitutional provisions did not eliminate the minority problems, and in each region, the relationship between the majority and minority groups remained strained. The tug of war among the groups continued till military intervention in 1966, and has continued since, often taking on more violent forms.

The most dramatic impact of military rule on Nigerian federalism is the extreme centralization it has occasioned. Every aspect of the structure and operation of federalism in Nigeria has been affected. The states have been substantially weakened. Minor decisions such as the location of local government headquarters, which are supposed to be state government responsibilities, are made in Abuja rather than the state capital. States have been denied their individual peculiarities. They exist today only to carry out directives from the center. Since the north had traditionally dominated the military, which in turn has dominated Nigerian politics, northern domination of the rest of the country has been enhanced by military rule.

Canadian Federalism

The Canadian federal system was established in 1867 through the British North America Act (BNA Act), passed by the British Parliament. Before the passage of the BNA Act, extensive consultations among the British North American colonies had taken place. The Quebec resolutions, which formed the basis of the Act, were referred to as the Compact of Confederation or Treaty among the provinces that originated the Dominion. At the time of the union, there were two main proposals of a widely different nature. There were those who considered that the most advantageous arrangement would be a legislative union under which law making would be centralized in one Parliament, following the British precedent. There were also those who charged that a federal arrangement would best satisfy the aspirations of the various groups.

At the beginning of the deliberations the leaders stated their positions. John A Macdonald declared himself in favor of a powerful central government, under which people from each section must feel protected. Others expressed the view that the rights and privileges of the people would be best protected if left to the local legislatures. In the end, a federal system to protect the "diversified interests of the several provinces and secure efficiency, harmony, and permanency in the working of the nation" was drafted (Beck, 1971:1-39). The delegates agreed to a federal union with a federal parliament charged with authority over matters of general interest (Section 91), while the provinces were accorded legislative control over local objects and guardianship of provincial interests (Section 92).

A lot has been written about the Canadian federation. It is often referred to as a pact among the provinces. The emphasis is on the fact that the British North America Act "embodies a compromise under which the original provinces agreed to federate"(Beck, 1971:41). In other words, the powers of the provincial governments do not flow from the central government. Quite the contrary, it is the Central Government, which owes its very existence to the willing consent of the provinces. The provinces predated the federal government.

The particular circumstances of the period 1864-67, namely, the American Civil War, the failure of the Province of Canada to gain control of Rupertsland, the failure to agree upon an inter-colonial railway, the threatened abrogation of the Reciprocity Treaty, the Fenian raids, and above all, British pressure for the consolidation of the colonies created a favorable political climate for a federal constitution with a strong center and centralizing potentials. The fear that a weak federation might degenerate into civil war like the American experiment pushed in the direction of a highly centralized federal arrangement. John A. MacDonald who became the first Prime Minister of Canada saw to this. The provinces were granted only a moderate list of powers, essentially of a local or private nature. K.C. Wheare later described the Canadian constitution as quasi-federal because of the many instruments available to the national government to intervene in provincial arenas. These included disallowance and declaratory powers, appointment of the lieutenant governor, the latter's discretionary power to reserve provincial legislation, and federal appointment of superior, district, and county court judges.

The Canadian federation was not without its own share of divisive forces. Ethnic, linguistic and religious differences existed in the United Canada, consisting of Ontario and Quebec. The disparities in size and what was seen as competitive rather than complementary economies played havoc on the desire for unity. Finally, despite common membership of the British Empire and similarities in their political institutions, the Maritimes saw themselves as sufficiently different either to reject Confederation outright or to hold back joining, as was the case in Prince Edward Island and Newfoundland.

The BNA Act and Rights

The BNA Act made no specific mention (or enumeration) of civil rights and liberties, no explicit reference to freedom of religion, speech, the press and assembly, and no bill of rights comparable to the American Constitution. These were implied in the declaration that the BNA Act was establishing a constitution "similar in principle to that of the United Kingdom". It was only in the 1930s that the Supreme Court declared that the BNA Act did contain an "implied bill of rights" (Valpy & Coyne, 1998: 53). However, these rights were implied and not made explicit.

From Biculturalism to Multiculturalism and the recognition of Rights in Canada

As explained above, Confederation was initially viewed as a pact between the English and the French, since these were the two European groups in the Canadian colonies as of that time. Section 133 of the BNA Act protected the use of English and French in Parliament and in the Quebec legislature. Section 93 also guaranteed separate denominational schools, a clause demanded by English Protestants in Quebec. The Quebec civil code was also protected in Sections 92 and 94. These guarantees were extended to the new provinces and territories of the Dominion of Canada when there was expansion to British Columbia (1871) Prince Edward Island (1873) the North West Territories (1880) Alberta and Saskatchewan (1905) and Newfoundland (1949). No official recognition was given to the aboriginal or native population, comprising the Indians, Inuit and Metis.

Since Confederation, Canada has expanded geographically, and has opened her doors to immigration from all over the world. At Confederation, the settlers had come primarily from Europe. Soon thereafter, Asians were allowed in to provide labor for the construction of the trans-continental railway lines. Similarly, new immigrants came from Eastern Europe, the Indian sub-continent and Africa. The diversity of the population brought about conflict. The dominant white majority used every available opportunity to discriminate against other races. Those discriminated against could not be sure of the protection of the judiciary. For example, in 1902, noted (Greene, 1989:18), the Judicial Committee of the Privy Council which served as the highest court until 1949, upheld British Columbia legislation that denied the vote to Canadians of Asiatic stock as being within the proper bounds of provincial jurisdiction. Similarly, in 1921, the Quebec Court of Appeal found that racial segregation in theatres was acceptable as an exercise of the private rights of theatre owners. (Ibid:18)

During the Second World War, the treatment meted to Canadians from countries that were at war with the mother countries showed that the new immigrants were regarded with suspicion. The rights of Canadians from Japan and Germany were violated during the war. This embarrassment led to post-war attempts at establishing a bill of rights. The Bill of Rights sought to place all Canadians regardless of original place of origin, on the same legal and political level. Multiculturalism replaced bi-culturalism. The Canadian government had to take a hard look at how an all-inclusive multi-cultural society based on the equality of the various groups could be established. The lessons of this experiment in peaceful co-existence and mutual respect for group rights are the central theme of this essay, which will provide useful lessons to Nigeria.

As indicated above, the Canadian provinces that negotiated Confederation were divisible into two linguistic groups: the French in Quebec, and the English in the other provinces. Prior to Confederation, the Indian nations had negotiated treaties with the Crown, and there were several Royal Proclamations and ordinary federal laws such as Indian Acts, which defined the relationship between the Indian and the new settlers. Under a typical treaty, an Indian tribe would cede land to the Crown in exchange for the Crown promising some annual payments, grants and other supplies to the Indians, and also permitting Indians to hunt, fish and log throughout the surrendered land. Beyond this, the white settlers did not treat Indians with a great deal of respect. And collectively, Indians were confined to pieces of land designated as Indian Reserves. The Indian Act, which governed life on the reserves, was to say the least cruel. For example, Section 12(1) (b) of the Indian Act stated that "Any

Indian woman who married a non-Indian, would automatically lose her Indian status, and so would her children". The 1867 Constitution treated the Indian and Indian lands as coming under federal jurisdiction. With the prevailing attitude after the Charter of Rights was enacted, most of the discriminatory clauses in the Canadian constitution have been amended (Bill C-31 of 1986).

It is important to reiterate that Confederation was seen as a pact between the English and the French cultures. With time, however, the ethnic composition of Canada changed due to the arrival of immigrants from other parts of the world. The attempt to define a more inclusive Canada led indirectly to the enhancement of the powers of the federal government. In the 1960's John Diefenbaker, the Canadian Prime Minister of German extraction, and a Prairie populist felt that Canada needed a bill of rights. He thought such a bill could become a symbol that would transcend regional identities and apply to all Canadians. He succeeded in making Parliament pass the Canadian Bill of Rights. This bill was simple in its goals, which stated in Section 1

> *Several rights and freedoms have existed and shall continue to exist. They include the following: the right to life, liberty, security of the person and enjoyment of property, unless deprived thereof "by due process of law"; the right to equality before the law and the protection of the law"; and the freedoms of religion, speech, assembly, association and the press. These rights and freedoms are "to exists without discrimination by reason of race, national origin, color, religion or sex.*

Despite this brave effort by the government, the Supreme Court interpreted the Canadian bill of rights narrowly, as applying only to federal laws and administrative activities, but not to provincial laws and actions. This posture by the Supreme Court prompted pro-civil liberty activists to campaign for an entrenched Charter of Rights that would take precedence over all legislation, and in effect undermine the notion of parliamentary sovereignty. The road to the charter was a long and arduous one. The goal of entrenching the Charter of rights became a key ingredient in the federal government's nation-building strategy of the Trudeau regime from 1967 to 1982. That strategy evolved to contain three important elements that impacted on the rights of Canadians. These were:

(a) To create the conditions that would encourage a stronger national identity to counteract the forces of provincialism

(b) To patriate the constitutional amendment process, and provide for an entirely Canadian amending procedure, and,

(c) To extend language rights and to create new "mobility rights" so that Canadians would feel at home in any province, and would not be deterred from moving within the country.

In 1968, Justice Minister Trudeau tabled before the Federal Provincial Conference a proposal for a Constitutional Bill of Rights. The Conference did not succeed. In 1970, the Federal Government established a special committee of Parliament (the Molgat MacGuigan Committee) to consider a package of constitutional reforms. The Committee received 1,700 briefs, from the public, many of them recommending that the proposed charter should include protection for groups with special needs, such as the handicapped, women, senior citizens, aboriginal people, minorities, and the poor.

Each time the federal and provincial first ministers met after 1970, proposals for constitutional reform featured prominently in the deliberations. The meetings deliberated on the Canadian Charter of Rights and Freedoms. The Charter was intended to entrench the shared political values of all Canadians in Constitutional law, and to protect the rights of all Canadians against their governments. The larger political purpose was to strengthen national unity by providing constitutional support to a new definition of Canadians as right-bearing citizens. The Charter contained clauses of special interest to women, aboriginal, multi-cultural Canadians, the disabled and others. Their recognition was a change from the traditional view that the only important communities were those directly linked as national and provincial communities to the governments in the Canadian federal set up.

The eight sections of the Charter dealt with fundamental freedoms, democratic rights, mobility rights, legal rights, equality rights, language rights, minority language rights and aboriginal rights. Section 25 specifically directed judges to interpret the Charter so as not to abrogate or derogate from any aboriginal treaty or other rights of freedoms that pertain to the aboriginal peoples of Canada. Similarly, Section 35 re-affirmed existing (rather than the original) aboriginal treaty rights of the Aboriginal peoples of Canada, and made a promise of a future constitutional conference that would include the first ministers and the leaders of native organizations. Following this, at the 1983 Constitutional Conference, an agreement was reached that gave the Indian Bands the right to negotiate self-government agreement with Ottawa and provincial governments. After protracted negotiations, the first in the series of land treaties between Indians and the other levels of government. The Nisga's Treaty (Doerr, 1997) - was reached in British Columbia in 1998. The Nisga Agreement gave the Indians extensive land and resources, self-government, fisheries and taxation rights. It gave the Nisgas 1930 square kilometers of land to be owned communally by Nisgas Nation, with title vested in the Nisga government. The Nisga government would also own surface and subsurface resources on these lands. The Agreement also stated that the primary institution of government of the Nisga nation would be the Nisgas central government, and a series of Nisga village governments. The Nisgas central government will be responsible for relations between the Nisga and British Columbia and Federal Governments. Subject to the approval of the British Columbia Government, the Nisgas will have their own police force and court to enforce and rule on Nisga laws on Nisga lands. The Canadian Charter of Rights and Freedoms will apply to the Nisgas government and institutions in relation to all matters within its jurisdiction and authority.

Another significant development is the establishment of the government of Nunavut in April 1999. By taking this step, the Canadian Government recognized the native population of the North, and accorded them self-government in all internal matters. Such respect and recognition are important in the building of a federal partnership.

What is most significant about the Canadian federation is that the leaders at all levels of government have come to accept that the process of renewing the federation is a never-ending one requiring patience, negotiation and bargaining and a spirit of give and take. This process is multifaceted. While there are parliamentary committees and Royal Commissions looking into a renewal of federalism, federal and provincial officials are also meeting to work of agreements which from time to time hit the headlines when they are presented to the Conference of First Ministers for deliberation. Examples of these are the Meech Lake Accord (1987), the Charlottetown Accord (1992) and the Calgary Declaration (1997). It is also important to note that these agreements by the first ministers were in most cases submitted to the people for further public debate and ratification in form of referendum. Another example is the Special Joint Committee of the Senate and the House of Commons on A Renewed Canada (1991-1992) Gerald A. Beaudoin & Dobbie Committee. This Committee took the proposals by the government to the people and held a national debate on constitutional proposals.

It is not our intention to give the impression that everything is fine with the Canadian political system. What we are saying is that the political actors seem to accept the need for change that may be in form of non-constitutional amendments. The political reality is that the provinces cannot protect themselves from the overlapping of federal programs given the fact that the federal government is able to spend in areas of provincial jurisdiction. However, federal officials have refrained from pressing this advantage, and have operated through regular consultation with their provincial counterparts. This is the hallmark of the **deconcentration** suggested above. **Deconcentration** has been used to fight regional disparities, and has produced very imaginative solutions to cope with deep societal cleavages. This has allowed federal and provincial governments to strike deals on power sharing, based on the many differences of culture and language, and to work out national policies in new areas. Let us illustrate with a few examples:

The National Energy Policy

In Canada, the provinces depend on natural resource exploitation for their economic well being, and most of these resources are regionally specific: Oil and gas principally in Alberta, forest products in British Columbia, Wheat and Potash in Saskatchewan, and so on. The marker for most of the resources lie outside Canada, predominantly in the United States to the south. Due to the fact that the constitution grants the federal government control over inter-provincial and international trade, Ottawa is able to get directly involved. Ottawa has not made any effort to appropriate provincial powers, or change the distribution of jurisdiction through constitutional amendment. It has merely used its taxation powers to ensure some redistribution of the benefits of natural resources. This is what Nigeria should contemplate doing.

The Social Union

A new form of federal/provincial relations emerging in the Canadian federation is officially described as a Social Union. The essence of the social union is a new form of federalism that allows the federal government to continue with its leadership role in social programs for the benefit of all Canadians. This by logical extension means some form of centralization. However, the Canadian authorities want to prevent undue centralization while leading the provinces in the provision of social programs for all Canadians regardless of where they reside. The rationale is that the availability of social programs would facilitate mobility throughout Canada and help the process of nation building. However, there was also the realization that federal leadership and programs may have the unintended consequences of stifling the Provinces. The social union is a way out of this predicament. It incorporates the opting out formula. While the federal government prescribes national standards and modes of delivery of federal services, provinces are allowed to maintain their independence and individuality. They can opt out of the federal plan and set up theirs without losing the financial advantage other provinces get by participating in the federal program. (Howse 1997: 311-331). In this way, if the federal program gets corrupted, not all provinces will be affected. The right to participate is married to the right to differ. This is true federalism.

Constitutional Safety Valves

In Canada, there have always existed conflicts between the English and the French, or the whites and the Aboriginal populations. There are also regional, economic and religious differences. Canadian groups have used the freedom of association to express their discontent or to solve their political problems. Groups have frequently transformed into political parties to promote specific regional or sectional interests. Farmers in Alberta and Manitoba organized protest parties at different times to show their displeasure about Ottawa's policies (The Progressive Movement 1919-1920). Today, Western alienation explains the strength of the Reform Party in Canada. Quebec voters have at different times voted together against the policies of the two traditional parties in Canada. Quebec is at present governed by a separatist Party Quebecois, formed mainly to show Quebec's disenchantment with the Canadian federal system. Groups have the freedom to form and dissolve without any level of government attempting to regulate them. The ability to organize such groups allows disenchanted groups to let off steam before their disenchantment boils over.

Nigeria's groups and political rights

In Nigeria prior to military intervention in 1966, political associations formed freely, and the freedom of association was one of the rights guaranteed in the constitution. While the NPC, the NCNC and the AG were dominant in their respective regions, minorities and the political opposition in the regions and at the center were able to organize in pursuit of their group interests. The large number of political parties was blamed for the political instability of the First Republic. In an attempt to eliminate what it regarded as splinter or sectional parties, Nigerian constitutions since 1979 have made it impossible for sectional groups to organize and function as political parties. Sections 202-204 of the 1979 Constitution ban regional or sectional parties. These provisions impact negatively on the nature of political protest and the freedom of association in Nigeria. All the constitutions and constitutional proposals since then have duplicated these restrictions. Even the 1999 Constitution of the Federal Republic of Nigeria (sections 221-226) duplicated the restrictions on political party formation. While appreciative of the reasons for these restrictions in the first place, one must note that they are undemocratic. The restrictions on party formation only allow political frustrations to boil over.

Southern marginalization, northern domination, power shift, true federalism, and so on are concepts that attempt to explain the perversion of federalism under military rule in Nigeria. Military rule brought about extreme centralization of power, which makes observers conclude that Nigeria can no longer be described as operating a federal system of government despite official pretensions. Unfortunately, the Nigerian political system has not found means of relating to groups unless they are constituted into states. Each time a group wants recognition, they start by agitating for their reconstitution into a separate state. Governments have responded to such pressures by creating new states to please group leaders. The people themselves are rarely consulted in state-creation exercises, giving the impression that the creation of states is a political reward to the leaders who are now given their own empire for economic exploitation. The leaders at the center also feel they have a right to partition the country into states, as they find politically convenient. Nigeria will need to take a closer look at other federations such as Canada, Australia and the United States where the territorial integrity of the component units of the federation have been preserved. The increase in the number of political units in the more stable federations came about through the expansion into the frontier, rather than the subdivision of existing units.

Through decrees already discussed, the Nigerian federal government appropriated what belonged to the states, namely, mineral resources. The appropriation of oil revenue by the northern controlled federal government dispossessed the producers, thus making Nigeria a classic case of **internal colonialism.** The unholy alliance between the military rulers, the northern political elite and the multinational oil exploration firms in the southern sections of the country has only led to the victimization of the people from whose land oil is found. The details of these acts of official repression need not be repeated here.

Protests and agitation for redress were either ignored or brutally suppressed. As of the time of writing, the conflict has worsened. Ijaw youths gave both the federal government and the oil companies a deadline within which to vacate their land. By the last day of the ultimatum, the state government had declared a state of emergency over Ijaw territory. Following this, there were reports of confrontation during which several Ijaw youths were killed. Dialogue would have prevented this bloodshed. To the Niger Delta area, the discovery of oil from their land appears to be a curse rather than the blessing it ought to be.

The similarities between the Canadian and the Nigerian systems are many. The Province of Alberta produces a good deal of the Canadian oil. Most of this is exported to the United States and the eastern provinces. Instead of appropriation, the Canadian federal government hiding under the jurisdictional powers of inter-provincial trade, imposed an export tax on Alberta oil being exported to the United States, and froze the domestic price to the benefit of all Canadians. These accomplishments were as a result of negotiation.

The Nigerian Civil Society

The Military not only destroyed the states, but also brought all other groups under their control. First, the labor unions were forced through decrees to come under the umbrella of the Nigerian Labor Congress. Following this, the government infiltrated labor by sponsoring favored candidates for the leadership of the organization. This converted labor into a subsidiary of the ministry. All trade union activities came under government regulation and control. From 1976 to date (March 1999), the Nigerian Labor Congress has been unable to organize any successful protest in the interest of the workers. Wages are not negotiated between labor and governments, but decreed by the federal government. The current industrial unrest in Nigeria is a result of the announcement of a minimum wage for all workers in the federation by the federal authorities without the courtesy of a prior discussion with the various state administrations. Ironically, it was the decimation of the Nigerian labor that facilitated the emergence of the civil society. Interest groups such as the National Association of Democratic Lawyers were formed initially to protest perceived high handedness of the military government and human rights abuses. If labor had been effective, many of the organizations in the civil society probably would not have existed.

Religious Groups

Section 10 of the 1979 Constitution of the Republic of Nigeria, stated explicitly that "the Government of the Federation or of a state shall not adopt any religion as state religion." The intent of this provision was to assert the secular nature of Nigeria, and give all religious groups an even playing field. The various religions, namely, traditional, Islam and Christian religious faiths, which had coexisted before colonialism, were treated as equal during colonial rule. The occasional religious clashes were brought about by attempts to impose Islam on minorities in the north, or by attempts at imposing Islamic Sharia laws and dress codes on other parts of Nigeria (Constituent Assembly Debates, 1978). There were religious conflicts in Tiv areas, in Zango-Kataf, Southern Zaria and in Kano (the Maitatsine riots 1980-1985), but these were isolated cases and were regional in scope. They were minor compared to the nationwide suspicion which flared in 1986 after the government of General Babangida dragged Nigeria into full membership of the Organization of Islamic Conference (OIC). Understandably, Christians and others were unhappy with the attempt to relegate their religions and they put up a spirited fight to restore the country to its secular position. Attempts to deal with some of the problems emanating from religious conflicts and placate the various groups have revolved around reiterating Nigeria's secularity, equity and balance in the allocation of air time for religious programs, the establishment of an inter-religious advisory body, and so on. These have not been very effective because it is perceived that government still favors Islam in many respects.

The Ogoni and Ijaw Crises

It will be incomplete to discuss groups without mentioning the on-going crisis in the oil producing areas of the Niger Delta which some see as the challenge of exclusion. Due to acts of omission and commission, and the seeming inability of the federal authorities to listen to genuine complaints of marginalization and economic degradation, the problems of oil producing minorities have recently taken on more serious dimensions. In the Nigerian case, oil, which accounts for a large portion of the federal revenue, is extracted from the south-eastern portion of the federation. Political power is perceived to remain permanently in the north. Decisions as to how the wealth is allocated and to whom are all made without reference to the oil producing areas. Worst, the producers who are subjected to the ecological dangers of exploration do not enjoy the benefits of the wealth. Leaders from the oil producing areas have consistently articulated demands for redress of this perceived injustice. Several groups have been formed, the most vocal and most resolute have been the Movement for the Survival of Ogoni Peoples (MOSOP) and the Ijaw National Congress (INC). The government's responses have shown apparent lack of understanding. The repression of Ogoni leaders culminating in the judicial murder of the nine MOSOP leaders in 1995 can never be the solution to the problem. The inability of the state governments in the oil producing states of Ondo, Bayelsa, Akwa Ibom, Rivers, Delta and Edo States to address the problems of the oil producing communities is itself a reflection of how weak and irrelevant state governments have become in the Nigerian federal system. The establishment of the Oil Mineral Producing Areas Development Commission (OMPADEC) by decree 23 of 1992 to manage funds allocated from the Federation Account for the oil producing areas is another case of imposition from above. Members of the Commission are appointed by the federal government and are responsible only to it. OMPADEC further dramatized the colonial status of the oil producing areas. The money meant for the oil producing areas does not get to the suffering masses, and are not spent on infrastructures in those areas.

The Constitutional Conference of 1995 (Resolution 19) by consensus agreement, recommended that revenue allocation shall constantly reflect the principle of derivation, provided that the approved formula shall not be less than 13% of the revenue accruing to the Federation Account. (Report, 1995, vol.: 141-142). This recommendation would have gone a long way to appease the oil producing areas, but the Nigerian Military Government, refused to act on the report, while Abacha embarked on a self-succession mis-adventure.

The oil companies take their orders from Abuja and operate as if the state governments do not exist. For any meaningful dialogue to begin there is a need to put power back to the oil producing states and the local communities. A good beginning will be the dismantling of OMPADEC as presently constituted. The Oil producing states should receive their allocations **based on agreed** principles and be allowed to determine how the resources are to be allocated and for which projects. Federal interference has been detrimental to the development of democracy and effective grassroots participation.

Nigerians to date have not been participants in the political process. They have been mere spectators to it. None of the constitutions foisted on Nigeria has gone through a process of ratification in a national referendum. The key members (Chairmen and officers) of the Constitution Drafting Committees and the Constituent Assemblies have been appointees of the federal government. The agenda for the deliberations of the various committees were set by the federal government, in most cases, pre-empting certain discussions by indicating "no go" areas. To add insult to injury, the military governments have unilaterally modified these documents even after deliberation by its chosen representatives. Unlike the practice in other societies, no Nigerian constitution has been presented to the people for ratification in a referendum. State governments that are supposed to be the constituent units of the federation have not been consulted on constitutional matters. In other words, the Nigerian federal (military) governments have refused to trust the people to make meaningful contributions or input into the process of constitution making, even though it is the people who have to live with the consequences of those decisions.

The National Conference Idea

The sprouting of the civil society and the pro-democracy movement in Nigeria can be traced directly to the high-handedness and mismanagement by the various military administrations. The earliest examples were the Committee for the Defense of Human Rights (CDHR) the National Association of Democratic Lawyers (NADL), and the Association of Trial Lawyers of Nigeria, (ATLN). These various groups initially did not coordinate their activities. Each group challenged the military in its own ways using labor union tactics. For example, the NADL, the NBA, the CDHR members were collectively opposed to the inhumane prison and detention conditions in

Nigeria, the establishment of military tribunals, government's disregard for court verdicts. Similarly, the NBA fought against retroactive decrees and the ouster clauses in the various decrees. Other groups such as the National Association of Nigerian Students (NANS), the Academic Staff Union of Universities (ASUU) also addressed government policies as they impacted on the educational system.

The initial attempt at collective action by the various groups was in 1990 when they broached the idea of a National Conference, primarily to put pressure on Babangida to honor his disengagement plan, and to provide a forum for the discussion of the national political agenda. The issues listed for discussion included the pursuit of economic justice, fundamental human rights, the freedom of the judiciary, and the national political agenda.

Sixty-nine associations were invited to the National Conference scheduled for September 6-9, 1990. On the day the Conference was to open, security agents were sent to disrupt the proposed conference and seal off the venue. The regime of Babangida did not allow the national conference to hold until it left office in 1993. But before then, the political crisis precipitated by the annulment of the Presidential election has engulfed all of Nigeria. More groups felt frustrated by the annulment, and joined their voices to those who were already agitating for a conference. In fact, when General Abacha seized power on November 17, 1993, he sought the support of the pro-democracy forces by promising to hold a Sovereign National Conference, and he also appointed one of the most outspoken proponents of the national conference (Dr. Olu Onagoruwa), as the Attorney General. Like Babangida, General Abacha reneged on the idea of the national conference.

General Abubakar had a golden opportunity to initiate discussions on the future of the federation when he prepared his transition agenda in August 1998. Like the others he ruled out a national conference. The conclusion that Nigerian military leaders have a phobia of dialogue is therefore inescapable. Responsible opinion from different parts of the country, by NADECO, the United Nigeria Democratic Front, JACON, Group of 34, have suggested holding a national conference or the conference of nationalities to debate issues about the future if the Nigerian federation. Rather than seeing the conference as a threat to corporate existence of Nigeria, government ought to view it as a safety valve or a forum for groups to air their frustrations about perceived imperfections of the Nigerian federal system. Until those imperfections are openly acknowledged, Nigerians cannot begin to discuss solutions. An open forum, which is not manipulated, or teleguided by the government will be a meeting place for the various nationalities to reaffirm their faith in Nigeria, and this definitely will strengthen Nigeria.

Concluding Remarks

Our effort has not been directed at an analysis of the issues in both Canadian and Nigerian federations. Both have powerful conflict-generating components. The Canadian political system has been more successful, not so much in resolving conflicts, as in managing it, and striking a balance between various proponents. As Alain Gagnon (1993: 12) argued, " the principal means of preserving the Canadian polity has been the evolution of instruments of conflict management, and the tremendous flexibility allowed the political system, permitting a pendulum movement between centripetal and centrifugal federalism". The commitment to achieving a working balance between the requirements of national unity, and the desire by the constituent units for their distinct status remains the guiding principle for keeping Canada together. The willingness of the center to share responsibilities, and allow other levels of government to participate in decision-making and in federal projects is the **deconcentration**, which keeps Canada moving.

As for Nigeria, there has been a movement from a highly decentralized to a highly centralized political system. This development occurred primarily because of military style centralism. Unfortunately, this centralization has not been accompanied by a high degree of efficiency. Instead, the center became incompetent and corrupt and the corruption infested the rest of the country.

The Nigerian Constitution of 1960 was a very progressive document in that it listed some fundamental rights for all Nigerians. The various governments have oppressed the citizens as if those rights do not exist. Under the military, decrees have been passed that denied citizens of many of their rights. Imprisonment without trial is a common feature of life in Nigeria. In short, Nigerian governments have consistently acted arbitrarily in their dealings with the public. In most instances of state creation, the constitutional provisions for the exercise were not followed. In situations where the judiciary has shown courage and ruled against government actions, those rulings have been ignored with impunity. One is therefore tempted to conclude that governmental lawlessness is more of a threat to liberty in Nigeria than the non-specification of those rights. Government must learn to operate within and respect the constitution, and not tinker with it at will. What Nigeria urgently needs is a return to both the spirit and the letter of the federal system adopted at the time of political independence. To begin with, the new civilian government must initiate an all-inclusive process of participation that will address the concerns of ethnic groups, the civil society and of individuals. This cannot be achieved if government does not open the dialogue to all citizens and at all levels of government. An acceptable constitution would emerge from such dialogue, and the various groups in Nigeria will have the opportunity to present their cases. This is the essence of federalism and of self-government.

REFERENCES:

Akande, J.O. 1988. "The Minorities and the Challenge of Federalism" in R.O. Olaniyan ed. *Federalism in a Changing World*. Ile-Ife: Obafemi Awolowo University Press.

Beck, J. M. 1971. ed. *The Shaping of Canadian Federalism: Central Authority or Provincial Rights*. Toronto: The Copp Clark Publishing Company.

Burgess, Michael 1990. ed. *Canadian Federalism, Past, Present and Future*. Leicester University Press, London.

Burgess, Michael & Gagnon, Alain.1993. *Comparative Federalism and Federation: Competing Traditions and Future Directions*. Toronto: University Press.

Byers, R.B. & Redford R.W. 1979. *Canada Challenged: The Viability of Confederation* Toronto: Canadian Institute of International Affairs.

Cairns, Alan. 1992. *Charter Versus Federalism: The Dilemmas of Constitutional Reform*. Montreal: McGill-Queens University Press.

Coyne, Deborah & Valpy, Michael. 1998. *To Match a Dream: A Practical Guide to Canada's Constitution*. Toronto: McClelland & Stewart.

Dare, Leo. 1998 "Hegemonic Military and Democratic Pressures in Nigeria", Paper Presented at the Canadian Political Science Association, 1998 Annual Conference University of Ottawa, June 1998.

Doerr, Audrey. 1997. "Federalism and Aboriginal Relations," in Harvey Lazar ed., *Canada: The State of the Federation*, Kingston, Ontario: Institute of Intergovernmental Relations.

Elaigwu, Isawa J. 1986. *Gowon; The Biography of a Soldier-Statesman*. Ibadan: West Books.

Elazar, Daniel. 1987. *Exploring Federalism*. Tuscaloosa: University of Alabama Press.

Federal Republic of Nigeria: *1979 Constitution of the Federal Republic of Nigeria*. Lagos: The Federal Government Press.

Fafard, Patrick & Brown, Douglas eds. 1996. *Canada: The State of the Federation*. Kingston: Institute of Intergovernmental Relations, Queens University.

Forsyth, Murray, ed. 1989. *Federalism and Nationalism*. New York: St Martins Press.

Gagne, Marie-Anik. 1994. *A Nation Within a Nation: Dependency and the Cree*. Montreal: Black Rose Books.

Harles, John. 1997. "Integration Before Assimilation: Immigration, Multiculturalism and the Canadian Polity", *Canadian Journal of Political Science*, XXX:4 (December, 1997), pp. 711-736.

Lazar, Harvey. 1998. ed. *Canada: The State of the Federation*, 1997: non-constitutional Renewal. Institute of Intergovernmental Relations, Queens University.

Howse, Robert. 1997. "National Unity and the Chretien Government's New Federalism." Harvey Lazar. Op. Cit. pp. 311-331.

Kallen, Evelyn. 1995. *Ethnicity and Human Rights in Canada*. Toronto: Oxford University Press.

Katz, Ellis & Taro, Alan. 1996. *Federalism and Rights*. Maryland: Rowman and Littlefield

Publishers.

Kilgour, David. 1990. *Inside Outer Canada*. Edmonton: Lone Pine Publishing Inc.

Murray, Forsyth. 1989. *Federalism and Nationalism*. New York: St Martins Press.

Nice, David. 1987. *Federalism, The Politics of Intergovernmental Relations*. New York: St. Martins Press.

Report of the Commission Appointed into the Fears of Minorities and the Means of Allaying Them. London: HMSO, 1958, Federal Republic of Nigeria: Report of the Constitutional Conference. 1995. (2volumes), No publisher. The Constitution of the Federal Republic of Nigeria, 1979, Times Press, Apapa, Lagos.

Report of the Special Joint Committee on a Renewed Canada (Joint Chairmen: Gerald Beaudoin & Dorothy Dobbie), Ottawa, 1992

Rocher, Francois & Christian Rouillard. 1996. "Using the concept of Deconcentration to Overcome Centralization/Decentralization Dichotomy", in Fafard & Brown, *Canada: The State of the Federation*. Kingston, Ontario: Institute of Intergovernmental Relations.

Whitaker, Reginald. 1992. *A Sovereign Idea: Essays on Canada as a Democratic Community*. Montreal: McGill University Press.

CHAPTER 6

Ethno-Religious Limits To The Construction Of Federalism In Africa: Yugoslavia And Nigeria Compared

Jibrin Ibrahim

Introduction

The central object of federalism is the extension and expansion of political space, autonomy and institutions to the benefit of geo-political units in a context in which the political community accepts that ethnic, religious and cultural differences exist and that their management would benefit from differential levels of governance. The point of departure of the theory and practice of federalism therefore is that such differences are legitimate and should be accepted and incorporated into the structure of governance. The political systems of federal states are therefore constructed in such a way as to accommodate such differences. Institutions for managing the differences, for seeking compromises and for negotiating conditions for living together are therefore central to federal politics. Our concern in this chapter is about the dangers of pushing ethnic and religious differences too far to the point at which they become dysfunctional in sustaining federal arrangements. If federalism requires the abandonment of the notion of the unitary state and the recognition of ethnic and religious difference, ethnicity and religion cannot be the sole basis for the construction of federalism. This is especially true in Africa where ethnic and religious differences have been very central to the continent's political crisis.

The nation-state that emerged following the Peace of Westphalia is in trouble. In so many parts of the world, the nation is finding it difficult and/ or impossible to co-exist with the state. Nationalist, regional, ethnic and religious sentiments are rising, and the state is being challenged by these forces (Fleiner,

1996, Olukoshi & Laakso, 1996). The result of this development on humankind is devastating. Terms such as pogrom, genocide, ethnocide and ethnic cleansing are becoming common adjectives for describing current events in some African and European countries and indeed in other parts of the world.[1] Nazi style destructive political pathology, characterized by excessively high levels of human destruction, has re-emerged with full force on different points of the globe. The conflicts between the Somali clans, Hutu and Tutsi in Rwanda and Burundi and between the Serbs, Croats, Albanian and Muslim Slav populations in the former Yugoslavia, have become some of the most devastating cases of human tragedy in recent history (Lemarchand, 1994, Samatar, 1994, Ignatieff, 1993). Such conflicts pose serious challenges to the existence of states and to strategies of political resolution of conflicts because their dynamics tend to block attempts at political engineering. The pathologization of the political process certainly makes the operation of federal systems of government impossible. Identity issues are usually at the center of such processes, but the problem is not so much with the identities themselves, but in the way in which they are used to define historical categories of destruction and survival.

It has been argued by Salamone, that identities are masks which change often in reaction to different situations. People tend to employ multiple identities, which at various moments are translated as tribalism, ethnic conflict, regionalism, statism, religious bigotry, nationalism, etc. (Salamone, 1992:70). In any case, our argument in this paper is that identities are not based on objective cultural categories, they are cognitive categories based on in and out-group identification (Cynthia Mahmoud, 1992:6). If the problem is not in the identities themselves, why then have communities that have lived together for long periods, under conditions of "normal" conflict and cooperation suddenly amplify their differences and mutual suspicion, transform them into hatred and start engaging in genocidal activities. The answer can only be found in the specific historical trajectories taken by the societies in question (Ibrahim & Pereira, 1998).

The crises of the state, nation, community and contesting cultures is particularly profound in contemporary Africa and the continent must confront the necessity of redesigning and saving its political future or face the risk of systemic collapse. For a very long period, African ruling classes have been propagating the virtues of national unity and the necessity of developing the nation-state. The reality of the continent, however, is that commitment to and identity with the state has always been very low. Indeed, the post-colonial state is currently undergoing an existential crisis. The African continent has been subjected to such terrible forces of repression, of exclusion of ethnic and religious groups, of destruction of her human and natural resources, that anarchy, ethnic cleansing, warlordism and the decomposition of political communities have become an integral part of the political agenda for many countries. That is the path of despair and hopelessness that must be averted. The way forward is the struggle for renewal in which democracy is a critical instrument that could lead to the reconstruction of politics and the state, culture, economic organization and production. At the heart of that search for democratic renewal, in the context of rising identity conflicts, is the question of federalism.

Federation and Federalism

After the euphoric hopes for Grand African Federations of the late 1950's died down, the federal idea has since been systematically dismissed as a serious solution to African problems. The basis for the dismissal is allegedly empirical, that federalism does not work in Africa. Indeed, there is a lot of evidence on the apparent failure of federalism. All of the attempts at establishing federal governments have failed. If Africa's federal experiments have failed, the failures are directly related to the unwillingness of ruling cabals to accept the limits placed on their powers by democratic federal constitutions. The unitary states that the various ruling cabals have tried to impose on their people have also collapsed. Jacobinism as a state ideology has been an even more glaring failure than federalism, because it has been tried and it did not work, while democratic federalism, has not really been tried over a sustained period. The time has come for Africa to revisit federalism, but in so doing, we should be careful and avoid some of its pitfalls.

The federal principle arises when a political community is characterized by significant territorial cleavages, which are usually reinforced by primordial divisions such as linguistic, religious and ethnic ones. The federal idea is to evolve political institutions that reflect the reality of the simultaneous necessity of unity and diversity. When national unity is over-emphasized, the polity moves towards a centralized state and when diversity is pushed to its logical limit, the federal state decomposes and splits into its constitutive units. Federalism is therefore a process of a constant search for equilibrium between the poles of unity and diversity. A federation may develop either as a result of centrifugal political forces the breaking down of a unitary form of government, or from centripetal action, the building up of different units into a new entity (Maddox, 1941:1121). The fundamental difference between unitary and federal states is that in the former, conflicts tend to be resolved through administrative fiat by the central government and in the latter, they are formalized and negotiated between central and regional governments through legal-constitutional means (Bakvis & Chandler, 1987:4). Indeed, in federal regimes, neither the federal nor regional governments are supreme, the constitution is the only supreme organ (Wheare, 1963:53). Each level of government has constitutionally guaranteed areas of competence. The classic reasons for the formation of federal states are very applicable to contemporary Africa. They include the desire to constrain the excesses of the use of political power, especially that of the executive, the need to protect group identities and rights, the fear that small political communities have of external control or aggression and the calculated expectation of economic advantage that could be obtained through larger economies of scale.

The only federal systems that have survived and prospered such as those in the United States, Switzerland and Canada, have been the ones that have developed democratic systems of political organization. In Africa, it is often argued that divisive ethnic mobilization develops from democratization and this is used as an argument against multiparty democracy, which, it is oft repeated, is bound to degenerate into inter-ethnic strife. This position is questionable:

> The argument that multiparty democracy exacerbates ethnic tension links the worst situation of ethnicity with the worst practice of multiparty democracy. On the other hand, the belief in the positive impact of democracy on ethnicity links the least tense ethnic situation with the most successful form of democracy. (Nnoli, 1992:51)

Nnoli argues convincingly that the persistence of the ethnic problem in Africa is linked to the failure of democracy:

> There is a democratic side to the ethnic question in Africa. It concerns the right of each ethnic group to be treated equally with all the others, for their members to be secure in their lives and property, from arbitrary arrest and punishment, and for them to enjoy equal opportunity in trade, business, employment, schooling and enjoyment of social amenities (Nnoli, 1989:206).

Nations, nationalities, tribes, clans and ethnic groups have the right to opt out of states that deny them their democratic rights. They also have the democratic right to unite with others if they so wish. The key to Africa's future could very well be found in the expansion of democratic space and the spread of the federal idea.

In the current demands and struggles for reconstructing African political systems, federalism has occupied a prominent place. It is true that currently, only Nigeria and Ethiopia define themselves as federal countries, and that Nigeria's claim to a federal status is unjustified while Ethiopia's new ethnic federalism has offered little real autonomy to the federating units contrary to the constitutional stipulations. South Africa's post apartheid political arrangement is also quasi federal even if the word federal is unacceptable to many powerful political actors in that country. In spite of the limited cases of "really existing federation" in the continent, what is important in the present context is that there are strong movements in many African countries demanding for and in many cases, engaged in armed struggles for a federal solution. In Uganda, Kenya, Sudan, Niger, Nigeria, South Africa, Congo Kinshasa, Senegal, and Chad, there are very powerful political movements campaigning or fighting for federalism.

We believe that federalism is the system of government that best fits the political reality of contemporary Africa. Yet, even a cursory glance at the recent political history of the continent reveals that the various experiments aimed at instituting federal polities seemed to have failed consistently. The Ugandan quasi-federal arrangement lasted from 1961 to 1966 when Obote reneged on the special status he had agreed to give Baganda at the 1961 London Constitutional Conference. The Ethiopian federation lasted from 1952 to 1962 when Eritrea was annexed as the 19th region of Ethiopia. The Libyan Federation lasted from 1951 to 1963 while that of Cameroon lasted from 1961 to 1972. The Central African Federation lasted from 1953 to 1963 while the Mali Federation lasted for less than two years, between 1959 and 1960. The East African Federation did not even take off. African ruling elites have not allowed federalism to function. They made sure that all attempts failed. They were not the only ones. In Eastern Europe, attempts at federalism failed because the political elites were unwilling to share power and when they tried to share power, they placed too much emphasis on ethnic and religious difference, and by so doing, the equilibrium between unity and diversity so necessary for federalism was broken. We will present the Yugoslavian example.

Yugoslavia and the Narcissism of Minor Difference

The Yugoslavian case is an excellent illustration of how identity conflicts can easily degenerate into pathological destruction. One important factor that tends to recur in such instances of serious identity conflict leading to war and pathological destruction is that there is the fear that "the other" would carry out atrocities against one's group, so a preventive offensive move is easily justified. This fear of "the other" worsens when the state is perceived as the weapon of one group against the other or too weak to offer protection to any group. The focus of analysis should therefore be the role and the nature of the state rather than essentialist notions of ethnic, cultural and religious difference. Indeed, we are reminded by Ignatieff (1993) that when the real sociological differences among ethno-religious groups are rather tenuous, they tend to multiply their minor differences in an effort to clearly separate the friend from the foe, an effect Freud called the narcissism of minor difference.

Our argument is that it is not the difference between ethnic, cultural and religious groups that are important in conflictual political situations. We know that there are a lot of bloody and brutal conflicts between groups that are culturally, religiously and ethnically similar such as the Ogonis and Andonis in the Niger river delta in Nigeria, the warring clans of Somalia and the Hutu and Tutsi of Rwanda and Burundi. What is important is the initiation of and subsequent accumulation of acts of mutual punishment, deprivation and destruction of groups which builds up hate memories and a self perpetuating dynamics of more destruction and punishment as groups, however defined, accumulate the fear that they could be annihilated. Yugoslavia is a very good example of this process. Cultural and identity difference in the country is less pronounced than is often assumed even if it looms large in the imagination:

> *For many Croatian nationalists, for example, the Serbian minority in Croatia had no real reason to declare itself Serbian; these people lived on Croatian territory, looked no different from Croats and spoke the same language. Serbs in turn often had to be persuaded that Croats were not Catholic Serbs, but people with a different national identity. The refusal of most Muslims to regard themselves as either Croats or Serbs has often been met by angry disbelief from Croatian and Serbian nationalists. (Djilas, 1995:87)*

Ignatieff's interesting essay on nationalism, blood and belonging in Yugoslavia draws upon Freudian analysis to offer an insight into the nature of the problem:

> *Freud once argued that the smaller the real difference between two peoples the larger it was bound to loom in their imagination. He called this effect the narcissism of minor difference. Its corollary must be that enemies need each other to remind themselves of who they really are. A Croat, thus is someone who is not a Serb. A Serb is someone who is not a Croat... All Croats become Ustashe assassins; all Serbs become Chetnik beasts. (Ignatieff, 1993:14-15)*

The development of violent conflict between neighbors whose differences are rather plastic easily produces devastating results because there is a tendency to reducing one's own security to the destruction of the other. Indeed, once fear combines with hate memory in a context in which political authority is seen as illegitimate and partial, "senseless" massacres are easily justified as the fault of the other as has been the case between the culturally close communities in Bosnia.[2] Some elements are essential in building up the frenzy that justifies mass massacres:

> *What Hobbes would have said, having lived through religious civil war himself, is that when people are sufficiently afraid, they will do anything. There is one type of fear that is more devastating in its impact than any other, the systemic fear that arises when a state begins to collapse. Ethnic hatred is the result of the terror which arises when legitimate authority disintegrates (Ignatieff, 1993:16).*

The legitimacy of the modern state is linked to its capacity to present itself as a provider of necessary public goods and more important, a neutral arbiter that guarantees the security of all sections of society. When the state is generally perceived as serving the particularistic interests of one group, it starts losing its legitimacy, and indeed, its authority. As state capacity declines, fear of "the other" rises and becomes an objective factor of survival and people are forced to resort to other levels of solidarity - religious, ethnic, regional etc, in search of security. It is therefore necessary to rehabilitate the analysis of the state in understanding extreme forms of identity conflicts. As the focus of this case study is on socialist states, it is necessary to pose questions about the socialist state and federalism.

The Socialist State and Federalism

According to the former Soviet President, Mikhail Gorbachev, federalism failed in the Soviet Union because of the adoption of unitarism. He contends that Lenin was a committed unitarist until the October Revolution when the various peoples of the Russian Empire declared their independence and the idea of a federative union became the only way of saving the revolution. Lenin converted to the federal idea and the Union of Soviet Socialist Republics might have prospered had Stalin not imposed unitarism:

> *Later, Stalin, while preserving the name, essentially created a unitary state. Thus, he suppressed the new approach that emerged from the revolution. (Gorbachev, 1994:5)*

The real question however was whether the communist system, based as it was on the principles of the dictatorship of the proletariat and democratic centralism, could have allowed for a genuine federal polity. The former was authoritarian and anti-democratic and the latter, centralist and by definition, anti-federal.

The Soviet "federal" model was bequeathed to Yugoslavia and Czechoslovakia. At the formal level, sovereignty was shared between the federal and federating units but in realty, all power was centralized in the central state, and above all, in the ruling party (Dimitrov, 1996:77). The three systems were uniform at the formal level up till 1963, and to some extent, up till 1971-74. The three so-called federal systems had legal/constitutional systems that ensured that most laws were made at the federal level, the judiciary was unified and state control of the means of production as well as central economic planning ensured that all important decisions were taken at the central level. The absence of political pluralism meant that no divergent interests or voices could be expressed. All powers were concentrated in the hands of the leadership of the communist party.

For Lidija Basta, it was not a coincidence that in all three ex-socialist federations, the Soviet Union, Czechoslovakia and Yugoslavia, state collapse occurred simultaneously with regime collapse. None of the states survived regime collapse. In the socialist federal states, the exercise of civil rights had been limited to the selected leadership of the party at the tip of the pyramid, all decision-making was under party control and there was neither a democratic consensus nor a federal pact. The federal system was organized in a peculiar way. The principle of the equality of nations/ethnic groups was constitutionally proclaimed but was not constitutionally guaranteed. What occurred was an authoritarian process of balancing inter-ethnic relations. The fact that the constitutional principle of ethnic self determination was enshrined legitimated the belief that all ethnic groups ultimately had a right to their own states (Basta, 1996:99).[3]

Explaining the Failure of Federalism in Yugoslavia

Samuel Huntington has offered an explanation of the failure of federalism in Yugoslavia. It is based on an essentialist reading of the nature of the people themselves and their religions. His basic contention is that civilized European Christian peoples could not cohabit with primitive Orthodox and Muslim peoples because of a fault-line separating them since the break-up of the Roman Empire in the fourth century. As he put it "Europe ends where Western Christianity ends and Islam and Orthodoxy begins" (Huntington, 1997:158). His basic thesis is that following the break-up of the authoritarian communist system, civilizational battles took over from ideological ones. Catholic and Protestant Baltic communities constituted their states as did the Orthodox and Muslim ones because religious differences were too strong to allow the communities continue together of their own free will.

He attributes the rapidity with which the Federation broke up in 1991 to the decisive role played by the German Government in supporting the independence of Croatia. Bonn acted decisively because it was under pressure from the German Catholic hierarchy and its Catholic political ally, the Christian

Social Union party in Bavarian. He also stresses the role played by the Pope who had "declared that Croatia is to be the rampart of Western Christianity" (Huntington, 1997:282). He adds that the Orthodox world also felt compelled to support the Serbs under the leadership of the Russians and the Muslim world supported their co-religionists in Bosnia. The whole issue was reduced to a fault-line conflict between Islam, Christian Orthodox religion and Catholicism. It is not at all clear why Huntington attributed the collapse of the Yugoslavian state to the fault-line thesis, except for his prejudice. Given the historical, sociological and political factors leading to the collapse, did it need non-Catholics to produce the result that we have? Would the same process not produce the same result in a purely Western Catholic or Protestant setting? It is necessary to go beyond describing this pattern of decomposition that Huntington stressed to understand what failed in Yugoslavia and why it failed.

It is misleading to claim that religious difference is the main cause of the Yugoslavian crisis even if religion is one of the factors that led to its rapid escalation (Djilas, 1995:87). There is a significant burden of the legacy of history in Yugoslavia linked to ethnic histories and perceptions of injustice, impunity and inequity spread over a thousand years of contending ethnic political histories and incorporations into either the Austro-Hungarian or the Ottoman Empires that play an important role on the memories of the various peoples. In more recent history, the Second World War in particular was a very traumatic period for the Yugoslavians. The country was invaded by Germany, Italy, Bulgaria, Hungary and Albania and large chunks of the territory were occupied. There was also ideological civil war between fascists, royalists and communists. Finally there were local inter-ethnic civil wars in areas of mixed populations – Serbs and Croats, Serbs and Slavic Muslims, Croats and Slavic Muslims and Serbs and Albanians and these three series of wars led to the perpetuation of unimaginable atrocities on all sides (Critchley, 1993:102). That was the period in which the hate memories that fuelled the coronet bitterness were produced or reproduced. A very large number of Serbs for example were killed and brutalized by Nazi Urstace in Croatia and Bosnia during the Second World War.[4] In 1991, the same flags, currency and uniforms that the Serbs associated with the injustice done to them re-appeared so their alarm and determination to defend themselves is not without reason.

From 1971, the Yugoslavian federation was constituted on the basis of ethnic Republics – Serbia, Croatia, Slovenia, Bosnia-Herzegovina, Montenegro, and Macedonia, and the two provinces of Kosovo and Vojvodina. Although the federating units were virtually "allocated" to ethnic groups, the units were in reality all mixed:

Table I: Ethnic Composition of Republics and Provinces

Republic/Province	Population	Major Ethnic Groups
Serbia	5.8 million	Serb – 66%
Albania	14 million	Muslim Slav – 2.3%
Croatia	4.6 million	Croat – 70%
		Serb – 11%
Bosnia-Herzegovina	4.4 million	Muslim Slav – 43%
		Serb – 32%
		Croat 18%
Slovenia	2 million	Slovene – 90%
		Croat – 2.9%
		Serb – 2.2%
Macedonia	2 million	Macedonian - 28%
		Albanian – 20%
Vojvodina	1.8 million	Serb - 54%
		Hungarian - 19%
Kosovo	1.8 million	Albanian – 85%
		Serb – 13%
Montenegro	0.6 million	Montenegrin – 67
		Muslim Serb – 13.5%
		Serb – 9.2

Source: Compiled from Critchley, 1993:105

Note that percentages do not add up to 100 due to other minorities that are not indicated.

Except for Slovenia, all the Republics and Provinces had substantial minority populations. About 40% of the Serb population for example lived outside Serbia. All such minority populations became the target of ethnic cleansing in the 1990s.

Table 2: Ethnic proportions and religious denominations in the former Yugoslavia

Serbs	36%	Eastern Orthodox Church
Croats	20%	Roman Catholic Church
Muslim Slavs	9%	Islam
Slovenes	8%	Roman Catholic Church
Albanians	8%	Islam
Macedonians	6%	Eastern Orthodox Church
Montenegrins	3%	Eastern Orthodox Church
Hungarians	2%	Roman Catholic
Others	9%	-

Source: Compiled mainly from Critchley, 1993:104

The fact that the federating units in Yugoslavia had been constituted on ethnic grounds following the Soviet model meant that the majority/minority perceptions were bound to play an important role in the strategies of the political elite.[5] The Croats and the Slovenes felt that the majority Serb population were dominating the country politically and militarily. The Serbs on the other hand were unhappy at the fact that two provinces had been carved out of their Republic in 1968 and although they were still defined as part of Serbia, they were also considered as part of the federal *pouvoir constituent* and effectively had veto powers over Serbia as equal members of the Federation:[6]

> *The Socialist Federal Republic of Serbia is a state having the form of a state community of voluntarily united nations and their Socialist Republics, and of the Socialist Autonomous Provinces of Vojvodina and Kosovo, which are constituent parts of the Socialist Republic of Serbia. (article one of the 1974 Constitution cited in Basta, 1998:104)*

In addition, the Serbs thus were the only ones that lost political control of part of their own territory to a minority group. At the same time, Serb minorities in other Republics were not constituted into autonomous provinces or provided any specific protection. In spite of that, the Serbs were committed to the survival of the Yugoslavian Federation because they were conscious that precisely because forty per cent of their population lived outside Serbia, they needed the larger territorial framework to protect their people. The others however interpreted Serb commitment to the Federation as a sign of Serb determination to continue dominating them. In 1987, Milosevic reversed the constitutional relegation of Serbia by organizing a putsch against the party leadership of Kosovo and Vojvodina and replaced them with his clients. From then on, rather than have two of "his" provinces voting against him, he commanded three votes at the federal level, a change that alarmed the leadership in Croatia and Slovenia, who had assumed the special status of the two Provinces will always keep Serbia in check (Basta, 1998:105). An important dimension of the Yugoslavian conflict was the reckless roles played by the political leadership. According to Stanovcic (1995:6), President Tito carried out some measures that strengthened the position of hard-liners and weakened reformers in Croatia and Serbia. In 1971, he got the ruling party to exclude the Croatian leaders behind the pro-nationalist mass movement as well as the leaders of the pro-liberal movement in Serbia from the political arena. Intellectuals who had criticized his constitutional proposals and tried to initiate a political debate were repressed. Within the Republics themselves, very authoritarian leaders, whose legitimacy reposed solely on their roles as ethnic champions were buttressed. Serbia's Slobodan Milosevic and Croatia's Franjo Tudgman were very skilled but irresponsible manipulators of ethnic sentiments. They deliberately pursued a political line of brinkmanship so as to keep out reason and moderation from the political arena and thereby sustain their control over the authoritarian enclaves they were trying to carve out from Yugoslavia.

The most important explanatory factor for the collapse of the Yugoslavian state and the civil wars that followed was the nature of the federal institutions that were adopted. The Yugoslavian federal system had evolved through three distinct phases. The first phase embodied in the 1946 constitution lasted until 1963 and was modeled on the Soviet experience. It has been labeled as *façade federalism* because it was a highly centralized system of decision-making and was not therefore federal in its operation. The second phase, from 1963 to 1971 was the period of *communal federalism* when the emphasis was on local self-management at the enterprise level. The federal units were marginalized on the assumption that the nationality question had been resolved. The third phase, from 1971 to 1991 (formalized by the 1974 Constitution) was the *federal/confederal* period characterized by extensive autonomy for the Republics and two Provinces. In this phase, the Yugoslavian Federation lost virtually all constitutional, legislative, and to some extent, even executive autonomy. All powers were jointly exercised by the Republics and Provinces (Stanovvcic, 1995:4-6; Basta, 1987:114-118).

The 1974 constitution was thus virtually confederal and required consensus as a mode of operation. All component units, regardless of their population size and economic power were equally represented not only in both Chambers of the Federal Assembly, but also in all Federal decision making bodies such as the Presidency, Federal Executive Council and the Federal Constitutional Court. Provinces however had less representatives than Republics. All the eight federating units, six nations and two minorities (Hungarian and Albanian), had to agree to all major decisions so the Yugoslav system was transformed from a very centralized to a loose, almost confederal system. This transformation led to the erosion of the authority and legitimacy of the state. The Yugoslavian crisis was therefore essentially a crisis of state formation where we witness the consequences of the failure of building a coherent state.

The country has existed as an independent state only since the end of the first World War. Marshal Tito, had a sufficiently large aura and authoritarian grip to hold it together but following his death in 1980, things started falling apart. "The late Yugoslavian state was a permanently constituting and not a constituted state" (Basta, 1996:99). In its constantly changing configurations, the constitutive principle was inter-ethnic relations and balance so each political or constitutional conflict was automatically transformed into an inter-ethnic confrontation. The power of the ethnos could not be transformed into that of the demos. By generating loyalty almost exclusively through ethnicity and religion, the common state was emptied out of its legitimacy. This state crisis was unavoidable because the absence of political pluralism, coupled with the absence of individual citizens as political actors meant that political space was occupied only by ethnic leaders of the ruling party (Basta, 1996:101). It cannot be over-emphasized that federalism is a political devise for establishing viable institutions and flexible relationships between political units (Gognon, 1993:15). If the institutions are not viable, the system fails. The fault line was not so much in the blood flowing through Slav veins, it was in the institutions that they adopted.

Yugoslavia did not have to decompose violently, it could have taken a pacific route similar to that of Czechoslovakia. There were however a number of serious problems. It was difficult reconciling growing extremist nationalism with peaceful democratic resolution of the conflict. With Serbs, Croats and Slovenes having 36.3, 19.7 and 7.8 per cent of the population respectively, it was easy for extremist politicians to blow up the minority problems especially as apart from the Slovenes, each group had minority populations in the area of the other groups who were presented as threatened minorities. It cannot be overemphasized however that the disintegration of the Yugoslavian state was not primarily due to federalism but to wider political and institutional arrangements that blocked the evolution of a wider Yugoslavian identity and social consensus (Stanovcic, 1995:8-9). The form of federalism that was adopted was virtually bound to fail because of the excessive emphasis placed on the ethnic composition of the federation. The League of Communists of Yugoslavia, the ruling party, gradually fragmented into eight republican/ provincial ethnic organizations, formalized by the unfinished 14th Congress of 1990. The thread holding the Yugoslavian master narrative was cut to pieces – that the country had six republics, five nations, four languages, three religions, two alphabets and one party (Stanovcic, 1990:26). The party that had fragmented the society to increase its ruling capacity itself fell victim of the process it set in motion.

Lessons from the Yugoslavian Experience

In multi-ethnic states, ethnic communities have a significant potential for the political mobilization of their members. When this potential is realized, the political stability of the state is eroded. The extent of the erosion of political stability through ethnic mobilization is often a function of the democratic/ authoritarian nature of the regime :

> *In a democratic multinational State, stability is generally maintained by means of political bargaining and compromise between ethnic subgroups whereas in authoritarian systems it is maintained principally through the elimination of the possibility of subsystem political mobilisation by coercion and by the regime's appeals to supra-ethnic issues and policies. (Prazauskas, 1991:581-2)*

In periods of transition from authoritarian to more democratic systems, there is a certain decomposition of the coercive state apparatus. The authoritarian control mechanism that prevents the conflagration of inter-ethnic group relations collapses and there is rapid growth of political instability.

Political actors can easily develop radically different cognitive maps, each connecting past and present through divergent paths and each based on the politics of numbers (Lemarchand, 1994:17). The case in question might be Yugoslavia, Somalia, Burundi or Rwanda. In the case of Burundi for example, the Tutsi ruling minority insist that there are no ethnic differences between them and the Hutu and that Hutu demands for full participation is an unjustified and unacceptable expression of tribalism that is breeding division and ultimately trying to lead to their extermination. For the Hutu majority, Tutsi rule can only mean repressive minority rule that cannot acquire legitimacy. Justice, for them, is majoritarian democracy that would enable them take over power from their "hamitic" oppressors. Each group only sees its side of the story, so while the past creates the conditions for contemporary happenings, current actors recreate and manipulate history to support and justify their present actions. The Hutu for example make no reference to the Hutu instigated insurgency that led to thousands of Tutsi deaths in 1972, they only remember the Tutsi led repression that followed and resulted in the massacre of hundreds of thousands of Hutu. Similarly, the Tutsi will not concede that the discriminatory policies of the Micombero regime (1966-76) was what led to the Hutu insurgency (Lemarchand, 1994:1719).

What is the future of the state? It is difficult to disagree with Fleiner that:

> *The nation-state based on friend-enemy concepts cannot be the state concept of the future. State authority must be linked to political objectives and to political issues such as police protection, defence and possibly social security..... The nation is a reality which cannot be denied. It has to be recognised. Nonetheless, nations should never be builders of state authority, but they should be recognised as communities which seek to pursue cultural objectives necessary for the identity of individuals and families living within the political society: the state. (Fleiner, 1996:38)*

The lesson we can learn from the experience of Eastern Europe is not as Huntington would have us believe, that they got it wrong because they come from the wrong stock of the human race. It is that they committed two crimes – they tried to constitute states based on amalgamating ethnically defined political communities and they tried to run states on purely authoritarian principles, forgetting the importance of consent, legitimacy and civil and political rights. It was a formula that was bound to fail. It was a failure genuine federalism would have helped in preventing. In reconstructing the future of Africa, these lessons must be taken into account:

1. Repression and authoritarianism cannot be the basis for the construction of legitimate political communities or states. States must pursue policies that convince rather than constrain their populations into believing that they have a stake as well as an identity in the political community.

2 The creation of ethno-religious domains cannot be the basis for resolving identity related political conflicts because the plasticity of ethnic identities can create a process of amplification of minor differences to sustain and indeed intensify ethnic differences and conflicts.

3 Secession and the fabrication of new "ethnically constituted" states cannot on its own resolve the "ethnic question" because new "ethnic" categories can emerge in the new polity as long as the factors that exacerbate ethnic

tensions remain.

These lessons have a lot of significance for Nigeria's current political conjuncture in which there are widespread calls for the re-structuring of our federal arrangement along ethnic lines.

The Promise and Failure of Nigerian Federalism

The area now known as Nigeria came into being in 1914 when the British Protectorates to the north and south of the Niger and the Lagos Colony were amalgamated. Some political actors have referred to the amalgamation as the mistake of 1914. Nigeria is a large and varied country with a national land area of 922,789 square kilometers. The country has maximum dimensions of 1,200 kilometers from east to west and also from north to south. Nigeria is a country tailor-made for federalism due to its size and diversity.[7] With half the population of West Africa, petroleum and gas resources, a high level of educational achievement and relatively advanced infrastructure, Nigeria is a major player in the region and its governability has implications for its neighbors.

Nigeria's colonial legacy was "federal". Lord Lugard established a system of 'indirect rule' that was based on a policy of non-centralized administration or separate government for 'different peoples'. This policy led to the evolution of certain structures and institutions which to a certain extent still characterize the contemporary Nigerian state. The basic principle of "Indirect Rule" was 'divide and rule'. In the Emirates of northern Nigeria and in the Yoruba kingdoms of the southwest, indigenous political structures were retained and often reinforced by the colonial administration as the primary level of government, while in the south east as well as among some of the acephalous 'Middle Belt' societies, a new order of colonial chiefs known as 'warrant chiefs' was imposed. The system of 'Indirect Rule' had a profound impact on the evolution of Nigerian elites. In the north, traditional elites were fully involved in the administration of British imperialism, thanks to the system of 'Native Administration' (NA), and were therefore allies of the Crown. Secondly, they had a pact with Lord Lugard to keep Christian missionaries and by extension, western education, out of the Emirates. The result was that the pace of development of western education in the Muslim part of the north was very slow and the few that were chosen for the western schools were all employed in the NA. Thus, virtually the totality of the elite in the Muslim north collaborated with colonialism and had a stake in it. In the other parts of the country, Christian missionaries were given full freedom for proselytization and virtually exclusive control of Western education. It resulted in a fairly rapid evolution of a Western educated elite, to the detriment of traditional ruling elites. The new elite, however, had very limited chances of integrating into the upper echelons of the civil service even when they had high levels of education. Given their educational background and the frustrations of exclusion, they naturally drifted into political agitation and adversary journalism.

In 1938 the South was divided into two regions, the West and East while the North was left intact - hence the origins of the tripartite political system. This system was formalized with the Richards Constitution of 1946 and five years later, Governor Macpherson's constitution 'federated' the three regions by creating a central assembly in addition to the regional ones and devolving effective executive power and autonomy to the regionally constituted elites. The guiding principle of this tripartite Federation was that each Region had a 'majority ethnic group', which was to play the role of the leading actor: in the North the Hausa, in the West the Yoruba, and in the East the Igbo. In fact the whole process of constitution-making between 1946 and 1958 was an elaborate bargaining pantomime to find an equilibrium between the three regions, or rather, between the leading elites of the majority ethnic groups. No wonder the process resulted in the emergence of three major political parties, each allied to a majority group.

Nigeria is not composed of three cultural groups but of hundreds of cultural and ethnic groups the majority of which are dominated by the so-called majority groups. The country is profoundly multipolar, in spite of its apparent tripolarity. None of the three regions of the First Republic represented a historic political bloc. In the East, immediately the Igbo State Union was formed, it was confronted by the Ibibio State Union. The anti-Igbo feeling in the Delta was so strong that in February 1966, Major Isaac Boro declared the secession of the 'Niger Delta Peoples Republic' in protest against Igbo leadership and this first formal succession attempt in Nigeria also resulted in the first declared civil war, the now forgotten "twelve-day war". Political differences in the West are more well known and need not be repeated here. In the North, many political poles exist, some of which could briefly be mentioned. The dominant pole is rooted in the Sokoto Caliphate zone and it was this group that the British maneuvered to place in power between 1946 and 1951, because they had co-operated so closely in the system of 'Native Administration' (NA). The second pole in the same zone is the radical anti-aristocratic tendency that was expressed by the Northern Elements Progressive Union/People's Redemption Party (NEPU/PRP) heritage. The third pole is the Bornu tendency expressed in the Bornu Youth Movement (BYM) and to some extent in the Great Nigeria People's Party (GNPP) while the fourth one is the Northern minorities tendency expressed in the Northern Nigeria non-Muslim League formed in 1950 and transformed into the United Middle Belt Peoples Congress in 1953. This movement formed part of the constituent groups that formed the Nigerian People's Party (NPP) in 1978.

All these political divisions were violently repressed by the WAZOBIA[8] domination in the three regions especially as the Westminster Federalism of the First Republic evolved with the center of political power being the regions rather than the center, contrary to the British case. The refusal of the British to create more regions in 1958 when the Willink Commission affirmed that fears of domination of the 'minorities' by the 'majorities' were justified was virtually a dis-enfranchisement of at least 45 per cent of the population. The politics of the First Republic evolved in a contradictory manner with the multi-polar tendency being simultaneously suppressed and supported. In each region, it was suppressed by the Regional Government but then encouraged and supported by the other Regional Governments, hence the elaborate system of shifting national alliances. The domination of political power by the Northern pole meant that a democratic change of Government at the center was virtually impossible for the simple reason that internal regional democracy was impossible and in each region, the minorities were the excluded ones. The Caliphate Oligarchy in control of the NPC could maintain perpetual control of federal power, although it was an aggregate minority even in the North, its base, thanks to the principle that the elite of the dominant ethnic group in each region had become the inheritors of political power. The North, with 54 per cent of official representatives, could always thwart shifting bipolar alliances by destabilizing them. That was the structural basis that weakened, but did not destroy federalism in Nigeria.

It was the military that subsequently succeeded in completely destroying Nigerian federalism, by sacrificing it on the alter of centralization. The military are structurally incapable of running a federal system because their unified command structure is incapable of accepting that a state government, which they consider to be hierarchically subordinate to the federal government, could have domains over which she is sovereign. This, as is generally recognized, is the essence of federalism. Nigeria's geo-political realities have been completely modified. The tripartite structure which had become quadripartite with the creation of the Mid-West in 1963, has been significantly transformed. In 1967, just before the advent of the civil war, the Gowon Military Administration created 12 states from the four existing regions. The move appeared to have been a political advance because it was addressed at correcting the structural imbalances and ethno-regional inequities of the inherited federal structure. In 1976, the Mohammed-Obasanjo Administration increased the number of states from 12 to 19, General Babangida raised the number of states to 21 in 1987 and to 30 in 1991 while the regime of General Abacha increased the number of states in the country to 36.

The multiplication of States has produced a Jacobin effect that strengthens the center by eroding the autonomy of the regions. Rather than correct the ethno-regional balance in the country, the fissiparous state-creation tendency has concentrated enormous powers at the center and weakened all groups except those who directly control federal power. Nigeria thus finds itself now with a so-called Federation that is for all practical purposes a unitary state with some limited devolution of power to the states. This tendency was reinforced with the so-called decentralization policy of the Babangida regime carried out between 1987 and 1991 with the declared aim of increasing the autonomy, democratizing, improving the finance and strengthening the political and administrative capacities of local governments. The number of local governments was increased from 301 to 449 in 1989 and to 589 in 1991 and again to 776 in 1996. Their share from the Federation account was increased from 10% to 20%. They were constituted as "proper" governments with executive and legislative branches and "liberated" from the control of state governments with the 1988 decision to scrap Ministries of Local Governments and establish a Directorate in the Presidency to directly finance and supervise local governments. This has resulted in a situation in which the central government now has direct control over virtually all aspects of the governance of the 776 local governments in the country.

This military culture gradually impacted on public law and resulted in the disastrous allocation of enormous powers, hitherto held by the regions or the cabinet, to the President or the Governor in the 1979, 1989 and the 1999 Constitutions. The military have even succeeded in making the civilian politicians accept the principles of military government as a basis for Nigeria's "Democratization". The political class forgot that Nigerians had accepted federalism as a guarantee that would help reduce the fears of ethno-regional domination and that these fears could only be allayed if the federating units had real powers that could guarantee people some autonomy in their local operations. The result was that Nigeria's heritage of a federal and parliamentary tradition, both of which tend to encourage the dispersal of power, were replaced, not by the American style presidential system which is based on effective separation of powers, but on an excessively centralized executive system that concentrated power in one person, thus opening the gates, not for the over-acclaimed American system, but for the worst form of Jacobin dictatorship.

The result of the destruction of Nigerian federalism and the imposition of an over-centralized state has been increasing disaffection of groups and calls for secession or re-negotiation of the federal arrangement. One expression of that tendency was the attempted coup d'etat of 22 April 1990 in which officers, mostly from Southern Nigeria and the Minority areas unsuccessfully tried to overthrow the authoritarian Babangida regime and expel seven Hausa-

Fulani states from the Federation. Political groups, such as the Movement for National Reformation campaigned for a Confederation of eight ethnically constituted groups of political communities. Over the past few years, ethnic minorities have been very active in their campaign against majority domination. The most well known one is the Movement for the Survival of the Ogoni People (MOSOP), based in the petroleum producing riverine area and which was recognized by the United Nations as the representative of an "endangered ethnic group". In January 1993, MOSOP organized a demonstration of 300,000 supporters, witnessed by Greenpeace and other observers (Naanen, 1995:63). In November 1995, nine MOSOP leaders, including their charismatic spokes-person, Ken Saro Wiwa were hanged in a manner the world has characterized as judicial murder. Despite the persecution of the leaders of MOSOP, the issues that they raise of political domination and economic exploitation remain. The latest minority group to take up the struggle are the Ijaws, who have become very militant over the past few years. Indeed, as has been observed:

> *The prevailing opinion in Nigeria is that to survive as a nation-state, the country must restructure its political relations vesting a substantial degree of autonomy in the component units. (Naanen, 1995:75)*

Unfortunately, this is not being done. The military have successfully thwarted popular efforts to convene a Sovereign National Conference to re-negotiate the country's power sharing mechanism.

Nigeria's political climate has worsened due to the refusal of the military to hand over power to a democratically elected civilian administration. It may be recalled that after a lot of procrastination by government and determined protest against another postponement of elections by the people, presidential elections were finally held on 12th June 1993. The candidate of the Social Democratic Party, M. K. O. Abiola, a southerner and Yoruba won neatly in an election that was surprisingly generally considered free and fair. General Babangida however annulled the elections and tried to initiate yet another round of "political crafting", but there was so much mass protests against the cancellation that he had to leave power in haste and handover to an incompetent and powerless civilian without any mandate, creating the basis for yet another coup d'etat in November 1993 by his former second in command and another northerner, General Abacha.

The Abacha Administration was determined to keep to the Babangida policy of perpetuating military rule by other means. Rather than relying solely on the ruse of an interminable transition program to keep the democrats and politicians occupied, General Abacha tried to follow the footsteps of Rawlings in Ghana, the late Mainasara in Niger and Jammeh in the Gambia to get himself either elected President or even to be declared President by "consensus".[9] This attempt reinforced the belief that the northern military and political establishment are unwilling to allow a southerner access to the highest office in the land. At the same time, virtually all powers were concentrated in the Presidency, so it became the only office worth fighting for. A government sponsored Constitutional Conference was convened in the second half of 1994 and it finished its deliberations in June 1995. The military Junta had announced that it will hand over to an elected administration in October 1998 and all the indications were that Abacha would hand-over power to himself. Abacha however died a few months before the hand-over date, thus creating an opportunity for re-opening the political field.

Meanwhile, a lot of serious damage had already been done to the nation's body politic. The continued existence of the Nigerian state is being threatened by numerous ethnic revolts and conflicts. Religious fundamentalism and bloody inter-confessional conflicts have become a major problem (Ibrahim, 1991 & 1994). Low intensity warfare is spreading in many parts of the country (Olukoshi and Agbu, 1996; Bonat, 1994; and Naanen, 1995). In multi-ethnic states, ethnic communities have significant potential for the political mobilization of their members. When this potential is realized, the stability of the state could be threatened. There is a strong link between the democratic or authoritarian nature of regimes and the capacity of segments of society to increase their political participation through ethnic mobilization:

> *In a democratic multinational State, stability is usually maintained by means of political bargaining and compromise between ethnic subgroups whereas in authoritarian systems it is maintained principally through the elimination of subsystem political mobilisation by coercion and by the regime's appeals to supra-ethnic issues and policies. (Prazauskas, 1991:581-2)*

Authoritarianism and exclusion in Nigeria have led to the failure of federalism and indeed are leading to the decomposition of the state itself. Successive Nigerian Heads of State have accumulated enormous powers in the office, but the powers are more apparent than real. They do indeed control the petroleum rent and the repressive apparatus of the state, but little else. The state has lost its control over the people. Every community and group is virtually doing its own thing and there is a serious problem about the governability of Nigeria under the current dispensation. There are fundamental problems relating to access to political power and petroleum rent, and problems of equity and social justice posed by the domination of political power by one group. These are leading many to renounce their commitment to the Nigerian state. The most serious aspect of this development is that more groups are now seeking their political futures in ethnically or religiously defined citadels.

In December 1998 for example, a Conference of Nationalities was organized by the Campaign for Democracy in which ethnically defined regions were proposed as a solution to the crisis of Nigerian federalism. The communiqué published at the end of the meeting proposed: "That the ethnic nationalities should be the building blocks of the Federation, with the right to self-determination". This was the principle upon which the Soviet, Yugoslavian and Czechoslovakian Federations were constructed and as we have argued above, it is a system that cannot but lead to disintegration of the state. Members of Nigerian ethnic groups must be spared the political future of ethnic dictatorship, it is usually worse than pan-ethnic dictatorship. The same is true of religious groups. Calls for the establishment of an Islamic Republic or of Christendom, pose serious threats to the members of the two religious groups. The dictator who acts on the basis that you are all his people can do more damage than the others. Today in the former Yugoslavian Republics, no criticism of the regimes in place are allowed because the enemies are supposed to have been removed, cleansed. Any critic from within is immediately equated to be an agent of external enemies and eliminated.

Conclusion

Federalism and federation have not failed in Africa, they have not been tried, except for the Nigerian example where it functioned for some years. Most of the so-called African experiments at federation were engaged upon as a strategy or a stepping stone to unitarism. Federation was therefore understood by those negotiating it as a transitory phase to a more derivable political form. In many of the cases we have reviewed above Mali, Senegambia, Cameroon - the contracting parties did not have a common understanding of what pact they were signing, but the stronger party has always understood that the objective was the establishment of a unitary state. While reviewing the first decade of federal experiments in Africa, Donald Rothchild contends that:

> Federalism evokes little enthusiasm in Africa as a whole and, as might be anticipated, has less appeal for the ideologue than for the pragmatist. Its overlaps, duplications, compromises, excessive legalism and lack of symmetry offend the ideologically-oriented person, who seems almost to instinctively recoil from proposals for federalism, except, perhaps, at the pan-African level. (Rothchild, 1968:5)

The nationalist idealism of the first generation of African leaders was coupled by the voluntarist belief that the concentration of power was the surest and fastest path to national unity, democracy and development. As the Mwalimu, maybe the most sincere and committed amongst them, asserted:

> *A strong Executive is essential to stability in any young state, be it in Europe or in Africa... a system where there is only one legal Party may be a better safeguard of democracy and Human Rights than a multi-party system, because it can simultaneously strengthen national unity and help to build a national identity. (Nyerere, 1993:18)*

The real failure in the political history of postcolonial Africa has been that of the strong and centralized state. It has not produced what it has promised - national unity, democracy and development. After four decades of failure of the strategy based on negating pluralism and trying to impose unitarism, the time for a genuine experiment with federalism has arrived.

In constructing federalism in Africa, the ethnic and religious factors must be taken into account. The historical legacies of discrimination against groups based on their ethnic or religious origins must be addressed. In so doing, the granting of autonomy to regions must be real and power must be shared, not shifted. However, the federating units cannot be defined on ethnic and religious basis. Ethnic and religious enclaves are dangerous for their members and even more dangerous for the minorities that find themselves within. And it should be remembered when the basis for group definition narrows down and follows primordial criteria, the production of minorities increases. Groups that thought they belong start discovering that they do not quite belong. The construction of federalism requires that political basis for the construction of legitimacy should be discovered.

ENDNOTES

1. For a long time, the literature on the impossibility of the nation-state has been focused primarily on Africa. Numerous Africanists have argued for decades that the "tribal essence" of African society has made the consolidation of the nation state impossible. Now that the same optic is being popularized for parts of Europe, suitable conditions for a scientific comparative analysis have been created.

2. Ignatieff explains that he grew up as the child of a Canadian diplomat living in Bosnia and that the cultural differences between the communities were not apparent, as there appeared to have been a common secular, Western, and linguistic culture.

3. The socialist experience of ethnic federal units is of great pedagogic interest for contemporary Africans where Ethiopia has recently adopted the model of ethnic federalism and there are demands in many other African countries for the ethnic federal model.

4. Independent estimates of the number of people killed vary from 400,000 to 700,000 although Serb militants claim it is up to a million and Croat militants allege it could be as low as 60,000 – Interview with Lidija Basta, 10/7/1998.

5. According to Vojislav Stanovcic, a recurrent joke over the years in Yugoslavia was that by the year 2000, there will be ten states in Europe - one in Western Europe, one in Eastern Europe and eight in the former Yugoslavia, Interview, Fribourg, 5th May 1998.

6. On almost every concrete issue discussed at the federal level, the two autonomous "Serb" Provinces voted against Serbia thus fomenting Serb nationalism (Basta, 1998:105).

7. See J. Ibrahim (ed) *Population, Space and Development*, WALTPS Report of the Nigeria Team, Club du Sahel, Paris, 1994, for a detailed exposition of the complexity and diversity of the Nigerian population.

8. WAZOBIA - a composite word from the verb to come in the three major languages - Yoruba (wa), Hausa (zo) and Igbo (bia). It has become a symbol of the political domination of the numerous minority groups in the country by the majority groups.

9. The idea was that the new Constitution would have a provision allowing all political parties, if they so wish, to choose a President (Abacha) by 'consensus" without having to go through elections. Abacha was thus not ready to go the Rawlings way of getting himself elected.

REFERENCES

Awa, Eme O. 1976. *Issues in Federalism*. Benin City: Ethiope Press.

Ayoade, J. A. A. 1978. "Federalism in Africa: Some Chequered Fortunes, *Plural Societies*, vol 9, no 1.

Bakvis, H. & Chandler, W. eds. 1987. *Federalism and the Role of the State*. Toronto: University of Toronto Press.

Basta, Lidija 1987. "The Yugoslav Federation (also) as a Common Function of the Republics and Provinces – The New Content of Autonomy of the Federal Units" in Fleiner, T. & Hutter S. eds *Federalism and Decentralisation* Fribourg: Editions Universitaires.

————. 1996. "Federalism without Democracy, Political Rights without Citizen" in Fleiner, T. & Schmitt eds *Towards a European Constitution*, Institut du Fédéralisme, Fribourg.

————. 1998. "Constitutional Background of the Kosovo Conflict."

Burgess, M & Gognon, A.G. eds. 1993. *Comparative Federalism and Federation: Competing Traditions and Future Directions*. New York: Harvester.

Critchley, W. H. 1994. "The Failure of Federalism: Yugoslavia" in Randall S. and Gibbens R. eds. *Federalism and the New World Order*. Calgary: University of Calgary Press.

Dimitrov, E. 1996. "L'unification de l'Europe et les expériences du fédéralisme multinational dans les pays ex-socialistes" in Fleiner, T. & Schmitt eds. *Towards a European Constitution*. Fribourg: Institut du Fédéralisme.

Djilas, Aleksa. 1995. "Fear Thy Neighbor: The Break-up of Yugoslavia" in C. A. Kupchan ed *Nationalism and Nationalities in the New Europe*. Ithaca: Cornell University Press.

Fleiner, T. & Schmitt eds. 1996. *Towards a European Constitution*. FribourgInstitut du Fédéralisme.

Fleiner, Thomas. 1996. "State – Nation – Nationalities – Minorities: New Nation State Concept for a European Constitution" in Fleiner, T. & Schmitt eds *Towards a European Constitution*, Fribourg: Institut du Fédéralisme.

Gognon, A.G. 1993. "The Political Uses of Federalism" in Burgess, M & Gognon, A-G eds *Comparative Federalism and Federation: Competing Traditions and Future Directions*. New York: Harvester.

Gorbachev, Mikhail. 1994. "On New Federalism" in S. Randall and R. Gibbens eds *Federalism and the New World Order*. Calgary: University of Calgary Press.

Hicks, U. K. 1978. *Federalism: Failure and Success*. London: Macmillan.

Huntington, Samuel. 1997. *The Clash of Civilisations and the Remaking of the World Order*, New Delhi: Penguin.

Ibrahim, J. & Pereira C. 1998. "On Dividing and Uniting: Ethnicity, Racism and Nationalism in Africa" *Nethra: Journal of the International Centre for Ethnic Studies*, vol 3, no 1.

Ibrahim, Jibrin. 1991. "Religion and Political Turbulence in Nigeria" *Journal of Modern African Studies*, no. 29 (1).

———. 1995. "Democratic Transition in Africa: The Challenge of a New Agenda" in Chole, E. & Ibrahim, J. eds *Democratization Processes in Africa*. Dakar: CODESRIA

Ignatieff, M. 1993. *Blood and Belonging: Journeys into the New Nationalism*. Toronto: Viking Penguin, .

Lemarchand, Rene. 1994. *Burundi: Ethnocide as Discourse and Practice* New York: Woodrow Wilson Centre & Cambridge University Press.

———. (1997) "Patterns of State Collapse and Reconstruction in Central Africa" *African Studies Quarterly*, vol 1, no 3.

Maddox, W. P. 1941. "The Political Basis of Federalism" *The American Political Science Review*, vol XXXV, no 6.

Mahmood, Cynthia. 1992. "Do Ethnic Groups Exist? A Cognitive Perspective on the Concept of Cultures" *Ethnology*, vol. XXXI (1).

Naanen, Ben. 1995 "Oil-Producing Minorities and the Restructuring of Nigerian Federalism: The Case of the Ogoni People", *Journal of Commonwealth and Comparative Politics*, vol. 33, no 1.

Nnoli, Okwudiba. 1989. *Ethnic Politics in Africa*, Ibadan: Vantage Publishers.

———. 1992. "Reflections on Ethnicity and Multiparty Democracy in Africa" CODESRIA/Rockefeller Reflections on Development Programme.

Olukoshi, A. O. & Agbu, O. (1996) "The Deepening Crisis of Nigerian Federalism and the Future of the Nation-State" in Olukoshi, A. O. & Laakso, L. eds. *Challenges to the Nation-State in Africa*, Nordiska Afrikainistitutet, Uppsala.

———. & Laakso, L. eds. 1996. *Challenges to the Nation-State in Africa*, Nordiska Afrikainistitutet, Uppsala.

Osaghae, E. E. 1992. "Managing Ethnic Conflicts Under Democratic Transition in

Africa" in B Caron et al eds. *Democratic Transition in Africa*. Ibadan: CREDU.

Otite, O. 1990. *Ethnic Pluralism and Ethnicity in Nigeria*. Ibadan: Shoneson.

Prazauski, A. 1991. "Ethnic Conflicts in the Context of Democratising Political Systems," *Theory and Society*, vol. 20.

Rothchild, Donald. 1968. "From Federalism to Neo-Federalism" in D. Rothchild ed. *Politics of Integration: An East African Documentation*. Nairobi: East African House, Nairobi.

Salamone, F. A. 1976. "Becoming Hausa: Ethnic Identity Change and its Implications For the Study of Ethnic Pluralism and Stratification" in Sanda, A. O. ed. *Ethnic Relations in Nigeria*. Ibadan: Sociology Department, University of Ibadan.

Samatar, A. I. ed. 1994. *The Somali Challenge: From Catastrophe to Renewal* Boulder; Lynne Rienner.

Sardamov, Ivelin. 1996. "Modern Dilemma: Detribalisation or Ethnic Intolerance?" *Michigan Journal of Political Science*, no 21.

Stanovcic, Vogislav. 1990. Federalism and Pluralism in a Democratic Society: A view from the Yugoslav Experience and Perspective" in P. Simlé et al eds. *American and Yugoslav Views on the 1990s*. Belgrade: Institute of International Politics.

Stanovcic, Vogislav. 1995. "Searching for New Designs: Alternatives to Federalism, The Yugoslavian Experience" Paper for IPSA Research Committee on Comparative Federalism, Florida: Atlanta Beach.

Tindigarukayo, J. K. 1989. "The Viability of Federalism and Consociationalism in Cultural Plural Societies of Post-Colonial States: A Theoretical Exploration", *Plural Societies*, vol. XIX, no 1.

Wheare, K. C. 1963. *Federal Government*. London: Oxford University Press.

Woodward, P. and Forsyth, M. eds. 1994 *Conflict and Peace in the Horn of Africa: Federalism and Its Alternatives*. Aldershot: Dartmouth.

SECTION III:
MANAGING ACCUMULATION IN FEDERAL POLITIES

CHAPTER 7

Towards An Enduring Economic Foundation For Democratic Federalism In Africa: Some Notes

Adebayo Olukoshi

Introduction: Contextual and Conceptual Considerations

T he debates on the reform process that has been going on in Africa have been mainly concentrated, in a very narrow manner, on the twin issues of economic structural adjustment and political liberalization, with the latter increasingly reduced to a discussion of the politico-administrative prerequisites for the successful establishment and consolidation of the "free" market (Haggard et al, 1995; Haggard and Webb, 1994; Nelson, 1989). Only in a few cases have the implications of the reforms for the overall framework of national-territorial administration been addressed beyond technicist notions of "good"/"bad" governance and strategies for infusing public sector management with "free" market principles and practices (Bangura, 1999; Olukoshi, 1998; Mkandawire, 1996; Gibbon et al, 1992). But even where efforts have been made to address the implications of contemporary economic and political reforms for national-territorial administration, these have mostly been limited to an assessment of the consequences for the success or failure of orthodox economic reform implementation of presidential and parliamentary as well as majoritarian versus non-majoritarian/power sharing/ coalition forms of government (Stepan and Skach, 1994). Studies have also been published in a similar vein on the effects of the first-past-the-post electoral regime and the different variants of proportional representation on the process of "effective" national economic and political governance. As it is, the task of tackling the challenges of national-territorial administration in the context of political and economic reforms of varying magnitudes, and beyond narrow concerns with subordinating the politico-institutional framework to the goals of orthodox adjustment or the requirements of a technocratic policy elite, is one which remains to be adequately addressed. This essay is partly intended as a contribution to the realization of that task. That the implications of structural adjustment and recent political reforms for the national-territorial framework of political and economic governance in Africa has not been sufficiently addressed in the literature must be surprising to the casual observer. This is because there has been no shortage of attention focused on the role of the state in the political economy of contemporary Africa and this is attested to by the proliferation of adjectival epithets invented during the 1980s and 1990s to try to capture its essence. Among the better known of these epithets are the "prebendal state," the "(neo-)patrimonial state," "the rentier state," the "unsteady state," the "sultanist state," the "over-extended state," the "crony state," the "inverted state," the "predatory state," the "lame leviathan," and the "kleptocratic state." Indeed, one of the remarkable things about the literature is that most of the contributors to the discussions on the sources of the continent's problems point, in one way or another, to the state and the top-heavy, centralizing logic of the post-colonial model of accumulation that underpinned efforts, from the 1960s and throughout the 1970s,at promoting socio-economic development and national unity (World Bank, 1984;Bates, 1981; Sandbrook, 1985, 1986). Also, the outbreak of popular pressures for political and socio-economic reforms that have been witnessed across the continent since the late 1980s are, in many respects, directly connected to popular disenchantment with the way in which the post-colonial development and unity projects were organized. In many countries, this disenchantment has resulted in direct challenges to the nation-state itself, even if these challenges are not mainly expressed in secessionist terms or through a resort to armed violence and have not produced many more cases of outright state collapse(Olukoshi and Laakso, 1996). Out of these challenges have emerged a variety of proposals for reforming national-territorial politics. On the whole, the accent of the proposals have centered on federalism and decentralization.

In retrospect, it would seem that the spirited attacks on the state in contemporary Africa by the Bretton Woods institutions and their organic intellectuals had less to do with responding to popular yearnings for the creation of a more representative and accountable set of political institutions and more with narrow institutional concerns to promote an externally-designed program of economic and governance reform. Little wonder then that some of the centralizing, top-down structures and components of national-territorial administration associated with the much-attacked post-colonial model of accumulation were simply re-deployed in support of structural adjustment implementation, even if it meant trying to insulate them from local pressures for political and managerial accountability. It was, after all, the hey day of donor Machiavellianism whereby successful adjustment implementation was directly equated with the capacity of a "strong" central state to override interest group opposition to orthodox market reforms (Gibbon et al, 1992). Even after some importance began to be attached to the insulation of central banks and the economic bureaucracy from the rest of the governmental machinery and wider interest group politics, the emphasis still remained on how a "strong" state could be enabled to implement top-down policies of economic reform imposed by the leading international financial institutions.

Thus, for all the attack which the Bretton Woods institutions launched against the African state, they relied on it and its centralized logic for the prosecution of their market reform agenda. The only difference in this regard between the pre-adjustment and adjustment periods was that, paradoxically, the very state on which the Bretton woods institutions relied in order to force through their preferred structural adjustment policies was itself increasingly weakened as an administrative organ and a political institution by the adjustment experience. The reasons for this paradox are discussed further later in this essay. What is really important for our purposes at this point is to note that even as it retained its centralized political and economic decision-making/governance institutions during the adjustment years, the state was increasingly exposed to a legitimacy deficit which fed into a widespread feeling that it was both remote and increasingly unrepresentative. This deficit was, among others, directly linked to the decline of social citizenship in much of Africa and the demoralization of the ranks of the administrative cadres of the state as real incomes collapsed, retrenchments were effected, and key policy decisions were usurped by the IMF and World Bank in what some have described as the second colonialism.

While the opening up of the political space through the implementation of reforms connected to civil liberties and multi-party politics may help to redress some of the problems that are at the heart of the feeling of popular disempowerment and disenchantment, it can only represent a first step in the search for a more representative and participatory political order that is capable of accommodating the diverse and competing interests in African polities. For, at the heart of the challenges to the nation-state in contemporary Africa is the failure to satisfactorily resolve the citizenship question; the restoration of political pluralism addresses only one dimension of that question. This essay is premised, therefore, on the assumption that wider reforms in the basis of the post-colonial nation-state project are crucial to a rounded democratic resolution of the African crisis; the effort at reforming the African political space, in order for it to be complete, will have to go beyond the recognition/ restoration of (individual) civil liberties and political pluralism to embrace the effective devolution of power in the economy and polity side by side with the simultaneous institution of locally-rooted mechanisms for making the exercise of power representative and accountable. Such a devolution of power should not be confused with the ideology-driven market populism of the political right which, in many countries, has translated into the wholesale privatization of public enterprises, the systematic dismantling of trade unions, and the atomization of civic associations. Instead, it is premised on the need for African countries to move beyond formal constitutionalism and imbue their polities with structures of popular sovereignty that guarantee that the citizenry have a say in all matters that affect them at all levels of local, intermediate and national administration and governance.

To pose the challenges of democratization in Africa in terms not just of the struggle for political liberties and rights but also for politico-administrative decentralization and regional/group autonomy is to position ourselves in a discourse that raises a variety of questions which cannot be fully or sufficiently tackled here. Some of the questions which arise, as they have been posed in the debates, relate to whether the key priority in contemporary Africa centers on issues of social (especially class) inequality and re-distribution as opposed to the quest for group autonomy and administrative decentralization. Flowing from this is the question of whether what Africa should be aiming to achieve is the elimination of (class/social) difference which has so stymied the task of national integration and equitable development as opposed to the establishment of institutions and processes that recognize(ethnic/socio-cultural) difference where it exists as a demographic-political factor and use it as a building block in the nation-state project, i.e. integrationism versus multi-culturalism. The questions are endless but it would seem that what is called for is not an "either-or" formulation that attempts a subjective, pre-determined hierarchy of priorities but rather, a wholistic approach which simultaneously takes on board the need for a politics of re-distribution, equity, representation, participation, autonomy and recognition as the basic ingredients for a project of national renewal. In other words, there is a need to simultaneously address the political issues raised by the social and the National questions if an enduring basis is to be created for stability. This is not to deny the necessity for attention to be paid to historical context. Without doubt, the nature and history of the specific context will always play a crucial role in shaping the national reform agenda. What often becomes problematic is the tendency among students of Africa either to deny the autonomous relevance of the National/Minority Question or, where they acknowledge its importance to, nevertheless, subordinate it to the class question in the faulty assumption that the latter, *ab initio*, has an historic primacy for all time and that once it is resolved, the former will automatically also be sorted out. On the other hand, the extreme approach of seeking to understand all African realities through the prism of "tribe"/tribalism or ethnicity and the nation as if this is the only cleavage that matters needs to be discarded. For, there is a great deal of ambiguity around ethnicity and ethnic identities in contemporary Africa on account of a variety of historical and demographic factors and the conditioning role which social conditions like poverty and inequality and political factors like dictatorship play in shaping political attitudes. Thus, as the experience of many African countries has shown, there can be no question of a trade-off between class and nation in the quest for a durable and stable polity. Similarly, it will not do simply to root a reform agenda solely on narrow considerations of "tribe" and ethnicity. Nor can it be taken for granted that the resolution of class contradictions will lead, automatically, to the settlement of the National Question and vice versa. Taken together in an integrated framework though, it is plausible that efforts at tackling class-based inequality will profit from the redressing of regional inequalities, the de-concentration and devolution of decision-making and the accommodation of local aspirations for socio-cultural and/or administrative autonomy. To be sure, decentralization and local autonomy are not in, by, and of themselves, democratic or necessarily indicative of the embrace of a democratic path: As has been suggested by several commentators, a project of devolution which is not simultaneously accompanied by the reform of the structures of economic, political, social and cultural power can only result in the decentralization of authoritarian rule. Indeed, decentralization and regional autonomy are not only not inherently incompatible with dictatorship - did not the colonial powers in Africa adopt different variants of indirect rule as part of their bid to reinforce colonial domination? (Mamdani, 1996) - but could also be undertaken as exercises in the consolidation of unrepresentative and non-participatory governance. For us, therefore, the issue in federalism is not so much that it is by definition a more democratic form than centralism and/or unitarism - that would be a wrong way of posing the question and the issue involved is not simply a conceptual but an empirical one- as that its democratizing potential should be closely tied, in theory and practice, to the institutionalized submission of power to popular democratic prescription both at the national, intermediate and local levels (Wamba-dia-Wamba, 1995). This implies that if the object of decentralization and local autonomy is the enhancement of representative and accountable governance, the institutions and processes of democracy have to be integral to the entire exercise in a manner which ensures that the citizenry is able to exercise rights and =responsibilities, as well as demand representation and accountability, at every point of contact with the state and

147

its representatives. It is in such a context that we can meaningfully distinguish democratic federalism from any other kind of federalism.

Considered closely, and set against the fact that the federal mode of national-territorial administration is always shaped by the history and context of different countries, it would seem that the really important issue to focus on is not so much the extent to which a federal political system is centralized or decentralized as the extent to which it is democratic or undemocratic, flexible or rigid. No two federal systems are the same and the different federations that exist display varying and shifting degrees of centralization and decentralization. To be federal, a political system must, of course, contain certain minimum elements of administrative and political decentralization but such decentralization can never get to a point where the very basis of association within a defined national-territorial space is completely nullified. Given, therefore, that federal systems will embody elements both of centralization and decentralization in differing mixes, and some systems could and do move over time from more decentralized to less decentralized forms and vice versa, the critical issue then becomes the extent to which the particular mix that prevails in a given polity embodies the popular democratic aspirations of the citizenry as defined by the historical juncture. It is for this reason that greater attention needs to be focused on the democratic form and content of federal systems in order to gauge not just the degree of the devolution of power but also the extent to which the use of devolved power is representative of the will and aspirations of the citizenry. The institutional mechanisms of the federal order must also not be too rigid as to deny the system the necessary flexibility for responding to the shifting demands of the pace and content of development which, by their nature, inevitably produce and reproduce the structures of opportunity in the economy and society.

Coming to grips with the democratic content of a federal political order also requires a careful unbundling of democracy as a category. Apart from its liberal components which include individual liberties, political pluralism, universal suffrage, the right of association, the rule of law, respect for the due process and the independence of the judicial system, there is also its republican component which places emphasis on public service, accountability (both political and non-political), and a sense of civic duty and responsibility. Furthermore, democracy carries social democratic components which form a crucial part of the social contract between the citizenry and the state and encapsulates the obligations of the latter in the areas of social livelihood, education, and security of life. The content and meaning of the social bargain between the citizenry and the state are crucial to the grounding of the political order in the sovereignty which democratic systems invest in the people. Finally, and particularly crucial for federal systems, is the existence of representative institutional channels and mechanisms for redressing not just citizen grievances but also disputes among the layers of government over competences and actions. The flexibility of these institutional channels to cope with shifts in the jurisdictions of different tiers of government as the pace and content of the development process changes constitutes a crucial element of the representative capacity of the federal system.

The Post-Colonial Model of Accumulation and the Logic of Centralism

At independence, most African countries embarked on the twin projects of development (mainly defined in socio-economic terms) and national integration (mainly defined in politico-cultural terms) on the premise that both endeavors required a central direction and that only the state was best placed to constitute them (Olukoshi and Laakso, 1996). Not surprisingly, the post-colonial model of accumulation that was developed to serve as the overarching framework for the developmental and unity projects reserved a commanding role in the economy and polity for the public sector in general and the central government in particular. Through exercises that ranged from the nationalization/indigenization/Africanization of foreign enterprises to the establishment of parastatal organizations to undertake commercial, financial, agricultural and industrial investments aimed at accelerating the pace of economic development, and the promotion of public sector investments in social and physical infrastructure, the state attempted, with varying degrees of success, to push through its vision of what it thought was necessary for the goal of endowing the nationalist project with a substantive socio-economic content and achieving rapid economic development. Although different regimes defined the ideological framework for this project differently - the appellations ranged from authenticity and humanitarianism to mixed economy, (African/scientific/ujamaa) socialism, and market liberalism - they were united by the fact that they all endowed the state with a central, commanding role in the socio-economic development process. This is what has been referred to in the literature as the regime of dirigism or developmentalism that prevailed in post-colonial Africa until the early 1980s.

The post-colonial model of accumulation had the logical consequence of, almost inexorably, centralizing the revenue mobilization and allocation mechanism in much of Africa. This was as true for the predominantly agrarian economies that depended mainly on agricultural exports for their revenue receipts as it was for the resource-rich, rentier economies that increasingly relied on rents from the minerals extracted from them by transnational companies. Control of monetary instruments and policies by the central government which was crucial to efforts at creating a national market was reinforced by the virtual monopolization of the most important fiscal levers and policies by the central authorities. Coupled with the dominant capacity of the central state to allocate investible resources as well as influence the direction of foreign capital flows, it is not hard to see why the post-colonial model of economic development easily translated into the reinforcement of centralizing trends in the economy. Those trends themselves were strengthened by the integrating logic built into efforts at creating/consolidating a national market. Thus it was that, in time, the central state became the source of all the patronage that mattered and to be on the wrong side of the elite in control of the state apparatus was to suffer marginalization and even reprisals. With the central state occupying such a paramount position, relative access to it and the resources it controlled became measures of individual and group integration into the post-colonial nation-state project; those who lost out in the intense competition for access either as individuals or groups, whether defined in class or regional, ethnic, or religious terms, easily saw their lot in terms of a disenfranchisement. This was especially so where exclusion, often accompanied with subtle and direct forms of discrimination, took on a systematic and sustained pattern (Olukoshi and Laakso,1996). The dominance of the central state in the post-colonial model of accumulation also brought to the fore the question of its capacity to establish and sustain over the long-term, a level of performance that would be capable of responding to the needs and aspirations of the society in general.

In the early post-independence years when growth levels were healthy, revenue receipts rising in real terms, thanks in part to the favorable prices enjoyed by most primary commodities in the world market, and investment resources/inflows growing, the state was, by and large, able to maintain its overall credibility before the various constituencies that vied for its attention; it had the resources with which to weld together the broad anti-colonial coalition on which it rested even if the distribution of the resources was marked by clearly discernible inequality and unevenness along class, gender, ethnic, religious and regional lines. Furthermore, its internal coherence as an administrative apparatus, and, moreover, one with a clear "statist-developmentalist" ideology, was, in retrospect, much sharper than what was to follow during the crisis and adjustment years of the 1980s and 1990s. Clearly, both in the definition of its mission and in terms of the articulation of a vision, the early post-colonial state in most cases displayed a degree of coherence and mission around which it attempted to rally a populace that was also eager to advance the gains of independence. The issue here is not so much the initial success or even universal agreement which attended this effort, important though that was to become, as that there were clearly articulated organizing principles and projects around which the populace was mobilized and a legitimate framework for doing so.

However, when during the course of the 1970s, the post-colonial economy began to slide into crisis, a crisis which crippled the capacity of the state to fulfill its socio-economic developmental plans, cracks inevitably opened up in the polity as questions of corruption, nepotism, inequality, and systematic exclusion appeared more starkly and began to be posed in political terms that had implications for the way in which power was organized and exercised. It marked the beginning of the end of the post-colonial social contract that underpinned state-society relations. The declining capacity of the state to fulfill its basic social-welfare obligations to the citizenry, an objective that was central to the national anti-colonial struggle, combined with growing problems of internal governance to undermine the legitimacy of many incumbent regimes. Yet, the political framework within which the post-colonial developmental model was being pursued was not one which easily permitted an open and direct contestation of the state's record. Little wonder then that in response to the growing crisis of legitimation that it confronted, the state became not only more authoritarian but also distrustful of independent political action and the contestation of its policies. In many countries, the trend was towards an acceleration of the centralization of decision-making, the concentration of power in the hands of a small coterie of officials which, in turn, facilitated the emergence of personal rule, the erosion of local autonomy, and the consolidation of political monopoly. The implication of this was that the legitimate space for the airing of grievances or mobilization of aspirations, both individual and group, was narrowed.

The Post-Colonial Unity Project and National Integration from Above

The political difficulties associated with the collapse of the post-colonial social contract that defined the framework for state-society relations and the context for state interventionism were exacerbated by the way in which the unity project was defined and pursued. The socio-economic components of the post-colonial model of development were backed up at the political level with a unity project that first defined multi-ethnicity and political pluralism as essentially problematic and then proceeded to seek ways of containing them. In most cases, the latter quest resulted in the abolition of the multi-party political frameworks on the basis of which most countries attained independence and, in their place, the institutionalization of single party or military regimes that purported to represent the "national interest." The thinking that lay behind this was quite straight forward: African countries that are the products of the arbitrary colonial boundary-drawing that resulted in disparate groups being brought together, mostly for the first time, under one territorial administration needed to forge a new national identity that would transcend the ethnic and other non-secular (sub-) identities of their peoples and create a strong basis for national unity. This was never going to be an easy task, especially given that colonial domination rested on a system of divide-and-rule which created or intensified suspicion among different ethnic groups, religions, and regions and also privileged some groups, religions and regions politically, economically, and even culturally at the expense of others (Olukoshi and Laakso, 1996; Olukoshi, 1998).

The self-serving invention of stereotypes about different groups - some ethnic groups were characterized as "courageous", others as "lazy", still others as "entrepreneurial" both in a positive and negative sense and some as "unreliable" - by the colonizing powers carried over into the post-colonial period and fed into an unhealthy pattern of competing ethnicities which made the task of creating a national identity that much more daunting. Matters were not helped by the fact that as they were confronted with the inevitability of independence for their colonies, the departing colonial powers set about constructing coalitions and regime types to which they could safely hand over day to day governance whilst retaining neo-colonial control and/or influence. In class terms, this entailed spirited attempts aimed at clearing the political playing field of radical trade unionists and nationalists - those "undesirables" who were thought to be the local agents of international communist expansionism. Not a few wars were fought on the continent, especially but not exclusively in the white settler colonies, as part of this struggle against the radical nationalists. The flip side of the campaign against radical nationalism was the grooming of "moderates" who were often steeped in ethnic or regionalist politics or who were encouraged to define their constituencies in those terms if they were to have a chance of achieving power. Thus, while the colonial authorities were not universally successful in implementing their neo-colonial designs in this regard, where they did succeed, the coalitions to which they handed over power often had strong ethnic and regionalist undertones that were certain to pose threats to the entire nation-state project either because the groups that were excluded sought to contest their exclusion or those that were included tried to consolidate their grip in the face of mounting opposition (Olukoshi,1998). The contestation of the lop-sided "order" which the colonial powers left behind in Africa on class and non-class, secular and non-secular grounds, has been a major factor underlying the chronic instability of the countries of Africa. Against the background of the foregoing, it is not surprising that in responding to the challenges of nation-building, the post-colonial authorities increasingly sought to bring their diverse peoples under one umbrella in the assumption that the task of creating a new national identity was incompatible with the demands of the various sub-national identities prevalent in the polity. This was all the more so as it was thought that the goal of rapid economic and social modernization that was central to the post-colonial model of accumulation was very likely to profit from political efforts at concentrating national energies on the task of development, instead of dissipating them through the cultivation and encouragement of structures and processes of domestic competition for power and influence. If the task of rapid socio-economic modernization was successfully realized through the harnessing of the energies of all the peoples of the country, it was also hoped that this would have the added benefit of undermining the "primordial" identities that, as we noted earlier, were seen as being, by definition, detrimental to national unity. Across the continent, the political correlate of the socio-economic development program of the state soon took the form of de facto and de jure single party rule or the inauguration of corporatist military and military-dominated/-backed regimes to which all sectors of society were supposed to belong: One nation, one destiny, under one leader and, in some cases, one God. Various theories of consociationalism and modernizing oligarchs/elites were spurned to give intellectual backing to this particular approach to the post-colonial unity project (Olukoshi and Laakso,1996; Olukoshi, 1998).

The post-colonial unity project, in the way in which it was constituted and operationalized, carried some authoritarian seeds in it from the outset. It not only required strong central direction but also functioned in a top-down manner which gave little real space for local initiatives and action. Furthermore, in many countries, the autonomous platforms of the people, ranging from trade, students, and youth unions to professional associations, women's groups and co-operatives were eroded and reduced to branches of the single party or movement. Yet, in spite of all of the official protestations to the contrary, many of these parties and movements, as well as the national security apparatus that guaranteed them, carried clear ethnic, regional, religious insignias, often corresponding to those of the incumbent leader, and which, in perception and reality, were widely seen as conditioning relative access and inclusion and at what level. Together with the onset in the decline in national socio-economic fortunes which most countries began to suffer during the 1970s, this factor reinforced disillusionment with the nation-state and yet, as we noted earlier, the political structure was such that it tended to stifle the airing of concerns and the organization of alternatives. The formally-established political mode, in this instance, became an obstacle to internal reform even as the developmentalist project on which it was built faltered and the class, ethno-regional, and religious basis of power was exposed. In this climate, the seeds of authoritarianism that inhered in the unity project soon germinated into full-blown repression until the onset of the new popular pressures for change that engulfed the continent from the late 1980s onwards.

Structural Adjustment and Political Reforms in Africa

The pressures for political reform in Africa that have been the subject of much discussion in recent times occurred within the framework of the abandonment by most countries of the crisis-ridden post-colonial developmentalist model and the adoption of International Monetary Fund (IMF)/World Bank structural adjustment programs, often under donor conditionality and cross-conditionality. These programs began to make their entry into the African policy terrain during the early 1980s as the economic crisis confronting the countries of the continent deepened. By the end of the decade of the 1980s, virtually every African country was implementing the program; even those countries that did not have formal agreements with the IMF and the World Bank - Botswana, Namibia and South Africa- had shadow policies that mirrored the standard reform prescriptions of the Bretton Woods twins. In this fundamental sense, structural adjustment has become the foundation upon which efforts at developing African economies and societies are now premised. This is so in spite of the fact that the program was initially meant to represent only a temporary diversion from "development", aimed as it was at allowing governments to correct short-term economic distortions before returning to their medium- and long-term developmental goals. Indeed, from being a short-term instrument for reform, structural adjustment has been transformed into the very essence of development, with all of the implications which that shift carries for the economy, polity, and society in Africa. Structural adjustment, in design and content, represented a conscious and systematic attack on the entire post-colonial model of accumulation. Its objectives could be summarized as follows: The relentless retrenchment of the state and the simultaneous liberation of the forces of the market. Not surprisingly, the component elements of the program consisted of policies and instruments designed to facilitate the realization of these objectives: Repeated currency devaluation, trade, foreign exchange market, interest rate, and price liberalization, subsidy withdrawal/cost recovery, public enterprise privatization/commercialization/liquidation, the liberalization of (foreign) investment regimes, the scaling back of public expenditures, the retrenchment of workers in the public sector as part of the bid to trim the state and balance the budget, and the enforcement of wage restraint. In attacking the state interventionism that was built into the post-colonial model of development, the authors of the adjustment program tended to interpret popular disillusionment with the performance of public institutions and enterprises in Africa to mean a plea for their dismantling or privatization and an unalloyed vote for the market. This one-sided interpretation, together with the efforts at market liberalization carried multi-level adverse implications for the post-colonial nation-state project.

At one level, in its workings, structural adjustment not only became part and parcel of the dynamic of economic crisis and social decline in Africa but also tended to reinforce them in several respects. This is so in spite of the fact that by the end of the 1980s, in response to sustained and compelling criticisms of the social costs of their adjustment policies which also failed to produce economic growth, the IMF and the World Bank grafted a social dimension to the program. The various programs for the mitigation/alleviation of the social costs of adjustment, narrow in scope and grossly under-funded as they were, failed to make a major difference on the problem of social decline, widening inequality, and growing poverty in Africa. Thus, the erosion of the basis for the social citizenship that had been integral to the post-colonial social contract was further accelerated during the structural adjustment years. This emptying of citizenship of its social content fed into and was reinforced by the distinct anti-statism of structural adjustment, an anti-statism that, impractical terms, meant the abdication by the state of its most basic responsibilities to the citizenry, a development which found new ideological justification in neo-liberalism. Several students of contemporary African politics have attempted to capture this situation through notions of "disengagement" and the "irrelevant state" (Chazan, 1988; Ihonvbere, 1993). While there are strong grounds for questioning the accuracy of these formulations, what is important to underline here for the purposes of our discourse is the erosion of key elements of the social basis of state-society relations in Africa which they point to. Increasingly, citizens encountered and experienced the state in terms of its raw coerciveness and rampant corruption: The era of predation had arrived.

At another level, the anti-statist orientation of structural adjustment had negative implications for those whose livelihood was tied to the public sector, and that meant a majority of the working people since in most African countries, the public sector was, and in spite of massive retrenchments, still remains the biggest employer of labor. Not surprisingly, some of the biggest losers from the adjustment process have included labor, students, and various categories of professionals - in a word, those groups in society that have, historically, been the bearers and defenders of the national-territorial and secular state project in spite of the struggles which they waged against incumbent regimes for a variety of reasons. Denigrated as urban parasites by the high priests of adjustment theory, the attacks on their interests, partially through the delegitimation of their struggles and aspirations, and the shrinking and disorganization of their ranks, uneven though this was within sectors and between countries, had adverse consequences for the nation-state project.

For, the weakening of the social forces capable of defending the national-territorial space in the context of the collapse of social citizenship opened the way for the revival of ethnic, regional and religious networks and structures that not only increasingly played a role in the basic livelihood strategies of their members but also challenged the entire nation-state project in the process (Adekanye, 1995; Osaghae, 1995). Also, the exodus of many skilled personnel from a public sector where morale and remuneration had collapsed and the immersion of those who remained into multiple modes of livelihood (Mustapha, 1992) dealt a severe blow to state capacity.

Furthermore, in the eagerness to strip the state of its assets and cut it down to size literally and metaphorically, the authors of structural adjustment were completely unmindful of the implications of their policy prescriptions for national identity. Public institutions which had been created in the post-colonial period and which had assumed an important place in the national psyche as much for their symbolism as for the actual functions which they performed or failed to perform were remorselessly torn down with scant regard to the impact of such action for national identity. The choice that was placed before Africa was posed in terms of the state versus the market; the authors of adjustment, in pushing the case for the market not only did not address questions of how it might be governed in the interest of the citizen - even as citizen-consumer - but also threw away the symbols and values of nationhood and identity that were constructed at independence. Furthermore, the reform of public enterprises mainly through privatization cemented the impression that under structural adjustment, every national asset that had any worth, actual and potential, was up for sale to the highest bidder. With the highest bidders being mostly expatriates whose buying power was significantly boosted by the collapse of national currencies, privatization easily translated into a full re-instatement of foreign domination which indigenization/nationalization/Africanization had been designed to curtail. Privatization, therefore, went hand in hand with the de-nationalization of economies. The market not only failed to deliver economic and social recovery, it also failed to produce new symbols that could serve as a basis for re-establishing/re-building national identity.

In terms of the territorial-administrative structure of the adjusting states of Africa, IMF/World Bank market reform efforts tended to feed into and reinforce the top-down, centralizing mode of rule that was in place in most countries. For a start, the implementation of the adjustment policies depended heavily, indeed solely on the central government; it was only with the central government of the adjusting country that negotiations were held and agreements signed. The task of ensuring the implementation of the measures prescribed by the donors also rested with the central authorities who had the responsibility of compelling compliance by all levels and arms of government. Furthermore, within the governmental bureaucracy, only the key economic ministries were party/privy to the full discussions involved in the market reform project. Moreover, relative to other branches of government, the adjustment years have witnessed the reinforcement of the relative weight of the executive branch vis-à-vis the legislative and judicial arms. Thus, within the central government and between it and other layers of administration, structural adjustment has meant the reinforcement of economic centralism generally, and one with a narrow and weakened bureaucratic base in particular, in spite of the market liberating ideology that underlies it. In part, this is also because in most of the countries of the continent, the program was the product of outright donor imposition or, in any case, was not the outcome of a domestic social consensus.

The adjustment years have, additionally, witnessed the abandonment of conscious policy efforts aimed at redressing uneven regional development across various economic and social spheres in the adjusting countries of Africa. Uneven development, which was a legacy of colonial capitalism, has always been a potent, underlying source of conflict in many African countries, affecting issues of revenue mobilization and allocation, the channeling of investment capital, and the distribution of physical and social infrastructural projects, among others. For all the weakness of the post-colonial state interventionist model of development, an effort was made to tackle some of the manifestations of this unevenness, even if not as vigorously, even-handedly and comprehensively as may have been possible or desired. The neglect of this problem during the adjustment years has resulted in the widening of gaps between regions and ethnicities as well as within regions and ethnicities in such areas as access to educational and medical facilities, potable water and electricity, and roads, among others. Thus, although the post-colonial unity project may have had a clearly discernible class, ethnic, regional and religious base, what seems to be happening under the regime of structural adjustment is the expansion of a market-generated structure of domination, exclusion and neglect that has adverse implications for national cohesion. State retrenchment and the quest for the enthronement of the market has, for many communities, mainly meant the closure or collapse of the only non-coercive evidence of state presence and the symbol of inclusion in a political and economic community.

Towards an Enduring Economic Foundation for National-Territorial Administration in Africa

It seems clear from all of the foregoing that in seeking an enduring economic foundation for a project of democratic federalism in Africa, orthodox structural adjustment does not offer us a viable path; we must look beyond it. In doing so, certain basic principles must, of necessity, be taken on board. These include the need for the adoption of a reform package that encourages, rather than stifles growth and development - no federal arrangement can endure on the basis of prolonged economic stagnation and social decay; the creation of a domestic social consensus around the reform package by taking greater account of class, gender, and ethno-regional concerns; the establishment of a new social contract to underpin state-society relations, if only to ensure that there is a concrete bargain in being a member of the political community; the rehabilitation of state capacity for policy formulation and implementation; the entrenchment of the rights of the members of society to impose democratic prescriptions on the state at all the levels where its actions touch their lives; the recognition of political pluralism as a basic prerequisite for national political re-birth; and the accommodation of cultural and regional autonomy in the recognition that where an objective and/or subjective need for it exists, it could be a positive input into the securing of national unity.

The political reforms which have taken place in many African countries since the late 1980s represent important developments that could, in some cases, serve as a new beginning but these are not yet complete and, in any case, are not sufficient in themselves especially as the crucial question of restoration of social citizenship remains unanswered. Indeed, the faltering of several of the projects of political liberalization that has already been observed is not unconnected to the fact that the reforms, like structural adjustment, have been slow in delivering concrete improvements in the lives of the generality of the people. Clearly, the task of re-establishing social citizenship directly broaches the issue of economic reform for growth and development just as it also involves political bargaining for a new contract between the state and society. On the basis of the lessons of experience with post-colonial statist-developmentalism and neo-liberal market fundamentalism, it would seem that the reform path that is open to Africa consists of a creative and dynamic combination of measures aimed at greater economic rationality and policies that cater for the social-welfare needs and aspirations of the populace. Inevitably, such an enterprise is bound to be attended by tensions between the demands of economic rationality and the popular welfare of the citizenry; it is precisely this fact that makes it necessary for the revamped reform project to be embarked upon within a political framework that is democratic.

Decentralization of economic activity, including revenue mobilization and allocation, the encouragement of private individual and autonomous co-operative economic activities, and the establishment of a credible public regulatory mechanism may well be included as elements in the effort at reconstituting the basis for development in Africa. Whatever the combination of measures that is adopted, what is important to underline is that in the end, if economic decentralization is not to be hollow, it has to be accompanied with the restoration of economic growth and social citizenship as well as political democracy and administrative decentralization. The import of all this is that the construction of an enduring economic foundation for a project of democratic federalism in contemporary Africa may well have to begin in the arena of politics where the agenda for the democratization of the polity would have to be set out.

REFERENCES

Adekanye, J.B., 1995. "Structural Adjustment, Democratisation and Rising Ethnic Tensions in Africa". *Development and Change*, Vol. 26, No. 2.
Bangura, Y., 1999 "Globalisation, Technocratic Policy-Making and Democratisation", (Mimeo), Geneva.
Bates, R., 1981. *Markets and States in Tropical Africa.* Berkeley: University of California Press).
Chazan, N., 1988. "Ghana: Problems of Governance and the Emergence of Civil Society", in L. Diamond *et al* eds., *Democracy in Developing Countries*, Vol. 2, Africa. Boulder: Lynne Rienner.
Gibbon, P. 1992 *et al* eds., *Authoritarianism, Democracy and Adjustment* (Uppsala: NA)
Haggard, S. J-D. Lafay, and C. Morrison, 1995 *The Political Feasibility of Adjustment in Developing Countries*. Paris: OECD Development Centre.
———-. and S. Webb 1994 eds., *Voting for Reform: Democracy, Political Liberalisation and Economic Adjustment* (Oxford: Oxford University Press).
Ihonvebere, J., 1993 "Economic Crisis, Structural Adjustment and Social Crisis in Nigeria", *World Development*, Vol. 21, No. 1.
Mamdani, M., 1996 *Citizen and Subject: Contemporary Africa and the Legacy of Late Colonialism*. Princeton, NJ.: Princeton University Press.
Mkandawire, T., 1996 "Economic Policy-Making and the Consolidation of Democratic Institutions in Africa", in K. Havnevik and B.V. Arkadie eds., *Domination or Dialogue? Experiences and Prospects for African Development.* Uppsala: NAI.
Mustapha, A.R., "Structural Adjustment and Multiple Modes of Livelihood in Nigeria", in P. Gibbon *et al*, op. cit.
Nelson, J. 1989 ed., *Fragile Coalitions: The Politics of Economic Adjustment.* New Brunswick and Oxford: Transaction Books.
Olukoshi, A., 1998 The Elusive Prince of Denmark: Structural Adjustment and the Crisis of Governance in Africa. Uppsala: NAI.
———-. and L. Laakso. 1996. eds. Challenges to the Nation-State in Africa. Uppsala: NAI.
———-. 1988 ed., *The Politics of Opposition in Contemporary Africa.* Uppsala: NAI.

Osaghae, E., 1995 *Structural Adjustment and Ethnicity in Nigeria*, Research Report No. 98, Nordiska Afrikainstitutet.

Sandbrook, R. 1985. *The Politics of Africa's Economic Stagnation.* Cambridge: Cambridge University Press.

Sandbrook, R. 1986 "The State and Economic Stagnation in Tropical Africa", World Development, Vol. 14, No. 3.

Stepan, A. and C. Skach. 1994. *"Presidentialism and Parliamentarianism in Comparative Perspective"* in J.L. Linz and A. Valenzuela eds., *The Failure of Presidential Democracy: Comparative Perspectives*, Vol. 1. Baltimore and London: Johns Hopkins University Press.

Wamba-dia-Wamba, E., 1995 "From the National Conference to the Federal republic of the Congo?", Development Dialogue, No. 2.

World Bank, 1984 *Sub-Saharan Africa: From Crisis to Sustainable Growth.* Washington, DC.: World Bank.

CHAPTER 8

Fiscal Federalism in the 21st Century: Options for Nigeria

Bade Onimode

Prologue

Nigerian federalism is about the only one in Africa and it has been under strains for some years. Different commentators attribute the stresses to the combined pressures of military dictatorship and its unified military command that imposes a unitary state, and the increasing dominance of the federal government, with the corresponding marginalization of the states and local governments. Then there have been persistent complaints over the substitution of fiscal federalism for fiscal unitarism and the relegation of the derivation formula in national revenue allocation. All these have been compounded by the politics of Federal character, ethnicity and indigeneity. These are the collective backgrounds to the increasing tensions of federalism in the country.

They are quite surmountable problems that demand serious national priority, a collective sense of social justice and honesty of purpose. But it is essential to situate the systematic restructuring of Nigerian federalism within the wider context of African and global geo-politics.

In this wider setting, the increasing demands for new federal options and democratization in Nigeria can be related to the growing impetus of the African Democratic Movement that has been energized by the World Democratic Revolution, that burst upon the world stage around 1989. Since then, popular struggles for democracy and good governance across Africa have increasingly challenged the existing structures of the nation-state on the continent - and, indeed, elsewhere in the world. Arbitrary colonial boundaries that merged different nationalities haphazardly abusive denial of democratic rights to nationalities, communities and individuals under authoritarian regimes, and perceived repression with denial of equitable access to state resources, have galvanized most of the agitations for democratic restructuring.

As we approach the 21st century against this problematic background, and as the military disengages from governance to yield space for the socio-economic re-construction of Nigeria, what are the possible options for federalism in the country? The identification of such options should be informed by the re-construction of the evolution of Nigerian federalism, the major problems associated with this history, the relevant lessons of comparative federal experiments in other parts of the world, and insights into the possible political culture of the 21st century.

The Evolution of Nigerian Federalism

Four dominant changes or developments are identifiable in the evolution of Nigerian federalism. These are the original status quo; the redivisions of the polity into increasing numbers of states and local governments; changes in national revenue allocation and the introduction of federal character, and the protection of animosity interests.

The original federal system in Nigeria from 1945 to 1966 consisted of a tricolor regional system with asymmetrical domination by the former Northern Region; provision for competitive politics based on the West Minister model; and revenue distribution based mainly on the principle of derivation. Under the original regional system, there was constitutional division of powers between the federal, state and local governments.

While some of these powers were under the exclusive legislative list, others were under a concurrent legislative list that could be exercised by both the federal and state governments together with a residual list. Each tier of federal and state governments was essentially autonomous within its own sphere. The logic of this statutory division of powers was to satisfy the basic idea of unity in diversity, allow different nationalities to give political expression to their separate identities as the country federated from aggregate in to parts (as in the USA, India and Canada), rather than from a central core to additional political units.

The competitive political system also allowed all the component units constitutional access to political leadership of the federation. But this was attenuated by the dominant size of the former Northern Region, so that coalition political behavior became inevitable, especially under the zero - sum game (winner-take-all) of the West Minister model

The early federal system also based regional access to national revenue mainly on the principle of derivation. Other revenue allocation criteria were secondary to this, and this ensured that the former regions could use revenue from commodity exports for their rapid development.

All these changed with the intervention of the military into politics from the coup of 1966, which led to civil war during 1967/70. With the unified common structure of the Federal Military Government, which then dictated structural and other changes in the federal systems to state governors that were political appointees of the military head of state. Thus successive federal military governments re-divided the polity into many states and local governments on the demands of elite groups in different geo-political areas of the country. These involved the creation of 12 states by 1967, 19 by 1976, 21 by 1987, 30 by 1991 and 36 states plus the Abuja Federal Capital Territory by 1992. Correspondingly, there were 301 local governments by 1976, 450 from 1988; 587 by 1991 and 774 by 1992.

These political creations were facilitated by the country's greatly increased oil wealth from 1976. The main arguments for state creation were to minimize any threat to the federation from any state, to create growth poles and provide for greater ethnic identities; while additional local governments were supposed to be for taking government closer to the grassroots.

From the principle of derivation to those of equality of states and demographic strength was the other major federal shift after the civil war in 1970. The new egalitarian principle also led to the federal government's domination of the federal system through the provision of periodic grants to the other tiers of government. This distributive change was also associated with the introduction of the doctrine of Federal character into the 1979 and 1992 constitutions. This federal character stated that... "there shall be no predominance of persons from a few states or from a few ethnic or other sectional groups in that government (of the federation) or in any of its agencies" (1979) Constitution, p. 8). This federal character was used for elections, employment in government's establishments, and educational admission by quota system, the location of federal establishments, etc.

Though this was one of the original motivations for federalism, this principle was introduced explicitly into the federal system after the civil war and the emergence of oil. There was to be a minimum level of resources for each state and local government, almost on the basis of the consociational model or grand coalition for national management.

This underscored the view that Nigeria's federalism evolved fissiparously rather than by aggregation. Moreover, this consociational arrangement was associated with increasing tendency towards a unitary system of government through the increasing concentration of powers and resources at the federal level. Indeed, by 1988, this trend had gone so far under the Babangida regime that the federal government started giving financial grants directly to local governments, without bothering to go through the increasingly marginalized states.

The Current State of Nigerian Federalism

It is important to emphasize that the most important single factor in the development of Nigerian federalism up to its present state has been the unified command of the military. This is what gave administrative fiat to some of the fundamental changes in the federal system with little resistance from the states and local governments - the endless re-divisions of the polity, relegation of the derivation formula in revenue allocation, the predominance of the federal tier of government and the massive concentration of powers - political and economic - and resources at the federal level and at the expense of the states. Hence the current state of Nigerian federalism is characterized by five main features. These are unitarism rather than decentralization and national integration; distributive federalism; the controversies over federal character and indigeneity; the politicization of ethnicity; and the increasing tensions of federalism marked with sporadic conflicts.

First, is unitarism and national integration. The unified command structure of the military typically demands a unitary state under military dictatorship. This started from the 1966 coup and seems to have reached a climax under the maximum state apparatus of the Abacha regime. The process involved a dialectical asymmetry. While the commitment to minority interest pandered to the consociational model of coalition in national management, the fissiparous tendencies involved in persistent re-divisions of the polity, through five phases of state creation since 1967, progressively wreaked the states and simultaneously strengthened the forces of unitarism.

But while this enforced military unitarism has been making it more difficult for individual states or groups of states to challenge the federal system effectively as in the civil war, this federal security seems to have been purchased at the expense of its political relevance. This is because unitary rule and centralized authority has persistently failed to become synonymous with national integration in all but a formal sense. While the states and local governments became weaker and more dependent on the increasingly predominant federal center, these small states tried to keep their distance from the center and, therefore, from the heart of the nation as much as possible. The federal center has thus tended to become more politically and psychological remote from the states. Federal character and indigeneity made this national integration even more problematic.

There is also the issue of federal character and indigeneity. Taken together (and they both developed from the 1979 Constitution), the principles of federal character and its notorious quota system and indignity made individual and group integration into the Nigerian nation-state even more problematic. The quota system in the practice of federal character made Nigerian citizens unequal in places of employment, educational placement, etc.

As critics have pointed out, the principle of federal character panders to mediocrity and promotes universal incompetence, as it strikes at the heart of high standards and professionalism. It also tends to enable elites from the disadvantaged areas to exploit the political system by gaining access to socio-economic opportunities to which they are not entitled by merit. While the principle helps the indigenous of some areas, it undermines the development of national elites. Observers argue that these aberrations arise because there are no legitimate and objective criteria for the objectives sought by federal character. It has thus tended to become an arbitrary instrument of patronage, abuse of office and political alienation, in many instances. Curiously also, this federal character hardly protects minority interests.

Indigeneity compounds these problems by giving a preference to primordiality over national integration. If individuals cannot claim equal rights across the country on the basis of residence, birth and marriage, what is to be the melting pot for the development of Nigeria's nationhood and national integration? If Nigerians must go back to their states of origin before they can exercise basic constitutional rights and privileges, how can they be expected to identify with Nigeria wherever they live in the country?

But some concessions are possible in these arguments. It is true that Nigerians in the less-developed states and parts of the country have legitimate fears of domination and lack of access, if all activities were open to free competition without reservations. But is this not a legitimate case for the careful articulation of affirmative action programs as in South Africa, for marginalized areas and social groups?

Third, is the distributive approach to federalism. Observers of Nigeria's federalism insist that the country has adopted a distributive approach to federalism. This is said to be evident from the re-divisions of states and local governments in the polity; the predominant status of fiscal sharing or revenue allocation formula; the application of the consociational model with minimum resource allocation to each state and local government; and the looming status of federal character and its quota system in the sharing of jobs, educational placement, federal investments, etc.

The problems with this distributive obsession in federalism are first, that it panders to economics, yet people do not live by bread alone. There are also important constitutional, political, cultural, historical and other factors, which induce nationalities to federate. When these non-distributive fundamentals in federalism are undermined, they tend to vitiate the distributive rewards of federating. Thus, if states are forced into unitarism and lose their relative federal autonomy, there is hardly any distributive material compensation or grants that can offset this.

This is clearly one reason why with the emasculation of the constitutional basis of federalism by military unitarism in Nigeria, no satisfactory distributive formula has been found to restore confidence in the imposed centralized system and ensure social justice, peace and stability in the polity. Hence questions of political and legislative powers, relative state autonomy and participatory development by all geo-political units, have to be settled amicably before mundane distributive politics can be of undying significance.

Again, a concession is required. As Nigerian federalism has evolved from the desegregation of a whole, rather than the aggregation of fissiparous units, the logic of distribution is naturally inherent in the federal system. So the real issue is how to ensure the correct balance between this distributive approach and other relevant modalities for federalism in Nigeria.

The political mobilization of ethnicity and the tensions associated is yet another key feature. Observers of Nigerian federalism have been warning about the dangers of the politicization of ethnicity in the country. There are two issues here. One is the persistent conflict between ethnicity and citizenship, especially when ethnogenesis becomes a self-perpetuating phenomenon. Put differently, how can the Nigerian socio-economic melting pot ensure that though Nigerians belong to different ethnic groups, their loyalties as citizens of Nigeria (as members of the Nigerian federal nation-state) can become superior and transcend the primordiality of their narrow ethnic identity and loyalty?

How does a Nigerian develop from being a Yoruba, Ijaw, Ibo, Hausa, Efik, Edo, etc. into becoming first and foremost a Nigerian citizen? One clear way is to play down the political uses of ethnicity for educational placement, job, etc. Clearly, the insistence on state of origin, indigeneity and quota systems pander to this politicization of ethnicity.

The attributes of the current federal system in the country have culminated in the emergence of serious tensions, and even conflicts. The generic cause of these tensions of federalism may be traced to the question of social justice. When nationalities, communities and individuals perceive a pattern of systematic social injustice in the functioning of any political system, this generates alienation, tensions and conflicts. Questions of us and them geo-political or ethnic domination, exploitation and even repression will arise.

These questions have been raised since the initial phase of Nigerian federalism with respect to northern domination, arising from the pre-dominant size and population of the then Northern Region. Then between 1966 and 1970, this cry of domination was compounded by the imposition of military unitarism, and these led to civil war.

In the post-civil war period, persistent tensions have been generated from:

166

- the re-imposition of centralized authority by the military, again with associated fiscal unitarism;

- jettisoning of the principle of derivation in federal revenue allocation for less equitable principles;

- fissiparous re-divisions of the states and local governments which marginalized them further;

- controversies over the principle of federal character and its alienating quota system;

- the non-integrating impact of the politics of indigeneity and ethnicity;

- increasing concentration of power and resources in the federal center and their corresponding denial to the states and local governments.

The politics of militarism have exacerbated these tensions and prompted current demands for the re-structuring of the federal system.

Nigeria's Federal Options in the 21st Century

These issues prompt the elaboration of Nigeria's federal options for the 21st century in order to meet some objectives. One of these is that these options should be consonant with the dominant political (and even economic) values and paradigms of the next millennium as we can project them. Second, these federal options must in some ways provide significant solutions to the major problems and tensions of federalism in the country. Third, these options must provide fresh dynamism for the closer integration and essential transformation of Nigeria as a competitive polity in the next century.

Several studies and related endeavors have preceeded some critical insights into the socio-economic contours of the next millennium. The on-going mega-trends of a world on the threshold of the 21st century reveal that the next century will be an era of cultural nationalism and the triumph of the individual.

These mean that the political values and ideals of human rights, freedom of cultural expression and group identity in language, democracy, individualism and a sense of community as well as entrepreneurial politics, will dominate the political landscape of the next century. Hence political structures and systems that are inconsistent or hostile to these political values and ideals will be swept away, or come under intense pressures, which the nation-state may not survive.

The implied paradigm shift by these unfolding political values and ideals, therefore, emphasize democratization, abiding respect for human rights, individual and community autonomy and greater political space for pluralism and cultural nationalism. The demands for people-centered development, open accountability, participatory politics, putting the people first, people's empowerment, the politics of consensus rather than authoritarianism, and cultural pluralism will dictate the priorities of public policy.

How will these political transformations of the 21st Century affect Nigerian federalism? The answer is in several ways. First and foremost, the paradigm shift of the next millennium will be incompatible with the current structures of military dictatorship and authoritarian governance. They will also be inconsistent with the current political and fiscal unitarism in the country. Similarly, the structures and patterns of geo-political dominance in the country will be incompatible with the competitive politics and democratic spirit of popular participation and cultural nationalism or the next millennium. And so will the individualism, human rights posture and entrepreneurial politics of the future be incompatible with the current practice of federal character, the politics of ethnicity and the relegation of the principles of derivation in national revenue allocation.

Quebec in Canadian Federalism has been giving examples of the paradigm shift of the 21st century. The cultural nationalism, separatist sentiments and pressures for greater equity and pluralist expression in the Quebec experience are clear lessons for the re-structuring of Nigerian federalism.

There are two sets of options involved in reshaping Nigerian federalism for the challenges of the next millennium that are indicated above. These are:

(a) options for alternative forms of federalism or for the practice of federalism and

(b) options for realizing these changes in terms of the alternative political programs for erecting the alternative federalist structures and practices.

These should be separated because (b) is a set of means for realizing federal goals in (a).

With respect to the first option, there are about six challenges and policy options to address, viz:

(1) return to the status quo ex ante or return to the pre-1966 federal system;

(2) redistribution of federal and state powers with respect to the exclusive,

concurrent and residual legislative lists;

(3) political-security re-structuring: this is a sub-set of option (2) and has to be combined with option (4);

(4) practice of fiscal federalism;

(5) Confederalism;

(6) Termination of military dictatorship and institution of rotational presidency.

Though option (6) on the termination of military dictatorship is not inherently federal, it is relevant because the perversion of options (1) to (4) and the strongest and most persistent assaults on Nigerian federalism, have come from military dictatorships whose regimes are incompatible with the practice of federalism. The issue of rotational presidency arises in connection with the concentration of powers and resources in the federal government, which makes access to the presidency so critical for access to national resources and power. The denial of access to the presidency is also one of the dominant sources of allegations of geo-political domination of the country - whether as a federal or unitary system. Rotational presidency removes this source of acrimony in the polity, though it must be admitted that the presidency per se has not been a source of major changes in the federal system. So we now discuss option (1) to (5), by noting that options (3) and (4) cannot stand-alone. A unitary system is excluded from these options because it negates federalism.

Options (1) on return to the pre-1966 federal system and option (5) on a confederal system can be easily settled. The pre-1966 federal system was based on a tricolor regional system that has atrophied, and that system pre-dates the era of oil wealth. The creation of so many states since 1967 makes it difficult to imagine the abolition of these states and a return to the old regional system, though its distribution of powers and fiscal system may still have valid attributes. Such attributes can be captured in options (2), (3) and (4). The country's present level of oil wealth and development have also become too complex to be adequately captured by the pre-1966 federal system.

The confederal option (5) is typically demanded as a result of frustrations over the refusal or inability to operate the other federal options. This implies that if the country can negotiate seriously over options (2) to (4) then confederacy could be discounted. But there are those who argue that the country's agonies over political and fiscal unitarism, federal dominance, federal character, uneven development and related problems do not suggest that the right choices will be made over options (2) to (4). In the circumstances, therefore, they feel that the confederal option is relevant. Yet, it is possible to regard this confederal option as a threat that should force political actors to choose among options (2) to (4). So the confederal option arises when the other options on federal restructuring fail.

The second option dealing with power redistribution and decentralization is an up-dated version of the pre-1966 federal system in which the country re-negotiates the distribution of legislative powers and resource allocation among the three tiers of government. This redistribution and decentralization is necessitated by the current unitary deformities of the original federal system, the increased number of states and local governments, and the post-1973 oil wealth in the country.

In this re-distribution, the concentration of powers and resources at the federal level has to be whittled down in favor of the states and local governments. The original autonomy of each tier of government in its sphere of authority has to be restored. Then which powers should be on the exclusive legislative, recurrent and residual legislative lists have to be negotiated among representatives of the different parts of the country. The precise outcome will depend on the interplay of geo-political and social forces in the country.

But at the very minimum, this re-distribution and decentralization of powers and resources must restore credible control over the development of each tier of government to it with adequate statutory resources for such development. Hence there should be no question of the federal center lording it over the states and local governments in virtually all matters, as has been the case for years under military dictatorship. This option allows for the operation of the consociational model without its current recessive integration.

Option (3), political - military restructuring is a version of option (2) and it arises if the country were to opt for option (1) of adopting the pre-1966 federal system. On account of the existing horrendous distortions and massive concentrations of power and resources in the federal system, this option requires national negotiations to eliminate these distortions. The specific areas requiring restructuring here include:

- reduction of the exclusive legislative powers of the federal government, e.g. over internal security, national revenue and control over resources located within each state and local government;

- expansion of the recurrent legislative powers in order to give states and local governments greater relative autonomy;

- provision for fairer representation and control of all states over the military and security organs (police, prisons, customs, etc) at all levels of command;

- ensuring fairer distribution of top positions in all public services and parastatals in order to terminate geo-political domination;

- review of the principles of federal character, protection f minority interests and indignity, which have been abused in the past, in order to make these principles more consistent with equitable access to national resources and with the socio-economic integration of the country.

Hence this option is wider than option (2), with respect to its security, access, equity and integrative objectives and practices.

Fiscal federalism is the fourth option. Ideally, this is part of option (1) to (3) above. But because of the intense bitterness and tensions over the massive concentration of national resources at the federal level under the fiscal unitarism of the military dictatorships, this option bears spelling out separately. In reality, it does not constitute a complete federal system, but is a part of options (1) to (3) above.

In the pre-1966 federal system, fiscal federalism was based mainly on the principle of derivation in revenue allocation, its basic tenet is that each tier of government should:

- enjoy adequate statutory revenue allocation for the discharge of its constitutional functions;

- the principles of revenue allocation among the federal, state and local governments are to be determined democratically, and not imposed by the federal government.

- the fiscal functions of each tier of government are to derive from the constitution, so that they cannot be emasculated or changed through administrative fiat by any sphere of government.

- all the tax and expenditure powers of each tier of government have to be approved by the National Assembly for each fiscal year in accordance with the constitution, in order to check the abusive extra-budgetary fiscal operations that were so common under the military dictatorships.

Table 1

Recent Revenue Allocation under Fiscal Unitarism (N Billion)

Distribution of Federation Account Revenue

	1995	1996	1997	1998	1999 (%)
Federal Governments (48.5%)	79	87	101	92	48.5
State Governments (24%)	38	43	50	45	24.0
Local Government (20%)	32	36	42	37	20
Special Fund (7.5%)	12	13	15	15	7.5
	189	189	208	189	

Source: Obtained from various budgets of the Federal Governments of Nigeria 1996/98.

Table 2: VAT Revenue Sharing Formula

	1998	1999
Federal Government	25	15
State Government	45	50
Local Government	30	35

Source: Obtained from various budgets of the Federal Governments of Nigeria 1996/98.

Tables 1 and 2 depict the revenue allocation formulas in recent years under the fiscal unitarism of the military. They have been starving the states of revenue, stunting the growth of the economies of state and causing excessive dependence on the federal government for fiscal bail-out by the states and local governments. All these have been severely undermining the autonomy of the states and local governments.

For the more appropriate bases of fiscal federalism in the earlier years of the federal systems, see Tables A, B, C in the Appendix. They each depict a more robust revenue basis for the states than Tables 1 and 2.

Given the options in (1) to (6) above, which should Nigeria choose as we enter the 21st century? The answer depends on the make of choice adopted and the relative weights that Nigerians as individuals, and groups, political parties and tiers of government want to attach to the various elements and criteria in these options. But it would seem that option (6) is undesirable, while option (1) on the pre-1966 federal system is out-dated and option (5) weakens the federation excessively. So the real alternatives are between options

(2) and (3), with option (4) as a sub-set of either. Both options lead to a relatively weaker federal center than the country has known so far, and to the existence of more vigorous states and local governments. This coincides with the emerging trends of democratic participation, more binding human and community rights, cultural nationalism and people's empowerment towards 21st century.

It is important to emphasize that whichever option is chosen, should be necessarily subject to periodic review, say, every five years. This should be in the light of the dynamics of national development and integration. There can be no permanent solution to the problem of appropriate choice of the best structures for a nation - state; the structures evolve in time according to the historical experiences of the country. Constitutional amendments, referenda and similar mechanisms are used for these periodic reviews. Nigeria needs the exclusion of military dictatorship so that a democratic enabling environment can be created for what is essentially a political process of learning by doing. This is how federal systems develop and endure around the world.

Approaches to the choice of Federal Options for the 21st Century

The next set of options to deal with are those dealing with the modalities for choosing among the different options (1) to (6) discussed above.

If we exclude the approach of military imposition or totalitarian fiat as undemocratic (and ruled out by option (6) above), then four conceivable methods of choosing among these federal options are:

1.   Constitutional amendment;

2.   Constitutional commission followed by a full constitutional conference for re-working a federal constitution;

3.   Sovereign national conference;

4.   National plebiscites.

The (1) and (4) options have been included for the sake of completeness.

For the purpose of choosing federal option for the 21st century, some major modalities have been identified. These include constitutional amendment, constitutional commission and conferences and Sovereign National Conference.

Constitutional Amendment

A mere Constitutional Amendment can hardly reshape Nigeria's federal system fundamentally and satisfactorily. The constitution itself is still being finalized - and there are debates about whether we should be trying to use the 1992 or 1979 constitution. So the constitutional amendments required for either of these constitutions will be so many that they may amount to re-writing a new constitution. Then there are those who consider both constitutions as basically inadequate and would want a brand new constitution.

Constitutional Commission and Conference

On the face of it, this looks like a plausible approach to federal restructuring in Nigeria. But it is not generally favored for some reasons. One is that the basis for representation at a conference will be determined by an extant federal government, which some may feel is not genuinely democratic and representative of the cross -section of political forces in the country. Second, the critics of this approach argue that if the existing federal government is not itself democratic or legitimate, then it can hardly be relied upon to fairly choose the true representatives of the people for a constitutional conference. Third, for these reasons, the critics feel that a federal constitution that will be fashioned through this faulty approach will itself be seriously flawed. It will not be able to command the full confidence and respect of the entire national population.

The burden of this argumentation is also that the existing political structures of representation in the country - census, states, local governments, electoral registers, political parties etc - are so badly distorted through years of military distortion of the federal system, that any constituent assembly that they produce are also likely to be severely distorted.

Sovereign National Conference

Many sections of the population demand the direct representation of the different nationalities in the country at a national conference for federal restructuring. These nationalities are the units that have federated, and are required to federate better in future. So it is the direct representatives of these nationalities (about 250 of them) that should meet to fashion a new federal system for the country.

The rights to be negotiated at a sovereign national conference belong collectively to these nationalities, and not to individuals. Hence it is these nationalities bearing rights that are to be represented, and not amorphous and atomistic selfish individuals. This is reconstituting the nation - state, not merely restructuring it.

The sovereignty of this national conference is equally significant. It is supposed to be independent of the existing governments in the country, which is regarded as greatly flawed on many grounds. The colonial government that first created the Nigerian federation was severely flawed in this regard. The government is regarded as inadequately representative of all major nationality groups and their interests; it is not genuinely democratic; and it is also viewed as inequitable by critics with respect to its unequal composition, unequal access to the state and class - partisan character as an executive committee of the ruling class and its allies.

For these and related reasons, the sovereign national conference (SNC) is not just to re-shape, restructure, or modify the nation - state on the basis of the existing social contract. Rather, the SNC is to re-born or re-constitute the nation-state afresh. The entire basis of association in the state is to be re-examined, re-negotiated and reformulated. This is a fundamental overhauling of the state and building it from scratch, or on the basis of entirely new and democratic principles.

This suggests that the tensions and cleavages in the existing nation state are too deep to be settled without direct negotiations among the nationality stake-holders in the state. The entire basis upon which sovereignty was bestowed on the nation-state is to be re-examined and re-enacted.

The choice of the best modality again depends on the political setting in the country. If the various stake-holders in Nigerian federalism—state governments, civil society and the private sector—can agree to be persuaded to trust the government to ensure equitable election of representatives and unfettered choice at a constituent assembly, then this modality is cheaper than the other two. But its outcome hinges critically on the democratic commitment and sincerity of the government as well as the confidence of the populace in the government.

Where these conditions are not met because of the depth of tensions and insidious nature of cleavages, then a sovereign national conference is required. Nigerians themselves should be allowed and encouraged to make the choice.

Epilogue

The urgent imperative for a change of Nigeria's federalism for the 21st century has been evident for some time. This derives from the massive distortions and severe tensions and conflicts of the current federal system. Its inability to endure for much longer and the need for re-tooling the country for the challenges of democratization, human rights, participatory development and cultural nationalism of the next millennium are familiar.

The deformities of the current federal system include its military perversion towards a unitary system; the associated massive concentration of powers and resources at the federal level that dominates the country excessively; the uneven access to national resources; the abuses of the principles of federal character and indignity; and the parochialism of ethnic politics in the system. All these have nearly pushed the country to the brink under the pressures of military dictatorships.

The main options for restructuring the federation include a return to the pre-1966 federal system, the redistribution and decentralization of powers under this system, politico-military restructuring, fiscal federalism, confederalism, and the replacement of military dictatorship with rotational presidency.

The possible political approaches for choosing among these options are constitutional amendment, constitutional commission and conference, a sovereign national conference and plebiscite. The country should create the democratic enabling environment for the unfettered debate and choices among these alternatives. These choices and the restructuring of the federal system should be seen as part of a periodic process of learning by doing, which is central to the establishment of viable and durable political systems around the world.

REFERENCES

Achebe, C. 1983. *The Trouble with Nigeria.* Enugu: Fourth Dimension Publishers.

Ayoade, J.A. 1993. *Federalism in Nigeria – Problems with the Solution*, Faculty Lecture. University of Ibadan.

Awa, E.O. 1983. *National Integration in Nigeria – Problems and Prospects.* Ibadan: NISER Distinguished Lectures, No 5.

_____. 1991 "Federalism in Nigeria – Agenda for its Future Development" *The Centre for the Study of Federalism Notebook*, Philadelphia, Vol. XVI, 3, Winter.

Adamolekun, L. and Ayo, S.B. 1989. "The Evolution of the Nigerian Federal System", *Publius*, 19 Winter.

Batch, Daniel. 1997. "Indigeneity, Ethnicity and Federalism" in O. Oyediran *et al* eds. *Transition Without End.* Ibadan: Vantage Publishers, Ch. 14.

Federal Republic of Nigeria 1987, *Report of the Political Bureau* (Lagos).

————. *The Constitution of the Federal Republic of Nigeria*, 1959, 1979 and 1992 (Lagos).

Jinadu, L.A. 1985. "Federalism, the Consociational State and Ethnic Conflict in Nigeria" *Publius*, 15, Spring 1985.

Mbanefoh, G.F. 1989 "Public Finance" in M.O. Kayode and Bala Usman eds. *Nigeria Since Independence – The First 25 Years – The Economy*, Vol. II. Ibadan: Heinemann Educational Books.

Naisbitt, J. and Aburdene, P. 1990. *Megatrends 2000.* London: Pan Books.

Olugbemi, S.O. ed. *Alternative Political Futures for Nigeria.* (Lagos; NPSA).

Onimode, Bade 1998. "Revenue Allocation Formula – Putting the Issue in Proper Perspective" in J.D. Ojo ed. *Proceedings of the Conference on the 1995 Nigerian Draft Constitution.* Ibadan: Only Child Prints.

CHAPTER 9

Pluralism, Federalism and Economic Development: A Comparative Analysis of Brazil and Nigeria

Tade O. Okediji

Introduction

For much of its existence as a subject of economic inquiry, scholarly analysis of economic development did not include examinations of non-quantifiable variables such as ethnicity, culture or religion. The difficulty in quantifying these variables created a dearth in economic analysis of their impact on economic development potential. [1]

Despite recent advances in incorporating socio-economic variables in the scholarly discourse on economic development, there remains much work to be done. For example, the relationship between ethnicity and the viability of economic development is one that, while not clearly evident, can be powerfully influential on the country's prospects for development. This is due especially to the complex and embedded idiosyncrasies that exist between and among ethnic aggregations (Collier 2000; Easterly and Levine 1997; Alesina and Perotti 1996; Alesina, Ozler, Roubini and Swagel 1996; Mauro 1995). Ethnic identity may be religious, as in the case of Northern Ireland between the Catholics and Protestants or in India among Hindus, Muslims and Christians. It can also be cultural whereby a group of individuals, through shared traditional customs, identify themselves as an ethnic group. In this case ethnic identity can be considered as "tribalistic", that is, identity is constructed through a shared sense of kinship. Finally, ethnic identity can be linguistic as members of a group share the same language or dialect such as the Yorubas in southwestern Nigeria or the Igbos in southeastern Nigeria. Ethnic identity is frequently based on primordiality, that is, physical attributes shared by members of the group such as tribal marks, skin complexion, height and/or certain dialects spoken within a language. Of course, none of these distinctions are exact or finite: ethnic identity may derive from any combination of the individual characteristic as much as from one single characteristic. Societies that are ethnically heterogeneous are more susceptible to ethnic conflict as a result of social dualism (Boeke 1953). The potential for ethnic conflict is heightened the greater the number of ethnic groups vying for control or access to limited economic resources, as witnessed in sub-Saharan African countries in the last few decades.[2]

The influence of ethnic fragmentation on the climate for economic development in heterogeneous societies can be manifested in one or both of the following cases. First, if the form of governance is perceived by members of the polity to yield a disproportionate amount of political power or control to certain ethnic group(s), the threat of ethnic hegemony potentially undermines the unity of the polity. Ethnic conflict at the local or regional level leads to entrenched cycles of civil conflict, engendering a climate of chronic political instability. Second, if the distribution of economic resources between or among the regions of the country is disparate, and exhibits a correlation to ethnic orientation, the skewed distribution of wealth will effect uneven economic development. Additionally, it can exacerbate ethnic conflict due to rent-seeking behavior by the dominant ethnic groups (Alesina and Tabellini 1989; Alesina and Drazen 1991).

This paper is a comparative analysis of the significance of ethnic/racial heterogeneity on the economic development of Nigeria and Brazil. It focuses explicitly on the question of whether a particular structure of democratic government, in this case federalism, is especially suited for economic development objectives in multi ethnic/racial societies. The paper posits that these countries are likely to derive a higher premium from democratic governance if a federal system is employed. To the extent that a legitimate democracy stems from the mandate of the people, federalism offers the prospect of minimizing the sense of alienation that often is the impetus for civil strife and threats of secession. One of the particular advantages of a federal system is the simultaneous protection of group and individual rights against the tyranny of the majority. This can be accomplished through institutional devices such as a bicameral legislature in which one house is elected on the basis of population, while in the other house the sub-units are represented equally.

Federalism is generally defined as the distribution of powers among the various levels of government within a country, often rooted in a constitutional division of power among the federal, state and local governments. Within a democratic system, a federal structure may be strategic in sustaining economic development by providing an effective framework for the management and allocation of resources. Riker's characteristics of federalism in the United States suggests three notable properties of a federal system namely: (i) coming-together-federalism, (ii) demos constraining federalism and (iii) symmetrical federalism (Stepan 1999). The first, coming-together-federalism, involves a bargain in which previously sovereign polities make a conscious decision to concede aspects of their sovereignty in order to pool resources for increasing collective security and to facilitate the accomplishment of social and economic goals. In the second, 'the demos' is fully represented and no one individual or group may act except through these representatives hence the term, 'demos-constraining federalism'. Finally, a symmetrically federal state guarantees each state within the federation the same constitutional powers. For Nigeria in particular, as well as other African countries, a federal system with any of these three properties have the potential, at least in theory to effectively counter historical forces unleashed through the colonial process, that continue to generate ethnic strife and retard prospects for economic development.

Nigeria and Brazil share important characteristics that facilitate meaningful comparative study. From a demographic perspective these countries rank first and second, respectively, as having the largest number of peoples of African descent in the world.[3]

Additionally, of all non-African countries in the world that have a significant population of peoples of African descent, Brazil is the one in which cultural ties to Africa are the strongest. These cultural ties are expressed in linguistic forms such as the Yoruba language, syncretic religion such as Umbanda, and through practices that range from agro-dietary methods to musical rhythms. These strong ties represent the basis of ethnic identification for most Afro-Brazilians. Nigeria and Brazil have histories of military rule and both are currently under democratic regimes. Additionally, both countries have adopted federal systems though the impetus for adoption was different in each case. In Brazil a federal structure was adopted to promote national integration and provide a political framework for the management of large territories. In Nigeria, the adoption of a federal structure was primarily intended to facilitate political unity in a highly fractured society.

In terms of economic development the countries exhibit an uneven regional economic development pattern that, in Brazil, has a racial dimension and, in Nigeria, an ethnic dimension. Brazil and Nigeria represent significant economies in their respective continents and in the global economy. Brazil, the sixth most populous nation and the eighth largest economy in the world is, by far, the largest economy in South America and was considered at the 'take-off' stage in sixties (Rostow 1961). In spite of its status as an emerging economy, World Bank (1997) reports indicate that Brazil has one of the highest levels of income inequality in the world. Nigeria, the most populous country on the African continent is the second largest economy in sub-Saharan Africa. Yet, despite a fairly large endowment of natural resources, predominantly oil and natural gas, Nigeria is still considered one of the least developed countries in the world. Among the most significant reasons for this marked state of underdevelopment is a history of political instability due to military coups that have been justified primarily by ethno-religious differences.

This chapter evaluates the use of a federal system as an instrument of containment and/ or management in advancing economic development objectives in large heterogeneous societies. The organization of the paper is as follows: Sections II and III, respectively, discuss ethnic heterogeneity in Brazil and Nigeria, and sketches the development of the current governance structure in each country with a particular emphasis on the evolution of the federal structure. Section IV places the discussion in the previous two sections in context of an analysis of several theories of federalism. It then examines the efficacy of the federal structure adopted by each country in light of their respective histories, and presents some implications for economic development. I present my conclusions in section V.

Ethnic Heterogeneity in the Brazilian Federal Context

Contemporary Brazilian society is a combination of features of the most sophisticated industrial nations as well as characteristics of the poor agricultural societies in the developing world (Eakin 1997). Brazil is divided into five geographic regions: the north, northeast, south, center-west and the southeast. Currently, the country is comprised of twenty-six states and a federal district. In 1996, the states were further subdivided into 5,581 municipalities. The country has been officially identified as a federal republic with a presidential form of government since 1946.

Heterogeneity and Economic Development

One of the lasting legacies of colonialism in Brazil is a highly stratified society in which socio-economic status is based on skin color. Racial categories in Brazil tend to serve as proxies for ethnicity. Thus for example, "White" includes Portuguese, German, Italian, Spanish, Polish, and inter-racial (mixed white and black), otherwise known as "Mulattoes" or "Pardos". The category "Black", and "other" includes Japanese, Arab and Amerindian. In the nineteenth century there were concerted efforts to create a more 'Europeanized' Brazil, or better known as the 'whitening' of Brazil. This was accomplished through a liberal immigration policy dedicated to the specific purpose of increasing the number of European immigrants[4] to eliminate blacks through miscegenation (Skidmore, 1999a; Lesser, 1999). Miscegenation was initiated and promoted by the Brazilian elite as part of a policy of presenting Brazil to the western world as a "modernized" country in order to encourage continued European immigration. In a sense, the government feigned racial inclusion and perpetuated a myth of a racial democracy (Hasenbalg 1984: 2).

Unlike the United States and most European societies racial categorization in Brazil is not 'bi-polar', that is, racial categorization is not defined primarily as black or white. The 1999 socio-economic indicators reported by the Brazilian Institute for Geography and Statistics indicate that, of Brazil's 158.2 million inhabitants, 54% are white, 39.5% mulatto, 5.7% black, .8% Asian, and Indian. These ostensibly definitive figures and categories obscure the multifaceted nature of racial categorization. For example, a "mulatto" in one region of Brazil could be considered "white" in another region, while a "white" individual from Bahia would not necessarily be considered "white" in Santa Catarina, a southern state with a large German population (Hanchard 1999). These ethnically derived distinctions convolute racial stereotypes and compound racial categorization/definition within the country. It also illustrates the preoccupation of the society with skin color classifications. Although Brazil characterizes itself as a racially democratic or race-neutral state, socio-economic indicators demonstrate that race plays a prominent role in Brazilian society. Haselbalg (1983) demonstrates a strong correlation between skin color and social status in Brazil. Socio-economic inequalities based on race are evident in employment, levels of educational attainment, quality of health care and standard of living (Costa, 1983; Silva, 1985). Whites have better access to jobs than other racial groups, due to their better access to education. They are also able to advance on the occupational ladder at a much faster pace than any other racial group (Lovell 1999). Indeed, Brazil stands out among developing as well as developed countries for its stark regional and social disparities. For an industrialized state, it has one of the most unequal income distributions of any country (See tables 1-2).

Table 1

Some Socioeconomic Characteristics of Brazil

	South	South East	Center West	North East	North
Percentage of National Territory	6.75%	10.8%	18.8%	18.3%	45.2%
Percentage of Total Population	15.3%	43.7%	7%	29%	5%
[a]Income Inequality (Gini Coefficient)	.545	.546	.584	.590	.564
[b]Illiteracy Rate of People 15 years or older	8.1%	8.1%	11.1%	27.5%	11.8%
[c]Average monthly Income (U.S. $, 1999)	$210.58	$227	$191.76	$104.11	$145.88
Percentage Contribution to GDP	15.72%	62.60%	5.86%	12.58%	3.24%

[a]The Gini Coefficient for Brazil is .575.
[b]Average Illiteracy Rate for Brazil is 13.8%.
[c]For employed population 10 years and older.
[d]Urban areas only.
Sources: IBGE, PNAD, 1999-2000

Table 2

Income Inequality in Brazil, 1960-1990

	1960	1970	1980	1990
Lowest 20%	3.5%	3.2%	3.0%	2.3%
Middle 60%	42.1%	34.6%	30.9%	31.6%
Top 20%	54.4%	62.2%	66.1%	66.1%
	100%	100%	100%	100%
Top 10%	39.7%	47.8%	51.0%	49.7%
Top 5%	27.7%	34.9%	33.8%	35.8%

Source: S. Kaufman Purcell and R. Roett, *Brazil under Cardoso* (Boulder: Rienner Publishers, 1997), P.73.

Historically, the migrant patterns to the country may have left subtle racial/ethnic characteristics or perceptions regarding the different regions (see tables 3 and 4).

The industrial revolution that occurred in the Brazil of 1940's and 50's created an uneven regional economic development pattern and also influenced race relations (Bastide 1965; Van den Berghe 1967; Fernandes 1969). By this time, regions within the country had become synonymous with a certain racial presence. Europeans dominated the south, blacks the northeast, native Indians the Amazon and the southeast was a melting pot of different races. Today, however, it has a majority white population as it did during the colonial period. Industrialization was confined to the south and southeast, especially in Sao Paulo, Rio de Janeiro and Minas Gerais where the White majority was and remains concentrated. The region represents the heart of the industrial triangle, which accounts for over half of the nation's manufactured products.

On the other hand, the northeastern region which accounts for 30% of the population and about 15% of the gross domestic product (Eakin 1997: 69-75), is populated primarily by non-whites. Although this region was the first major colonial settlement in Brazil, and served as the bedrock of the sugar plantation, today, it is the most impoverished region with wide spread poverty. Most of the population is comprised of blacks and mulattos, the vast majority of whom are employed in agriculture. The literacy rate in this region is about 60%, compared to the national average of 88% (Eakin 1997: 69-75). The impoverished conditions have led to high levels of migration to the interior of the country.

Southern Brazil has the highest standard of living in the country. Income per capita in some areas in the south, such as Teutonia, is about triple that of the national average (Eakin 1997: 85).[5] Additionally, in terms of economic development, both the south and the southeast benefited significantly from the presence of industries such as manufacturing and large-scale agriculture, which in turn is attributed to the fact that European migration to Brazil in the eighteenth and nineteenth century was to the south and southeast (Skidmore 1999). The south also boasts the worlds' largest hydroelectric dam near Iguacu Falls. Culturally and ethnically, the southeast is a transition zone between the northeast, which is dominated by people of African descent, and the south, which is dominated by people of European descent.

Table 3

Total Population and Distribution by Color/Racial Groups and by Region: Brazil, 1999

	Color Group				
Region	White (%)	Brown (%)	Black (%)	Native Indians & Asians (%)	Total
North	28.4	68.3	2.3	1.03	100.3
Northeast	29.7	64.5	5.6	.16	99.9
Southeast	64.0	28.4	6.7	.82	99.9
South	83.6	12.6	3.0	.70	99.9
Center West	46.2	49.4	3.5	.83	100.0
Total	**(54.0)**	**(39.5)**	**(5.7)**	**(0.8)**	**100.0**

Source: PNAD, IBGE, 2000

Table 4

Distribution of Color/Racial Groups by Region: Brazil, 1999

Region	White (%)	Brown (%)	Black (%)	Native Indians & Asians (%)
		Color Group		
North	1.38	3.33	.114	.05
Northeast	8.60	18.60	1.63	.048
Southeast	28.00	12.41	2.94	.361
South	12.78	1.93	.464	.107
Center West	3.24	3.48	.250	.059
Total	(54.00)	(39.75)	(5.39)	(.625)

Source: PNAD, IBGE, 2000.

The preceding overview illustrates the historical pattern of unbalanced regional development in Brazil. A sense of well-being increases as one moves from the northeast to southern Brazil. The northeast, as a whole, accounts for half of Brazil's poor. About 27.5% of the population over the age of 15 in the northeast is considered illiterate compared to the rate of 14% for all of Brazil. About 90% of all institutions of higher learning are located in the south and southeast again dominated by a racial "white" majority. This regional imbalance has produced large rural to urban migration which led to an increase in the urban crime rate due to social dislocation and economic deprivation.

The Evolution of a Federal State[6]

The centrifugal force of regionalism provided justification for the adoption of a federal structure in Brazil (Roett 1992: 5). Regionalism resulted from the distinct patterns of colonization, settlement, and economic growth during the colonial period (1500-1822) which was also accompanied by the accumulation of social influence and economic wealth by dominant families of the regions (Roett 1992: 5). The initial post-independence state was essentially a centralized bureaucratic empire that was continuously confronted with revolts in the form of secessionist threats by the different states and regions. These revolts reflected primary identification by citizens with the regions instead of the state. While the empire provided a central focus for national unity, it was clear that the autonomy, and ethnic concentration of the states and regions gave them significant power and influence in the political arena.

The Vargas era (1930-45) witnessed a decline in the autonomy of the states and regions attributed in part, to the manipulation of political power through the agency of an authoritarian government. Vargas successfully suppressed revolts that challenged the authority of centralized power. He accomplished this by building a corporatist state (one based on a hierarchical, organic view of society). In particular, a corporatist labor movement, with symmetrical associations of employees and workers, with the state as the arbiter between them, provided an important part of the built-in support he needed to remain in power (Skidmore 1999: 93). The federal structure evolved out of the 1945 election that initiated the fifth Brazilian constitution. The federal system accommodated the independence of the various regions, and their provinces or states, while preserving the core unity of the federation. Thus the federal structure served as a framework within which administrative and political objectives, as well as the social and economic demands of the states, were managed without posing a threat to national political identity. What may have appeared as nation-building was, instead, a strategic move by the drafters of the fifth Brazilian constitution to constrain threats of secession by promising a degree of autonomy to the various regions that comprised the old empire in a bid to secure the unity of the nation. For instance, the constitution recognized the predominant role of the central government, but restrictions were placed on its jurisdiction in an effort to prevent abusive intervention in the internal affairs of the states (Burns 1999: 387). Federalism thus addressed the issue of political instability without any substantive commitment to economic and social equality. Since its inception, then, the federal structure in Brazil has created a dependence on the central government rather than building the capacity of states to respond to local needs.

Under military rule (1964-1985), Brazil experienced centralized government or "strong" federalism in which the autonomy of states and municipalities were reduced and the powers of the state governors were restricted. Between 1964-1979 the military regime weakened the national congress through a combination of strategies which included repression and constitutional changes that strengthened the executive at the expense of the legislature. Further, an electoral system was designed to favor the government party (Mainwaring and Samuels 1999). This action diminished the capacity of the states to initiate socio-economic programs necessary to improve the standard and quality of life of the citizens in the respective regions. Additionally, centralization likely furthered the existing regional inequalities since the federal government was the dominant actor with respect to economic development objectives and initiatives. Without an established economic policy to address socio-economic conditions, centralization was certain to exacerbate existing inequalities, particularly since some of the poorer states depended heavily on the federal government for revenue transfers. For example, 12 of the 27 states in Brazil, all of whom are in the northeast and the Amazon, rely on the federal government for the majority of their revenues in form of revenue transfers (Mendes 2000).

The post-military Brazilian state went through a process of political liberalization that restructured the federal models of the Vargas and military eras. This occurred with the return to democratic government in the midst of severe economic crises. During the transition to democracy, state governors acquired increased political clout. This was partly due to the fact that for the first time since 1965 they were popularly elected, which gave them political power. Direct popular election created an incentive to be more attentive to state needs and less subservient to the federal government (Abrucio and Samuels 1997). State governors had control over employment policies for a wide array of positions ranging from unskilled labor to cabinet positions. The Governors also controlled nominations to many of the federal government posts within their states (Abrucio 1998). Finally, political power over mayors was also reserved to the governors. This also gave them increased political power as the number of municipalities increased from 4,198 in 1988 to 5,500 in 1995.

Post-1985 federalism most significantly altered the balance of power among the federal, state and local governments in the fiscal realm. Fiscal decentralization entailed the transfer of significant resources from the federal level to the states and municipalities. From 1980 to 1995 the total revenue available to state governments increased by 50%, and for municipalities by 130% (Noguera 1995: 32). While states gained political autonomy with these resources, fiscal decentralization simultaneously limited the capacity of the federal government to balance the national budget, pay off Brazil's significant debt, and maintain funds needed for investment programs to facilitate economic development. The 1988 constitutional convention devolved financial resources to the states without assigning them accompanying responsibilities (Bonfim and Shah 1991). Particularly, the 1988 constitution was inexplicit about the division of responsibilities among the federal government and subnational governments regarding socio-economic needs such as health, education, housing and welfare. This incertitude fueled a conflict among the federal, state and local government with each claiming that certain issues were the responsibilities of another. Ultimately, the federal government has carried the bulk of the burden, leaving it with diminished financial resources but growing demands (Tavares de Almeida 1995; Sola 1993; Abrucio 1998). However, the financial crisis that erupted in January 1999, and which ultimately led to currency devaluation, is one manifestation of the federal governments' attempt to reassert its role within the federal system by curtailing the powers of the states and local governments (Sola, Garman, and Margues 1997). This was accomplished by tying debt relief for states to reduced spending.

The Cardoso administration in place since 1995 has attempted, with some success, to further curtail the power of the state governments through changes in the fiscal distribution of revenue among the federal, state and local governments. In 1995, Congress passed the "Camata Law" which required states to limit payroll expenditures to 60% of net receipts by 1999. Failure to do so would mean risking losing federal funds (Mainwaring and Samuels 1999). The increased leverage provided by the Camata Law is, however, countered by strategies and the governance structure employed by Brazil. Presidential initiatives have to pass through the congress and the state governors. According to Tsebelis (1995), powerful governors add the dimension of veto power to thwart presidential initiatives by acting in collusion to veto the initiatives. Further, state governors can instruct members of congress from their states to block presidential initiatives that potentially threaten the autonomy of state governments.

The pendular swings between centralization and decentralization in the federal system have created difficult conditions for governability in Brazil. Proponents of centralization stress the origins of Brazil in the Portuguese empire, with the extensive bureaucracy and concentrated land ownership, which permitted the Portuguese elites to control huge territories. Together with the surprising continuity of relationship between pre-independent and post-independent Brazil, centralization guaranteed the integrity of Brazil's enormous territory under the command of the traditional elites (Camargo 1993). On the other hand, those who favor decentralization point to the necessity of recognizing the pluralistic character of the country. Decentralization has brought progress in economically strong states such as Sao Paulo and Rio de Janeiro. However, in poorer regions such as the Northeast, it has served to strengthen the power of the local elite (Carmago 1993).

The federal system in Brazil has failed to correct the regional inequalities. In fact, it may have exacerbated the regional inequalities in growth. This is partly attributed to the pendular swings between centralization and decentralization. The lack of consistency in implementation of the federal structure has also contributed to the inertia regarding the socio-economic inequalities within the country.

Ethnic Heterogeneity in Nigeria's Federal Context

The Evolution of a Federal State

The formal adoption of a federal system in Nigeria occurred in 1954 during British rule. The British considered federalism as a means to accommodate the diverse ethnic, religious and linguistic composition of the country (Adamolekun and Ayo 1989: 1). Because a federal structure required a division of power sharing between the central, regional and local governments, federalism was deemed especially beneficial for plural societies seeking unity while retaining aspects of their individual identities (*Ibid*).

The federal structure adopted by the colonial administration divided power equally between the federal and the regional governments. The Nigerian federation comprised of the eastern region dominated by Igbos, the western region dominated by Yorubas and the northern region dominated by the Hausa-Fulani. The adoption of a federal system, while aimed at regulating ethno-political conflicts was itself based on ethnic heterogeneity rather than on factors such as geographic diversity (Jinadu 1985:2). In each of these regions a single party dominated the political arena. In the West, the Action Group was the dominant party from 1951-62, in the East, the National Council of Nigeria and the Cameroons (NCNC) from 1951-66, and in the North, the Northern Peoples Congress from 1951-66. Each dominant political party represented its dominant ethnic group both in terms of membership and political objectives. This result was ironic, given the fact that the objective of Nigerian federalism was precisely to avoid altogether, or at least minimize, the potential for political conflict stemming from ethnic divisions. The ineffectiveness of the federal structure to ameliorate ethnic divisions was evident in the fact that the regional governments were much stronger than the national government. The colonial arrangement was thus, in reality, a confederation and not a federal state.

It is clear today that this experiment with federalism both undermined the very purpose for which it was implemented, and exacerbated the tensions the colonial administration sought to address. One explanation for this gross failure was the failure of the colonial administration to recognize that the various ethnic groups historically were sovereign nations themselves, with distinct forms of government, modes of social and legal organization and other characteristics of geo-political entities. The regions that were created in the name of federalism, did not erase the political and social distinctions among the various ethnic groups in each region, neither could these diverse groups be suppressed under a regional authority where one hegemonic group ruled the others.

Thus, from its very inception as a nation-state, Nigeria's heterogeneous society seethed under the double yoke of colonial rule and hegemonic rule of particular ethnic groups. This "federal" arrangement continued through Nigeria's independence in 1960. Ethnicity is key to understanding Nigeria's pluralistic and often divisive society. The implementation of federalism, rooted in ethno-regional identity, inevitably led to the politicization of ethnicity in the

Nigerian political landscape and exacerbated ethnic conflict (see table 5). Eventually, ethnic discrimination and the regional struggle for wealth played a role in the events leading to the Nigerian civil War in 1967. The military takeover in 1966 marked a turning point in Nigeria's political history and ushered in a political framework of military rule that dominated Nigeria for the next three decades.[7]

Table 5

Nigeria: Socioeconomic Characteristics

Total Population	111 Million
Life Expectancy	51.5
Adult Literacy Rate	62.6%
GDP per capita PPP, 1999	US$ 853.00
No. of Ethnic Groups	490
Major Ethnic Groups	Yoruba, Igbo, Hausa, Fulani, Tiv, Kanuri, Nupe, Efik
Structure of the Economy	
Agriculture	29.5%
Industry	46%
Manufacturing	4.1%
Services	24.5%

Source: World Bank 2000, *World Christian Encyclopedia, 2001.

Military rule in Nigeria changed the balance of power between the central government and the regional governments in favor of the central government. Under some accounts of federalism such as the Jeffersonian model, a stronger central government undermines the federal system and should not be encouraged. However, given Nigeria's colonial legacy and its pernicious cycle of ethnic strife a stronger federal government vis-à-vis regional governments was an important step towards the creation of a stable environment necessary to sustain economic growth. The military government was strengthened through the use of decrees that granted increasing administrative powers to the federal government.

Another strategic step taken by the federal military government (FMG) under the leadership of General Gowon (1966-75) was the restructuring of the federation into twelve states. There was clearly an ethnic dimension involved in the creation of states under this regime. For instance, in 1966, the Eastern region attempted to secede from the federation. This threatened the economic viability of the country, as most of the petroleum resources of the country were concentrated in this region. To weaken the power of the Igbo dominated eastern regional government, the military government divided the region into three states, namely Rivers, Cross-River and East-Central states. The division was done along ethnic lines, which was expedient for the federal government's purposes. With this state creation, the petroleum reserves of the country were now concentrated in Rivers and Cross-River states. These two states were of a different ethnic composition from the East Central State and they generally opposed secession. State creation thus simultaneously weakened the region politically by diluting the hegemony of the ruling ethnic group and preserved the economic resources of the country within a localized area of the region. It also reflected pre-colonial ethnic identities which facilitated the participation of these ethnic groups in the country.

The Mohammed/Obasanjo military regime (1975-9) continued the trend of reconstructing the federal structure to give more administrative powers to the federal military government.[8] For example during the Gowon regime, the state governors were part of the governing council or supreme military council (SMC). During the Obasanjo regime, the state governors were removed from the SMC and subordinated to the office of the chief of staff, who was the second to the head of state. Another significant move by the federal government, in an effort to increase its administrative dominance, was the initiation of local government reforms in 1976 and the creation of seven additional states. Again, state creation was done more or less along ethnic lines, bringing the total number of states in the federation to nineteen. The local government reforms initiated by the federal government effectively ended the jurisdiction of the state governments over the local governments. By the end of the Obasanjo regime in 1979, federalism had taken on a new meaning in Nigeria. The role of the central government had evolved from one of passivity in the formative years of federalism under colonial rule to one of dominance in the years following independence. This had grave repercussions for future attempts to return to a democratic system.

Heterogeneity and Economic Development

From 1979-1983, there was a short-lived attempt to return to democratic rule under a presidential system. Most of the political parties and alliances remained rooted in ethnic identification. For example, the Yorubas in the west dominated the Unity part of Nigeria (UPN), while the Igbos in the East dominated the Nigerian Peoples party (NPP). The northerners of the Hausa and Fulani ethnic groups dominated the National Party of Nigeria (NPN), Peoples Redemption Party (PRP) and the Great Nigeria Peoples Party (GNPP) respectively. The National party of Nigeria (NPN) was an elitist party, perceived to have a strong northern base that also attracted wealthy individuals from the other dominant ethnic groups.

Each of these political parties was merely an extension of the political parties formed during the first republic (1960-1966). For instance, the UPN was an extension of the Action group, the NPN, an extension of the Northern Peoples Congress (NPC) and the NPP, an extension of the National Council of Nigeria (and the Cameroons), later of Nigerian Citizens (NCNC) thus reinforcing the ethnic dimensions, and suspicions that underlay each political party.

The demise of the second republic and the subsequent military take over of the government in 1983 returned Nigeria to the division of power that was established during the Obasanjo regime. The Babangida regime (1985-93) and the Abacha regime (1993-98) were the most tyrannical forms of rule in Nigeria's history and instituted a reign of despotic power. Mann (1993) defines despotic power as the repressive capacity of the state and infrastructural power as the capacity to penetrate society and actually implement decisions. In an authoritarian state, the objective is to combine these two sources of power, in order to suppress any potential challenge emanating from the civil society. The combination of these two forms of power sets the framework for a dictatorship and this was precisely what was depicted in military rule in Nigeria from 1985-98 (Sklar 1983).

The incipient federal structure under colonial rule, with equal co-sharing of political power between the regional governments and the national government, combined with the state creation process of the first military regime set the stage for extreme manipulation of ethnic heterogeneity. By the end of the Abacha regime, (1993-1998) the concept of a federal system (or its aberrations) as experienced in the Nigerian political context, and its potential as a mechanism for constraining the inherently destabilizing forces of ethnic heterogeneity, was subsumed in the struggle for democracy, basic human freedoms, and civil rights. In short, the role of ethnic heterogeneity in Nigeria's development was completely engulfed in the demands for freedom from tyrannical rule. Scholars and international institutions proposed macroeconomic policies that more often than not, were contingent on, or accompanied by, calls for a transition to democratic rule without attendant consideration to the form of its institutional expression.

In Nigeria, the question of ethnic heterogeneity and its role in facilitating a climate for economic growth is also inextricably linked to religion. Ethnic heterogeneity is particularly destabilizing to development efforts which is most evident when religion assumes a prominent place in the public sphere. The interplay of ethnicity, religion and political ideology ultimately affect patterns of economic development.[9] The greater the divergence between these non-economic variables, the more vulnerable economic development is to the forces of ethnic heterogeneity. In Nigeria, this divergence is particularly strong. The Hausas are predominantly Muslim, the Yorubas comprised of both Muslims and Christians and Igbos are predominantly Christians. Other ethnic groups in Nigeria represent a mix of Islam, Christianity, and animism or traditional worship.

Religious pluralism, expressed in ethnic terms, has had an unprecedented influence on Nigerian political life. Most of the major political groups formed during the first and second republics inevitably exhibited a religious dimension that correlated with ethnic identity. For instance, in the first republic the Northern People's Congress, (NPC) was the dominant party in the north with a strong Islamic base. In the eastern region, the dominant party was the National council of Nigeria and the Cameroons (NCNC) later changed to National Council of Nigerian Citizens, which had a strong Christian base specifically, Catholicism. In the western region, two political groups ruled at different times. The Action Group (AG) was the dominant party from 1951-62 and the Nigerian National Democratic Party (NNDP) was the ruling party from 1963-6. Both parties had a strong Christian base specifically, Protestantism. As mentioned previously, these ethnic alliances re-emerged during the second republic (1979-83), albeit it was not as pronounced as in the first republic.

It should not be surprising, then, that in the last few decades ethno-religious differences led to periodic outbreaks of conflicts within the country. Additionally, Nigeria's involvement in the Organization of Islamic Conference (OIC) in 1986, under the Babangida regime, served to widen the religious divide between Christians and Muslims, especially given the climate of distrust already existing based on the correlation between ethnic identity and religious affiliation. In 2001, one of the northern states- Kaduna- decided to implement Sharia law. This ultimately led to fears of persecution of non-Muslims by ethnic groups that did not adhere to the Islamic faith. It has raised questions concerning the separation of church and state and the jurisdictional allocation of powers within the federal system. Indeed, in Nigeria, it is almost impossible to determine where the ethnic line ends and the religious one begins and which is the cause or effect. What is clear, however, is that the divergence of the two has greatly heightened the level of political instability in the country. Even though major ethnic groups have courted the smaller groups in order to increase their political power base, ultimately religious strife has served to prevent the formation of strong inter-ethnic and inter-religious political alliances.

One of the most contentious issues influencing economic development in Nigeria, and which also has an ethnic dimension, is revenue allocation. The current revenue allocation formula appropriates a large allocation of revenues to the federal government, thus giving the federal government the power to set and execute the economic agenda of the country, as table 6 below shows.

Table 6

Revenue Sharing 1995-1999

Federal Government	48.5%
State Government	24%
Local government	20%
Special Fund	7.5%
TOTAL	100.0%

Source: B. Onimode, "Fiscal Federalism in the 21st Century-Options for Nigeria" (Discussion paper, University of Ibadan, Department of Political Science, 1999).

With this power, the federal government can target states for large-scale infrastructural development programs. While large revenue allocations are important for strengthening the federal government vis-à-vis the states, yet because the states are reflections of particular ethnic groups, ethnic bias is always suspected and sometimes detected, whenever a particular state or region is identified for development programs. Ethnic heterogeneity combined with religious pluralism, and a history of colonial rule that manipulated ethnic differences has created an environment where selection criteria, even when ostensibly objective, appear to favor one group over another. During the Babangida and Abacha years in particular (1985-1993, 1993-1988 respectively), the federal government's use of infrastructural funds seemed to reflect more of an ethnic bias than at any other time in Nigeria's history.

Another salient issue regarding the role of heterogeneity has been the criteria used to allocate revenues among states. A key element in the derivation principle was the census figures. The determination of state size was based largely on demographic factors. Consequently, the more populous states received a greater share of revenue even though the states did not contribute proportionally to the national income. This led to 'census rigging' to ensure that a larger share of the revenues went to certain states and, hence, ethnic groups. Ultimately, this created an uneven distribution of wealth among states and, thus, among ethnic groups. The federal character principle borne out of the 1979 constitution to prevent the domination of the government by any state(s) or ethnic group was rendered ineffective especially since states were already unevenly developed prior to this constitutional provision (Onimode 1999: 8). Major ethnic groups such as the Yoruba, Hausa-Fulani and Igbo are concentrated in certain states and have received a significant share of revenues. Other ethnic groups that were smaller and dispersed among states became increasingly economically marginalized since they received a smaller allocation of revenues. All these issues contributed to, and intensified, ethnic rivalry and perpetuated the climate of political instability.

Part of the decentralizing mechanism of the federal government in Nigeria, and its attempt to empower less dominant ethnic groups, has been the creation of new states. From 1976 to 1996, 24 additional states plus the federal capital were created in Nigeria. A possible rationale in the decision to create states was that the smaller ethnic groups were dominated and, at times, exploited by the major ethnic groups. However, an alternative perspective on state creation is that it weakens regional power and strengthens the central government (Khan 1994). This was certainly evident in the creation of states during the Babangida regime (1985-93). The creation of new states justified a revision of the revenue allocation formula and a lower appropriation since the revenue had to be distributed among more states. This strengthened the economic power of the federal government, which, with this increased power, could do greater damage to economic development viability as it exercised its power in favor of specific ethnic groups and the states in which they resided.

Given the history of ethnic strife and distrust within the Nigerian society it seems clear that federalism, at least its "coming together" and asymmetrical features is, in the short term, a viable option of governance. These features of federalism would recognize the distinct sovereignties each ethnic group represents, while also alleviating the concern that certain states would be left out of the national political process. Since identities in Nigeria are so heavily dependent on ethnic affiliation, a system of governance that makes room for each group is more likely to alleviate the unique problems presented by ethnic heterogeneity. Thus the institutional expression of democratic governance may be more important, in the short run, to economic development viability and is likely to help overcome the decades of ethnic distrust that have hindered the country's progress.

Finally, the specific problems of ethnic groups that have been economically marginalized and exploited, such as the environmental degradation and lack of infrastructural development in the Niger Delta, need to be addressed at the federal level. This is a sensitive issue with significant implications for the country's economy. The entire annual production of Nigeria's oil which accounts for 80% of the nation's revenue comes from the Niger Delta. Despite their significant contribution to national income, the Niger Delta has been subjected to abject poverty evidenced by the total absence of basic utilities and social infrastructure. This has intensified the political debate regarding the ownership of natural resources and the role of federalism in determining this ownership (Ejobowah 2000: 41). Additionally, there have been persistent demands by the ethnic groups in the Niger Delta for a constitutional conference to revise jurisdictional ownership of resources. These demands have escalated into violent protests by some of the marginalized groups in an attempt to force the federal government to address these concerns. To address the problem of jurisdictional rights between the central government and state governments, the 1994 national constitutional conference made a provision in the 1995 draft constitution requiring the national assembly to work out a revenue allocation criteria that combines the derivation principle with several other principles.[10] Additionally, the establishment of the Niger Delta Development Commission by the current president, Obasanjo, is regarded as an important step to address the development of this impoverished region (Ejobowah 2000: 43).

The initial political maneuvering from decentralization to centralization in Nigeria was a direct response to the political power of the regional governments and their threat to the unity of the federation. The creation of new states by the federal military government was aimed at diluting that threat. The subsequent proliferation of new states between 1976-1996 in the name of decentralization, in fact, enhanced the powers of the central government; the strategic creation of weak states ensured their dependence on the central government. Hence, the federal system failed to alleviate ethnic tensions in Nigeria. In fact, it may have served to exacerbate tensions given the heightened need by states to compete for federal revenues in order to remain economically viable. There was no incentive to act cooperatively because ethnic identification, which produced these states, remained the dominant consideration in governance strategies at the central government level. Thus federalism in Nigeria has created market- destabilizing heterogeneity.

Ethnic Heterogeneity Federalism and Economic Development

The continued challenge of economic development in Nigeria and Brazil is particularly difficult to rationalize given the significant human and natural resource-base of the two countries. Political instability in these countries is closely associated with the ethnic composition of the society and the related tensions of real and perceived ethnic differentiation in regards to economic opportunities. The similarities between the two countries facilitate comparisons that reveal the efficacy of federal structures to manage or contain the rivalries that retard economic development prospects.

A subtle but important distinction needs to be made regarding the intent of federal systems and its application/implementation in different countries. The original intent behind the adoption of federal systems was as a means for 'nation-building' such as the United States in which the various colonies independently agreed to give up their sovereignty in order to be part of a larger union or in Riker's terms 'coming-together-federalism'. For many developing and/or formerly colonized countries that are characterized either by a combination of ethnic, religious or linguistic diversity the adoption of a federal system was primarily a means of containment or management. That is, a means to manage the plurality of ethnic, linguistic or religious divisions with the ultimate goal of 'nation-building'. In this context, the success of 'nation-building' is primarily based on the ability to manage or contain these factors. This fundamental distinction affects how federal systems can be employed as a means to promote long-term economic development. In multiethnic societies the goal of the central government will be to reduce the incidence of political instability that is rooted in ethnic strife in order to advance economic development objectives.

At least three attributes of a federal system are directly related to promoting long term economic development. These are, (i) efficient allocation of resources, (ii) fostering political participation and (iii) the protection of basic liberties and freedoms (Rubinfeld 1997: 21). These attributes may be incorporated in any of four possible models of federal governance identified in political economy literature for their specific utility in fostering conditions suitable for long term economic growth and development. These are, market preserving federalism, economic federalism, cooperative federalism and democratic federalism.

Countries with large multiethnic/multi racial populations faced with uneven economic development can benefit from federal structures that emphasize a strong central government in order to correct social and economic inequalities and promote long-term growth. For Brazil and Nigeria, the utilities that economic federalism offer are valuable for the purposes of long-term economic development while redressing the regional inequalities in growth. Economic federalism seeks to promote economic efficiency by allocating to the central government the function of providing public services across all jurisdictions and correcting inefficiencies through the use of taxes, regulations or subsidies. Additionally, economic federalism recognizes the role of subnational governments in the development process by promoting a decentralized structure of government.

In Brazil and Nigeria, the market inefficiencies that have created regional inequalities in economic growth can be corrected via the agency of a strong central government. A strong central government through its political and fiscal mechanisms such as, grants-in-aid or subsidies can correct these inefficiencies. Even though this model of federalism tends towards centralization rather than decentralization, centralization may be a better strategy for developing countries that are still experimenting with democracy and are confronted with unbalanced growth. A decentralized structure gives more fiscal and political autonomy to states which can exacerbate unbalanced growth especially if there are already existing economic disparities among the states. Additionally, increased political and fiscal autonomy devolved to the states can lead to a weak central government which will be ineffective in executing economic policies since the states become more dominant players in the economic agenda. The economically more independent and richer states can dominate the economic agenda of the country. Exacerbated unbalanced growth among states and conflict between and among dominant and less dominant states (regarding the economic agenda and/or distribution of economic resources) can create a climate of political instability. Political instability can be instigated as weaker states (or less dominant players) may resort to threats of secession and/or other avenues to express their economic disenchantment.

Political and fiscal decentralization occurred in Brazil between 1985-1994 in which the states and local governments were given more economic resources. However, the lack of specification of responsibilities for which these additional resources were allocated, invariably created economic problems for the federal government which was, ultimately, financially responsible for the excesses of the state governments. For instance, in 1998, 34% of the entire federal debt were assumed state debts (Mendes 2000: 14). This left the federal government with diminished resources to promote economic policies (Abrucio 1998). Thus decentralization created a weak central government and exacerbated the existing regional inequalities in growth. In fact, richer states such as Rio de Janeiro and Sao Paulo have welcomed fiscal decentralization in order to exploit their tax base (Mendes 2000: 14). Decentralization in Brazil has given subnational governments increased political powers but has retarded the ability of the federal government to focus on macroeconomic variables that are needed for long-term economic growth. In this regard, economic federalism, which recognizes the federal government as the most effective institution responsible for providing public goods and correcting inter-jurisdictional externalities holds some promise for Brazil.

Given the plurality of the Nigerian polity coupled with the ethnic bias in the regional inequalities in growth, economic federalism can be employed as a means to promote economic development while redressing the regional inequalities in economic growth. In this regard, a strong central government within a decentralized federal structure can correct these inefficiencies through federal grants that are specifically aimed at developing the disadvantaged regions and other federal government programs aimed at promoting infrastructural development. Without a strong federal government, sub-national governments will have no incentive to correct these inequalities through cooperative strategies since they represent ethnic groups that are all competing for economic resources. This ethnic competition has typified the Nigerian federation especially since the discovery of oil in the 1960's and the creation of new states. Additionally, in Nigeria there has been a continued tension among the states and the federal government regarding the allocation of oil revenues. Again, there is an ethnic dimension to this tenuous situation. The oil producing states (Bayelsa, Cross Rivers, Akwa Ibown, Delta, Eboyin and Edo) are among the least developed in terms of infrastructural development and represent a number of minority ethnic groups. The tenuous situation has led to threats of secession by some of these states in an attempt to gain their sovereignty and have control over their natural resources. The larger states that represent majority ethnic groups and have been the recipient of a disproportionate share of the oil revenues have ensured to keep the Niger Delta states within the federation realizing the economic implications of dissolution. This tenuous ethnic climate in the country has created market-destabilizing heterogeneity which has posed detrimental consequences for economic development in Nigeria. To address some of the socio-economic concerns of the underdeveloped states, the current federal government established the Niger Delta Development Commission with the task of looking into ways of developing this impoverished region. In this regard, having a strong central government taking the initiative to address and correct these inefficiencies has helped to avert ethnic strife and a potentially destructive political climate.

Federalism has failed to contain/manage the ethnic diversity of Nigeria. In fact, it has created market-destabilizing heterogeneity through the creation of ethnic states. Even though state-creation was effected under the guise of decentralization, these states lack the resources to enable them develop and thus remain very underdeveloped. This has created a dichotomy between the rich and the poor states. More importantly, the ethnic groups in the poor states continue to remain marginalized politically.

For developing countries such as Brazil and Nigeria where democracy is still, for the most part an "experiment in progress", economic federalism holds some promise in redressing regional inequalities in economic performance. However, the success of economic federalism is partially dependent on the perceived legitimacy of the democratic system by the component units. The decentralized nature of the federal system recognizes the mutual interdependence of the different levels of government in the overall economic agenda of the country. This can also promote cooperative strategies between sub-national governments and the central government in exploring economic development initiatives. For instance, in Nigeria, since the sub-national governments represent certain ethnic groups, these cooperative arrangements may eventually eliminate the climate of distrust among ethnic groups. The continued cooperation will reduce ethnic strife stemming from competition for economic resources and reduce political instability which is inimical to economic growth. The cooperative strategies can create market-enabling heterogeneity and promote market-preserving federalism through the formation of common markets across jurisdictions.[11] In the case of Brazil, a strong federal government can utilize its powers to create incentives for states to address the socio-economic inequalities. Cooperative strategies between the central government and the state governments will be more difficult since there are two dimensions to the inequality problem, one is regional, that is, among the states and the second is the racial bias within and among states. However, the central government through its resources can correct the regional inequalities in growth.

An interesting analogy can be drawn between Brazil and Nigeria with regards to the pattern of decentralization of political power, specifically the location of the federal capital. The federal capital in Brazil was relocated from Rio de Janeiro in the southeast region to Brasilia in the center-west region in an attempt to open up the interior of Brazil. In Nigeria, the federal capital was moved from Lagos (south-western region) to the geographic center of the country (Abuja) based primarily on ethno-political considerations. Lagos was the second largest city in the southwest and was dominated by the Yoruba ethnic group. This concentration of one ethnic group in an economically viable part of the country made other ethnic groups, in the country especially the strategic elites in the north uneasy. Thus, the move to Abuja was a strategic attempt to dilute the political and economic base of one of the three dominant ethnic groups.

The most complex issue raised in this chapter is the relationship between economic development, political institutions and the overall structure of governance in a given country. In theory, democracy offers political freedoms that facilitate the operation of free markets that are indispensable to sustained economic growth. The thesis I advocate in this chapter is that political instability arising from ethnic heterogeneity will not necessarily respond to democracy without regard to its institutional form, at least for the purpose of mitigating political instability. Rather, the institutional expression of democratic governance, in particular federalism, may be more important to economic development in ethnically divided societies than the freedoms that advocates of democracy proffer as the primary factor vital to sustained economic growth, especially where market-destabilizing heterogeneity has been the principal cause of underdevelopment as is the case with Nigeria. Conversely, Brazil's economic development record has exhibited a race-regional bias. Given these market inefficiencies, a federal structure can be employed to redress the externalities as well as promote and sustain economic development by providing a proper governance structure. A proper governance structure is both a necessary and sufficient condition for the successful implementation of macroeconomic goals. A federal structure allocates roles and jurisdictional powers among the different tiers of government in order to create a proper institutional framework for sustainable economic development. By recognizing the contribution of the different tiers of government to the overall development process, economic policies can be successfully executed while simultaneously accomplishing the goal of 'nation building'. Thus, in a sense, a federal system promotes a cooperative relationship among the central government, the state governments and the municipal governments. Additionally, the assignment of roles in a federal structure guarantees both a macro as well as micro function. A macro function in the sense that the central government sets the economic agenda of the country and a micro function regarding the economic goals within each of the subnational governments.

There is yet another dimension to the democratization debate. The initial post-colonial independent states that were established in sub-Saharan Africa started out as democracies and then became authoritarian states. The leaders at the time sought to consolidate the process of nation-building while simultaneously pursuing economic development goals. With regard to the latter, post-colonial governments argued that competitive national politics, an intrinsic feature of democratic processes, would hold national development agenda hostage to sub-national interests based on ethnicity, region, religion or class (Ndulu and O' Connell 1999: 49). This conviction spawned ideologies that posited democratic regimes as subversive of economic development goals. The belief that democracy is not always consistent with a nation's pursuit of economic development has received an indicia of credence. For example, although unsupported by empirical evidence, the Lee hypothesis suggests that authoritarian regimes are more prone to produce rapid economic growth than democratic states (Sen 1999: 6). However, the dominant political formulae for sustained economic development remains democracy and its enabling institutions.

To the extent that economic development is concerned with the promotion and expansion of human and political freedoms, it requires the most appropriate form of governance to guarantee and facilitate the exercise of these freedoms. As Amartya Sen (1999) points out, the measure should not be whether societies are fit *for* democracy, but rather they should be made fit *through* democracy. Further, in culturally and ethnically diverse societies such as Nigeria and Brazil, democratic rule within a properly crafted federal structure is more likely to promote consociation among the various ethnic groups especially where, as in Nigeria, a three-party democracy was adopted. In this regard, a federal structure will serve to strengthen the democratic state given a large, ethnically diverse population.

There is empirical evidence suggesting that political instability is an impediment to economic growth (Scully 1988; Barro 1991; Fosu 1992; Easterly and Levine 1997). Additionally, the incidence of political instability is greater in multiethnic societies due to competition for economic resources (Alesina and Tabellini 1989; Alesina and Drazen 1991; Annett 1997). Since 1985, Brazil, after twenty-one years of military rule, has successfully practiced democracy. Yet the socioeconomic problems confronting its racial/ethnic minorities and the regions where they are concentrated remain a blight on Brazil's development record. Thus one may safely suggest that but for the existence of a racial majority that controls political power and dominates the developed regions (the industrial heartland) Brazil's 'development' would not be measurable.

Nigeria on, the other hand, has just recently returned to democratic rule. Within this newly democratic government, a properly crafted federal structure is needed. For both Nigeria and Brazil, government economic policies must address the already existing ethnic inequalities in political participation, distribution of resources and the regional imbalance in economic development. In this regard, the re-democratization of Brazil and the stable political structure has opened up opportunities for economic development and growth through the establishment of multinational ventures and other foreign investments. An example of this is Mercusol, the integration of the Brazilian markets with Argentina, Paraguay and Uruguay. One of the main objectives behind the formation of the common market through integration is to serve as a prerequisite for economic development.

Conclusion

This chapter examined the effect of particular forms of federal governance on ethnic diversity. In particular, my objective was to examine the possibility of alleviating racial/ethnic fragmentation by employing an institutional form of democratic governance, in particular federalism and the consequent effects on the economic development prospects of Nigeria and Brazil. Brazil has experienced measurable success in transforming its economy into a newly industrialized state in spite of ethnic and racial heterogeneity. The success experienced in Brazil can be partly attributed to the establishment of a stable democratic system, and the attempt by policymakers to address the macro-economic problems such as hyperinflation, the debt crisis and corruption. However, it is clear that since ethnic/racial fragmentation has not presented a threat to the unity of the federation, the central government has essentially been able to ignore the race-regional development bias. Hence, racial and regional inequalities still persist. On the other hand, ethnic heterogeneity has had a much more destabilizing effect on the Nigerian federation coupled with the fact that the central government has yet to develop a strategic economic development plan that addresses the socio-economic inequalities among the ethnic groups.[12]

In Brazil, a federal structure was employed as an instrument of management. Therefore, the regional inequalities in economic growth still persists. This is why Brazil possesses characteristics of developed as well as developing countries and has one of the most unequal income distributions in the world. Also, the decentralization of the federal system may have hindered the ability of the federal government to initiate and address regional inequalities in economic development due to the accumulation of large state debts that have left a financial burden on the federal government (Mainwaring and Samuels 1999). Thus decentralization in Brazil may have occurred at the expense of economic development.

In Nigeria, a federal structure was adopted as an instrument of containment and management. Political leaders at the time recognized that the plurality of the country had detrimental effects to the unity of the federation. Hence the ethnic configuration was vulnerable to any positive or negative manipulation of the federal structure. However, to the extent that the federal structure has not successfully contained ethnic diversity, it has failed in its management role. This explains the high incidence of ethnic strife and political instability in Nigeria. The different rationale for the adoption of the federal structure in Brazil and Nigeria may also explain how federalism has, thus far, impacted development viability and, particularly for Nigeria, how it may do so in the future.

ENDNOTES

1. The first attempt to quantify non-economic variables was by Irma Adelman and Cynthia Taft Morris, (1968). There have been subsequent attempts by other development economists such as Scully, (1988), Barro (1991), Fosu (1992) and Easterly and Levine (1997) to empirically examine the impact of non-economic variables on

economic development.

2. There is a large body of empirical work that demonstrates the link between ethnic diversity and economic development such as Shleifer and Vishney (1993), Mauro (1995), Easterly and Levine (1997), La Porta, Lopez de Silanes, Shleifer and Vishney (1998), Svensson (1998), and (Easterly 2001) to mention a few.

3. The racial classifications in Brazil are White, Black, Brown, Indian and other (Asian, Arab, Amerindian). "Browns" are mixed white and black. If Afro-Brazilians or people of African descent are considered "blacks" and "brown" this population will constitute the largest collection of people of African descent in the world second only to Nigeria.

4. There is a significant amount of literature on the 'whitening' epic in Brazil. Scholars such as Hasenbalg, Skidmore, and Nascimento, to mention a few, have written extensively on this controversial topic. See bibliography for more details.

5. This is partly due to the fact that Teutonia is a major center of dairy production in Brazil.

6. Section I benefited immensely from papers by Selcher (1998) and by Mainwaring and Samuels (1999). See bibliography for more details.

7. Although federalism assumes the existence of a democratic regime, in one sense Nigeria's military rule might be classified as 'military federalism'. In other words, a division of power between a central government, regional and local governments can also exist within the framework of non democratic governments as the colonial system demonstrated. To the extent that such a division of power successfully constrains ethnic strife (for example recognizing new states based on ethnic aggregations as the military in Nigeria has historically done), or facilitates the integration of otherwise invisible ethnic groups into the polity, then one or several of the characteristics of federalism may still serve an important function for development purposes, notwithstanding the militarization of the political system.

8. In 1975, through a military coup, General Gowon was ousted as head of state. The new head of state was General Mohammed who was assassinated in a coup d' etat in 1976. General Obasanjo became head of state and essentially continued the policies established in the Mohammed regime.

9. For more see Collier (2000), Easterly and Levine (1997), Alesina and Perotti (1996), Alesina, Ozler, Roubini and Swagel (1996), Perotti (1996), and Mauro (1995).

10. See *Draft Constitution of the Federal Republic of Nigeria* 1995: Vol. 1, section 153; vol. 2 Section 142.

11. Market-preserving federalism is an alternative theory of federalism which also recognizes a decentralized government structure. One of the characteristics of market-preserving federalism is the ensuring of a common market in which subnational governments are unable to use their regulatory power to erect trade barriers to prevent the mobility of goods from other political units. For more see Weingast (1995).

12. The creation of states in Nigeria has always had an ethnic motive, thus the term ethnic states. Consequently regional inequalities in economic growth represent ethnic inequalities regarding the distribution of wealth.

REFERENCES

Abrucio, Fernando Luiz. 1998. *Os barões da feracao: O poder dos governadores no Brasil pós-authoritário*. Sao Paulo: Editora Hucitec/Universidade de São Paulo.

——1997. *Jogos Federativos: O Modelo Predatório brasileiro*. Unpublished manuscript, CEDEC.

——and Samuels, David. 1997. "A 'nova' política dos governadores: Política subnacional e transição democrática no Brasil". *Lua Nova* (40/41): 137-166.

Adamolekun, L. and Ayo, B. 1989. " The Evolution of the Nigerian Federal Administration System." *Publius* 19: 157-176.

Adelman, I. and Morris, C. 1968. Performance Criteria for Evaluating Economic Development Potential: An Operational Approach. *Quarterly Journal of Economics* 82 (2): 260-280.

Alesina, A. and Perotti, R. 1996. "Income Distribution, Political Instability, and Investment." *European Economic Review* 40 (6): 1203-1228.

——Ozler, S., Roubini, N., and Swagel, P. 1996. "Political Instability and Economic Growth." *Journal of Economic Growth* 1: 189-211.

——and Drazen, A. 1991. "Why are Stabilizations Delayed?" *American Economic Review* 81 (5): 1170-1188.

——and Tabellini, G. 1989. "External Debt, Capital Flight and Political Risk." *Journal of International Economics* 37: 199-220.

Anett, A., 1997. "Ethnic and Religious Division, Political instability, and Government Consumption." Department of Economics, Columbia University.

Atlas Maradov Mira. 1964. Moscow: Miklukho-Makalai Ethnological Institute at the Department of Geodesy and Cartography of the State Geological Committee of the Soviet Union.

Barret, David, Kurian, George and Johnson, Todd. 2001. *World Christian Encyclopedia*. New York: Oxford University Press.

Barro, R. 1991. "Economic Growth in a Cross-Section of Countries." *Quarterly Journal of Economics* 106 (2): 407-443.

——1997. "Determinants of Economic Growth A Cross-Country Empirical Study." HIID Working Paper , No. 526.

Bastide, R. 1965. The Development of Race Relations in Brazil. Pp. 9-29 in *Industrialization and Race Relations*, ed. G. Hunter. London: Oxford university Press.

Bonfim, Antulio N., and Shah A. 1991. "Macroeconomic Management and the Division of Powers in Brazil: Perspectives for the Nineties." *Policy Research and External Affairs Working Paper*. Washington D.C. : The World Bank.

Boeke, J. H. 1953. *Economics and Economic Policy in Dual Societies*. New York: New York University Press.

Camargo, A. 1993. "Federalism and Inflation Why Brazil needs a New Federal Pact." Fernand Braudel Institute of World Economics Working Paper no. 2, Sao Paulo, Brazil.

Costa, D. ed. *The Second Brazil: Socio-Demographic Perspectives*. Rio de Janeiro Brazil: Ebano.

Eakin, M. 1997. *Brazil The Once and Future Country*. New York: St. Martins Press.

Easterly, W. and Levine, R. 1997. "Africa's Growth Tragedy." *Quarterly Journal of Economics*, 112 (4): 1203-1250.

——2001. Can Institutions Resolve Ethnic Conflict. *Economic Development and Cultural Change* 49(4): 687-706.

Ejobowah, J. B. 2000. "Who Owns the Oil? The Politics of Ethnicity in the Niger Delta of Nigeria." *Africa Today* 47 (1): 29-47.

Fernandes, F. 1969. *The Negro in Brazilian Society*. New York: Columbia University Press.

Fontaine, Pierre-Michel ed. 1985. *Race, Class, and Power*. Los-Angeles: Afro-American Studies Center.

Fosu, K. 1992. "Political Instability and Economic Growth: Evidence from Sub-Saharan Africa." *Economic Development and Cultural Change 43*(4): 829-841.

Greenstein, F. and Polsby, N. (eds.) 1975. *Handbook of Political Science*. Reading, Massachusetts: Addison Wesley.

Hudson, R. ed. 1998. *Brazil a Country Study*. Washington D.C.: United States Government Printing Office.

Hanchard, M. ed. 1999. *Racial Politics in Contemporary Brazil*. Durham, North Carolina: Duke University Press.

Hasenbalg, C. 1983. *Race and Socioeconomic Differences in Brazil*. Rio de Janeiro: IUPERJ.

Hanushek, E. and Gomes-Neto, J. 1994. Consequences of Grade Repetition: Evidence from Brazil. *Economic Development and Cultural Change 43*(1): 117-148.

Instituto Brasileiro de Geografia E Estatistica 1999. Sintese de Indicadores Socias. Rio de Janeiro: Brazil.

Instituto Brasileiro de Geografia E Estatistica 1999. Pequisa Nacional Por Amostra de Domicilios. Rio de Janeiro: Brazil.

Jinadu, A. 1985. "Federalism, The Consociational State, and Ethnic Conflict in Nigeria." *Publius 15*(2): 71-100.

Kaufman, P. and Riordan, P. (eds.) 1997. *Brazil Under Cardoso*. Boulder: L. Rienner Publishers.

Knack, S. and Keefer, P. 1995. "Institutions and Economic Performance: Cross-Country Tests Using Alternative Institutional Measures." *Economics and Politics* 7: 207-227.

La Porta, R., Lopez de Silanes, F., Shleifer, A., Vishny, R., 1998. The Quality of Government. National Bureau of Economic Research Working Paper Series 6727.

Lavinas, Lena. 1997. Abismo regional. Veja (Sao Paulo) (26 February):9-11.

Lesser, J. 1999. *Negotiating National Identity*. Durham, North Carolina: Duke University Press.

Lovell, P. 1999. "Development and the Persistence of Racial Inequality in Brazil." *Journal of Developing Areas 33*(3): 395-418.

Mainwaring, S. and Samuels, D. 1999. "Federalism, Constraints on the Central Government, and Economic Reform in Democratic Brazil." Kellog Institute for International Studies, Working paper no. 271, University of Notre Dame.

Perotti, R. 1996. "Democracy, Income Distribution and Growth: What the Data Says." *Journal of Economic Growth*. 1: 149-187.

Mauro, P. 1995. Corruption and Growth. *Quarterly Journal of Economics 110*(3): 681-712.

Mann, M. 1993. *The Sources of Political Power*. New York: Cambridge University Press.

Nascimento, Abdias do. 1982. *O Negro Revoltado (The Insurgent Black Man)*. Rio de Janeiro: Nova Fronteira.

Ndulu, B. and O' Connell, S. 1999. "Governance and Growth in Sub-Saharan Africa." *Journal of Economic Perspectives 13*(3): 41-66.

Nogueira, Julio Ceaser de A. 1995. O financiamento publico e descentralizacao fiscal no Brasil. Texto para Discussao 34. Rio de Janeiro: CEPP.

North, D. 1994. "Economic Performance Through Time." *American Economic Review* 84: 359-368.

Onimode, B. 1999. "Fiscal Federalism in the 21st Century." Department of Political Science: University of Ibadan, Nigeria.

Parikh, Sunita and Weingast, Barry. 1997. "A Comparative Theory of Federalism: India." *Virginia Law Review* 83: 1593-1610.

Political Risk Year book. 1998. Volumes III and IV.

Riker, W. 1975. Federalism. In F. Greenstein and N. Polsby. op.cit.

Roett, R. 1992. Brazil Politics in a Patrimonial Society. Connecticut: Praeger Publishers.

Rodden, Jonathan and Rose-Ackerman, Susan. 1997. "Does Federalism Preserve Markets? *Virginia Law Review* 83:1521-1543.

Rosenn, K. and Downes, R. eds. 1999. *Corruption and Politics of Reform in Brazil: The Impact of Collor's Impeachment*. Miami: North South Center Press.

Rostow, W. W. 1961. *Stages of Economic Growth: A Non-Communist Manifesto*. Cambridge: Cambridge University Press.

Rubinfeld, Daniel. 1997. "On Federalism and Economic Development." *Virginia Law Review* 83: 1581-1589.

Sawyer, D. 1988. "The Society and Its Environment." *Brazil a Country Study*. R. Hudson, ed. Washington D.C.: United States Government Printing Press Pp. 89-156 .

Scully, G.W., 1988. The Institutional Framework and Economic Development. *Journal of Political Economy* 96(3): 652-662.

Sen, A. 1999. "Democracy a Universal Value." *Journal of Democracy 10* (3): 19-34.

Selcher, W. A., 1998. "The Politics of Decentralized Federalism, National Diversification, and Regionalism in Brazil." *Journal of Inter-American Studies and World Affairs* 40(4), 25-50.

Shleifer, A., and Vishny, R., 1993. "Corruption." *Quarterly Journal of Economics* 108: 599-618.

Silva, N. 1985. "Updating the Cost of Not Being White in Brazil." in *Race, Class, and Power in Brazil*, ed. P.M. Fontaine. Los Angeles: Afro-American Studies Center Pp. 42-55.

Skidmore, T. 1999. Collors Downfall in Historical Perspective. Pp. 1-12 in *Corruption and Political Reform: The Impact of Collors Impeachment*. K. Rosenn and R. Downes, eds. Miami: North South Center Press.

———1999. *Brazil Five Centuries of Change*. New York: Oxford University Press.

———1974. *Black into White: Race and Nationality in Brazilian Thought*. New York: Oxford University Press.

Sklar, R. 1983. "Democracy in Africa," *African Studies Review, 26*, pp. 235-279.

Sola Lourdes. 1993. Estado, transformacao eonomica e democratizacao no Brasil. Pp.

235-279. *Estado, mercado e democracia,* ed. L. Sola. Rio de Janeiro: Paz e Terra.

Sola, A., Christopher Garman, and Moises Marques. 1997. "Central Banking, Democratic Governance and Political Authority: The Case of Brazil in a Regional Perspective." Paper for the 17th World Congress of the International Political Science Association, Seoul, South Korea, 17-21 August.

Stepan, A. 1999. "Federalism and Democracy: Beyond the U.S. Model." *Journal of Democracy 10*(3): 19-34.

Svensson, J., 1998. "Foreign Aid and Rent Seeking." World Bank Development Economics Research Group, *Policy Research Working Paper* 1880.

Svensson, J., 1998. Investment, Property Rights and Political instability: Theory and Evidence. *European Economic Review* 47(7): 1317-1342.

Tavares de Almeida, Maria Herminia. 1995 Federalismo e politicas socias, *Revista Braseileira de Ciencias Sociais* 10: 88-108.

Taylor, C. and Hudson, M. 1972. *World Handbook of Political and Social Indicators.* New Haven: Yale University Press.

Tisbelis, G. 1995. Decision Making in Political Systems: Veto Players in Presidentialism, Parliamentarism, Multicameralism, and Multipartysim. *British Journal of Political Science 10 (3):* 289-325.

Van den Berghe, P. 1967. *Race and Racism.* New York: Wiley.

Weingast, B. 1995. "The Economic Role of Political Institutions: Market-Preserving Federalism and Economic Development." *Journal of Law Economics and Organization* 8(1): 1-31.

Winant, H. 1999. "Racial Democracy and Racial Identity: Comparing the United States and Brazil." in *Racial Politics in Contemporary Brazil.* M. Hanchard, ed. Miami: North South Center Press pp. 86-88.

World Bank. 2001 & 1997. *World Development Report.* New York: Oxford University Press.

SECTION IV:
FEDERALISM IN COMPARATIVE PERSPECTIVE

CHAPTER 10

South Africa and The Federalist Logic

Eghosa E. Osaghae

D espite strong opposition to the federal option and its rejection at critical stages in South Africa's history, notably at the time of Union in 1910 and in the political negotiations that led to the inauguration of the post-apartheid state in 1994, the debate on federalism has not abated in the country. Not even the opprobrium of its association with apartheid in recent debates has dissuaded federalists within and outside the country from the view that the country needs one form of federal solution or the other. Indeed, in spite of opposition to the federal option, the theory and practice of government in the country since the formation of the union have had a strong federal flavor (Elazar, 1996). It is the logic of this federalist imperative that explains the gulf between unitarist preferences and near-federal constitutions and practice, as well as the incrementalist process of federal evolution, that this chapter analyses. The chapter is divided into four sections. Section one attempts a theoretical construction of the federalist logic. This informs the situational framework of the federalist logic in South Africa sketched in section two, while section three analyses the process of federal evolution since the transition to the post-apartheid state. Section four presents the conclusions.

The Federalist Logic: A Theoretical Overview

Considering the wide variety of political and governmental arrangements to which the term federal has been applied, ranging from unitarist arrangements like Nigeria's so-called military federalism to confederal set-ups such as the European Union, federalism has become a highly flexible and relative concept. Attempts at capturing its trajectories have varied from its conception as a degree of decentralization (Riker, 1975; and Elazar, 1976 and Osaghae, 1990, for a critique), to classifications of the varieties of the 'federal solution' into territorial and non-territorial, constitutional and non-constitutional forms of federalism (cf. Lijphart, 1985; Osaghae; 1997), as well as by traditions of federalism (Burgess & Gagnon, 1993), to more recent discrete categorizations such as post-modern federalism which refers to non-territorial power sharing involving emergent power actors such as women and linguistic minorities, evolutionary federalism or incremental federalization in non-formally federal states (Agranoff, 1996:386), and supra-state, international federations arising from the increasingly interdependent nature of the global system (Elazar, 1996).

In view of the variableness in conception, is it realistic to construct a federalist logic? The answer, perhaps surprisingly, is yes, because the flexibility of usage has not led to any fundamental disagreement on the meaning and essence of federalism. Students of federalism generally agree with King's (1982) distinction between federalism as an ideology incorporating several federal ideas or principles, and federation as an organizational or institutional arrangement, which corresponds to the relevant federal idea. More specifically, federal principle, as the operational representation of federalist ideology, refers to a cluster of techniques—constitutional, legal, political, administrative and financial—which serve to maintain or erode the balance between mutual independence and interdependence between levels of government (Vile, 1977:3).

In other words, the federal principle entails a method of marrying diversity and union, or "shared rule" and "self rule" (Elazar, 1987), and this can take various forms, including non-territorial and territorial power sharing, elite pacting, decentralization, asymmetrical federalism, consociationalism, and so on. It is in such terms that Burgess (1993) prefers to talk of federalism rather than federation.

Federation, on the other hand, is more specific: it refers to a system of government in which there are at least two tiers of government and, in which the relative autonomy of constituent units and their participation in central decision- making are constitutionally entrenched. In effect, federation is a "fully constitutional government" whose genius "lies in its infinite capacity to accommodate and reconcile the competing and sometimes conflicting array of diversities having political salience within a state" (Burgess, 1993:7).[1] The implication of the linkage between federalism and federation is that there are as many forms of federation as there are federal ideas, although King is quick to point out that not all federal ideas result in federation, meaning that it is possible for a state to be run according to federal principles without being a (full-fledged) federation.

Utilizing the federal principle does not necessarily mean establishing a federal system in the conventional sense of modern federation. Federalism is a phenomenon that provides many options for the organization of political authority and power; as long as the proper relations are created, a wide variety of political structures can be developed that are consistent with federal principles (Elazar, cited in Kotze, 1995:69).

In other words, as I have pointed out elsewhere, there is a whole category of federalism without federal government (Osaghae, 1997). Having seen that the essence of federalism has not been lost to the elasticity of usage, let us now return to the idea of a federalist logic. The presence of the logic involves the following attributes of federalism some of which follow from the points made thus far: (a) that it is applicable only under some conditions and to certain situations and not others; (b) that it is the product of careful design, bargain, and will; and (c) that it is purposive, that is, designed to solve certain problems and serve other purposes. We shall elaborate on each of these attributes.

With regard to (a), it was Livingston (1952, 1956) who championed the view that the essence of constitutional systems lies in the nature of society served by the constitutions, rather than the constitutions themselves. On this basis, it is argued, federalism is best suited to federal societies, a federal society being, according to Livingston (1952:90), a state in which "the major identifying diversities...are arranged territorially" (by contrast, "if the distribution of diversities follows a marble-cake pattern (i.e. scattered); the society is plural and non-federal"). The argument then follows: "Only when a society contains territorial groups so markedly different from one another that they require some instrumentality to protect and express their peculiar qualities, does the need for federalism generally arise" (ibid).

This explains why federalism has been associated with pluralism and plural societies which describe the federal character of states, although it is important to stress that the federal solution as such cannot make coherent a society in which the diversities are so great that there can be no basis for integration. Since Livingston wrote, the notion of federal society and, in effect, federal instrumentalities, has been broadened to include societies with marble cake diversities which are no less troubled by problems of diversity than those Livingston regarded as proper federal societies.

The federal society thesis is valid to the extent that countries where federal instrumentalities have been applied belong almost without exception to the expanded category of federal societies, but it does not tell us why, in terms of the federation-non federation distinction made earlier, some federal societies (cf. Nigeria, India, Malaysia) become full-fledged federations and others (cf. South Africa, Sudan, Uganda, Cameroun) do not. The point is that the fact of being a federal society is, generally speaking, a necessary but not sufficient condition for federalism. A lot depends on other crucial factors like the orientation of the political elite which shapes the federal idea, the economic configuration and relations among the component groups, the degree of social cohesion as conditioned by urbanization, literacy, industrialization; etc, and the history of inter-group relations.

This takes us to (b) which should be read in conjunction with (c). The import of this is that federalism is perceived as a political solution to problems of government, typically those arising from the contradictory pulls of union and diversity in multi-ethnic, multi-cultural and multi-racial societies, and the union of independent states, as in the European Union, Economic Community of West African States, and the Commonwealth of Independent States that followed the collapse of the old USSR, for purposes of collective security, economic union, and their like. There is no guarantee that it would succeed - indeed it requires enabling factors like the will to form a union, fiscal capacity, constitutional discipline, and the cultivation of a culture of tolerance and compromise to succeed - but the federal solution has proven to be reliable in the management of the problems of governing diverse societies. Along these lines, Gagnon (1993) has identified conflict-solving, protection of minority groups, expression of democratic practices, especially where balances are sought between centripetal and centrifugal forces, and where the politics of representation is very complex, as some of the political uses to which federalism has been put. Duchacek (1977) and Adamolekun & Kincaid (1991) have also emphasized the potency of the federal solution in reconciling seemingly irreconcilable interests in divided multi-ethnic situations, while Elazar (1996) has analyzed the relevance of federalism for supranational organizations in terms of a paradigm shift in the study of federalism.

Our focus is on federalism within the nation-state, which is the level at which federalism has remained popular. Perhaps the greatest exponents of the federal solution at this level in contemporary history have been British colonizers who applied it to hold together large multi-ethnic colony-states like Nigeria, India, Uganda, and to some extent South Africa, where different, unequal and antagonistic groups were forcibly incorporated into new states. Following the examples of Switzerland and Canada where federalism has proven to be a cure for micro-nationalism (Watts, 1970), it has been recommended for multi-cultural states, especially those seriously threatened by disintegration (Sudan, Ethiopia, Lebanon, South Africa at several points, and Bosnia Herzegovina are good examples). In these instances, the federal solution has been approached more as a means to an end (typically of national cohesion) than an end in itself, in contradistinction to older federations like the USA, and Switzerland where federalism is both end and means. This explains why the federal solution is less rigid, more malleable and pragmatic, and far more adaptive and innovative in the newer federations, even to the point where Wheare and his critics are hard put to regard some full-fledged federal systems as federal (the imperial-center federalism operated by military governments in Nigeria is a case in point).

The exact form of federal solution worked out, the manner of operation and its future direction, however depend on the constellation and configuration of forces and power relations in civil society, as well as the attitudes toward federalism by the strategic elites who participate in the bargain from which federalism usually emerges, and those who operate it afterwards. Federal forms that have been devised and operated include, on the full-fledged federation side, centralized and decentralized federal government and symmetrical and asymmetrical federation, and, on the federalism without full-fledged federal government side, a variety of consociational, territorial and non-territorial devices, including power sharing and decentralization or devolution of power.

A lot also depends on how the federation or other variant of federalism came into being. According to Friedrich (1963, 1968), the federalizing process can be aggregative, involving the coming together of previously independent units, or disaggregative, in which "a hitherto unitary political community...becomes differentiated into a number of separate and distinct political communities" (1963:9). In general, aggregative federations tend to be full-fledged federal systems, saddled with inter-governmental issues, constitutionally rigid and democracy-driven. Disaggregative federations, on the other hand, tend to be less full-fledged federal systems characterized by (a) emphasizing on administrative arrangements (devolution and decentralization schemes) in which the central government retains its propriety over the constituent units; (b) the search for effective ways of accommodating diversity and minimizing challenges to the central government by separatist dissatisfied constituents; and (c) constitutional experimentations.

The point that needs to be stressed about the disaggregative federalizing process which is applicable to South Africa, is that the resulting arrangement may be substantially federal without bearing that label. This may be due to an aversion to the label itself, especially where, as in Spain (Agranoff, 1996), and South Africa (Schlemmer, 1992; Kotze, 1995), federalism has a negative connotation and is associated with the strengthening of divisive tendencies. In the case of South Africa, its association with apartheid or separate development and other divisionist schemes such as the Kwa Zulu/Natal Tadaba of the Grand Apartheid era of the 1980s, underlies the sometimes vehement opposition to federalism by the nation-centrist African National Congress (ANC). Ironically, the National Party which authored apartheid was resolutely anti-federal, in part because federalism was seen as a British-inspired colonial device to halt Afrikaner ascendancy, as in the initial proposal to have a federation of Southern Africa, until its transmutation to an opposition party of minority white-Afrikaners forced it into bargaining for a federal state in the transition to the post-apartheid order (Kotze, 1995; Osaghae, 1998, 1999). And yet, as we shall see, the theory and practice of the constitutional order has been and is substantially federal, although many of the country's ANC leaders would deny such a reality.

To summarize, we may characterize the federalist logic as a logic that relates federalism to the nature of society (diversity), and the efforts to resolve the politico-administrative, social and economic problems arising therefrom, by political and constitutional means. While it is true that not all situations of diversity necessitate or are suited to full-fledged federal government, it is equally true that most of such situations are attuned to, and invite, the federal solution in one form or the other. The spectrum of the federal solution is quite broad, and ranges from non-territorial power sharing to complex varieties of full-fledged federal systems of government. Whichever variant of the federal solution is preferred or adopted, particularly in disaggregative situations, depends on a number of factors, chief amongst which are the depth of divisions and antagonisms that ensue from diversity, the constellation of economic and social forces, and the extent to which the economic structure is integrated, complementary or rivalrous, the character and orientation of the political and ruling elite, and the nature and history of political conflicts in the country.

South Africa and the Federalist Logic: A Situational Framework

It is against the background of the foregoing conceptual clarifications and theoretical postulates that the experience of South Africa with the federalist logic will be analyzed. To situate the discussion in the rest of the chapter in a proper perspective, we shall briefly examine why federalism has remained a dominant theme of political discourse in South Africa, and give an overview of the debate on federalism in the country.

The major attraction to federalism in South Africa lies in the fact that the country belongs to the genre of federal societies classified as (deeply) divided societies. In addition to possessing large and geographically diverse territory, and economic complementarity, the country has a long history of racial and ethnic divisions and conflicts and of attempts to territorialize political cleavages. A good example of the latter is the Bantustan policy by which the apartheid regime granted 'independence' to black homelands. According to Welsh (1989:250) "Advocates of federalism have long contended that South

218

Africa's unique racial and ethnic problems and its sheer geographical size would be best accommodated by the adoption of a federal form of government". The problem, however, is not so much diversity and large size, as it is the fact that the polity is a divided society, that is, a polity in which political mobilization follows the lines of primary cleavages (in this case, mutually reinforcing racial', ethnic, and class cleavages) which then constitute the basis for contestations for power and other politically significant relations of deeply divided societies in which one or few powerful groups enjoy exclusive control of power often present a stratified or hierarchical social structure in which power, holdership, wealth, and social status are unevenly distributed and over time develop into caste-like divisions between dominant and dominated groups, if not properly managed. (see Firsehman, 1981 for theories of ethnic inequality). In the case of South Africa, this aptly ,summarizes the legacy of the apartheid regime whose raison d'etre was the entrenchment of white Afrikaner power and privilege and under which blatant racism was the "ideological foundation of government" (Davidson & Strand, 1993; for the manipulation of racial and ethnic differences to these ends by the apartheid regime, see Adam & Giliomee, 1979). The challenge posed by the government of a divided society like South Africa then, is how to reduce the effects of division and inequality, without at the same time sacrificing the strong attachments to primary groups and identities. This explains the attraction of federalism in South Africa with its long history of deeply-rooted racial and ethnic divisions and inequalities.

Periods of political transition and transformation, which have been numerous, given South Africa's turbulent history of inter-group relations, have been auspicious for proposing, examining and re-examining, and of course rejecting federal options. The options and opposition to them have changed as often as the nature of society, the configuration of diversity, demands of political society, and power relations, have changed. At the time of union, federal government was demanded by Natal federalists mainly to, amongst others, preserve the integrity of the four colonial territories at the time. Before then, two unsuccessful attempts had been made to federate Southern African territories in the 1850s and 1870s by the British colonizers. Later, after the coming into power of the Afrikaner NP (National Party) in 1948, the Progressive Party and Progressive Federal Party which both derived their major support from English-speaking white liberals, kept the federalist advocacy alive. The loss of the status of official opposition by the PFP in 1987 however decimated support for federalism among whites. With regard to the majority blacks, a homelands policy was devised to support the system of racial discrimination and separate development. The relationship between the homelands and the republic can be likened to a federacy in which small states, "rather than seeking full independence...have sought an asymmetrical federal association with the larger state power on the basis of internal autonomy and self-government, in order to share in the benefits which come from association with a greater power..." (Elazar, 1979:29).

Then in the 1970s and 1980s when the demise of apartheid became imminent, consociationalism, with its full complement of power sharing, group more than individual rights, minority veto, segmental autonomy and. proportional representation, and other forms of federalism were widely advocated (cf. see Forsyth, 1984; Horowitz, 1991; Lijphart, 1985). There were also proposals for division into white-controlled, black-controlled and non-racial units, though it must be emphasized that capitalist development and consequent economic integration had rendered the full separation to keep out blacks from the republic an unrealistic option. At this stage Buthelezi and Jordan Ngubane, both KwaZulu leaders, and Arthur Keppel-Jones were the champions of a full-fledged federal system. For Buthelezi, the author of the KwaZulu-Natal Indaba which proposed extensive self-government and a single legislative body for the region[3], the overriding consideration was how to reduce cut-throat competition, for central power:

> *"The distribution or devolution of power from a unitary centre to a number of autonomous states would greatly reduce or even eliminate altogether for a long time, the obsession of all groups with central power and control thereof...The establishment of central and state parliaments would mean a shift of political attention from the single all-powerful parliament..."(cited in Welsh, 1989:265).*

In the negotiations and pacting processes that hallmarked the transition to the post-apartheid regime, federalism featured prominently as a guarantee for regional autonomy and the preservation of cultural identities, alongside consociational demands, by the converted NP and its allies. The tenor of the federal debate during the transition suggested that it was advocated to preserve and further entrench privileges. The fact that besides Mangosuthu Buthelezi's Inkatha Freedom Party (IFP) which was regarded as a collaborator of the apartheid regime, federalism had very little support amongst black people in general and black nationalists in particular, in effect that its main advocates were and continue to be white liberals and separatists, has therefore tended to polarize the debate in a manner that makes federalism central to the race-based ideological contestation in the country.

Despite its topicality and relevance, proposals for full-fledged federation were rejected and defeated at every turn, largely by forces of nationalist counter-ideology. At the National Convention where agreement was reached on the South African Union of 1910, the desire to create a united white republic to counteract the threat posed by black nationalists and the rise of Afrikaner nationalism underlay the position of the anti-federalists led by John X. Merriman, then prime minister of the Cape colony and General Jan Smuts, then colonial secretary in the Transvaal government. For Smuts, federalism was inappropriate because it involved a treaty or pact between <u>independent</u> powers, whereas in South Africa, the powers were white brothers, and because it gave great powers to the judiciary, an unelected and unrepresentative body.

A publication on the eve of the convention, which was to influence the thinking there, rejected the Whearan model of dual federalism (Wheare, 1967) which was projected as the essence of federalism, on the grounds that it created 'hard and fast' divisions between federal and regional governments, thereby creating endless litigation and conflict. Some of the views expressed, in the publication are worth citing at length because of their relevance to contemporary debates on federalism in general:

> *"We are led to think that the functions of government cannot be divided into two lists, one national and the other local. Most, if not all of these functions, have their national aspect on the one hand and their local aspect on the other. We cannot say that the nation is solely responsible for defense and the locality for education...an arrangement which gives each kind of work to the appropriate machine cannot be fixed for all time by the rigid provisions of a constitution. Its essential principle is adaptation to the facts and, unless society is to stand still, the facts will change, and the methods of administration will change as well (cited in Welsh, 1989:252)."*

But, by and large, what won the day for unitarists, besides the fact of the wasteful rivalrous policies on railway transportation, custom tariffs, non-white labor and other economic matters, was the need to formulate common policies to deal with the 'native' question and strengthen control over them. Already, the differences in policies towards blacks, coloreds and Indians, such as the non-racial franchise practiced in the Cape, to which the other less liberal colonies were opposed, had taken their toll on white unity and ability to respond to the assault of the natives. It required little logic to realize that "Divided control over Africans also meant weaker control" (Welsh, 1989:259; also Kriek, 1992). This, more than any other consideration, meant that the native Africans were to be kept out of the resulting union as much as possible, without jeopardizing the exploitation of their labor. This was the beginning of the separation of African labor reserves or homelands, and the system of racial discrimination and inequality which in essence denied citizenship to non-whites in the union.

In the transition to the post-apartheid order, spanning the Convention for a Democratic South Africa (CODESA) and other bargaining and pacting forums, the ANC which this time led the anti-federalist front with its avowed commitment to a united, democratic, non-racial and non-sexist country, held on to the unfavorable dual and divisive perception of federalism. It saw federalism, with its entrenchment of regional autonomy, power sharing and group rights as a ploy to freeze racial inequalities and discrimination and thereby weaken the central state. This was disenabling of the party's liberationist, nationalist and redistribution agenda, embodied in its National Democratic Revolution (NDR)[5]. Dullah Omar, the post-apartheid minister of justice, has summarized the objectives of NDR as follows: "re-uniting [the] country, moving away from fragmentation, and creating a single geographical and political entity...The second objective...is developing a national consciousness, moving away from separateness or apartheid and building a single nation" (Omar, 1997:4).

But Omar was quick to acknowledge the federal imperative, saying that in spite of all this, there was need to recognize the multi-religious, multiethnic and multicultural character of the country. Part of the ANC's strategy to deal with these divisive identities was to strengthen the countervailing non-racial, non-ethnic identities such as worker or labor (farmer, mine worker, factory worker) and gender identities, which the relatively advanced capitalist system had fostered. Following Agranoff's classification, this can be regarded as a variant of (post-modernist) federalism. Any more serious form of federalism, such as the federal flavor of the interim constitution of 1993 was acceptable only to the extent that it represented "a workable mix of recognizing ethnicity without reifying it" (Maphai, 1995:71). The party's first choice was a unitary government in which the central government would have overriding powers over constituent (subordinate) governments, the relationship being one of "overlapping or concurrent jurisdiction, rather than segmented and competitive powers" (ANC, 1992:18).

The more black nationalist Pan-Africanist Congress (PAC) which joined the negotiating processes very late, also favored a strong unitary arrangement, but one in which the blacks were in absolute (majoritarian) control, if possible with the forced expulsion of whites. The demands of the federalists, principally the NP, IFP, moderate right-wing parties, the homeland governments and some academics, on the other hand, was for regional autonomy, which would enable regional governments enjoy entrenched fiscal competency and original non-centralizable jurisdiction on certain matters, and group rights, including the consociational right to minority veto. The case of the NP which, to retain its hold on power, had consistently rejected a non-racial and geo-political ' form of federalism (it even went so far as abolishing provincial legislatures and replacing them with administrative executive councils in 1986 to halt federal tendencies), is very interesting. Its turn around to federalism (although the party refrained from using the word federation), group rights and all, was expedient, forced by its (at the time potential) loss of state power, and transmutation of its white-Afrikaner support group into a minority. As it was at the time of the union, it was nationalist forces that once again triumphed over those of (supposedly divisionist) federalists, though, this time around, the all-encompassing nature of the transition and the give-and take culture developed by the negotiating parties, saw more deliberate efforts being made to balance the positions. The ANC, for example, was forced to concede much ground on regional autonomy in exchange for concessions from the other parties on full-fledged federalism and consociational instrumentalities.

Yet, in spite of all the strong opposition it has elicited, strong elements of federalism have continuously found their ways into South African political practice and culture. Thus, although the 1909 Act of Union as well as the 1961 constitution which provided the framework for the union were essentially unitarist to the extent that the powers assigned to the provincial governments related only to matters "which, in the opinion of the Governor General-in Council are of a merely local and private nature in the province" (cited in Welsh, 1989:258), and because provincial ordinances required the assent of the Governor General-in-Council, there were a number of federal principles in operation[6]. These included the full complement of government - executive, bureaucratic, legislative and judiciary - enjoyed by the provinces; the relatively autonomous powers granted the provinces which enabled the Cape' province to retain its non-exclusive white franchise until 1936 in the case of blacks and 1956 in the case of Coloreds; the legal equality of the English and Dutch (subsequently Afrikaans) languages; and creation of a second legislative chamber (senate) in which each of the four provinces had equal representation of eight senators.

In the post-union years, the apartheid ideology of separate development which, amongst others, resonated in the creation of' Bantustans (the four "independent" homelands of Transkei, Venda,. Bophuthatswana, and Ciskei, as well as the six "self-governing" homelands of Kwa-Zulu, Gazankulu, Lebowa, Qwa-Qwa, KwaNdebele, and KaNgwane) were seen by some as possible units in a future South African federation, and the doctrine of "own affairs" and tri-cameralism which saw the creation of White, Colored and Indian legislatures and departments in the Grand apartheid era. The constitutional bases and governmental practices of the transition of the 1990s were even far more federal than those of previous arrangements. As we shall have more to say on this in the next section, all that is necessary at this stage is the following statement of the implicit federal character of the 1996 constitution:

> *[the] constitution recognizes duality, namely the equal citizenship of all in one South Africa on the one hand and the diversity of South Africa's people on the other. Hence [the] constitution makes provision for equal rights at every level. And then the constitution makes provision for protection of freedom of religion, belief and opinion, language and culture...as well as cultural, religious and linguistic communities. The constitution enjoins upon the state the obligation to respect persons of different ethnic and cultural origins (Omar, 1997:8).*

The question may then be asked: why has the practice of government not been consonant with the unitarism preferred by nationalists and expressed in the constitutions? The answer will be found in the following factors, which derive from what I have called the federal imperative in South Africa. The first is that, as Welsh (1989:263) puts it, it is unrealistic to suppose that a concept of South Africanism could be forged in the crucible of a unitary arrangement that attempts to sweep away the artificial and historical boundaries. The Anglo-Afrikaner conflict that underlay the union of 1910 could not be resolved in a non-federal context, just as the mesh of racial boundaries, ethnic homelands and administrative divisions could not fit into the sort of unipolar undivided political arrangement (originally) envisaged by the ANC for whom even cultural differences in art, music and so on, were to be fused into a popular national culture (Venter, 1996).

In short, the lasting legacy of what de Villiers (1992b) calls <u>apartheid federalism</u>, that is, a system of racial discrimination, territory, and ethnic and race-based separate development, and economic divisions, notably those between capitalist centers of the white republic and the labor reserves of the homelands periphery, was the politicization of the cleavages to an extent that rendered unitarism untenable and impracticable. The existence of avowedly federalist parties like the PFP, IFP and moderate right-wing white Afrikaner parties like the Freedom Front, kept the pressures for constitutional recognition of diversities alive.

The second factor is closely related to the first; namely, that unitary arrangements are not strong enough to withstand the onslaught of ethnic and racial mobilization, and are not capable of "standing up to the stresses of conflict that deeply divided societies most regularly manifest" (Welsh, 1989:263). The stresses unleashed by Afrikaner right-wing movements which demanded separation in a volkstaat, and for whom true federalism was a second best option, are particularly noteworthy in this regard. Third then, is the problem of racial and ethnic minorities, how to protect their rights to the cultures, languages and religions they held steadfastly unto, and also protect them from

the possible excesses of (black) majority rule. Fourth is the virtual impossibility of administering a country of South Africa's size and economic and territorial diversity, with a long history of politico-administrative autonomy without one form of entrenched decentralization or another. The result of this is
that although they reject political federalism, nation-centered ruling parties
such as the ANC and the Afrikaner NP before it, have found administrative
federalism expedient.

The final factor is the centrality of (elite) pacting and negotiation, which,
following Agranoff (1996), may be regarded as a necessary condition for
federalism. The transition to the post-apartheid order, in particular, was hinged
from the very beginning (the Groote Schuur and Pretoria Minutes of 1990
are generally regarded as the starting point of the transition) on elite pacting.
The negotiations involved nineteen political associations - parties, alliances,
homelands delegations, etc - representing the major stakeholders in the transition. Pacting was greatly enhanced by the establishment of constitutional
sanctity as the guiding principle of negotiations at CODBSA, and the realization by the negotiating parties that they stood to lose more if the negotiations
failed (see Giliomee & Schlemmer, 1989; and Adam & Moodley, 1989 for
the conditions for meaningful negotiations in South Africa).

So South Africa has never really been a unitary state. Its political and
administrative arrangements belong to the genre of federalisms without federal government although, as we analyze in the next section, developments
since the transition of 1994 suggest that the country is steadily moving towards more federal government federalism. All this has been in response to
the dynamics of the country's federal imperative, and in spite of deep-rooted
ideological opposition to federalism by nation-centered nationalists. From a
comparative standpoint, Agranoff (1996:386) groups South Africa together
with Belgium, Spain, Ethiopia and Russia as states "that appear to be meeting
the challenges of regime transformation, ethnic and regional diversity, and
problems of social and economic justice through federal evolution" . The
concept of federal evolution aptly captures the incrementalist manner in which
South African federalism has evolved and is still evolving, without constitu-
tion-makers, policy makers and the ruling classes setting out to deliberately
construct a federation (in fact they want to believe they are doing the opposite).

The essence of federal evolution is that "the act of creating a federation
is not the only means of federal design. Unitary states can differentiate themselves and build in arrangements representing a federation in process"
(Agranoff, 1996:386). This provides the situational framework within which
the federal evolution in South Africa since the historical transition to democracy in 1994, which built upon the federal infrastructure laid by the apartheid

regime will be analyzed. It should also be added that the liberationist, redistribution and all-inclusive democratic milieu which formally ended the several decades of ethno-racial discrimination, exclusion, and inequality, and peacefully installed new legal and constitutional processes, has proven to be very supportive of the process of federal evolution.

Federal Evolution in South Africa Since 1994

One of the hallmarks of South Africa's democratic transformation which began in 1990 with the release of Nelson Mandela and other political prisoners and the unbanning of the liberation movements, was constitutional negotiations. The all-inclusive negotiations took place under the aegis of CODESA and the Multi-Party Negotiating Forum and involved about nineteen political organizations that represented the diverse and competing political groupings (unlike the whites-only negotiations which led to the formation of the union in 1910). It was at these forums that different political choices were presented, bargained and traded, leading up to the 1993 interim constitution which guided the initial phase of the transition and the 1996 (or so-called final) constitution.

Although the 1996 constitution was negotiated and drawn up by a Constituent Assembly which was drawn from parliament and composed in proportion to party strengths, and notwithstanding the changes in party positions and power configurations as the transition progressed (such as the near hegemonic power enjoyed by the ANC and the withdrawal of the NP from the GNU and the crisis that subsequently split the party, it was not expected to deviate much from the interim constitution, as it was bound by section 71 of the interim constitution to the thirty-four constitutional principles set out in schedule 4 of that constitution. Some of the principles were that special majorities would be required to amend the constitution; that provision would be made for the participation of minority parties in the legislative process; that all forms of discrimination would be prohibited; and that the powers and functions of the national and provincial governments shall be defined in the constitution. Perhaps the only exceptions were the 'sunset clauses' such as the GNU, which were designed to meet the exigencies of the transition. The termination of these clauses did not however mean the end of consensus and bargaining politics, as we shall discuss below.

To understand the tenor of federal evolution in the period since the transition, we shall first highlight the political and constitutional preferences of the parties in the negotiation process, which were bargained to produce the constitutions. Next, we examine the federal features of the constitutions in comparative perspective. Finally, we examine how the federal framework provided by the constitutions has shaped the process of government to be more federal or more unitary.

To Be Federal Or Not Federal

Federalism and its correlate, regional autonomy became the point of division amongst parties in the constitutional negotiation process. Building further on the Indaba proposals of the 1980s, the IFP wanted a (con)federal state in which its Kwa Zulu-Natal region would enjoy substantial autonomy, including its own constitution and, if possible, veto power (the homeland governments of Ciskei and Bophuthatswana made similar proposals). The Democratic Party, which emerged from the demise of the Progressive Federal Party and derived its main support from liberal English whites, had perhaps the clearest federal proposal of all. It proposed a federation of between eight and twelve states, each with its own government and entrenched powers, in addition to bicameral parliament and proportional representation. The Conservative Party (CP), a moderate Afrikaner right wing party proposed a commonwealth of nations to include the volkstaat (an exclusive white Afrikaner nation). Although the CP did not propose to reinstate apartheid, it planned to restore, among other instruments of the system of racial segregation, exclusive white education, Group Areas Act, Mixed Marriages Act and influx control, ostensibly to preserve Afrikaner exclusiveness and identity. More extreme right-wing groups which refused to join the transition negotiations went further to demand a sovereign but no less amorphous volkstaat in terms of Afrikaner right to self-determination, a struggle for which they were ready to go to war.

The then ruling NP championed power sharing and a three-tier system in which regional and municipal governments would enjoy wide-ranging and entrenched powers, including fiscal competency, to reduce the dangers of majority rule in the short run, and to guarantee political relevance and privileges to its leaders in the post-apartheid order. Accordingly, the party became more interested in redefining 'power sharing' from a compulsory coalition government (which it now demanded for the interim period only) to constitutional checks and balances, a bill of rights, and devolution of power to the regions. It was moving from consociationalism which stresses power sharing between groups towards constitutionalism, a set of rules on which it could rely if it became an opposition party (Atkinson, 1994:95).

The NP's proposals came close to what Agranoff (1996:386) has described as "post-modern" federalism, that is, "reconstruction of states reflecting the paradigm shift to federal non-centralization based on forms of power sharing". Relative to the afore-mentioned parties whose proposals contained shades of full-fledged federalism, the ANC stood on the other (anti-federal) side of the debate. At one stage, it appeared as if the NP, DP, CP and IFP were building an anti-ANC coalition on the basis of common support for federalism, to reduce the party's chances of coming to power (de Villiers, 1992a:28). As we stated earlier, the ANC was for an undivided non-racial state and opposed to group rights, a position it upheld since its Freedom Charter was published in 1955. This greatly influenced section 3(1) of the 1996 constitution, which states that: "There is a common South African citizenship." Nevertheless, the liberation movement-turned political party found it expedient to embrace regional governments, as long as these were to operate within limits set by the central government. Its proposals also included judicial review, independent judiciary, bill of rights, bicameralism, and proportional representation, all of which indicated that despite its ideological opposition to federalism, the ANC was not averse to elements of federalism called, perhaps, by another name. Indeed, the chairperson of the ANC's constitutional committee, Zola Skweyiya, agreed that South Africa needed "a unitary government with some federal characteristics" (cited in de Villiers, 1992a:28).

As it were, there was a shift, in the course of negotiating the interim and 1996 constitutions, from "the previous ideologic, dogmatic approach to a more flexible pragmatic attitude [which) opened the doors for mutually acceptable solutions, containing elements of various models" (de Villiers, 1992). This was especially true of the ANC and NP, the principal negotiators, whose bilateral pacting overshadowed the inputs of the other parties, which mostly stuck to hard-line positions and pulled out from the negotiations at various points. On the question of regionalism around which the federalism question came to be hinged, for example, the ANC watered down its opposition to strong regions to an acceptance of regional governments with "original powers", although these were to be subject to the overriding authority of the central government. This shift suggested "an attempt to achieve some extent of common ground between federalist and unitary proposals" (Welsh, cited in Friedman & Humphries, 1993:67).

The NP, as we have seen also moved from a position of group rights for protection of minorities to consensus-driven constitutionalism which, amongst others, required the agreement of the leading parties for decisions to be taken. In the Constituent Assembly that produced the 1996 constitution, the NP turned fully around to agree with the ANC that the bill of rights, especially the right to private property, together with constitutional guarantee of language, religious and cultural diversity, were sufficient to protect the interests of minorities. Again, its proposals were clearly "a mixture of federal and consociative elements" (Kotze, 1995:61). Such pragmatic agreements were possible because the negotiating parties were sufficiently 'nationally mixed' to permit intricate balances, notwithstanding their recognizable ethno-racial affiliations. The scenario would arguably have been different if the parties represented territorially delineated divisions. It is instructive that the IFP, which had exclusive ethnic (Zulu) and territorial interests to defend, and the CP and other right-wing parties which looked forward to territorial autonomy, were the most unwavering in their demands for regional autonomy or outright separation.

The Constitutional Framework

The end-products of the negotiations were the 1993 interim constitution and the 1996 constitution. The main institutional manifestations of agreements reached were the government of national unity (GNU) at the national, provincial and local levels which was to last until 1999 when the next general elections were to be held; a system of proportional representation which assured minority parties of political relevance; affirmative action; re-composition and restructuring of important national institutions to reflect the changing balance of political forces; decentralization and other structural elements of power sharing which gave the nine new provinces and localities entrenched powers (Basson, 1995; du Toit, 1996).

In reflecting these agreements, both the interim and 1996 constitutions can be regarded as unitary with substantial federal features. The defining unitary character is found in the supremacy clauses (sections 4 of interim and 2 of the 1996 constitutions respectively) which define the constitution as the supreme law of the republic, binding on organs of state at all levels of government, the fact that the nine provinces are creations of the central government, the centralization of the police system, and the unitary character of the judiciary (Sono, 1995). But the federal features, which are more substantial and notable, included the following:

THREE-TIER GOVERNMENT

Alongside a powerful central government were two other relatively autonomous tiers of government - provincial and local. The distribution of powers and functions fell "within the range of federal-type models" (de Villiers, 1996:47) with national and provincial governments having exclusive and concurrent legislative lists. The nine provincial governments were autonomous within their spheres of competence, subject only to limitation by central parliament in affairs that required coordinated efficiency or in pursuance of enforcing minimum standards of service delivery throughout the country. In fact, section 126(3) of the interim constitution gave precedence to laws passed by provincial legislatures over parliamentary acts in matters enumerated in schedule 6, on which provincial governments had exclusive competence, although South African scholars contest the extent to which this section eroded the supremacy clause (section 4) referred to above (see Sono, 1995). Moreover, the revenue bases of the provinces were clearly defined, including their entitlement to an equitable share of individual income, value added tax and fuel levy collected by the central government, though they derive approximately 90 per cent of their incomes from the national government ' (a Financial and Fiscal Commission to, amongst others, advise on the fiscal aspects of inter-governmental relations was also provided for); the provinces were given the exclusive right to write their own 'constitutions; and they were empowered to appoint their own provincial service Commission as a first step in the establishment of their own public services. Also, the provinces had equal representation in the Senate where they were expected to protect provincial interests in central government; the assent of senate was required to pass national legislation that had to do with the provinces. The other tier of government comprised local governments whose functions, mainly devolved from the other tiers, were also constitutionally guaranteed.

These principles were basically consolidated and extended in some areas in the 1996 constitution. The three levels of government are defined in section 40(1) as "distinctive, interdependent and related". The powers and functions of local governments are more clearly defined (schedule 5(b), and section 151(4) forbids the national or provincial government from compromising or impeding, a municipality's ability or right to exercise its powers or perform its functions, though the provincial government retains the power to intervene when a local government is unable to fulfill its executive obligation (section 139(1)). Similarly, parliament has the power of intervention in matters of exclusive provincial competence under terms set out in section 44(2). To reduce the potentially conflictual and divisive trajectories of a three tier government, chapter 3 of the constitution introduces cooperative government as the framework for inter-governmental relations (IGR). In pursuance of this; parliament is empowered to establish structures to facilitate IGR and resolve disputes arising therefrom.

Perhaps the most significant development in the evolution towards constitutional federalism was the strengthening of provincial voice in the affairs of the national government. The senate is re-designated the National Council of Provinces which represents the provinces to ensure that provincial interests are taken into account in the national sphere of government. It does this mainly by participating in the national legislative process and by providing a national forum for public consideration of issues affecting the provinces (section

42(4).

As before, the provinces have equal representation (10 members each), selected in proportion to party electoral strengths in the provinces. Although the provinces have been strengthened in this way, the expansion of the concurrent legislative list and the corresponding shrinking of the areas of exclusive provincial competence (schedules 4 and 5, contrasted with schedules 4 and 6 of the interim constitution) suggest a balancing which gives the national government more leeway, especially as the country retains a single public service controlled by the national government.

Non-Territorial Federalism

In addition to these territorial and administrative dimensions of federalism, the interim and 1996 constitutions also contained several elements of non-territorial federalism. Foremost among these was executive power sharing through a Government of National Unity (GNU), which however applied only to the period of transition. Under the terms outlined in section 80 of the interim constitution, every party holding at least twenty seats in the National Assembly and which decided to participate in the GNU was entitled to one or more cabinet portfolios. Furthermore, if such a party held up to eighty seats, it was entitled to an executive vice president post. Following their performances in the April 1994 elections, ANC with 252 seats had the presidential and one executive vice- president post as well as 18 ministerial and 8 deputy ministerial portfolios; the NP with 82 seats was allocated an executive vice- president post, six ministerial and three deputy ministerial portfolios; while the TFP with 43 seats got three ministerial and one deputy ministerial portfolios. Similar patterns, which reflected party strengths, were in place in the provinces. Next was the electoral system of Proportional Representation (PR), which guaranteed representation for minority parties in the National Assembly and provincial legislatures in direct proportion to the share of votes won in elections. As a result of PR, parties like the Freedom Front, Democratic Party, and PAC, which won less than three per cent of the votes in the 1994 election were represented in the National Assembly.

Other non-territorial federal elements, which were aimed at pluri-national accommodation, include a bill of rights, and the constitutional recognition and protection of cultural, linguistic and religious diversity through virtual group rights. One underlying constitutional principle was that the composition of state institutions, including the judiciary, and the conduct of government business, should be cognizant of the need for representivity and diversity. Eleven official languages were adopted, and the 1996 constitution required the national and provincial governments to use at least two official languages (section 3(a). To divest these provisions of any inferred group rights, attempts were made in the 1996 constitution to de-racialize and de-ethnicize collective rights by making gender and class the bases of representivity and balance. Moreover, language and cultural rights were made a matter of personal choice, and cultural, linguistic and religious associations were designated, organs of civil society.

Perhaps then, the closest thing to a group right is the provision on self-determination in section 235, which deserves to be quoted in full: *"The right of the South African people as a whole to self-determination...does not preclude...recognition of the right of the notion of the right to self-determination of any community sharing a common cultural and language heritage, within a territorial entity in the Republic or in any other way determined by national legislation."*

This provision was an expedient response to the demands for a volkstaat, and to a lesser extent, the separatist agitations mobilized by the IFP in the Kwa-Zulu Natal province. The interim constitution had established a Volkstaat Council and charged it with seeking constitutional ways of actualizing the idea. But it remains to be seen how far the granting of a notion of the right to self-determination can satisfy Afrikaner nationalists and right-wing movements who demand explicit group rights - language rights, including right to education in the mother tongue, cultural autonomy, territorial autonomy and self-government - especially in the light of the contradictory attempt to de-collectivize group rights. Nevertheless, it is significant that both the interim and 1996 constitutions created regulatory and oversight institutions, which the 1996 constitution refers to as State Institutions for Constitutional Democracy, to ensure the protection of individual and notional group rights. The institutions include the Commission for the Promotion and Protection of the Rights of Cultural, Religious and Linguistic Communities, Pan-South African Languages Board, Human Rights Commission, Commission for Gender Equality, and the Independent Broadcasting Authority, all of which complement the Constitutional Court which has the final say on all constitutional problems.

Juridical Correlates of Federalism

The constitution was fairly rigid to the extent that it could only be amended with the concurrence of 75 per cent of members of the National Assembly and the supporting vote of at least 6 provinces in the National Council of Provinces (section 74 of 1996 constitution). Autonomy-seeking provinces and parties also had ample room for maneuver. Their boundaries, powers and functions could not be altered without the concurrence of at least six provinces in the National Council of Provinces, and they were entitled to provincial constitutions. Finally, the Constitutional Court served as the guardian of the constitution, and judicial review, widely regarded as a federal principle, was enshrined, as a core constitutional principle.

The Operation Of The Constitution(s)

The scope for federal practice and experimentation contained in the interim and 1996 constitutions was constrained by a number of factors, which worked in the opposite direction of strengthening the central government. Chief amongst these was control of seven of the nine provinces by the nation-centrist ANC, which also controlled the national government with a large majority. The centralization of ANC development policies within the framework of the Reconstruction and Development Program (RDP) practically reduced the provincial governments to administrative agencies of the national government, especially given their dependence on the national public service, and for up to 90 per cent of their revenues.

The only provinces which behaved "federally", by insisting on their autonomy from the center, were the two not controlled by the ANC, namely, the Western Cape (NP) and Kwa Zulu-Natal (IFP). Both were about the first to produce autonomy-asserting provincial constitutions, and seized every opportunity to attempt to wrest provincial rights in the name of inter-party competition; at several points, the Kwa Zulu-Natal government exhibited separatist tendencies, while the NP increasingly took on the character of a (Western Cape) regional party.

The fluidity of the transition process itself was another factor. The provinces (and local government councils which were constituted in 1995-96) had just come into being from the decomposition of the erstwhile regions in the white republic, 'own affairs' structures, and the homeland governments, including the erstwhile "independent" homelands of Transkei, Venda, Bophuthatswana and Ciskei. They were still struggling to establish viable structures, even in terms of administration. This gave leeway to the national government, especially as the provinces virtually depended on it for fiscal capacity and the establishment of provincial bureaucracies. The continuing uncertainties and violence that enveloped the first few years of transition and threatened the state (such as the violence in Kwa Zulu-Natal. and separatist and Third Force activities of right-wing Afrikaner movements) also provided the national government the ostensible grounds to insist on lording it over the provinces and local government areas in the name of national security.

Notwithstanding these constraints however, there were significant developments that served to galvanize the evolution of federalism in the country. First was the growing consciousness and assertiveness of provincial rights, and the clamor by premiers, including ANC premiers, for more clearly defined powers and less dependence on the national government. For example, Matthews Phosa, ANC premier of the Eastern Transvaal demanded exclusive and not only concurrent powers for the provinces (which the 1996 partially granted), as well as the enhancement of the fiscal and bureaucratic capacity of the provinces to enable them discharge their constitutional roles. His demands for expanded regional competency, especially for border provinces like the Eastern J Transvaal which houses the border with Mozambique, even extended to the foreign policy arena, as he sought provincial involvement in the control of illegal immigrants (Humphries, 1995) . Also, local government functionaries and scholars increasingly complained about the structural impediments to local government autonomy, and demanded greater fiscal and administrative capacities for that tier of government (de Beer & Lourens, 1995).

The process of federal evolution also saw the emergence of a voluntary inter-governmental consultative bodies which helped to foster the federal spirit by promoting inter-governmental cooperation. These included the Premiers' Forum which "developed from the need of premiers to discuss and plan common policy - especially with regard to their relationship with national government and to consult on matters which affect the provinces" (de Villiers, 1996:52), and the Inter-governmental Forum under whose aegis the president held regular consultations with premiers and Ministers, which brought together national and provincial ministers. These forums provided outlets through which provincial rights were claimed.

Then there were the sustained pressures which continued to be exerted by Afrikaner nationalists, especially members of the right-wing organizations. For example, the Volkstaat Council organized a conference on self-determination in 1996 as part of its mandate to seek constitutional ways of actualizing the volkstaat, at which federalism featured prominently as the most conducive political arrangement to cross-pressures of the assertions of the right to self-determination in a multi-national state. Most participants at the conference emphasized the utility of federalism for the protection of minorities (Volkstaat Council, 1996). As the post-apartheid order became consolidated, more and more came to be heard as complaints of marginalization, structured inequality and exclusion by black groups such as the Venda, Sotho and of course Zulu, who allege Xhosa preponderance (or domination) in the ANC and the running of the country's affairs. Such development only indicates that if steps are not taken to address these grievances, black federalists other than those in the IFP can be expected to increase in the future.

Conclusions

The federal nature of South African society has made federal solution in one form or the other necessary and expedient. This federal imperative has been the basis for the (disjointed) incrementalist evolution of federalism in the country, despite the vehement opposition of hegemonic nationalists - the NP - and its white Afrikaner constituency until the transition, and the avowedly non-racial ANC in the post-apartheid dispensation. The major conclusion from this analysis is that, with the opening of the previously closed South African political system in a manner that allows the competing identities full expression, the federal infrastructure built over the years, and especially in the interim and 1996 constitutions will be consolidated. The political and administrative arrangement in the country is already substantially federal both in theory and practice, and the probability is very high that a full-fledged federal system will come into being in the long run, though as is the case with India, it is not likely to be called federal.

ENDNOTES

1. It should however be pointed out that as much as constitutionality is the hallmark of federation, this is no guarantee that it would behave federally. The histories of several federations is replete with contradictions between formal structures and political practice (in terms of practice, some unitary states behave more federally than federal states). But this is not our immediate concern.
2. In fact; some scholars see federalism as a variant of pluralism, but, as Elazar (1987:87, 90-1) has clarified: "Federalism differs from pluralism because it bases its efforts to deal with the realities of human nature on a firm constitutional structure...pluralism in one form or another may indeed be a safeguard of liberty, but...it cannot be relied upon by itself unless properly institutionalized constitutionally...."
3. The Indaba proposal also included a bicameral legislature whose first chamber was to be composed proportionately among the racial groups; and the second, on the principle of equality; and the protection of minority rights in the areas of religion, culture and language.
4. An opinion poll conducted in the mid-1980s showed that 80 per cent of sampled urban blacks favored a unitary non-racial democracy (Welsh, 1989:271).
5. ANC leaders saw federalism and power sharing as entrenching the "group approach" as opposed to the one-man-one-vote approach to politics favored by white politicians and strategists. According to Oliver Tambo, "the idea of power sharing as well as that of federation or confederation is based on the notion of racial groups, each one of which must be treated as an organic political bloc which

must bargain for a modus vivendi with other racial political blocs" (cited in Welsh, 1989:270).

6.   Other unitarist defining elements included parliamentary sovereignty and flexibility of the constitution, which could be amended unilaterally by the central government.

7.   These are when it is necessary to maintain national security, economic unity, essential national standards, establish minimum standards, or prevent unreasonable action taken by a province which is prejudicial to other provinces or the country as a whole.

REFERENCES

Adam: H. & Giliomee, H. 1979. *Ethnic Power Mobilised: Can South Africa Change?*. New Haven, Yale University Press.

Adam, H. & Moodley, K. 1989 "Negotiations about what in South Africa?," *Journal of Modern African Studies*, vol. 27, no 3.

Adamolekun, L. & Kincaid, J. 1991 "The Federal Solution: An assessment and prognosis of Nigeria and Africa," *Publius: The Journal of Federalism*, vol. 21, no 3.

Agranoff, R.. 1996. "Federal Evolution in Spain*", International Political Science Review*, vol. 17, no 4.

ANC. 1992. "Ten Proposed Regions for South Africa," Discussion Document Bellville: CDS, UWC.

Atkinson, D. 1994. "Principle Born of Pragmatism? Central Government in the Constitution" in S. Friedman & D. Atkinson eds. *The Small Miracle: South Africa's Negotiated Settlement.* Johannesburg, Ravan Press.

Basson, D. 1995. *South Africa's Interim Constitution: Text and Notes.* Cape Town: Juta.

Burgess, M. 1993. "Federalism and Federation: A Reappraisal!' in M. Burgess & A-G. Gagnon eds. *Comparative Federalism and Federation: Competing Traditions and Future Directions.* Hertfordshire: Harvester Wheatsheaf

Davidson, P.I. & Strand, P. 1993. *The Path to Democracy: A Background to the Constitutional Negotiations in South Africa* Uppsala.

de Beer, J. & Lourens, L. 1995. *Local Government: The Road to Democracy.* Midrand: Educum.

de Villiers, B., 1992a. "Federalism in South Africa: Implications for Individual and Minority Protection" *Federalism: Making it Work.* Johannesburg: Konrad Adenauer.

————.1992b. "A Constitutional Scenario for Regional Government in South Africa: The Debate Continues", Konrad Adenauer's International Cooperation Occasional Papers Johannesburg: Konrad Adenauer.

————.1996. "The Role and Powers of Provincial and Local Governments in the New Constitution" in *Aspects of the Debate on the Draft of the new South African Constitution* Johannesburg, Konrad Adanauer.

Duchacek, I. 1977. "Antagonistic Cooperation: Territorial and Ethnic Communities," *Publius: The Journal of Federalism*, vol. 7, no 4.

du Toit, P. 1996. "Towards the Autonomous State? Comparing South Africa's 1993 Constitution and the 1996 Draft Constitution Bill" in *Aspects of the Debate on the Draft of the New South African Constitution*. Johannesburg: Konrad Adenauer

Elazar, D.J. 1976. "Federalism vs. Decentralisation: The Drift from Authenticity", *Publius: The Journal of Federalism*, vol. 6, no 3.

————.1979. "The Role of Federalism in Political Integration" in Elazar ed. *Federalism and Political Integration* Jerusalem: Turtle Dove.

————.1987. *Federalism,* Tuscaloosa: University of Alabama Press.

————.1996. "From Statism to Federalism - A Paradigm Shift", *International Political Science Review*, vol. 17, no 4.

Forsyth, M. 1984. *Federalism and the Future of South Africa.* Johannesburg: South African Institute of International Affairs.

Friedman, S. & Humphries, R.. 1993. *Federalism and its Faces.* Johannesburg: Centre for Policy Studies.

Friedrich, C.J. 1963. Federalism: *National and International London*: Oxford University Press.

.1968. *Trends of Federalism in Theory and Practice* London, Pall Mall

Gagnon, A. G. 1993. "The Political Uses of Federalism" in M. Burgess & A-G. Gagnon eds. op. cit.

Giliomee, H. & Schlemmer, L. eds. 1989. *Negotiating South Africa's Future.* Basingstoke & London: Macmillan.

Horowitz, D. 1991. *A Democratic South Africa? Constitutional Engineering for a Divided Society.* Cape Town, Oxford: Oxford University Press.

Humphries, R.. 1995. "Intergovernmental Coordination" in H. Kotze ed. *The Political Economy of Federalism in South Africa.* Stellenbosch, Centre for International & Comparative Polities, University of Stellenbosch.

King, P. 1982. *Federalism and Federation* London: Groom Heim.

Kotze, H. 1995. "Federalism in South Africa: An Overview" in H. Kotze ed. op. cit.

Kriek, D. J. 1992. "Federation Proposals before and during the National Convention, 1908-1909" in DJ. Kriek *et al, Federalism: The Solution? Principles and Proposals* Pretoria, HSRC.

Lijphart, A. 1985. "Non-Majoritarian Democracy: A Comparison of Federal and Consociational Theories," *Publius: The Journal of Federalism*, vol. 15, no 2.

Livingston, W. A., 1952 "A Note on the Nature of Federalism: Federalism as a Juridical Concept", *Political Science Quarterly*, vol. 67, no 1.

————.1956 *Federalism and Constitutional Change* Oxford, Clarendon Press.

Maphai, V.T. 1995. "Liberal Democracy and Ethnic Conflict in South Africa in H. Glickman ed. *Ethnic Conflict and Democratisation in Africa.* Atlanta: African Studies Association Press.

Omar, D., 1997, *Opening Address at the International Conference on National Identity and Democracy.* Cape Town.

Osaghae, E.E. 1990. "A Reassessment of Federalism as a Degree of Decentralisation," *Publius*, vol. 20, no 1.

————.1996. "The Federal Solution in Comparative Perspective" *Politeia*, vol. 16, no

1.

————.1998. "What Democratisation does to Minorities Displaced from Power: The Case of White Afrikaners in South Africa," *Report submitted to the CODESRIA Research Group on Ethnicity and Democratisation in Africa.*

————.1999. "Democracy and National Cohesion in Multiethnic African States: South Africa and Nigeria Compared," *Nations and Nationalism*, vol. 5, no 2.

Riker, W. 1975. "Federalism" in F. J. Greenstein & N. W. Polsby eds. *Handbook Political Science* vol. 5 Governmental Institutions and Processes. Reading: Addison-Wesley.

Schlemmer, L. 1992. "Federalism and Democracy: Propositions and Problems" in *Federalism: Making it Work* op. cit.

Sono, T. 1995. "How Federal is the Interim Constitution? Another View", in H. Kotze, op. cit.

Venter, D. 1996. "It may be Art, but is it Culture? The ANC's conceptions of Culture and Orientation towards Ethnicity in the 1994 RDP Booklet," *Politikon*, vol. 23, no 1.

Vile, M. J. G. 1977. "Federal Theory and the 'New Federalism'" in D Jaensch ed. *The Politics of New Federalism* Adelaide, Australian Political Studies Association.

Watts, R. L. 1970. *Multicultural Societies and Federalism.* Ottawa: Studies of the Royal Commission on Bilingualism and Biculturalism.

Welsh, D. 1989. "Federalism and the Problem of South Africa" in M. Forsyth ed. *Federalism and Nationalism.* Leicester: Leicester University Press.

Wheare, K.C. 1967, *Federal Government* 4th ed. London: Oxford University Press.

CHAPTER 11

The Sudan and The Federal Option

Awad Al-Sid Al-Karsani

Introduction

The search for good governance in post-colonial Africa through the blind and faithful adoption of others' traditions led to the rise of an African crisis of governance. For many of the African countries the postcolonial era is one of a search for a lost identity. Whatever "the causes of that crisis - "external", "internal", or a specific mix of the two- its solution can only be the result of initiative by organized social forces inside Africa" (Mamdani et al., 1988:16). The struggle for good governance is essentially to awake and liberate the African masses' consciousness to discover an African identity as a prelude to the solution of the governance crisis. The crisis of governance is a manifestation of the crisis of identity. The study of one pinpoints and highlights the problems inherent in the other.

For Sudan the crisis is essentially a political one. Since independence, the country has been suffering from a chronic state of political instability. A vicious circle of multi-party rule-authoritarian military governments - popular uprisings etc. civil war, ethnic strife, socio-economic and internal conflicts "indicate the questionable political legitimacy of most regimes that governed the country, including the so-called democratic regimes of the national political parties'. Decades of bad governance have been a primary cause of endemic conflicts and human suffering" (NHDR, 1988:80).

The federal option is not a new agenda in the politics of the Sudan. As early as 1949 calls for securing special safeguards for the Southern Sudan in an independent Sudan marked the country's move towards federalism and witnessed the birth of "non-centralization" as a means to handle the distribution of power. In the post-independence period, there developed a conviction that Sudan is ungovernable from the center. Decentralization became part

and parcel of the political game in the Sudan. The 1961 Provincial Administration Act accelerated the process of "power devolution". The 1971 People's
Government Act and the 1980 Regional Government Act listed specific matters as the exclusive reserve of the national government, while regional governments were allocated functions which had restricted geographical, political
and cultural impact. In the two decentralization experiences of the 1961 and
1980 the authoritarian nature of the regimes made the experiences fail to
achieve a modicum of popular participation. Furthermore, during the 1970s
and the 1980s "the cult of personality established by Nimeiri made the possibility of meaningful power sharing even more remote" (Fegley, 1986:167).
The link between authoritarian regimes and attempts towards experiencing a
degree of decentralization made a distinguished Sudanese political scientist to
sarcastically argue that :

> *It is hardly surprising therefore that many people in the Sudan today tend to think of
> federalism as merely another form of local or regional administration involving, perhaps,
> a greater degree of decentralization in the familiar unitary structure of the country
> (Abdel-Rahin, 1995:14).*

However, in 1991 the National Salvation regime advocated federalism as the
most suitable system for the Sudan.[1] What differentiates the National Salvation military regime from its predecessors (military or democratic regimes) is
that it has a philosophy of "Governance" and *Waltanchung*. Islam and the
dream to reincarnate the Rashidite Caliphs era of early Islam back on earth
acted as the ideological basis of the regime. And for Muslims over the ages
federalism means "proximity to people serves the maxim of Shura (consultation) which is a mandate in Sharia" (Abdalla, 1995:22).

Gradual Approach

The Sudan's Comprehensive National Strategy (CNS) states that:

> *"The main concern in the Sudan is to create a self reliant civil society satisfying human
> quest for dignity and freedom in balance with the advancement in economic, social and
> cultural life emanating from the national heritage. For Sudan, human development means
> participation and dialogue of all Sudanese in decision making based on freedom of
> thought and conscience" (CNS, 1992 vol. I: 7-8).*

For the implementation of federalism CNS adopted a gradual approach.
The process is carried in two stages:

a) Stage One (1992-1994): This stage was characterized by the concentration of work to complete the federal government structure and to filling the gaps that it suffers.

b) Stage Two (1995-1999): This stage is considered the stage of consolidating organizational and functional structures and the promotion of material as well as human resources (CNS, 1992 vol. I:217).

Dr. Ali El Haj Mohammed, the Minister of the Federal Government Chamber (Ministry of Federal Relations), described the first stage as aiming to achieve "equitable distribution of wealth and power, based on a solemn belief that "Justice is the foundation of good governance". Our federal system, therefore, provides an additional basis for justice, leading to political stability" (El Haj Mohammod, 1994:13-17). This first stage was started in February 1991 by issuing the Fourth Constitutional Decree which instituted the federal rule. The Decree was followed by some constitutional changes aiming at establishing the federal system up to the issuing of the Tenth Constitutional Decree, which re-divided the country's nine regions into twenty six states in 1994. On the same principle provinces were increased in number and given additional political roles, which were meant to deploy energies and goodness in people and to lead them into Local Government initiations in harmony with the whole federal system (the 1991 Local Government Act).

Besides the body of constitutional legislation which stipulated the powers and relations between various state organs, it is appropriate to describe this first stage as a transition from centralism to decentralization at the constitutional level. It required much effort to develop the concepts, establish new relations and compile the necessary literature from federal thought and other experiences.

The Eleventh Constitutional Decree, which was issued in 1994 came at the close of the first founding stage. It dealt with the relations between the federal and state governments, established full autonomy for each level of government regarding its relevant powers. It endowed the President of the Republic with the power to supervise the administration of the states through their governments and governors who are accountable to him. The President of the Republic exercises this supervision through the Federal Government Chamber. The role of this Chamber is one of co-ordination with both the states and the federal government. The Chamber's Minister is answerable to the National Assembly and the Federal Cabinet, as well as accountable to the President of the Republic.

Co-ordination is an important tool for the establishing and consolidation of the federal experiment. It is carried through direct contacts and regular visits to the states conducted by the Chamber officials, together with concerned federal ministers. During these visits meetings are held as follows:

a)   A meeting is held with the state's government and its Wali (Governor) where an appraisal is conducted of the state's plans vis-à-vis CNS, its achievements, its budget and the development of its relations with the federal government. The Chamber and the federal ministers suggest solutions to possible problems on new means of cooperation and coordination. The Chamber usually benefits from such meetings to explain conceptions and record remarks and recommendations to be passed to relevant authorities.

b)   A meeting is held with states legislative councils, Popular Committees, legal organs and the Civil Service, with a view to oversee development on their supervisory and legislative functions.

c)   Direct contact with the state's people, where there is a chance of discussing political issues and those relating to federal government in particular. These meetings enhance orientation and test the development of the experiment at the grass roots level.

The Eleventh Constitutional Decree has a great impact on the development of Sudan federal experience because it is "by all measures - a grand step forward and reflects political maturity as well as authenticity in effectuating the system of federalism" (Abdalla, 1995:222).

A negative impact of the first stage is that the country witnessed an increase in the number of federal ministries, which means that the federal level is still powerful. Also the administrative structures at the state level were drawn without considering the specific conditions of states. In every state there are six ministries and a seventh for Peace Affairs in the ten Southern states. The challenge is how to establish a small and capable government whose organization is based on the efficient utilization of the available resources in the state.

The second stage aims at:

i)   Strengthening of the federal systems' institutions and training of the necessary personnel to help these institutions to create and strengthen their autonomy independently of the central government.

ii)   Establishing and ensuring effective popular participation in the different levels of government from the grass roots.

iii) Contribute to the establishment of an effective government through elections accountable to the people.

The second stage started by the promulgation of the Twelfth Constitutional Decree. The Decree is considered a complement to the preceding one, No. 11. While No. 11 facilitated the process of power sharing in a three-tier federal system, the Twelfth Constitutional Decree addressed problems of wealth sharing.

It is not the first time that the center tried to share power and wealth with the other parts of the country. Nimeiri's regime (1969-1985) introduced Regionalism as a means to share power and wealth. However, this regionalism which was adopted at times (1980s) of a mounting economic crisis, acute shortage in daily consumption commodities and an aggravating political crisis, further distanced people from achieving their demands. T.C. Niblock criticized regionalism that its "policies required increased expenditure. The policies became simply instruments for diverting popular attention from economic failure and for ensuring the continued allegiance of those local influential individuals who could emerge as `ministers in the regional governments" (Niblock, 1987:287). Though regionalism was initially implemented to quell and court the "regional elite", it brought a negative impact. An African Right's Report noticed that 'The Kordofan Regional Government was dominated from outset by powerful Arab interests - a coalition of North Kordofan interests with South Kordofan Baggara and Jellaba - who were ruthless in distributing largesse to their local supporters (African Rights, 1995:42)." This alienation of the Nuba tribes from enjoying political participation and the fruits of their lands drove many of them to join SPLA/SPLM. The Twelfth Constitutional Decree had to remember and learn from this past experience.

The Twelfth Constitutional Decree divided the financial resources among the three levels of rule (federal, state and locality). For the first time a constitutional arrangement guaranteed distinct financial resources for the Local Government level. The 1995 Local Government Act reflected the importance of the locality, which became responsible for primary education, health care, economic and social development, payment of salaries, etc. Many parts of the Twelfth Constitutional Decree are embodied in the 1998 Constitution (Part VI, Chapter III, Articles 113- 115). The implementation of this Decree, as we shall see below, has led to different results.

It is clear from the above narration that the adoption and implementation of federalism has come through a gradual process. This is because the regime realized from the beginning that the application of federalism is conducive to its mere existence, broadening its base of support by courting the "regional elite" and thus contributes to ending the war in the South. This is why the move to apply federalism is also linked to the regime's endeavors to achieve peace in the South.

The South

Sudan has experienced one of the largest civil wars in the modern world. The root causes of the conflict lies in a host of factors: lack of sound governance and a clear vision of how to achieve national unity contributed to the continuity of the war as the most important agenda for all Sudanese governments in the post-colonial era.[2] On coming to power in 1989 the present government convened a National Dialogue Conference on Peace Issues. The Conference "declared for a peace plan based on a decentralization of power and resources, the protection of cultural diversity, and a clear understanding of the roles of state and religion. This was adopted by the Government as a national program for negotiations with the rebel movement (Sudan Foundation, 1998:1)." To fulfill this program the government held eighteen rounds of peace negotiations outside the Sudan with the rebel movement(s).

The application of federalism has induced many Southern forces inside the country to start dialogue with the government. The "Peace From Within" program became an important avenue for the consolidation of the atmosphere conducive to peace. Juba Convention of Southern Peace Forces praised the application of federalism as an important step towards the realization of peace. The application of the federal system of rule in the Sudan in general and in Southern Sudan in particular that led to the transfer of power from the center to the states, noting that federalism has been a demand of Southern Sudan citizens since Juba Conference in 1947.[3]

The various rounds of peace negotiations succeeded in laying the basis of certain principles which became pivotal for the realization of peace. For the purpose of implementing the principles discussed outside and inside the country the government in December 1995 "made the Twelfth and the Thirteenth Constitutional Decrees, setting up a federal structure of government for the whole country, and returning it to a sustainable version of democracy (Sudan Foundation, 1988:2)."

One of the achievements of the Twelfth Constitutional Decree is that the power to make and enforce criminal laws has been delegated to states. Every state can enact and enforce its own laws in accordance with the will of its citizens, i.e., Islamic laws are not applicable to non-Muslims. This official prominence of the Christians who make up 4% of the whole population, and only 15% of the Southern population (Sudan Foundation, 1996:4) found its full expression in the conclusion of the Political Charter (1996) and the Sudan Peace Agreement (1997) between the government and many rebel factions. Though these rebel factions are insignificant compared to the main faction of the rebels (SPLA/SPLM) led by Dr. John Garang, but the significance of the Political Charter and the Sudan Peace Agreement is that they represent "the boldest and most sustained effort in Sudanese history to bring about a just and lasting settlement to the Sudanese civil war," (Sean, 1998:8).

The Agreement contributed to the consolidation of the application of federalism. Like the Twelfth Constitutional Decree power is divided among the federal and state levels. The federal institutions are responsible for: armed forces and defense affairs, foreign affairs, national security, currency coinage and bills of exchange, federal legislation on matters within federal powers or on matters common to states, international boundaries and inter-state boundary disputes, inter-state waterways, federal railways and inter-state highways, Audit General, epidemic control, judiciary and emergency jurisdiction. The state powers include responsibility for: state security, public order and good governance, state taxes, wildlife, tourism, local government, agriculture, forestry and fisheries, promotion of cultures, folklore, arts, irrigation and embankment, state legislation in matters within states powers, customary laws or complementary to federal laws in matters peculiar to the state, Health, Statistics, state economic development and planning in accordance with the federal planning, education management, planning and training up to the university level within the framework of the national planning, missionaries activities, charities and endowments.[4] The exercise of residual powers is concurrent between the federal and the state level such as :

1. The State shall exercise the residual powers without prejudice to the powers allocated to the federal authorities.

2. The federal authorities shall exercise the residual powers without infringing on powers allocated to the states.

3. In case of dispute over residual powers between the state and federal authority, the dispute shall be referred to the federal (Supreme) court.

Regarding wealth sharing, the Agreement ensured the commitment of the government to "lay down a comprehensive economic and social plan to develop the country in general and to bridge the gap between the various states in particular, so that within a definite period, a parity in the provision of basic need such as security, employment, water, food, education, health and housing could be reached".[5] The parental outlook and hegemony of -the

245

center is clear in the Article that reads: "Major Federal development projects and big mining and oil projects shall be considered as national wealth and be managed on national basis".[6] This article became a source of controversy and it was understood that the center is still a dominant force in shaping and determining the future of federalism. Many voices were raised in the Constitutional National Committee demanding a revenue sharing formula to the benefit of the states. However, many observers of the application of federalism justify the hegemony of the centre at this stage to achieve national unity and to facilitate social and economic development in all states.

I have extended my analysis of the Agreement because it constitutes the culmination of the National Salvation regime's endeavors to install a new political system in the Sudan through the application of federalism. The Eleventh, and Twelfth Constitutional Decrees and the Agreement addressed problems of nation-building, i.e., the peaceful management of cultural, regional and ethnic diversity. The core of the matter - as summarized by a genuine scholar - is to find solutions to questions such as:

i.   How is the balance of power between the center and the constituent units of the federation to be maintained through the distribution of political and fiscal powers?

ii.   How is the relationship among the component units to be dynamically constituted and regulated?

iii. What is the implication of these relationships for group and individual rights?

It is clear that many of the principles of the Constitution were already laid in the Agreement and the Constitutional Decrees afore-mentioned. Article (2) of the Constitution described Sudan as a "federal republic governed at its highest level of authority on the basis of the federal system and in its base on local rule to ensure participation, *shura* and mobilization, respect for justice and division of wealth."

The application of federalism started, as argued above, in 1991. This date coincided with the adoption of the congress system as the basis of the political system. The building of the National Congress, the only legal political party in the country, started from the bottom. It made use of the existence of the Rationed Goods Committees (Services Committees) in the Quarter and Village level and upgraded them as the basic conferences of the National Congress. The flow of authority is supposed to be an upward process, where every level is permeated by an adjacent level of local (federal) government hierarchies.

Table 1
The Number of National Congress Basic Conferences, 1992-1996

Sessions	No. of Basic Conferences	No. of Attendants
First Session, 1992-1994	11,687	4,986,325
Second Session, 1994-1996	15,737	6,359,914
Third Session, 1996-1998	17,413	6,447,234

Source: Institute of Strategic Studies, Sudan Annual University Press, Khartoum, 1997, p. 15.

The Basic Conferences at the Quarter or village level are responsible for electing the Popular Committees - the basic units of federal government. The number of Basic Conferences witnessed an increase in their number from a session to another. Table 1 illustrates this. The number of the attendants of the Third Session (6,447,234) is more than the participants in the 1996 Presidential Elections (5,842,350). This does not mean the success of the experience. In a country like Sudan, where there is a strong tradition of a single-party or no-party rule, regional and tribal forces are accustomed to play political roles at the local and the national levels. In the absence of competition among political parties, regional elite and tribal dignitaries advent to play political roles. In the new realities of a federalized Sudan regional and tribal elite tried to use national politics to serve their own interests. It became a routine matter in Khartoum to see a delegation which represents a tribe or a region meeting the President of the Republic or the Minister of Federal Relations demanding the establishment of a locality, province or even a new state.[7] Table 2 shows the increase in the number of regions, provinces and localities between 1989-1997. Official reports describe the increase in the number of administrative units as ordinary, not alarming and that more of these units are to be established in the near future. However the performance of a large number of these new units is a failure at least in carrying their assigned duties in accordance to the 1995 Local Government Act.

The increase in the number of Provinces and Localities is responsible of igniting tribal warfare in Darfur states in Western Sudan. In this area the concept *dar* (tribal home land) is sacred. Tribes which are driven to stay in other tribes' *dars* are considered guests with no right to acquire permanent land titles or offices. However, in the light of administrative changes which accompanied the application of federalism and divided tribal *dars* among states the "guests' exploited the chance and demanded the establishment of separate tribal and administrative authorities independent of the host tribe. In some areas, like Southern Darfur State, they asked for establishing new Prov-

247

inces and Localities. War was inevitable among tribes. In some areas the old conflict between Arab and non-Arab tribes was ignited again and is escalating.[8]

Table 2
The Number of Administrative Units, 1989-1997

Year	Regions States	Provinces	Councils
1989	9	18	328
1993	26	98	493
1997	26	114	621
% increase between	166.7%	444.4%	50.3%
% increase between 1993-1997	—	16%	25%

Source: Federal Government Bureau Annual Report, 1995 and 1997.

A bright side of the implementation of federalism is the rise of the new states revenue. Voluntary work became an important means of community development. People are ready to support the new administrative structures. In Gederif State people voluntarily collected one billion Sudanese pounds to establish and develop their new state (Mohammed & Abu Sin, 1988:173). Many of the states witnessed substantial increases in the number of primary schools and the number of health care units. The increase in educational units is more than what has been achieved since independence in 1956. Popular Committees, local and foreign NGOs, Sudanese working abroad, rich and poor people contributed to the extension of basic services to their areas.[9]

In some of the new states local revenue from markets, auction markets and animal pounds became the property of the concerned state. On the other hand, many of the national projects within the states started to contribute to state budgets. Gezira Scheme paid 8% of its annual revenue in 1994-1995 to the Gezira State (Alkassani, 1988:162). Other states which have national projects within their boundaries started demanding the contribution of these projects to their budgets.

The increase of the revenue and volume of voluntary work in many states led to a negative impact. It weakened the states' ability to support many of the new established basic services. Many of the states suffer from financial deficit. This came at a time when the federal government official policy discouraged the extension of federal support to states. The march of the experiment in the first three years of the second stage (1995-1999) shows that the States' Support Fund - a federal organ established to assist poor states - succeeded in withdrawing its support from twelve states. A close examination of the figures of this support (Table 3) shows that it is very small and

248

usually goes to the payment of salaries in the states. The revenue of Southern Kordofan State in 1997 was LS 7.5 billions which is less than the state's expenditure in that year (LS 10.1 billions). Therefore, the support extended by the federal government (LS 2.51 billions) bridged the gap between revenue and expenditure.

Table 3
Federal Government Support Extended to some of the Poor Northern States in 1996-1997 (in Sudanese Pounds)

State	1996	1997
Southern Kordofan	1,450,000,000	2,510,000,000
Northern Darfur	2,000,000,000	1,819,000,000
Northern Kordofan	2,000,000,000	2,776,350,000
Blue Nile	—	2,000,000,000

Source: Compiled from the Institute of Strategic Studies, Sudan Annual Strategic Report, 1997, Khartoum, p. 39.

The Localities Support Fund is another device to ensure wealth sharing at the base of the federal setup. The Fund is composed of contributions - at the state level - by the rich localities and the state's government to help poor Localities. In Khartoum State out of its 36 Localities 16 are supported, 10 need partial support and 10 are considered rich. The experience of the Fund since its establishment in 1996 shows that its support is mainly used to pay the deficit in salaries, specially to primary school teachers. The federal government decision to shoulder the running of basic services to Localities (the 1995 Local Government Act) was behind the states and the Localities increasing impoverishment. The meager resources of these Localities are used to pay salaries. Table 4 illustrates the experience of the Fund in the relatively rich Gezira State. Out of the State's 19 Localities: 5 are considered rich, 9 are partially supported and 5 are poor. The table illustrates that the Provinces' revenues are less than the funds needed to pay for the cost of basic services in the state. In the rich Southern Darfur State 5 Localities are considered rich, while the other 14 receive regular support from the state.

It is evident that many Localities were established in response to political considerations. The stability and efficacy of federalism depends on the success of the Locality level to enjoy and practice the voluminous amount of power assigned to it. This could not be achieved unless these Localities are empowered with suitable resources and their areas of jurisdiction and functions are determined in accordance with the available resources.

Table 4
Province Contribution to Basic Services in Localities in Gezira State.[10]

Province	Population	Population % to Gerzira State	Province contribution in basic services Localities (%)
Gezira	763,254	29,6	34,4
Hassa Heisa	487,976	18,6	19,2
Kamlin	262,546	10,0	10,7
Butana	283,653	10,8	10,0
Umm El Gurra	199,156	07,6	04,9
Managil	626,961	23,9	20,9
Total	2,623,546	100	100

Source: Gezira State, "Localities Support Fund in Gezira State", paper presented to the Workshop on Localities Support Fund, Federal Government Chamber, Khartoum, June 1998, pp. 11-12.

It is clear that Nimeiri's policy during the application of Regionalism of absolving the government from its duties towards the people, especially those of underdeveloped regions is repeated again. Table 5 shows that the federal government has completely freed itself from extending services or executing development schedules in the states.

Table 5
State Government/Locality Expenditure in some sectors

Sector	Expenditure	Source of Federal Expenditure	Government (%)
Education	75 – 80	State Government	01 – 0.3
Water (Wells & Hafirs)	5 – 10		
Health	5 – 7	Locality	5 – 8
Roads & Bridges	2 - 3		

Source: Institute of Strategic Studies, Sudan Annual Report, 1997, op.cit., p. 40.

The 1998 Local Government Act came to remedy many of the deficiencies of application in the second stage. Concerning the establishment of Localities the Act stipulated that Localities are established by the state government by special warrants approved by the State Peoples' Assembly taking into consideration the following measures:

i.   A suitable number of population.

ii. Population is culturally, socially and economically homogenous.

iii. Availability of security and resources to implement and administer services and development in the locality[11]

On the other hand, the Warrant determines the geographical boundaries, number of members of the Locality Assembly, its functions and authorities.[12] This Article clearly uplifts many of the Localities from the burden of establishing and running basic services within their boundaries.

Political participation is pivotal to the success of federalism. The figures in table 1 above show that the number of attendants of the basic congresses increase from a session to another. In Kassala State in Eastern Sudan people's participation in Localities Conferences ranged between 89.4 - 97.4%.[13] However, this is a seasonal activity. The convening of ordinary meetings or sessions is occasional and came as a response to calls from above. Thus, political participation is still far lagging behind. There has always been a satisfaction gap at the grassroots level.

The revision of previous acts is important to achieve a better federalism. It is important to revise the Constitutional formula for wealth sharing. In the Constitution (Part VI, Chapter III, Articles 113-115) financial resources are divided among the three levels of rule. Table 6 illustrates the Constitution's division of financial resources.

Table 6
Division of Financial Resources

NO/ LEVEL	FEDERAL	STATE	LOCALITY
A	Custom revenues and revenues of international ports and airports	Business profit tax: provided that there shall be a percentage allocated to localities by a federal law	Estate tax
B	Companies profit tax, personal income tax, and stamp duty of federal and inter state dealings	State's industries excise duty	Sales Tax

C	Profits of national projects, provided that there shall be allocated to the states to which they extend the law may specify	State license returns	Agricultural and animal production tax, provided that there shall be allocated a percentage to the state by federal law
D	Federal ministries excise	States taxes and fees	Local and river means of transport
E	Expatriates' tax and foreign institution and	State's projects profits	Local industrial and artisan excise duties
F	Any such other taxes or fees that do not affect the state's or the local Government resources	Internal grants, loans and credit facilities	Any other local resources
G	Grants, loans and credit facilities		

Source: Constitution of the Republic of the Sudan, Part VI, Chapter III: Article 113-115.

The table shows that the federal level still controls major sources of revenue such as customs, companies profit tax, profits of national projects, expatriates and foreign institutions and activities taxes. M.H. Awad argued that:

> *"the share of the poorest states in Sudan (which has 70% of the population and contribute 30% of GDP) is 54 billion pounds of the government revenue from direct taxes, excise duties and profits of national projects which is estimated as 245 billion pounds in the Fiscal Year 1994-1995" (Awad, 1988:229).*

On the other hand, financial resources such as Zakat and bank deposits collected from these poor states are mainly expended or invested beyond them. Therefore, for the achievement of equitable division of resources and wealth sharing this constitutional arrangement should be revised and amended to the benefit of the poor states.

The availability of trained personnel in many of the peripheral states is a soaring problem for the strengthening of federalism. Many states paid high salaries and incentives to attract qualified personnel, especially in the health and educational departments. For the middle-aged Civil Servants the lack of proper housing, education and health care is behind their refusal to be transferred to many of the new states. To solve this problem the federal government applied many measures to provide poor states with the needed personnel. However, most of these measures are of temporary nature and resulted in creating problems in the concerned states, e.g. payment of salaries. There is a need for the adoption of capacity-building programs at the three levels of the federal setup. Training of upper and middle brackets of the Civil Service is important to assist the states and Localities to bridge this gap.

The Future

One cannot speak about the future of federalism in the Sudan in isolation of the present political developments in the country. As early as April 1998 a constitution was ratified through a popular referendum. The constitution recognizes and upholds international human rights and equality before the law:

> *"All are equal before the law. Sudanese are equal in rights and duties and entitled to public offices without discrimination based on race, ethnic origin or religion, are equal in eligibility for public office and civil service positions and to be elected without preference due to wealth."[4]*

Article 26 of the Constitution recognizes the right of association as an important individual right. The Article reads as follows:

1. All the citizens have the right to freedom of succession and organization for cultural, social, economic or professional purpose and restricted only according to law.

2. All the citizens have the right to form political organizations. This may be only limited by the conditions of shura and democracy in the leadership of the organization. Everyone has the right to campaign for their political party without using material wealth and bound by the provisions of the Constitution as implemented by the law.

This return of multi-partism in the form of political association *(Attawali Assiyasi)* necessitated changes in the federal structure. In the third tier—the Locality—the 1998 Local Government Act stipulated that the Locality Assembly is directly elected from the people,[(15)] and not as representatives of Popular Committees. The latter are preserved by the Act (Article 9: 1 and 2), but they were established under the approval of the Locality. This change is a radical restructuring of Local Government. Under the system of political associations one expects severe competition to win the Locality's Assembly seats. Thus, the Act ensures a healthy atmosphere and more freedom for the liberation of the individual to choose his representatives away from the yokes of old influences and loyalties. However, at this level - the Locality - it is important to combat the drive towards ethnic and tribal parochialism, which encourages the fragmentation of the country and accelerates the centrifugal forces responsible for the weakening of the Sudanese state.

Conclusion

From the above analysis it is clear that the Sudanese federal experience is far away from achieving its goals. It is still an infant experience which is gradually built from one stage to another. An important feature of this experience is that it is an open one. It exposes itself to other experiences and tries to learn from them to rectify the practice as a means to fulfill its ideals.

This gradual approach is important. In a country like Sudan, where the civil society institutions are weak one expects that the liberation of the masses consciousness is a gradual process. It is important to diffuse new values in the society such as accountability, transparency and the commitment to build communal rules and values which respect individual and groups rights. The adoption of such a gradual approach guarantees the solution of the crisis of governance at the eve of the third millennium.

ENDNOTES

1. The federal experience evolved gradually during 1991-1995 through a number of Constitutional Decrees the most prominent among them being Nos. 4, 7, 10, 11 and 12. Dr. Ali El-Haj Mohammed, the ex-Minister of Federal Government Chamber, described the experiment as "The states were thus redivisioned from nine into twenty six states on area - population basis, strictly avoiding any tribal or ethnic criteria... This is hoped to furnish a sincere start for a sustainable socio-economic development based on unity in diversity".

2. The Addis Ababa Agreement of 1972 brought about unity and peace in the Sudan. However, the need to secure "national unity" at any cost made the signatories of the Agreement content themselves with middle range solutions which proved to be of temporary nature

3. Excerpts from the Final Communiqué of Juba Convention of Southern Forces, May 1994.

4. For more information on power and wealth sharing see *Sudan Peace Agreement*, Chapter Three, pp. 5-10. This section of the Agreement became part of Sudan's Constitution (Articles 110-111).

5. Sudan Peace Agreement, op.cit., p. 7 (The Constitution of the Sudan, Chapter VI, Section 2, Article 112(1) and (3)). Furthermore the Agreement provided for the establishment of a Revenue Allocation Commission to recommend revenue sharing formula for the whole country. Article 116(2) of the Constitution established this organ under the auspices of the Federal Government Bureau.

6. The Federal Government replied its critics that it shall observe the following for the purpose of distribution of national revenue among the states and for site selection of major development projects:

a. Giving priority to the less developed states according to their state of underdevelopment.

b. Economic feasibility of project and their efficient functioning.

c. Effect of the project in the realization of self sufficiency in the basic needs of the country.

d. Balance relationship between development and density of population and environment.

e. Establishment of special fund to take care of crash development programs and maintenance of peace.

7. In November 1998 a delegation of the Qimr tribe of Southern Kordofan State met the President of the Republic and asked for the establishment of a new Province in their area. As a result Rashad Province, which was established in 1994, was re-divided into three Provinces.

8. In Western Darfur State the old conflict between the Masaleet tribe and the Arabs was renewed because of the former's fear that the administrative changes might infringe their Dar's inherited rights to the benefit of the Arab tribes.

9. A common type of voluntary work among the people is to collect funds necessary for the accomplishment of needed services through the sale of rationed goods (usually sugar) to big merchants. In 1997 the amount of money expended at the Popular Committees level was estimated as more than LS 40 billion, which was more than the whole support fund given by the federal government to the states.

10. In Sudan's federal structure the Province is not an administrative level. However, in Gezira State the provision of services is historically linked to the administrative divisions of the Gezira Schemes. These divisions are similar to the present division of the state into provinces.

11. The Local Government Act, 1998, Chapter III, Article (8) - Establishment of Localities.

12. Ibid., Article (10) - Function and Authority of the Locality.

13. Institute of strategic Studies, *Sudan Strategic Report*, 1997, op. cit., p. 63.
M.H. Awad, "Federalism Revisited", in Al-Karsani, Awad Al-Sid, (ed.), op.cit., p. 229.

14. The Constitution of the Sudan, Chapter II, Section I, Article (21).

15. The Local Government Act, 1998, Chapter III, Article (18) - 1 and 2

REFERENCES

Abdalla, Al-Hadi Abdal Samad. 1995. "Inter-governmental Relationships in the Sudan Federal System: Cooperation Conflict or Covariance" in Hassan M. Sahih *et al* eds. *Federalism in the Sudan*. Khartoum: KUP.
_____. Ibid.
Abdel-Rahuir, Muddathir. 1995. "Principles and Characteristic Features of Federal Gov-

ernment" in Ibid.

African Rights. 1995. *Facing Genocide: The Nuba of Sudan.* London.

Alkarsani, Awad Al-Sid. 1988. *Federalism in Sudan.* Khartoum KUP.

Awad, M.H. 1988. "Federalism Revisited" in Ibid., p. 229.

Fegley, R. 1988. "Decentralization in the Sudan: The Administration of the Northern Region" Unpublished Ph.D. Thesis, University of Reading.

Mamdani, M., Mkandawire, T. and Wamba-dia-Wamba D. 1988. "Social Movements, Social Transformation and the Struggle for Democracy in Africa," Working Paper 1/88, Darkar: CODESRIA.

Ministry of Social Planning & UNDP, 1998, Sudan: 1st National Human Development Report (NHDR) Khartoum.

Mohammed, Ahmad A & Abu Sin. 1988. "Some Reflections on the Division of New States" in Ibid.

Mohammed El-Haj Ali. 1994. "Major Federal Experiences with Special Reference to Sudan" Address at the Opening Session of the Conference hosted by the Department of Political Science with the support of Friedrich Ebert Foundation, Khartoum.

Niblock, T.C. 1987. *Class and Power in Sudan: The Dynamic of Sudanese Politics 1898-1995.* London: Macmillan Press.

Republic of Sudan. 1992. *The Comprehensive National Strategy, 1992-2002* Vol. I, Khartoum, KUP.

————. Ibid. pp. 215-217.

The Sudan Foundation. 1996. *Politics File No. 2,* "Anglo-Sudanese" in *Economist Intelligence Unit: Country Profile 1994-1995.*

————. 1998. "Europe and the Peace Process in Sudan," *Europe File No. 2,* London

————. 1998. Ibid. p. 2.

CHAPTER 12

The Politics of Federalism in Ethiopia: Some Reflections

Asnake Kefale

Introduction

T he post 1991 political developments in Ethiopia not only brought about change of a military regime but also significant changes in the structure of the Ethiopian state and its underlying ideological foundations. The victors that caused the downfall of the military regime (Dergue) in May 1991 came up with remarkably different visions about the future of the Ethiopian state and modalities of managing its diverse ethnic and linguistic groups. In other words, previous projects of Ethiopian regimes, which focused on centralization, and consolidation of power were rebuffed. The institutionalization of ethnic based federalism and the constitutional recognition of rights of ethnic and linguistic groups for "self-determination up to and including secession" was the culmination of decades of conflicts that overly consumed the nation's human and material resources. Ethiopia is presently experimenting an "innovative" form of governance, which officially advocates decentralization of power from the center to the (ethno-linguistic) regions and multi-party (ethnic) democracy. Fellow African scholars and policymakers cautiously observe these experiments and especially the present regime's policy of promoting ethnicity as the most important determinant for political and economic activities.

This chapter analyses the institutionalization of federalism in Ethiopia and the challenges and opportunities of the new system have brought. The paper is divided into three main parts. The first section deals with the problem of the "national question" and the reconstruction of the Ethiopian State. The second section analyses the political and legal bases of federalism in Ethiopia. The third part of the paper assesses some of the basic advantages and problems of federalism in Ethiopia. Finally a brief conclusion will be made.

Reconstructing the Ethiopian State and the National Question

Since the downfall of the military regime (Dergue) in 1991, a massive and radical reorganization of the structures of the Ethiopian state and its relations with the society has been underway. Ethnicity has been the pivotal factor in these multi-dimensional processes. The Ethiopian Peoples Revolutionary Front (EPRDF) which came to power after the demise of the Dergue follows a policy that gives pre-eminence to ethnicity. It should, however, be noted that ethnicity and "the national question" were not the concerns of a particular political force in Ethiopia. The national question in Ethiopia is strongly related to the circumstances that led to the expansion of the Ethiopian state towards the south and the emergence of a highly centralized state since the beginning of the twentieth century under the suzerainty of the ruling elite of the Amhara. The expansion of the Ethiopian state towards the South under the leadership of Emperor Menelik resulted in the creation of a multi-ethnic state. In other words, because of this expansion, various ethnic and national groups became subjects of a predominantly Christian and northern state.

The consequences of this process of empire-building by Menelik and his predecessors were manifold. The peoples of the newly conquered territories were subjected to economic, political, and national oppression. In addition to economic exploitation and loss of land, the peoples of the newly conquered lands became subjects of ethnic domination. In Clapham's words, the pattern of modern state formation in Ethiopia gave the Amharic language, culture, and identity a quasi-national and superior status through the imposition of central control and a substantial level of physical brutality and economic exploitation (1994: 31). The project of building a strong and modern Ethiopian state as entertained by pre-Revolutionary Ethiopian leaders relied on the promotion of the language and cultural values of the ruling Amhara elite at the expense of the diverse people of the country. The Amhara elite had also effectively used assimilation as an important strategy of sustaining their dominance. This was partly facilitated by the plasticity of Amhara ethnicity, which equally places emphasis on both maternal and paternal ties of descent (Young, 1997: 46).

Policies of pre-Revolutionary Ethiopian leaders with respect to language and religion were highly discriminatory. The Haile Selassie regime, for example, prohibited publication in the Oromo language, and contained publication in Tigrenna and heavily favored Orthodox Christianity (Crummey, 1994:4). The project of building a highly centralized state by subduing various ethnic groups and regions, however, faced multifarious challenges from different corners of the country. Redressing the national problem along with the question of land was among the essential slogans of the Ethiopian student movement and almost all of the political groups that emerged on the political spectrum later. Left leaning nationalist movements that emerged on the Ethiopian political scene opposed the domination of the Ethiopian state by the Amhara. Young, for example, argued that opposition in Tigray during the beginning of the 1960's started because of Tigrayan teachers discontent of Haile Selassie government's policies of centralization and homogenization of the empire around a Shoan Amhara base (1997:76). The same was true for other ethnic or national groups, whose interests and identities were undermined by the overly centralized state. Lewis, for instance, attributes the development of Oromo political consciousness to the systematic denial of the economic, political, and cultural rights of the Oromos (1996:47).

Though there were philosophical and political differences among the various contending forces, the demand for the recognition of the rights of "nations and nationalities" to self-determination was one of the very few denominators of the diverse and mutually antagonistic political forces in Ethiopian contemporary history. Hence, various nationalist movements in Ethiopian politics either sought the reconstruction of the Ethiopian state or their separation from it. The Tigrayan Peoples Liberation Front (TPLF), for example, in its formative years "claimed that it was fighting for self-determination which could result in anything from autonomy, federation, confederation, up to and including independence" (Markakis, 1987:254). All of the Eritrean separatist movements considered Eritrea as Ethiopian colony and sought its independence through armed struggle. The Oromo Liberation Front (OLF) which emerged in 1974 also aimed at the creation of an independent state called Oromia. Accordingly, the 1976 political program of the OLF aimed at the liberation of the Oromo people from oppression and exploitation, and an establishment of the Peoples Democratic Republic of Oromia through self-determination. The expression of these nationalist aspirations through various means including armed struggle and because of the uncompromising centralist stances of Ethiopian regimes led to decades of devastating civil wars.

The long struggle of the Ethiopian people for changing the feudal state led to the 1974 revolution. Left leaning political groupings played a prominent role in the circumstances that led to the revolution. Because of the absence of organized political force that could direct the revolution, the military came to power. Socialism that had been the favored ideology of almost all of the political forces of the revolution was officially adopted as state ideology. After its assumption of power, the military regime followed some policies that attempted to redress the longstanding demands of the Ethiopian people and the left. In 1974, the military regime nationalized land. The nationalization of land had a shattering impact on the socio-economic and political bases of feudal Ethiopia. The Dergue's land policy, which still substantially persists long after the demise of its architect is a subject of numerous criticisms and debates. It has, however, been instrumental in the liberation of the Ethiopian peasants particularly those of the newly conquered lands from decades of servitude.

The Dergue also gave a lip service to the problem of nationalities by formally recognizing the rights of nations and nationalities in its National Democratic Revolution Program of 1976. Section five of the program states: " the right of self-determination of all nationalities will be recognized and fully respected. No nationality will dominate another one since the history, culture, language and religion of each nationality will have equal recognition in accordance with the spirit of socialism" (PMAC, 1976). But the Dergue's formal acceptance of the right of national self-determination did not lead to the reorganization of the structures of the Ethiopian state. Despite the military regime's unwillingness to decentralize political power, it allowed the use of some non-Amharic languages as mediums of instruction for the regime's much acclaimed national literacy campaign. Radio broadcastings in Affan Oromo and Tigrayan were also started. The Dergue's pledge of recognizing the rights of nations was not, however, expressed in matters of self-governance.

Later in 1989 when the military regime officially transformed itself to socialist style peoples' democracy, it attempted to reorganize the nation's administrative structures. The country was divided into several zones and autonomous status was in principle granted to the rebellious provinces of Eritrea, Tigray, Assab, Dire Dawa and Ogaden. This did not, however, appease the rebellious groups and prolonged the regime's grip on power. In general terms, the attempt of the Dergue to create a new social and political basis for the Ethiopian state was not successful. It did not also make little difference to a political structure in which the state was overwhelmingly in the hands of Christian highlanders (Clapham, 1994: 34). Reconstruction of the Ethiopian state was thus left for the political forces that came to the helm of state power in the aftermath of the Dergue's military debacle.

The EPRDF and other political forces that established an interim government in July 1991 endorsed a transitional charter that contained rights and civil liberties. Eritrea's right to secede was recognized by the July Conference. With regard to the right to self-determination the Charter declares:

The rights of nations, nationalities, people to self determination is affirmed. To this
end, each nation, nationality and people is guaranteed the right to: (a) preserve its identity

and have it respected, promote its culture and history and use and develop its language; (b)
administer its own affairs within its owned defined territory and effectively participate in
the central government on the basis of freedom and fair and proper representation: (c)
exercise its right to self-determination of independence, when the concerned nation/
nationality and people is convinced that the above rights are denied, abridged or abrogated
(TGE 1991:2)

The Charter was thus a major departure from the hitherto unitary state structure. The Transitional Government's Proclamation No. 7/1992 also laid the foundation for the establishment of national and regional governments. This proclamation was the precursor of the Federal Constitution of 1995. According to Proclamation No. 7/1992 fourteen regional governments were established on ethno-linguistic bases, while Addis Ababa and Harar were accorded special status on political and population composition considerations. In addition to territorial re-organizations, this proclamation conferred upon regional governments both of legislative, executive and judicial responsibilities.

The 1995 Constitution of the Federal Democratic Republic of Ethiopia is also another major reflection of Ethiopia's new elite strategy of solving the "national question" by reconstructing the state. The Federal Constitution lists nine regional states as members of the new federation (FDRE Constitution, 1995:17). These regional states are largely established on ethno-linguistic bases. The rights of the constituting units to self-determination and including secession are enumerated in the constitution.

The new regime's policies of ethnic federalism and " ethnic democratization" are of significant interest for many scholars. There are various debates about the problems and advantages of Ethiopia's ethnic federation, which will be discussed later in this paper. With regard to redressing the problem of nationalities in Ethiopia, ethnic federalism has enabled the diverse peoples of Ethiopia to use their own languages for education and self-administration. This is not, however, to suggest that the nationality problem is completely solved in today's Ethiopia. There are still many nationalist movements opposing government policies alleging that the rights of the nations they claim to represent are not respected.

In summary, the adoption of ethnic federalism in Ethiopia is closely related to the problems of creating a working and manageable state structure consistent with the enormous diversity along linguistic, ethnic and religious lines in the country. Hence, the success and failures of this system of governance are strongly related to the national question.

The political and Legal Bases of Federalism in Ethiopia

Ethiopia's federalism is the result of several socio-economic processes. In fact, federal systems of governance in any country are unique as they are grounded in unique historical experiences. In Ethiopia's case, federalism is an out come of top-down processes. Though there were demands for the re-structuring of the Ethiopian state from different corners, the process of federalism was heavily dominated by the EPRDF. Thus the EPRDF guided the overall process of engineering the federal structure in Ethiopia with no wider participation of the public and that of other political groups.

Federalism in its present kind was established in Ethiopia because the EPRDF conceived it as the only viable form of governance that would solve age-old problems of the country. In this connection, a 1994 publication from the Prime Minister's Office reads:

> *In our case, when one refuses to accept federalism, it means, he refuses to accept the right to self-determination, i.e. a right exercisable only under federal order (Office of the Prime Minster, 1994: 4).*

There are two contending views about the politics of federalizing Ethiopia. The EPRDF considers the present structure of the Ethiopian state as an assurance for the continuity of the Ethiopian state and building democracy, while some skeptics question the true intentions of the ruling party to decentralize power and democratize state-society relationships. Ottaway as cited by Joseph, for instance, argues that the Tigrayan Peoples Liberation Front (TPLF) pursued strategies of proliferating ethnic political parties and transforming Ethiopia into a federation of ethnic states in order to make up for its weak power base (Joseph, 1994:6). Post-1991 political developments and the adoption of the federal system in Ethiopia could not, however, conclude as mere instruments of the EPRDF to stay in power. Building a democratic political system and a truly decentralized federal government in a country which did not have these experiences, could not be expected to be a smooth process. The successes of such undertakings of course require commitment from all political forces and most importantly from the regime in power.

The legal bases of federalism in Ethiopia basically emanate from the constitution. The federal constitution divides power between the federal government and member states. It, in effect, created a two-tier government, federal and regional (FDRE Constitution, 1995: 18). Both the federal and the regional governments are given the power of legislation, execution and adjudication.

The federal government in Ethiopia like other federal governments elsewhere in the world is responsible for national defense, foreign policy, printing of money, and some other matters, which require uniform application throughout the country such as nationality and fiscal policies, (FDRE Constitution, 1995). The member states or regional governments are also accorded with legislative, executive and judicial responsibilities. According to the constitution, "all powers not given expressly to the Federal government alone, or concurrently to the Federal Government and the States are reserved to the States" (Ibid. 19). Member states of the federation are also entitled to adopt their own constitutions, flags and anthems. The capabilities of regional states to effectively dispose their responsibilities are, however, limited because of lack of experience and adequate finance.

As a reflection of the new system's commitment of recognizing the equality of nations and nationalities languages, regional states and in some cases zonal administrations are allowed to designate their languages for both administrative and educational purposes. So far from the nine constituting units of the Ethiopian federation the Harai, Oromia, Somali, and Tigray regional states have started using their own languages. Some zonal administrations of the South Nations, Nationalities and Peoples region have also started using their languages for both administrative matters and primary education.

Structurally, member-states of the federation have legislative, executive and judicial institutions. State councils of regional states assume the highest authority. With the exception of *Harari* regional state, all of the remaining regional states' councils are unicameral and are filled by elected officials for a five-year term. The executive committees of regional states, which are elected by regional state councils, are responsible for managing the day to day activities of the states. The executive committees also elect the president and other key executive officials of regional states.

Territorially and administratively, regional states are in many cases divided hierarchically into *Zonal, Woreda,* and *Kebele* levels. These administrative structures are staffed by elected officials and are responsible for their own constituencies and the immediate higher authority in the hierarchy. Usually zonal administrations have their own councils. *Woreda* and *Kebele* levels of administrations constitute the lowest structures in federal Ethiopia. They are very instrumental for implementing policies, politicization of the public and control.

In sum the institutionalization of ethnic federalism in Ethiopia is strongly related to the EPRDF's ideology of promoting ethnicity as valid instrument of reconstructing the Ethiopian body politic. The legal foundations of federalism are enshrined in the constitution. Regional governments like many constituting units of federal systems are given power to manage their own affairs. In actual practice, implementing the intents of the constitution with

regard to federalism and decentralization are circumscribed by several political, economic and other problems. This will be discussed in the next section
of the paper.

Assessing the Federal Experiment in Ethiopia

Changing the body politic of traditional and old polities like Ethiopia is a very
challenging and often contentious task. In this regard assessing Ethiopia's federal experiment appears to be troublesome as the processes of federalizing the
Ethiopian state are going on and the federal system of governance is still in its
infancy.

The adoption of the federal system of governance in the multinational
Ethiopia is the logical outcome of the failure of building a centralized state. The
recognition of the importance of a decentralized administration which recognizes the cultural heritages of the diverse ethnic groups of Ethiopia by itself is
a major shift in Ethiopian political history. Federalism thus provides a number
of opportunities for the Ethiopian people and helps redress past problems and
pave the way for building a better future.

Federalism could also enable the diverse peoples of Ethiopia to manage
their own affairs and develop their cultures. The institutionalization of a federal system of governance has thus the potential for the mitigation of the age-
old contradictions between the uncompromising political center and the regions. In Ethiopia, the question and ways of the accommodation of cultural,
ethnic, and religious diversities have been the most perennial problems of
state building and its reconstruction. The adoption of federalism has thus
created an avenue for addressing ethnic and regional domination. In addition
to the advantage of providing the opportunity for the citizenry to participate
in local and regional affairs, the federal system of governance permits the use
of the peoples' languages for purposes of administration and education. In
what follows below some of the salient features of Ethiopian federalism will
be critically assessed.

The Centrality of Ethnicity in Ethiopia's Federalism

Leaving aside the academic, legal and political questions about defining groups
of people as either nations, nationalities, or peoples, it is evident that Ethiopia
has adopted a federal system of governance, which is largely based upon
ethnic and linguistic differences. As it is discussed above, the federal project in
Ethiopia is deeply intertwined with the issue of ethnic self-determination and
administration. The pre-eminence of ethnicity in the re-construction of the
Ethiopian state on the basis of federalism seems to have some undesirable

implications with economic and political dimensions. As regards distribution of economic resources, there are significant disparities among the nine constituting states of the new Ethiopian federation. Some of the regional states are well endowed with both economic and human resources, whereas some other regional states are densely populated. Unless the problem of imbalance is appropriately dealt with by encouraging mobility of citizens across regions and integrating economic activities of the different parts of the country, the new federal project, which overly relies on ethnicity, may jeopardize economic development.

The unique aspect of the new Ethiopia's federal constitution, i.e. the recognition of nations, nationalities and peoples to self-determination including secession still invites a wide variety of views. Ugo Mate, for example, argues that federalism and secession are not compatible categories (Mate, 1995:7). Considering Ethiopia's inability to steadfastly meet the constitutional rights of nations and nationalities because of lack of adequate resources and experience of democratic governance, the assumption that the recognition of the right of secession as an assurance of the rights of nations, nationalities and peoples is farfetched. In actual fact, the new federal constitution might not either correspond to actual power relationships and political realities in Ethiopia or the constitution introduces so many incentives to secession that the unity of Ethiopia as a federal state is not going to last much" (Ibid.)

The seemingly academic problem of defining the entities that are entitled to exercise the right to secede makes the constitutional procedures of secession vague. Article 39 of the Constitution, does not clearly indicate at what level of the federal government, whether at the level of regional states or other levels of governments that the demand to secession should be initiated. As experience has showed from different parts of the world, creating new states through a peaceful secession is not usual because of several economic and political problems. Even if the EPRDF and some other political groups considered the inclusion of the right to secession in the constitution as major stride in Ethiopia's political history, the recognition of the right to secede might probably lead to instability, instead of cementing the new federation on the basis of equality and autonomy. Because of the continued centralist propensity in Ethiopia's political economy the possibility of breaking away from the new federation peacefully and amicably seems unrealistic. Thus the inclusion of the right to secede might signal undeliverable promise and cause conflicts.

The creation of the members of the federation on ethno-linguistic bases does not also take in to account the incessant movement of peoples of Ethiopia and their interactions. No Ethiopian region or regional state as such is completely inhabited by one linguistic or ethnic group. The basic rationale for dividing the country into different regional states and the essence of ethnic federalism itself are greatly confronted by this glaring fact on the ground. The federalization of Ethiopia on the basis of ethnic affiliation did not also permit many ethnic groups, especially in the southern and western parts of the country to establish their own regional states. The state of southern nations, nationalities and peoples, for example, is the host of many ethnic groups that creating state structures that would enable all of the ethnic groups to self-administration proved impossible.

The new federation has also been confronted with the problem of striking the balance between group and individual rights. This is particularly true in many of the regional towns of Southern, and Eastern Ethiopia. Many of the regional towns in Ethiopia are multinational in their population make-up. The majority populations of the regional states are not in some cases necessarily the majority in the towns. Managing such towns by accommodating the interests of the "settler" population proved to be controversial. In some instances the individual rights of people living in such areas are being violated. It seems here worthwhile to mention the case of the Harari regional state. As cited by Asmelash, the population of the Harari regional state is 131,139 people, of whom 68,564 are Oromos and 42, 781 are Amharas. The Harari in whose name the regional state is established are only 9734 (Asmelash, 1997:14). Despite the multinational character of Harari regional state and the evident numerical majority of non-Hararis, the Harari monopolize political power. The very heated debate between non-Oromos and the Oromia regional administration about the issue of medium of instructions in some towns of Oromia also illustrates the problem of appropriately managing individual rights and group rights.

The difficulty of applying the ethnic-federalism project across the board is also attested to by the present status of the town of *Dire Dawa*, which is located in Eastern Ethiopia along the Ethio-Djibouti railroad. This town geographically either falls in the State of Somalia or Oromia. But the federal government directly administers it from Addis Ababa. The population of this town is a mixture of the various ethnic groups of the country. Though the way it is presently being managed from the center does not conform to the constitution, it gives an impression that the federal government might be contemplating other factors in addition to ethnicity in organizing local governments in multinational places. In sum, federalism through the parameters of ethnicity, in addition to the problem of viability of the entities created, may unnecessarily make citizens minorities in larger ethnic federations. The practice of some regional states that bars people who do not have knowledge of the regional languages from running for offices also tends to be discriminatory and contradicts the constitutional provisions about human rights and the various international human rights conventions and treaties which Ethiopia has recently endorsed.

Even if some years have elapsed since Ethiopia became a federal republic, the exact territorial jurisdictions of each of the nine members of the federation are not yet properly recognized. In fact, no official political map showing the internal divisions of Federal Ethiopia is yet produced. From experiences of other federal systems, the success of federalism depends on the availability of clear territorial and legal jurisdictions. Lack of recognized territorial borders might exacerbate traditional conflicts over waters and grazing lands. As such in dividing the internal boundaries of the federation, adequate care should be taken with regard to shared resources.

Political Power and Federalism

Successes of federalist projects are closely tied with the extent to which state-society relationships are democratized and the presence of effective and functional democratic institutions. Without the prevalence of democratic governance delivering the promises of federalism to self-rule, decentralization of power and citizen participation in decision making is unthinkable. As such assessing the extent to which the new federal system is really federal requires deciphering the power relationships and the political processes of post-1991 Ethiopia. Though some steps have been taken towards establishing a democratic system of governance since 1991, political power remains to be concentrated in favor of the ruling coalition, i.e. the EPRDF. All of the elections that were held since the downfall of the Dergue regime were invariably won by the EPRDF. The limited experience of the country in political pluralism, mutual suspicion and alienation between the government and opposition political parties and some other related socio-political factors are responsible for the low level of participation by non -EPRDF parties in the political life of the country in the past eight years.

The party structure of the ruling coalition gives much light to the structure of power and influence in the new Ethiopian, federation. In accordance with the official policy of the regime in today's Ethiopia establishing political parties along ethnic lines is not only permissible but also strongly encouraged. The TPLF, which constitutes the core of the EPRDF, has been engaged in establishing ethnic political parties under its tutelage since the late 1980's obviously to facilitate its grip on political power. The TPLF/EPRDF also helped the establishment of some ethnic political parties for the 1991 July national conference. This process has further been accelerated. There are as a result many EPRDF affiliated political parties significantly controlling regional administrations. With the exception of few regional states, power is controlled by EPRDF's coalition partners and its affiliates. In view of the experiences Ethiopian regimes in manipulating political groups and the real power situation in today's Ethiopia, it will be clear that the TPLF uses the various ethnic parties affiliated to the EPRDF to consolidate its power throughout the country. This in fact casts doubts on the project of decentralizing power. Even if power is decentralized constitutionally there is an apparent tendency to re-centralize power through party structures of the ruling coalition.

Fiscal Federalism

Economic viability and financial autonomy of federating units are crucial for the success of federalist projects. Experience has shown that decentralization efforts if they are not backed by financial decentralization would be constrained. According to Asmelash, "many failures in decentralization programs have been attributed to inadequate funding" (Asmelash, 1997:15).

In the Ethiopian case, along with the decentralization of political power, financial decentralization is underway. The federal constitution and other legislations provide for the division of revenue between the federal government and the regional states. Accordingly regional states are both entitled to raise revenue and receive grants or subsidy from the federal government.

Because of the generally underdeveloped nature of the Ethiopian economy and the legal basis of sharing revenue between the federal government and the regional states, fiscal autonomy by regional states is not yet realized. The federating units heavily depend upon the central government for funding. As Befekadu pointed out the most important source of revenue to the regional governments remains to be subsidy or grants from the central government (Befekadu, 1994:75). This is mainly because of the fact that the federal government reserves taxation of the most lucrative sectors of the economy to itself.

Unless revenue-sharing schemes between the federal government and that of the regional states is re-categorized in favor of the regions, regions autonomy in self-administration could be jeopardized. Thus steps have to be taken to make the regional states more self-reliant in terms of financing their recurrent and capital expenditures.

Federalism and Regional Disparities

In many regional states the magnitude of the problem of efficiently using funds allocated for development is paramount. Perhaps regional and local officials have squandered millions of Birr. The problem of appropriately using resources varies from regions to regions on the basis of their infrastructural capacity and trained personnel.

The extent of corruption in some of the regional states, which do not have adequate trained manpower such as the Afar and Somalia regional state, is alarming. The lack of the political will and ability to counter such delinquency blurs the wishes of the Ethiopian peoples for economic development.

Ali Said, for example, observes the problem of corruption in the Afar regional state as follows:

> *Realizing that the political right of self-rule is meaningless without economic support, the government hands over to regions a share of the central budget and the Afar region is one of the beneficiaries. Unfortunately, economic management went wrong from the beginning. Corruption and embezzlement became watchdogs of everyday life in the region. What funds remained were left and the proportion of the capital budget used during 1993 and 1994 was well below 30 percent, one of the lowest in all the regions. The problems of needs of the people were virtually ignored, no significant development activities having taken place, except a few initiated by the federal government, and the general economic picture of the region is dim (Ali, 1998:113-114).*

Unless the problem of corruption of misuse of funds is timely corrected, it could jeopardize the federal system of government which is in place in Ethiopia.

Conclusion

Every federal system of government is unique in so far that the issues it is instituted to tackle are different. The success and failures of federal projects thus could only be judged with regard to the problems that they are established to tackle. The experience of Ethiopia with federalism is yet very limited. It is both academically and realistically difficult to put the advantages and disadvantages of Ethiopia's federalism on a balance sheet. It is, however, possible to point out the following issues.

The institutionalization of a federal type of government in a hitherto highly centralized and autocratic state is an achievement. Establishing ethnic based entities is also a major departure which is anxiously observed by both Ethiopians and non-Ethiopians. The ethnicization of politics could be criticized on many counts. But the bold decision of the new Ethiopian regime to allow ethnic groups to use their languages for administrative and educational purposes is a positive outcome of the federalizing process in this country. Such official recognition of ethnic and national differences could help mitigate age-old tensions. After all it is not the diversity that exist between or among peoples and cultures of a given country that causes conflicts, it is in stead the way one manages or mis-manages differences. The path of Ethiopia in this regard can be a lesson for multi-lingual and multi-racial nations of Africa. But attempts should also be made in Ethiopia to rectify some of the problems which ethnic federalism has created especially the status of minorities living and working in some regional governments.

It is also equally dangerous to pose a federal system of government as if it is intrinsically democratic. In Ethiopia, there are suggestions which assume that the institutionalization of federalism had solved the age-old cries of the Ethiopian people for democracy, transparency and equity. But this is obviously farfetched. It is indeed very important to continually examine the limitations of the present federal system and craft alternative ways for its improvements and successes.

ENDNOTES

1. The Ethiopian Peoples Revolutionary Front is a coalition of the Tigrayan People Liberation Front (TPLF), the Amhara National Democratic Movement (ANDM), the Oromo People Democratic Organization (OPDO) and the Southern Nations, Nationalities and Peoples Democratic Organization. The main force within the organization coalition that significantly contributed to the downfall of the military regime in 1991 is the TPLF.

2. In the context of this paper the national question broadly refers to the call of various political forces in Ethiopia to redress problems of ethnic domination and oppression. In fact, the "national question" was one of the crucial issues of the Ethiopian revolution and its antecedent the Ethiopian student movement. Almost all of the revolutionary forces of Ethiopia attempted to address the problem of national oppression, though there were differences about the way to solve the problem.

3. Ethiopia is a multinational state. There are about 85 linguistic or ethnic groups in the country.

4. The July 1991 conference was summoned by the EPRDF for the establishment of the Transitional Government of Ethiopia and to approve the Transitional Charter.

5. See the recent debates by US based scholars about Democracy in Ethiopia. *Journal of Democracy, Volume 9, Number 4, October 1998.*

6. Article 39 of the Constitution of the Federal Democratic Republic of Ethiopia provides: "The right to self-determination, including secession of every Nation, Nationality and People shall come into effect: When a demand for secession has been approved by a two-thirds majority of the members of the Legislative Council of the Nation, Nationality or People concerned; When the Federal Government has organized a referendum which must take place within three years from the time it received the concerned council's decision for secession; When the demand for secession is supported by majority vote in the referendum; When the Federal

Government will have transferred its powers to the council of the Nation, Nationality or People who has voted to secede; and When the division of assets is effected in a manner prescribed by law. "

REFERENCES

Said, Ali. 1998. "Afar Ethnicity in Ethiopian Politics," in Mohammed, Salih and Markakis, John eds., *Ethnicity and the State in Eastern Africa*. Sweden: Elanders Gotab.

Beyene, Asmelash. 1997. " Decentralization as a strategy for Resolving the Nationality Problem: The Ethiopian Experiment" -Unpublished paper presented at the 18th AAPAM Roundtable conference on the theme: " Decentralization as a Principle of Democratic Governance." Nairobi: Kenya 17-21 March 1997.

Degfe, Befakadu. 1994. " The Legal Framework for Fiscal Decentralization in Ethiopia During the Transition Period" in Eshetu Chole, ed., *Fiscal Decentralization in Ethiopia*. Addis Ababa, Ethiopia.

Clapham, Christopher. 1994. "Ethnicity and the national question in Ethiopia" in Peter Woodward and Murray Forsyth eds. *Conflict and Peace in the Horn of Africa: Federalism and its Alternatives*. Great Britain: Dartmouth.

Crummey, Donald. 1994. " Ethnic Democracy? The Ethiopian case," A paper presented to the Annual Meeting of the African Studies Association, Toronto, November 4 FDRE (1995).

FDRE. 1995. The Constitution of the Federal Democratic Republic of Ethiopia. *Federal Negarit Gazetta*. 1st year, No.1. Addis Ababa. BSPP.

Joseph, Richard. 1998. "Is Ethiopia Democratic? Oldspeak Vs. Newspeak", *Journal of Democracy*, Volume 9, Number 4, October 1998.

Lewis, Herbert S. 1996. "The Development of Oromo Political Consciousness from 1958-1994"- in Baxter, P.T.W, et al. eds. *Being and Becoming Oromo: Historical and Anthropological Inquiries*. Uppsala: Nordiska Afrika Institutet.

Markakis, John. 1987. *National and Class conflict in the Horn of Africa*. Cambridge: Cambridge University Press.

Organ of Office of the Prime Minister (1994). *Schemes for Regional Development in Ethiopia* Addis Ababa.

Provisional Military Advisory Council (PMAC). 1976. *The Programme of National Democratic Revolution*. Addis Ababa: Berhanena Selam.

TGE. 1991. "The Transitional Period Charter of Ethiopia," *Negarit Gazetta*, 51st. year, No.1. Addis Ababa. BSPP.

Ugo, Mattei. 1995. " The New Ethiopian Constitution: First Thoughts on Ethnical Federalism and the Reception of Western Institutions", Unpublished.

Young, John. 1997. *Peasant Revolution in Ethiopia: The Tigray People's Liberation Front*. Cambridge: Cambridge University Press.

CHAPTER 13

Federalism in India: The Quest for Stability in Democratic Governance

R. B. Jain

When after independence in 1947, India embarked on the experiment to constitute itself into a sovereign republic and modernize the state and its administration through the adoption of a 'parliamentary democracy', not many scholars and analysts in the world had believed that India will survive as a democratic nation negating John Stuart Mill's contention that 'democracy is "next to impossible in multi-ethnic societies and completely impossible in linguistically divided countries" as well as Robert Dahl's belief "that widespread poverty and illiteracy are anathema to "stable democracy" a concept that is supposedly linked with the level of socio-economic development." However (see Lijphart, 1996) these early forebodings and later predictions that "the odds are almost wholly against the survival of freedom and... the issue is, in fact, whether any Indian state can survive at all" (Quoted in ibid.) have not only been proven wrong, but India's existence as a democratic state since the last 53 years of its independence in 1947 has compelled scholars to evolve a new consociational interpretation of the survival of democracy in deeply divided societies.

However, the functioning of the parliamentary-federal-democratic system during the last 50 years has led to the emergence of tendencies, which have not only challenged the national authority, but have raised a number of questions concerning the stability of governance? Has the Indian Federation succeeded in promoting 'unity in diversity' or has it encouraged more diversities of various kinds: ethnic, social and religions. Has it been able to accurately identify and accommodate the growing needs and requirement of its vast population? Is it conceptually and structurally equipped to handle the emerging challenges of a development process in which new technologies with their integrative compulsions are destined to play a growing role? Has the central and state governments become so gigantic making them indifferent to the varied local needs of the vast populace at the grassroots level. Has the existence of a series of minority governments at the center during the last one decade led to a reversal of the role of center and state governments. Has the federalizing process resulted in the crisis of governance and the stability of the government? (Murkaji and Arora, 119) This chapter is a modest attempt to analyze the growing strains in the process of federalization in a highly plural society like India, and assess their impact on the stability of democratic governance with a view to discuss any relevance that it may have for the emerging societies in Africa, struggling to solve the problem of competing ethnicities.

The Societal Mosaic

In terms of socio-ethnic diversities and cultural pluralism, India is perhaps the most confusing and complex society in the world full of a number of contradictions. Having a semblance of geographical unity and an uninterrupted historical past extending back to almost 5000 years, it is a vast sub-continent, composed of a huge population with geographical, linguistic, religious, social, regional and other kinds of diversities. (Jain and Sharma, 1997) It presents a sort of mosaic of innumerable human beings, each one of them separated from each other through ethnic, cultural, sub-cultural and other kinds of diversities yet presenting a pattern of political unity. Thus, in terms of essential components of a nation - a common language, a historical past, a common ethnic or religious homogeneity, etc. India could never fulfill the requirements of a nation state. Yet, paradoxically, while the British imperialism of the 19th century highlighted the multiplicity of castes, communities, tribes and groups, the national movement against the colonial rule that emerged at the close of the last century helped consolidate the various linguistic-cultural groups into distinct nationalities forging a sense of homogeneity and nationhood through a number of traditions and common elements of culture and religion. Thus behind the struggle between the nationalists who raised the slogan of "India a United Nation" and the British rulers who flourished on highlighting such conflicts, India was evolving its own national identity against the British, at the same time, however, unconsciously consolidating the various linguistic sub-cultural groups into distinct nationalities.

India's Approach to the Nation-Building Process

At the eve of independence in 1947, the political leadership in India was

274

confronted with the challenge to frame a well-conceived strategy of change, development, and nation-building, and to forge instrumentalities thereof - both mobilizational and institutional. While Mahatma Gandhi, the undisputed leader of the masses and the father of the nation put his faith in the reformed, ethnically refined individual in creating a better, if not an ideal society, Jawaharlal Nehru, the first Prime Minister of India and some other leaders in the country conceived the evolving of suitable political institutions such as the centralized nation-state as the best means to achieve the same goal and the principal instrument of social change.

To bring about this type of integration, four principles were formulated: (1) gradual "harmonious" change; (2) mechanical solidarity; (3) unity in diversity; and (4) discriminative egalitarianism. (Kahame, 1982; Narang, 1965)

The Nehruvian strategy of institution and nation building was based on the concept of liberal democratic ideology of freedom and equality, parliamentary system of government and concept of economic planning. It aimed at securing consensus, willing cooperation and enlightened participation of all sections of the society in the task of national reconstruction through the creation of federal structure of government and decentralized grassroot level political institutions for mass participation in political process. It accepted and tried to sustain and strengthen the hard reality of cultural plurality. The political structure not only guaranteed minority rights and provided constitutional guarantees to each segment of the population for the preservation of their distinct cultural identities, but also made provisions for their socio-economic and political upliftment through various types of concessions, aids, subsidies, etc.

The impact of Nehru's leadership, however, did not last long. Soon after his death, the strategies adopted for nation-building - the contradictory process of a centralized federalism strengthened by the belief that a strong and well-integrated polity controlled by a more enlightened, progressive and patriotic leadership, requires the exclusion of or at least the subordination of all sub-national loyalties, parochial and primordial in nature implicit in the known diversities became counter-productive. Even in Nehru's own times, the language issue emerged as the most volatile national crisis resulting in the reorganization of states in India in 1956 on linguistic basis and the adoption of a three-language formula. The consequences of the centralization of politics and the imposition of an alien process of nation-building in the framework of a single political community have led to the creation of different types of dichotomies of majority-minority, linguistic, caste and religious communities. In this process, economic issues remained more in the background than the socio-cultural issues which came into force and have further strengthened the various fissiparous tendencies and separatist movement in various parts of the country during the last three decades.

Despite the response of the various governments at the center and the states in appeasing and suppressing these centrifugal tendencies through the adoption of new strategies like creation of Minority Commissions and policy of increased affirmative actions for deprived communities, the establishment of Human Rights Commissions, etc, the pattern of development of the past five decades brings out clearly two diametrically opposite tendencies. As described by the Sarkaria Commission, while on the one hand, a number of facts, primarily centripetal economic forces, have strengthened the impulses of centralization, modernization, growth and development, on the other, very strong centrifugal forces have been unleashed in the country on account of break-up of the old political order, split of national parties, ever increasing exploitation of populist slogans and caste, language, money and muscle power in elections. (Commission, 1988)

Modernizing The State

The evolution and formation of state in India is deeply rooted in its history, and may be seen to have gone through three major transformations: (1) from lineage-based, primitive political systems to the origin of the state in the post-Vedic period and on the tribal peripheries of Brahmanical, Indo-Islamic, and Indo-British civilizations throughout Indian history; (2) from regional kingdoms to sub-continental imperial states dotting the entire historical landscape, beginning at least with the Maurya empire in Magadha in the fourth to second centuries B.C. and culminating in the British colonial state in the nineteenth and twentieth centuries; and (3) from empire to nation-state following the British withdrawal in 1947. The third transformation also witnessed the steady transition from a centralized bureaucratic empire within the feudal or colonial mode of production to liberal-democratic political institutions within the framework of a "mixed" economy (Singh, 1990) i.e. "mixed" in the sense of combining the role of the state and private sectors for economic development.

The Constitutional/Institutional Strategies

India was one of the first of the British colonies to gain independence from the yoke of an imperial power. To attempt to achieve a modicum of economic and political development in the aftermath of partition, through a democratic political system, while undertaking at the same time the reconstruction of a hardened social structure not only deeply rooted in the age-old traditions, but highly fragmented was indeed a formidable task. The four basic objectives of socio-economic and political development uppermost in the minds of political leaders at that time were (a) creation of a stable democratic polity; (b) laying the foundations of a self-reliant economy for rapid growth; (c) attainment of social justice through the elimination of discrimination based on class, caste, sex and religion and eradication of poverty, and (d) rebuilding of the dilapidated administrative structure to be able to withstand the pressures generated by the growing demands and aspirations of expectant masses.

The leadership in India responded by channeling the processes of change through the creation of a state system based on Western liberal democratic ideology of freedom and equality, incorporating the parliamentary system of government, reconciling it with the concept of economic planning, and reforming the administrative machinery to enable it respond to the growing exigencies and requirements of a social system divided by a variety of socio-cultural identities. Although the framing of a new political set up with its institutions, structures and rules of the game has proved to be a matter of incalculable difficulty for many of the new nations of Asia and Africa, India presented a striking contrast. Not only was an elaborate state system created with speed, but the democratic structure it established was institutionalized in considerable detail. This had been possible because of both antecedent agreement on fundamentals and continuing diffusion of these agreements in the generation that followed the independence. Even as early as 1928, the Motilal Nehru Committee had framed a complete draft of the constitution spelling out the features of (free) India polity. It recommended, among other things, a parliamentary form and federal structure of government and an exhaustive list of fundamental rights. These recommendations found overwhelming support among the members of the Constituent Assembly in the late 1940s.

However, decision-making on India's institutional strategy was not wholly a product of agreements that were reached during the national movement. The framers did consider the emerging framework anew. Certain occasions did occur when the members of the Constituent Assembly ran into serious disagreements. But debate was avoided at most opportunities. Viable compromises were sought on fundamental provisions such as the federal structure of the country, the importance of the judiciary in interpreting the constitution, and the role of "due process", the question of a proper balance between the personal liberties of the citizen and the integrity of the nation, between the right to property and the goal of social and economic development, between the need for centralization and the extent of decentralization to lower levels of the polity, between the right to equality and the question of special rights and privileges of minorities and tribal religious groups and so on. (Kothari, 1972)

In order to prevent the country from falling into pieces, certain restraints on the power of some institutions and the freedom of individuals were introduced. For example, the central government was armed with effective powers against the constituent states under Article 356. Similarly, preventive detention to strengthen the government's hand came to be accepted as a necessary provision despite its restrictions on the most fundamental rights of citizens. It was dubbed a "necessary evil". Again, while defining the relationship between Parliament and the courts, due consideration had to be given to the need to arm the state with powers to reduce social and economic disparities; consequently the "due process" clause was modified to suit Indian conditions. (Ibid.) Efforts were also made to elicit the maximum consensus in order to lay down a strong foundation for the nation. What emerged, as a result, was a federal structure of parliamentary government with a cabinet form of executive at the national and state levels directed to liberal democratic goals of individual freedom and social justice in the fulfillment of which government was assigned a positive role. The institutional structure that came into being was essentially modernist in character but with important departures from the Western model designed to facilitate national integration and social assimilation. (Singh, 1996)

The Indian leadership, in fact, borrowed the Western liberal philosophy and Indianized it according to unfamiliar and unique Indian practices and attitudes. Grant of "special privileges" to the backward groups in society and the "Scheduled Castes and Tribes" was an innovation designed to help the economically and socially weaker sections of the community. Similarly, the linguistic diversity of the country was given constitutional support through the granting of legal status to all the major regional languages. The system also provided for flexible methods of adaptation to changing social needs and demands by making the amendment procedure relatively easy to effect. This was a deviation from strictly orthodox federal practices. The constitution made provisions for a more balanced and cooperative federation as a dynamic functional unity through instituting significant forums for inter-governmental consultations and cooperation. There were (i) Inter-Governmental Councils (Art-263), bringing together the Prime Minister, the Chief Minister of States and Executive Heads of the Union Territories, (ii) The Finance Commission appointed after every 5 years to recommend the pattern of revenue-sharing between the Union and the State, and grants-in-aid from the consolidated fund of India (iii) an Authority to regulate inter-state trade and commerce (Act, 307), (iv) Authority to regulate and develop inter-state river valleys, (v) Tribunals under (Art 262) of Inter-State River Water Disputes Act, 1956, (vi) The Election Commission and (vii) Governor - the two vital constitutional links between the two levels of governments. (Pulparampil)

Within the federal structure, the states were reorganized on a linguistic-cultural basis to integrate heterogeneous communities into a nation, yet at the same time given an opportunity to maintain and promote their own regional language and culture. The dream of achieving unity in diversity was actually pursued. The launching of community development programs and the establishment of the Panchayati Raj institutions which have since been accorded constitutional status in 1993, were other measures within the framework of the Indian political process that were undertaken to secure democratic decentralization for the purpose of social and economic development at the grassroots level and in relation to the processes of nation-building.

The arena of power in India has not been limited to a ruling oligarchy or an aristocracy of birth, it has increasingly spread to the society as a whole by gradually drawing new sections into its ambit. This is what differentiates the Indian political system both from the European systems where, during the phase of rapid industrialization and social change, political participation was confined to the upper classes of society, and from the revolutionary experiments of both communist and non-communist varieties, where barring intra-party feuds and military coups, political competition was generally not allowed to interfere with the process of development. In India, politics is neither suppressed nor confined to a small aristocracy. On the contrary, it provides the larger setting within which decision-making in regard to social and economic development takes place, (Singh, 1996).

The launching of the new governmental organization and the inauguration of the Indian Republic in January 1950 did not complete the process of institutionalization. The emergence of further consensus on the political system involved new developments in the institutional layout of the country and important modifications of the formal structure of authority. The evolution of centralized cooperative federalism in India has largely grown outside the framework of the basic constitutional document. The institutional innovations like the National Planning Commission, the National Development Council, the Chief Ministers/Governors/Ministers/Secretaries Conferences, etc, how all developed as a result of the Union executive resolutions or informal actions, not even through the parliamentary enactments. These are all exercises in the so-called 'executive federation', in the sense that these bodies bring together within consultative framework the executive heads of the two levels of Governments. "Legislative federation" via the Second Chambers of the Parliament has not gone beyond Speaker's Conferences and legislative forums that have occasionally discussed generalities and their procedural framework. However, the organ that has greatly expanded its federal role and relevance has been the judiciary, which has emerged as the federal organ par excellence, establishing the supremacy of judicial review over the "sovereign" pretensions of the Parliament and the aggregate legislature, including the state legislative wings. In recent times, the Head of the State, the President of India has also been instrumental in preserving the federal spirit by directing the union executive (the Prime Minister) not to unnecessarily infringe upon the jurisdiction of the State Governments for merely political reasons (e.g. in returning the advice of the Union Executive of Prime

Minister Inder Gujral in 1997, and Prime Minister A. B. Vajpayee in 1998, to use Article 356 for dismissing the duly constituted governments in the states of Tamil Nadu and Bihar respectively).

Despite indigenous and foreign criticism, the story of Indian polity since independence has been one of remarkable stability. Except for a brief aberration, the state of emergency in 1975-7, which paradoxically was not legally unconstitutional, the past fifty one years of independence have seen remarkable performance of twelve general elections, reasonably efficient political and administrative institutions, and basic political stability.

Federalizing the State

After independence, India opted for a secular and federal democracy. Whereas secularism promised equal place to all religious groups, federalism aimed at seeking political justice to the identities of various cultural and linguistic groups. In other words, this was regarded as the formula for forging national unity. Federalism had a checkered history in independent India. During the first phase (1950-67), the issue of a center-state relations was relatively dormant because the India National Congress was in power both at the center and majority of states. Conflicts between the center and the states were dealt with at the party level rather than through formally established agencies.

With the 1967 General Elections there came a qualitative change in the pattern of center-state relations. For the first time, the dominance of the Congress party met with a stiff challenge. It failed to seek an absolute majority in the Union Parliament and was reduced to majority only in 8 out of 16 states, which went to the polls. The considerable reduced majority in the Lok Sabha (the lower house of the Parliament) gave a jolt to the Congress and the need for a kind of cooperative federalism was felt. Thus, a period of co-existence (1967-71) began to emerge, wherein states started asking for more autonomy. The organizational machinery of the Congress could no longer be used to resolve centre-state differences. The provision of the constitution, for the first time, were put to severe test and center-state relations became a burning issue. A new dimension was added to the role of the Governor of the states especially in those states where non-Congress governments were in power. Here, federal character was being re-asserted as against the unitary bias with which it began.

The landslide victory of the Congress in 1971 led to a change in attitude and a reversal of trend towards cooperative federalism. The period 1971-77 witnessed a swing towards centralism. Mrs. Indira Gandhi, the then Prime Minister, was of the opinion that state governments could accept and willingly implement policies and programs of the central government. Declaration of Emergency and the 42nd Constitutional Amendment carried forward the process of over-centralization to its extreme. The General Elections of 1977 marked the end of single party domination in Indian politics. The Janata Party came to power at the center along with regional parties in several states. During this phase (1977-80), states reasserted their right to more freedom to manage their own affairs. Vociferous demands were made to review the whole gamut of center-state relations.

With the coming back of Mrs. Indira Gandhi to power with a massive majority in 1980, no qualitative change took place in the governments of various states. Several states were ruled by non-Congress governments. Since then, the same situation had been continuing states asserting their rights and demanding for more autonomy and wanting to have full share in the governance of the country and full implementation of various provisions in the constitution in this respect. The possibility of this scenario continuing indefinitely brought a new focus to the problem of center-state relations. Mrs. Ghandhi appointed a Commission, headed by Justice Sarkaria, to examine and review the Union-states relations and make recommendations as to the changes and measures needed within the existing constitutional framework. The Sarkaria Commission went into the whole gamut of center-state relations and made a number of recommendations. It regarded federalism "a functional arrangement for cooperative action" and believed that liberal use of Article 258 can help in the realization of the concept of cooperative federalism envisaged by the Fathers of the Constitution. It asked for a more liberal use of this tool, i.e. Article 258 (under which the President may, with the consent of the government of a state, entrust certain functions in relation to any matter to the state) than has been done so far for "progressive decentralization of powers to the Governments of the State". (Manor, 1995; Sigh, 1992)

Recent elections to the eleventh Lok Sabha (1996) and twelfth Lok Sabha (1998) have thrown up new questions about the federal structure of India. They ended the era of single-party majority rule at the center and ushered in the era of coalition politics. This new era of coalition politics will be that of decentralization of power; where there would be a greater role for regional parties and accommodation of their legitimate interest. This is expected to replace the model of centrally dominated federal structure with a state sensitive coalition government wherein center-state relations will be conducted on the basis of equality. However, in actual practice the fate of federation hangs in balance. Regional parties are asking for as much autonomy as they can get in exchange for their crucial support to the party which has formed the Government at the center. This trend to appropriating as much autonomy as they can get in exchange for their crucial support to those who are in power and who wish to come to power at the center, is dangerous for the unity and integrity of the country as whole. A weak center being ruled by a hastily put together coalition of various political parties as happened in 1996 of the Deva Gowda government and later of Guhral government and as at present (1998) of the Vajpayee government for the sole purpose of grabbing power is an ideal breeding ground for extremist and secessionist tendencies.

There is yet another dimension of center-state relations in the changed environment, which pertains to relations among states and its impact on the coalition-based federal government. The rivalry between states is not a new phenomenon in India. There are already a good number of inter state/states disputes. The concerned regional parties would like to solve them in accordance with their formulas, which may not be quite acceptable to other concerned regional parties. In such a situation each regional party will try to pressure the federal government to help in settling the dispute(s) according to their wishes. Here, it would be difficult for the coalition government to take sides with any particular regional party because of the threat of withdrawal of support by other concerned regional parties. Apart from the mounting pressures in the 1990s for federalizing the predominantly parliamentary system to accommodate a greater degree of autonomy for the states in the Indian federal union, another direction of change, which has affected the Indian state in the past decade has been the policy of economic liberalization in the 1980s and the 1990s. Powerful alternative ideologies favoring the market and state government have come to the fore though the public sector and the center still continue to be entrenched. The move is cautious and gradual in both dimensions (Kothori, 1976).

Certainly, Indian federal structure needs a new center-state relationship but whether the present Vajpayee government at the center will be able to work it out is doubtful. This is so because it suffers from the inherent problem of unity, which in actual practice means a government whose future includes neither strength nor stability. But such a situation might result in the present government evolving new parameters of center-state cooperation on the basis of cooperative federalism. However, as observed by an eminent political scientist, it can be said that the Indian model of state-building, evolved against the background of a highly diverse society with a long history of disunity, presents a different conception of unity, true more to India's own traditions than to any prevailing theories of development. Most of these theories look upon both integration and modernization in essentially aggregative terms, as something that over-riders diversities and local autonomies and demands total loyalty. The Indian leadership has taken integration through open interaction and competition. The main characteristic of this approach is its centripetality through open interaction, a strong and visible "center", towards which the various "peripheries" were drawn through the competitive mechanisms of democratic politics, interspersed by adult franchise and other representative mechanism, such as the policy of protective discrimination mentioned above (Ibid. p. 223).

Another redeeming feature of Indian model of state-building has been the continued accent on the autonomy of Indian state and its general refusal to become a dependency of any external power, even if this meant a slower rate of aggregate of economic growth. India has striven hard and succeeded to establish its autonomy and it occupies a strategic position in the global political system. Both these factors—the logic of democracy and the logic of national autonomy—have always been a source of strength as well as weakness, which have many times led to a crisis of performance that has in recent years occupied the center of Indian political debate. (Krishna, 1992:74)

The Impediments to Federalism in India

However, there have been a number of socio-cultural and political factors which have at times proved impediments to the process of federalization and have also simultaneously shaped the character of federalism to change from a dominant centralized pattern to that of a model of 'cooperative federalism.' These can be grouped under the following headings:

(i)   The Linguistic Multiplicity

An element of social infrastructure which has made inroads in the nation-building process in India is linguistic multiplicity, which is unique in many respects than in comparison to many other countries of the world, such as Canada, Belgium, Russia, and Switzerland. Their example is, however, irrelevant in understanding the language problem in India. According to the linguistic survey published in 1927, there were 179 languages and 544 dialects in the erstwhile Indian subcontinent, which in 1981 grew into 1018 languages. Despite the multilingualism prevailing in India, the last phase of the Indian national struggle for independence witnessed the demand for one national language. But the emergence of a neat and acceptable formula of single national language has not been easy. The state in India recognized linguistic multiplicity when it accorded legal status to fourteen languages of India listed in the Eighth Schedule of the constitutional document (later amended to include sixteen languages) and recognized Hindi to be the national language. Such provisions, however, did not satisfy many leaders, especially in the eastern and southern parts of the country. The politicians recognized, propagated, and exploited the economic importance of a language being the official one. It was argued that any section of the society belonging to the official language group was also able to capture most of the job opportunities in the country. This created strong sub-regional movements directed against the officially recognized national language. The language problem became a live political issue. Hindi became the scapegoat in the larger politics of state autonomy. Many a time it led to violent outbreaks in the country and unprecedented acts of self-immolation and the like. The linguistic configuration was thus responsible for the creation of more regional diversities and many more states as sub units of the political system, expanding the responsibilities of a vast administrative machinery and leading to further drains on the already limited state resources and delays in the implementation of public policies. Linguistic differences have also prevented the growth of a consistent national policy on language and education. This has in turn led to lowering of educational standards and a greater strain on human resource development.

That, as far as language is concerned, India is not a "neat mosaic". (Galanter, 1984). Though the Indian states were largely carved out on the basis of language but at the ground level this relationship does not appear to be valid. Because of the presence of a large number of linguistic minorities and the presence of intermixture of language groups on the borders between adjacent states, the concept of a single national language is fraught with difficulties. Therefore, the western concept of "one language-one state" does not hold true in the case of India.

(ii)   Minority Rights

While framing the constitution of India, the constitution makers showed their sensitivity to and awareness of the importance of language and the strength of the roots of linguistic diversity. Article 29 of the constitution was regarded as the "Charter of Rights" for linguistic minorities. However, these rights did not seek to satisfy the linguistic communities' aspirations for "political justice". In order to further safeguard the rights of the linguistic mosaic, the framers of the constitution provided for some additional provisions in the constitution. Article 347 of the constitution provides that the President may, if he is satisfied that a substantial proportion of the population of a state desires the use of any language spoken by them to be recognized by that state, direct that such language shall also be officially recognized for such purposes and in such areas as he may specify. Second, irrespective of such directive every person shall be entitled to submit his representation for the redress of any grievance in any of the languages in use in the Union or the state, as the case may be (Article 350).

With the reorganization of states in 1956, two other provisions were made. The first one was that it shall be the endeavor of every state to provide adequate facilities of instruction at the primary stage to children belonging to linguistic minority groups. The President is also empowered to issue directive in this respect (Article 350A). The second one is by way of institutional safeguards and provides for the appointment of a Commissioner for Linguistic Minorities to investigate all matters pertaining to safeguards provided for them and submit the findings (Article 350B). Further, the Government of India set up two institutions - the Minorities Commission and the Human Rights Commission—in 1992 and 1993 respectively—to look into the grievances of minority communities with a view to bringing them into the socio-cultural mainstream of the Indian society so that they do not feel any sense of discrimination, alienation or isolation from the majority communities. Although it is too early to assess the impact of these institutions, they have been regarded as important steps taken by the government towards forging unity amongst minority and majority communities.

Despite these constitutional problems, the pressures exerted by linguistic minorities and the problems faced by them are numerous. This is so, not because any state has indulged in any deliberate discrimination. The reasons mainly responsible for this could be attributed to the psychological ingredients of the relations between different linguistic communities and the nature of implementation of policies. The various reports of the Commissioner for Linguistic Minorities echoes the same sentiments by pointing out major shortcomings in the implementation of the safeguards for linguistic minorities.

(iii) The Caste Divisions

Caste is one of the divisive forces which affects India's national life in many ways. It not only disrupts the bonds of unity among the people but also affects their development. Caste confrontations leading to violence have become quite common now-a-days. However, a qualitative change has recently been noticed in its role. The influence of caste has been decreasing in the socio-economic field but increasing in political sphere. Emergence of new caste-based organizations, growing polarization along caste lines, violence and reservation conflicts have given a new dimension to its role in India.

Since Independence caste started playing an ever-increasing role in the electoral politics of India. Before 1990s, the newly franchised Indians caste groups were not aware of the power of their members. Realizing the potentialities of the weapon of votes, various caste groups have in recent years made their influence felt in organized politics. As a matter of fact, a type of revolution has occurred in the minds of the so-called untouchable groups and the people belonging to the lower castes. Since the government has failed to bring out changes in the lives of the lower classes and caste groups, they thought that only they alone can undo this injustice. Different groups acquiring legitimacy and importance in politics have led all the political parties to nurse their "vote banks" based on regional, linguistic, religious and caste appeals.

The Strategy of Reservations on the basis of Castes

During the freedom struggle it was realized and recognized that those sections amongst the Hindus who were for centuries regarded as untouchables and outside the pale of Hindu society would require special attention to raise them from their existing level of poverty, backwardness and all forms of exploitation. Accordingly, a specific provision was included in the Directive Principles of State Policy in Article 46. It states that the state should promote with special care the educational and economic interests of the weaker section of the people, particularly the Schedule Caste and Schedule Tribes, and to protect them from social injustice and all forms of exploitation. The arrangements for protective discrimination in favor of the Scheduled Castes are found in Articles 15(4) and 16(4) of the constitution. Article 330 and 332 provide for reservation in legislatures; Article 331 provides for claims in services and pests and in other forms (Articles 17, 338 and 339). The question of identification of other backward classes (OBCs) is dealt with by Article 340. Under this article, so far two commissions (Kaka Kalelkar and Mandal) have been appointed. Kalelkar Commission submitted its report in 1995 and the Mandal Commission in 1980. The Mandal Commission recommended 27 per cent reservation of all the government jobs for the OBCs. Though the report was submitted in 1980 but it was implemented only in August 1990. Its implementation gave rise to many protect movements throughout the country. This is not an appropriate place to go into the details here but suffice it to say that this still continues to be a topic of heated debates and great social divide.

Politics of Reservation and Integration

To what extent has the above attempts at positive discrimination have helped in bringing about integration? Empirical studies, reports, etc. indicate a mixed picture. Whereas these marginalized groups have done quite well in cultural and educational spheres, their achievements in economic and social mobility are far from satisfactory. The extent and nature of even this impact varies not only among the SCs, STs and OBCs but also within each category of these groups (caste, sub-castes). For example, in case of Scheduled Castes, the protective discrimination has contributed significantly to their status mobility. They have gained more and wider political influence in central and state politics. The Scheduled Caste Members of Parliament and Assemblies from the reserved constituencies and a few elected outside of it "have more effective power or influence only under wider varying alliances and co-operations," (Singh, 1995). The literacy rate of the SCs increased from 10.27 percent in 1961 to 37.41

percent in 1991. Male literacy rate increased from 16.95 percent in 1961 to 49.91 percent in 1991. Female literacy rate too has grown from 3.28 percent in 1961 to 23.76 percent in 1991.

Thus, we find that a new class has emerged among the Scheduled Castes which commands substantial influence, despite having limited power. The emergence of this group of people in bodies which are organized not on caste or religion but on cosmopolitan principles, puts heavy pressure for conformity "to the integration principles of a new India society founded on the norms and values of the constitution of India," (Smith, 1958). The policy of positive discrimination on the basis of reservation is leading to many problems. Reservation provided for the Scheduled Castes and the Scheduled Tribes is not what is resented by those who have not been given benefits of such reservations. What they are resenting is increasing reservations to so-called backward castes. This is because it is being done at their cost i.e. reducing the opportunities available for the forward castes. As the backward communities are getting increasingly organized on political lines, the policy of reservation has become functionally a means of political consolidation. A political process which is based and conditioned on caste identities carries with it the seeds of insidious political fragmentation which may be a source of social threat to democratic stability. Conflict and violence are inherent in such a situation. It is really an irony that the policy of reservation which was aimed at weakening the caste hierarchy is actually tending to reinforce and perpetuate this evil.

Religious Diversities and the Strategy of Secularism

Apart from the caste system, another major social factor that affects political and administrative development is religion. All the major religions of the world, Hinduism, Jainism, Buddhism, Christianity and Sikhism, are represented in India. The vast majority of the population, almost 83 percent, are however, Hindus, while Muslims constitute 12 percent of the total, the second largest concentration of Muslims in the world. The major source of conflicts in the society has been between these two major and important religions - Hinduism and Islam. All other religions practically have no role except in a limited context, for instance, Christianity in Kerala or eastern border areas and Sikhism in Punjab. The roots of the Hindu-Muslim resentment are deep and can be historically traced back to the Muslim period. During the last few centuries, however, the Hindus and Muslims had learned to live together and share in the development of social and cultural traditions. The political evolution of India under the British revived the old animosities, which gave rise to alienation and hostility and the demand for a separate state of Pakistan. This issue paralyzed the nationalist struggle under Mahatma Gandhi. It resulted in a deep schism in Indian society, leading to the division of the country and to an outbreak of violence and bloodshed. From time to time even after independence such communal riots have frequently occurred in various parts of India.

Secularism is one of the main strategies adopted by the leaders of the independent India for nation-building. It was basically reconciliatory in nature. It tried to mediate between the interests of various communities and postulated a united Indian state where the followers of any religion would not be favored or discriminated against by the state. Secularism in India arose, unlike Europe, not in the process of conflict with organized religions, but as an instrument to unite the followers of different religious faiths in India in their struggle against the British rule. Thus, secularism in India was "a pragmatic solution to the problem of religious diversity," (Sinha, 1990). It was to guide the political process in the new state to facilitate the growth of nationalism and democracy. It was to transform parochial-primordial life process into a holistic nationalist life process.

The Constitution and Secularism

Though the word "secular" was added to the preamble to the constitution by the 42nd amendment in 1976, the concept of secularism was imbibed in the constitution from the very beginning. Article 15 lays down that the state shall not discriminate against any citizen on the ground of religion. Article 16 provides for equality of opportunity in matters of employment under the state irrespective of religion. Article 25 provides for freedom of conscience and free profession, practice and propagation of religion. Article 26 allows freedom to manage religious affairs. Article 27 prohibits compulsion to pay taxes to benefit a religious denomination. Article 28 provides that while no religious instruction shall be provided in an educational institution wholly maintained out of state funds, the educational institutions recognized by the state and aided by it, are free to do so provided no one is compelled to take part in religious instructions. According to Article 30, all minorities, including religious ones, shall have right to set up educational institutions of their choice and such institutions shall not be discriminated against in the matter or government aid. Article 44 enjoins the state to endeavor to establish a uniform civil code throughout the territory of India.

Although the constitution provides religious freedom to all sections of Indian citizens, it does not provide for clearly and explicitly complete separation of spheres of religious activity and civil authority. There is hardly any remedy if the state acts in an "unsecular" way.

Secularism and Communalism

Communalism has a bad connotation. It is considered as something undesirable for a state or society as a factor undermining the health of a nation and, therefore, to be curbed or prevented. This is so because the growth of communalism has resulted in ill-feeling and bitterness between different communities in society. India is the classic example where communal awakening contributed to the loss of lives of millions apart from destruction of property on a colossal scale. In India communalism is invariably perceived in a dichotomous relationship with secularism. Before independence, communalism was perceived as the opposite, the negation of nationalism. Here, communalism is defined as a locus of covert or overt tension; as a manifestation of discrimination for or against an individual or group for reasons of religious identity. In an extreme case the tension would manifest itself in a communal riot. Secularism is understood as the negation of this tension, as acceptance and tolerance of separate religious identities.

Despite the fact that communalism is regarded as something bad and condemned by all, it still persists and flourishes in Indian society. As a matter of fact, Indian society continues to provide objective socio economic and political bases along with ideological and cultural soil for the rise and growth of communalism. Communalism has made serious inroads into the state apparatus. All the major political parties, ranging from the Congress to Janata, including the BJP and the Muslim League profess to be secular. However, the quality of secularism of most of them has had varying degrees of weakness. As a matter of fact, their secularism has seldom been sturdy. Moreover, many of the functionaries in government and middle-level political leaders have not only compromised openly or secretly, but even supported communal forces and many times practiced communalism. No government, central and state, has even tried to fight it seriously. They have not only tolerated but encouraged the intrusion of religion into politics. They have often compromised and even allied with communal parties and individuals.

Communalism is a long term and deep-rooted problem and, therefore, requires intense and complex struggle on all fronts. There is a need not only to eliminate the social conditions responsible for its rise and growth but also concentrate upon the economic system. It has to be dealt with at the political level because it is above all an ideology. Politics based on that ideology including its latest version-terrorism-can be successfully met only at the political level. This is the lesson that can be derived from the events in Punjab from 1984 to 1995 and in Kashmir and elsewhere since independence.

The Administrative Integration

An effective administrative system needs a band of capable officers belonging to the different cadre of civil services. They also provide continuity and political stability on a long-term basis. For this purpose, the British introduced the system of "merit-based" bureaucracy in India in 1854. The Indian Civil Service (ICS) and the Indian Police (IP) were two all-India Services created to run the administration. These two services were the steel frame or the backbone of the colonial administration. These were recruited and trained by the central government but worked both for the central government and the provincial government.

After debating for long, the Constituent Assembly decided in favor of retaining All-India Services in Independent India. First, it was felt that it would be the ideal one for a federal system of governance which was based on cooperation and coordination between the two levels of the government. It would also facilitate a joint action on the issues of common interest between the two levels of governments. Secondly, it would make available best talents of the country even to the less developed parts of the country thereby bringing uniform development of each and every area. Third, it would not only facilitate but also strengthen national integrity. It would successfully meet the challenges of divisive forces based on religion, caste and language. And last, it would provide an efficient administrative system. The diverse nature of experience, acquired by its members, would make them capable "to have a breadth of vision and outlook, a capacity to coordinate, synthesize mutually conflicting approaches and an understanding of socio-economic and political environment of states as well as centre" (Commission, 1988). Articles 308-314 were incorporated in the constitution for this purpose. These provisions provide not only for a constitutional status to the IAS and IPS but also for the creation of one or more All-India Services through a resolution of the Council of States. These services are common to the Union and the States.

The importance of the All India Services as a stabilizing and unifying factor has been recognized and appreciated by a number of Committees and Commissions set up after the Independence. The States Reorganization Commission (1955), the Study Team on center-state relations of the Administrative Reforms Commission (ARC –1970) and the Estimates Committee of Parliament (1985) favored the continuation of All-India Services. Some even suggested creation of more All-India Services. Despite the fact that these services have withstood the test-of-time, there have been criticisms of their role and even objections of their continuation. Most of the state governments, which responded to the questionnaire of the Sarkaria Commission, in the 1980s were of the opinion that these services by and large fulfilled their

Concluding Observations

It is clear from the above analysis that the central concern before the Indian polity has been to organize a system of governance which enables effective participation of people in a highly diverse and plural society. Along with that has been the commitment to the maintenance of a pluralist or composite culture-based society. These factors have been at the core of the endeavor to build a united federal nation. Thus federalism in India has been more than the mere construction framework of center-state relations which has been gradually shaped by the emerging socio-economic realities, of a stratified mosaic of linguistic, tribal and communal diversity. It has also been affected by the processes of population growth, economic change, administrative developments and increased politicization thus taking it to the paradigm of a multi-level federalism, not of a nation in the conventional sense, but of a Federal Nation. (Puri, 1998; Narant, 1995). The development and maintenance of a federal system, is thus directly related to the existence of a federal spirit and the creation of a civil society that accept the primacy of ethno-linguistic identities, the will to preserve regional beliefs values and interests, as well as a commitment to maintain a certain degree of federal unity (Embree, 1973).

The concept of national integration in Indian usage includes both political integration and the formation of common national identity, and it has tended to be an ascribed rather than an achieved status. (Hamison, 1960) Many of the western writers have noted the "fissiparous tendencies", such as the strife endangered by the demand for linguistic states and the role of caste in politics, and the enforcement of regionalism and regional antagonism in the recent past as signs of disintegration of the society, (Kothari, 1972). However, as observed above, a number of factors can be identified that have worked towards national integration, despite the extreme centrifugal pressures inherent in the society. Some of these are economic: a move toward economic self-sufficiency, especially in machine tools and consumer goods, indigenous production of armaments, the decentralization of industries, taking into account the "politics of scale" as well as "the economics of scale", the curbing of concentration of wealth in a few urban areas, with the prevention of the growth of "parasitic elites". Other factors working for national integration are more political; the development of the institutions of participatory democracy as a "mechanism for the change of elites and the availability of counter-elites", and most importantly the problem of ethnic pluralities, (Embree 1973:46). There is a well-justified awareness that the very precise factors that seem to be so inimical to nationhood have in fact contributed to it. In a curious way, as Embree puts it, "the bewildering complexities of Indian social life and historical experience have worked to maintain the fabric of the political structure. Those characteristic features of Indian society that are so patently divisive have apparently worked in a countervailing fashion to create a pluralistic political society, with the structural stains that have been so obvious to observers working to buttress each other," (ibid.).

It is also apparent that the four major components of the uneasy mosaic of India's plural society; the traditional Indian social structure, dominated by caste, language, religion and class divisions, have indeed paradoxically helped in its transformation into a modern industrialized nation and in fact have been integrative in India's plural society, (ibid.). However, the mechanical devices that made integration possible in modern India can be easily identified. These are (1) the bureaucratic structure of a modern state, especially the outlook and character of common All-India Administrative Service and Indian Police Service; (2) the control by the Central Government of the means of coercion and protection, that is an army, and the police based on secular character; (3) establishment of a Minorities commission and Human Rights Commission to look into the interests of minorities and victims of human rights violations; (4) methods of rewards for cooperation, tangible in economic terms and intangible in terms of prestige (5) a system of communication, i.e. a free and alert press; and above all (6) a pattern of education and an independent judiciary, (Puri, 1988:29). These devices have provided the basis for important linkages between the different groups in the India society. Thus India's pluralism has been more resilient in absorbing the pressures of external and internal traumas than many more homogenous societies have been. The Indian experience therefore emphatically points out that there are no better alternatives to federal and confederal arrangements of accommodation and managing conflicts. (Panjivani, 1996)

In answer to the often repeated question "Is India disintegrating?," it is apt to remember that although India cannot be a nation-state in the European sense, and should not even aspire to, because it is not one nation, India is too complex a society to be compressed within such narrow confines, but there seems to be no danger to its unity, if it continually strives to retain, sharpen and operationalize the power-sharing mechanism at all levels of its structure in a "multi-cultural civilizational (federal) state."

REFERENCES

Basu, A. and Kohali, A. 1998. *Community Conflicts of the State in India.* Delhi: Oxford University Press.
Commission. 1988. *India: Commission on Center-State Relations*, vol. I (Delhi).

Embree. 1973. "Pluralism and National Integration: The India Experience" *Journal of International Affairs*, vol. 27, no. 1.

Galanter, M. 1984. *Competing Equalities: Law and Backward Classes in India*. Delhi: Oxford University Press.

Harrison, S. 1960. *India: The Most Dangerous Decades*. Princeton: N.J.: Princeton University Press.

Jain, R. B. and Sharma, O. P. 1997. "Forging Unity Among Diversities: Nation-Building Strategies in India" *Journal of Behavioural and Social Sciences*, no. 1.

Kanie, R. 1982. *Legitimation and Integration in Developing Societies: The Case of India*. Boulder: Colorado: Lynne Rienner.

Kathari, R. 1972. *Politics in India*. New Delhi: Orient Longman.

————.1976. "Integration and Performance: Two Pivots of India's Model of Nation-Building", in R. Kothari ed. *State and Nation-Building: A Third World Perspective*" Delhi: Allied Publishers.

Kohli, A. 1991. *Democracy and Discontent: India's Growing Crises of Governability*. Cambridge: Cambridge University Press

Krihna, S. 1992. "The Language Situation: Mosaic or Melting Point" in N. Mokarji and A. Arora eds. *Federalism in India: Origin and Development*. New Delhi: Vika.

Lijphart, A.. 1996. "The Puzzle of Indian Democracy: A Consociational Interpretation" *American Political Science Review*, vol. 90, no. 2.

Manar, J. 1992. "The sustainability of Economic Liberation in India. Murkaji, N. and Arora, B. *The Future of Economic Reform*. Delhi: op. cit.

Narang, A. S. 1995. *Ethnic Identities and Federalism* Shimla: India Institute of Advanced Studies.

Pulmarampil, J. ed. 1976. *India Political System: A Reader in Continuity and Change*. New Delhi: NV Publications.

Singh, M.P. 1990. "The Crisis of the India State: From Quiet Development to Noisy Democracy" *Asian Survey* vol. xxx, no. 8.

————.1996. "New Federalism in India: Tradition of the United Front Coalition" *Politics India*, New Delhi (October).

Singh, Y. 1995. "Integration of Marginalised Groups into Indian Society: The Case of Scheduled Castes, Scheduled Tribes and Backward Classes" in M. Dubey ed. *Indian Society*.

CHAPTER 14

Devolution and the Elusive Quest for Peace in Sri Lanka

Tiruchelvam Neelan

Introduction

Leonard Woolf the literary critic and publisher was a colonial civil servant in Ceylon from 1904 to 1911, and served both in Jaffna in the extreme north and in Hambantota in the deep south. Many years later in 1938 as an advisor to the Labor Party, he reflected on the questions of minority protection and constitutional reform. He argued in favor of a constitutional arrangement, which ensured a large measure of devolution on the introduction of a federal system on the Swiss model. Woolfe added that "The Swiss federal canton system had proved extraordinarily successful under circumstances very similar to those in Ceylon, i.e. the co-existence in a single democratic state of communities of very different size, sharply distinguished from one another by race, language and religion."

Despite the foresight of Leonard Woolf almost six decades ago, Sri Lanka's failure to lay down the constitutional foundation of a multi-ethnic society based on equality, ethnic pluralism and the sharing of power has exacerbated the ethnic conflict. As a consequence Sri Lanka has been besieged for years by ethnic fratricide and political violence (Triuchevlam, 1996).

The purpose of this essay is to assess the recent efforts in Sri Lanka to establish a federal form of devolution of powers and to examine the legal and political constraints that need to be overcome to bring about comprehensive constitutional reform. The essay will also examine whether the proposals are likely to facilitate the resolution of protracted ethnic conflict, and the broader lessons that may be drawn from the Sri Lankan experience on the importance of federalism as means of resolving conflict in divided societies.

Minority Protection and Autonomy Demands

In recent years, there has been a growing awareness of the universality and complexities of ethnic problems and the need for concerted action to devise strategies, programs and structures for the management of ethnic conflicts. Several multi-ethnic polities have incorporated federal forms of devolution into constitutional and political orders. In the development of these constitutional models, there has been continuing conflict between unitary and federal efforts, and centralized and decentralized forms. In India, for example, the federal polity is based on division into linguistic states, while in Malaysia, a federation of states is led by local rulers and includes territories, which were given special concessions. The former Nigerian model overlapped certain regional and tribal groupings in its demarcation of states. Federal and quasi-federal models of devolution also have a relevance to strife-ridden societies such as the Philippines, Pakistan and Sri Lanka, which have enacted new constitutions, or are on the threshold of redesigning their present constitutional framework. Within these societies, each of the diverse ethnic, tribal and regional groupings have varying perceptions of federalism, which have tended to condition the conflicts and tensions within federal or confederal systems.

A growing debate has emerged within each of these societies regarding the need for structural re-arrangements to strengthen their federal character. These efforts have been directed towards the need to redefine center-state relations in educational and cultural policy, police powers, resource mobilization and redistribution, and emergency and residual powers. Such efforts and problems evoke basic issues concerning equitable power sharing among ethnic groups. The failure to address these issues boldly, has accentuated secessionist demands by disaffected ethnic and other sub-national groups.

Self-determination often sought by ethnic minorities in the course of armed struggle or non-violent political agitation, has been problematic. Nation states become notably defensive in the face of such assertions and often employ extreme measures of repression in order to contain ethnic demands, which they perceive would result in national disintegration.

Another focal point of ethnic conflict has been preference policies directed towards disparities in education; employment and economic opportunities. These policies are often founded on competing perceptions of deprivation, which in turn give rise to rival notions of social justice. India, one of the most complex and hierarchically structured societies, has a constitutionally mandated policy of preference towards weak and vulnerable minorities and tribal groups: Policy makers and judges have had to grapple with issues of bewildering complexity in defining the constitutional limits of such policies, balancing the interest of historically depressed caste and tribal groups with those of economically backward classes. Preference policies such as Malaysia's New Economic Policy (1971) directed in favor of a politically assertive and dominant majority, pose qualitatively different socio-political issues relating to the legitimate limits of preference policies based on proportionality.

The international community must accord highest priority to developing principles, and concepts with regard to minority protection, and these must gain universal acceptance and contribute to the peaceful resolution of conflicts. But, given the evolving and changing nature of ethnic identity, the content of ethnic demands and the shifting balance of power among ethnic groups, most structural arrangements will remain fluid and transient. Thus, these arrangements must continuously be renewed and reconstructed in order to respond to new challenges and demands.

Although the ethnic minorities in Sri Lanka were un-reconciled to the constitutional arrangements at the time of transfer of political power in 1948 from Britain to Sri Lanka - which have, since then singularly failed to establish the foundations of a multi-ethnic polity - few expected that majority rule would be quickly followed by discriminatory legislative measures. First related to new citizenship laws, which effectively disenfranchised estate Tamils of recent Indian origin. This legislation facilitated the formation of ethnically based Tamil parties to resist discriminatory citizenship laws. They advocated parity with respect to the status of the national languages and urged the creation of a federal constitution.

The second development related to the promulgation of Sinhala as the sole official language. In the early fifties, ethnic communities were becoming increasingly polarized, and ethnical political discourse was becoming strident and volatile. The political and ethnic polarization intensified during the run-up to the 1956 general election when the Sri Lanka Freedom Party was swept into power in all parts of the country except the north-east. The party's success symbolized the resurgence of the forces of Sinhala-Buddhist nationalism, while the Federal Party's success in the north-east represented the emergence of a new form of Tamil linguistic nationalism. Unfortunately, these events ensured that the assertion of one form of nationalism was viewed as a denial of the other. Colvin R. de Silva, the leading left politician involved in the legislative debates on the Official Language Act warned that the policy of imposing the language of the majority on the linguistic minority would have dangerous political consequences. He added "Two languages - one nation; one language - two nations". De Silva accurately predicted that the failure to resolve the language question in a manner satisfactory to the minority would eventually lead to a separatist movement (Triuchelvam, 1996b).

Collective Violence and its Impact on Ethnic Consciousness

Twenty years have lapsed since one of the cruelest weeks in the troubled history of modern Sri Lanka. The minorities of Sri Lanka have been exposed to collective violence in 1958, 1977, 1981 and 1983. There was however a qualitative difference in the intensity, brutality and organized nature of the violence of July '83. There is no other event which is so deeply etched in the collective memories of the victims and survivors. Neither time nor space has helped ease the pain, the trauma and the bitter memories.

It was estimated that about 2000 - 3000 defenseless people were brutally murdered, although official figures maintain that the death toll was about 400. Many were beaten or hacked to death, while several were torched to death. Thousands of homes and buildings were torched or destroyed. Within the city of Colombo almost a hundred thousand persons, more than half the city's Tamil population were displaced from their homes, many never returned to their neighborhoods or to their work places. Outside the country, it was estimated that there were about 175 thousand refugees and displaced persons. Hardly a family escaped the death of a relative, or the destruction of their houses or their livelihood and the dislocation of their families (ibid., p. 150). One woman who had been victimized by the repeated cycles of violence, reconstructed her Tamil identity, 'to be a Tamil is to live in fear', she exclaimed in despair (Kanapathillai, 1983).

Many observers were disturbed by the organized and systematic nature of the violence. The rampaging mobs were fed with precise information on the location of Tamil houses and businesses. Their leaders were often armed with voters Lists, and with detailed addresses of every Tamil-owned shop, house or factory. The business, entrepreneurial and professional classes were especially targeted, as part of the objective appeared to be to break the economic backbone of the Tamils. It was estimated that almost 100 industrial plants, including 20 garment factories were severely damaged or destroyed. The cost of industrial reconstruction was estimated at Rs.2 billion rupees. This did not include the hundreds of shops and small trading establishments (Triuchelvam 1996b:150).

Equally disturbing was the element of state complicity in the violence. The state not only mishandled the funeral of 13 soldiers who had been ambushed by the LTTE on July 23rd, 1983 but also allowed the inflammatory news to be projected in banner headlines in the newspapers on the 24th. On the other hand, the retaliatory violence of the security forces in Tirunelveli and Kantharmadu which resulted in an estimated 50 to 70 persons being killed was suppressed from the media. Army personnel appeared to have encouraged arson and looting and in some instances participated in the looting. Neither the army nor the police took any meaningful action to prevent the violence or to apprehend the culprits. No curfew was declared for almost two days. Neither the President nor any senior minister made a public appeal for calm and restraint. It was also widely believed that elements within the state or the ruling party had either orchestrated the violence or encouraged the blood letting. No Commission of Inquiry was ever appointed to clear the state of these allegations or to investigate the causes of violence (Bastian, 1983).

When however political leaders did speak four days later, there was a total identification of the state with the majority community. President Jayewardene said that the riots were not a product of urban mobs but a mass movement of the generality of the Sinhalese people. He spoke of the need to politically "appease" the natural desires and requests of the Sinhalese people. Similarly, none of the senior cabinet ministers who spoke on television including Mr. Lalith Athulathmudali, had a word of sympathy for the victims of this terrible outrage, nor did any of them visit the refugee camps to commiserate even briefly with those who had suffered. This conduct of the President was in sharp contrast with his more conciliatory behavior in the aftermath of the 1981 violence. He was quoted on September 11 , "I regret that some members of my party have spoken, in Parliament and outside, words that encourage violence and murders, rapes and arson that have been committed" (Tambiah, 1986:20). The President further stated that he would resign as the head of his party if its members continued to encourage ethnic violence and racial bigotry.

Clearly the most disturbing episode took place on the 25th of July 1983 at Welikade prison, when 35 Tamil political detainees were battered and hacked to death with clubs, pipes and iron rods by fellow prisoners with the complicity of prison guards. The government conducted a perfunctory magisterial inquiry but no attempt has yet been made to take legal action against those responsible. This incident was repeated again on Wednesday the 27th of July and it is shameful that the government has yet to pay compensation to the bereaved families and has pleaded immunity to the legal proceedings instituted by them (ibid., pp. 24-25).

Several scholars have written extensively on the causes and consequences of July 1983, which the British anthropologist, Jonathan Spencer, has described as 'the dark night of the collective soul (Spencer, 1990:192). How is it possible that an island society renowned for its scenic beauty and the warmth and hospitality of its inhabitants is capable of such collective evil and inhumanity? Some have referred to the crisis of competing nationalism of the Sinhalese and the Tamils as being a contributory factor. Both forms of nationalism were antagonistic and incompatible. The assertion of one was perceived to be a denial of the other.

Others have referred to the historical myths as embodied in the ancient chronicle that demonized the Tamils. Jonathan Spencer points out that in the popular imagination, the tigers were believed to be 'superhumanly cruel and cunning and like demons ubiquitous' and that ordinary Tamil workmates and neighbors also became vested with these attributes. They remind us, as Voltaire did, that if you believe in absurdities you will commit atrocities (Spencer, 1984). Others have pointed to the propensity for violence in authoritarian political structures which enthrone the majoritarian principle and provide for the bizarre entrenchment of the unitary state. The Referendum in December 1981 which extended the life of Parliament further exacerbated the climate of political animosity and of intolerance (Obeyesekere, 1984).

July '83 also contributed towards convulsive changes in the politics of the Tamil community and their methods of struggle. As the political leaders committed to constitutional means of agitation became marginalized, Tamil militancy assumed ascendancy. It was even asserted by some that violence of the victims was on a different moral plane from that of the oppressor. This was a dangerous doctrine for the violence of the victim soon consumed the victim, and the victims also became possessed by the demons of racial bigotry and intolerance, which had characterized the oppressor. These are seen in the fratricidal violence between Tamils and Muslims, the massacres at the Kathankudy mosque, in Welikanda and Medirigiya; and the forcible expulsion of Muslims from the Mannar and ,Taffna Districts (Tiruchelvam, 1966:152).

Provincial Councils and Their Failure

During the eighties belated efforts were made to address some of the underlying grievances of Tamils and Muslims which had been acknowledged in the manifesto of the United National Party in the General Elections of 1997. The first of such attempts was to address the residual issues relating to statelessness by the Grant of Citizenship to Stateless Persons Act No. S of 1986, and the Grant of Citizenship (Special Provisions) Act No.39 of 1988. In the realm of language, Tamil was progressively made a national language in the second Republican Constitution in 1978, and subsequently made an official language in 1987. As a consequence of these changes, Sinhala and Tamil are the languages of legislation, administration, and of the courts although many problems remain with regard to effective implementation of bilingualism.

However the most significant measure to redress the imbalance in the relationship between the different ethnic groups in the country was the devolution of power to Provincial Councils by the Thirteenth Amendment to the

Constitution. This scheme envisages the devolution of legislative and executive authority to eight provincial councils which were constituted within the country. The structure of the devolutionary system envisages the election on the proportionate representation system of a legislative body known as a Provincial Council. Each province would have a Governor appointed by the President. The Governor holds office during the pleasure of the President but may be impeached by the Council if he intentionally violates the constitution or is guilty of misconduct or corruption. The Governor shall also appoint a Chief Minister who in his opinion is best able to command the support of the majority members of that Council. There shall in addition be a Board of Ministers of which the Chief Minister shall be the head. The executive power in respect of the devolved subjects shall be vested in the Governor, who shall however in the exercise of the function act in accordance with the advice of the Board of Ministers unless he has been expressly required by the constitution to set on his own discretion.

The subjects and functions to be devolved on the Provincial Councils are set out in the 9th Schedule to the Constitution which is called the Provincial Council List. The subjects include police and public order, provincial planning, local government, provincial housing and construction, agriculture and agrarian service, rural development, health, indigenous medicine, cooperatives, and irrigation. In respect of subjects such as law and order, education and land, the scope of devolution is further defined in Appendix 1, 2 and 3. There is also a Concurrent List of subjects where the center and provinces enjoy concurrent authority. The Reserve List defines a sphere of exclusive authority of the center and includes areas such as defense and national security, foreign affairs, post and telecommunications, broadcasting, television, justice, foreign trade and commerce, ports and harbors, aviation, national transport, minerals and mines and elections. An unusual feature of the reserve list which has caused uncertainty is a provision that national policy on all subjects and functions shall belong to the center, (ibid.).

On the financing of devolution, it was envisaged that provincial councils would be financed through direct grants by the center, limited form of taxation, and revenue sharing arrangements. There is also a Finance Commission consisting of 5 members empowered to make recommendations with regard to allocations from the annual budget of funds adequate to meeting the needs of the province. The Commission has also the power to make recommendations with regard to making apportionment of funds between various provinces having regard to the objectives of balanced regional development in the country.

In addition, the devolutionary scheme envisages the establishment of high courts in each province to exercise original criminal jurisdiction and appellate and reversionary jurisdiction in respect of criminal matters. In addition, the Provincial High Court had been conferred the jurisdiction to issue preroga- tive writs such as habeas corpus, certiorari and prohibition in respect of any matter set out in the Provincial Council List.

The political and constitutional contexts within which the Provincial Council scheme was evolved has continued to constrain the effective working of Provincial Councils. The scheme was an integral part of the Indo-Sri Lanka Accord entered into on 29th July 1987 and signed by President J. R. Jayewardene of Sri Lanka and Prime Minister Rajiv Gandhi of India. The Accord endeavored to provide a conceptual framework for the resolution of the ethnic conflict and to outline institutional arrangements for the sharing of power between the Sinhala and Tamil communities. The Accord declared that Sri Lanka was "a multi-ethnic and multi-lingual plural society" consisting primarily of four ethnic groups - the Sinhalese, Tamils, Muslims, and Burghers. It further recognized that the northern province and the eastern province "had been areas of historical habitation of the Tamil speaking population". Both these statements had important ideological significance in framing the policies of bi-lingualism, the provincial council scheme; and the temporary merger of the northern and eastern province as the unit of devolution, (ibid.).

The framers of the Onto-Sri Lanka Accord had hoped that they would present the political groups in the north-east and the south of Sri Lanka with a 'fait accompli' and that they would progressively build elite a consensus around the main concepts and ideas embodied in the Accord. These expecta- tions however proved to be unrealistic. Both the LTTE, the dominant po- litico-military formation in the north-east and the JVP repudiated the Accord and questioned its legitimacy. A controversy surrounding the Accord ulti- mately led to an armed confrontation between the LTTE and the Indian Peace Keeping Force and to an insurgency in the south of Sri Lanka. These developments cast a dark shadow over the working of the Provincial Coun- cil system. Elections to the Provincial Councils were held in April and June 1988, but the Sri Lanka Freedom Party, the main Opposition party did not participate in this exercise. Similarly the elections to the North-east provincial council held in November 1988 were deprived of their legitimacy due to the opposition of the LTTE and the difficulties in conducting free and fair elec- tions. The devolutionary experiment in the north-east was short-lived and lasted from November 1988 and mid-March 1990. It remains a cruel irony that the north-east provincial council remains dissolved and all legislative and executive power is vested in the Governor of that province. The Constitu- tion framework also proved to be problematic. Section 2 of the Sri Lanka Constitution entrenches a unitary state and the conception of the unitary state has influenced the outlook of the bureaucracy and the judiciary in the resolution of center-provincial disputes. The executive presidency inevitably led to a concentration of power and authority in the center, and constrained the meaningful devolution of power to the provinces. The divisional secretariat system resulted in further extension of the authority of the center at the sub-district level.

Various disingenuous methods were employed to re-vest in the center powers relating to transportation and agrarian services. The center also exercised an excessive degree of control over finances, and devolution of power in the area of land and law and order were incomplete. These developments have led to concern that there was a reluctance on the part of the center to part with power and that there was consequently a lack of sincerity in implementing the scheme of devolution.

The Draft Constitution— Does it Represent a Paradigm Shift?

One of the constitutive principles of the draft Third Republican Constitution related to the redefinition of the nature of the state. Since the transfer of power, Sri Lanka has been regarded as a unitary state, save and except that it was explicitly recognized as a unitary state in the first Republican Constitution in 1972. The second Republican Constitution went one step further and entrenched this clause and provided that no law which was inconsistent with this principle could be enacted unless it was passed by a special majority in Parliament and approved by the People at a Referendum. The Thirteenth Amendment case highlighted the difficulties that the entrenchment of this clause would pose to any effort towards significantly devolving power on the provinces. Although the scheme was modified to conform to what were then perceived to be the requirements of a unitary state, the legislation's constitutional validity was questioned by four of the nine justices of the Supreme Court who adjudicated on the matter. With the result that there was considerable concern that any significant enlargement of the powers of the provinces would contravene the entrenched clause relating the unitary state (Edrihinsa, 1998).

One of the limitations of the Indo-Lanka Accord on which the Provincial Council scheme was based, was that while the Accord called for a redefinition of the Sri Lankan polity, it did not bring about a change in the unitary character of the Sri Lankan state. The Accord did acknowledge that Sri Lanka was a multi-ethnic, multi-lingual, plural society consisting primarily of four main groups - the Sinhalese, Tamils, Muslims and Burghers. However, no change was advocated to Section 2 of the Constitution, which entrenched the unitary state. As we noted above this conception of the unitary state influenced the legislature to adopt disingenuous methods to re-vest in the center powers relating to transportation and agrarian services. A major flaw in the

Thirteenth Amendment was that 'national policy on all subjects and functions' were to be determined by the center. This in effect meant that the center could under the guise of protecting national policy make legislative inroads into the sphere devolved to the provinces under the provincial list or the concurrent lists, (Tiruchelvam, 1996a:41). Rohan Edirisinghe has correctly observed that 'The constitutional provisions are fundamentally flawed. They permit the center both to retain, so much power and also undermine devolved powers so easily, that they cannot result in substantial devolution of power," (Tiruchelvam 1996b:24). The concept of the unitary state also became embedded in the consciousness of the bureaucracy and the judiciary. It influenced the approach of the bureaucracy and the judiciary to the resolution of center-provincial disputes. They did not perceive themselves as neutral arbiters but as an integral part of the centralized state.

The August 3rd proposals redefined the nature of the state as a 'union of regions'. Drawing on the language of the Indian constitution, Sri Lanka was further described as a 'united and sovereign Republic'. In the most recent legal text there is a reworking of the language without any significant deviation from the original intent and impact of this provision. The Republic of Sri Lanka is now described as 'indissoluble Union of Regions', thereby interpolating an archaic phrase drawn from the Australian Constitution. Article 3, which relates to sovereignty and its exercise also ensured that legislative and executive power would be directly vested in the Regional Council and its political executive in respect of subjects devolved.

With regard to the subject and function to be devolved on the region, most of the subjects and functions which were previously in the concurrent list were transferred to the regional list. This would significantly strengthen the capacity of the devolved authorities to adopt an integrated approach to social and economic development of the region and thereby seek to redress regional disparities in development. A contentious issue has been devolution of powers in relation to land. The legal text makes it clear that state land shall vest in the region and the Regional administration shall be entitled to transfer or alienate land and engage in land use and land settlement schemes. The center may however for the purpose of a reserved subject request a Regional administration to transfer state land to the center. There is an obligation in the part of the center to consult with regions in regard to such requirements. The legal text also provides that Interregional irrigation projects where the command area falls within two or more Regions would be the responsibility of the centre. This provision is also found in the Provincial Council Scheme although the selection of allottees and the alienation of land under such Schemes were within the powers of the Provincial Council. This is a matter which will require further clarification. Law and order including the maintenance of public order have been clearly devolved on the Region although there would be disputes as to whether the investigation of offences relating to the reserved list of subjects should be vested with the regional or national police service (Tiruchelvam, 1996a).

The issue arises whether the draft constitutional proposals would result in establishing a federal political system. Ronald Watts has pointed out that the term federal political system "refers to a broad category of political system in which, by contrast to the single source of authority in a unitary system there are two (or more) levels of governments which combine elements of shared rule through common institutions and regional self- rule for the governments of the constituent units." Having regard to the structural characteristic of the proposed power sharing arrangements, we can reach the following conclusions. Firstly, there are two orders of government at the national and regional level each acting directly on their citizens. Secondly, there is a constitutional distribution of legislative and executive authority and allocation of revenue resources between the national and the regional orders of government providing for areas of exclusivity and autonomy for each order. Thirdly, the proposed written constitution will not be unilaterally alterable in that no bill for the amendment or repeal of the provisions of the chapter relating to devolution or relating to the distribution of subjects and functions between the center and the region shall come into operation in respect of a region unless such act or provision has been approved by a resolution of a Regional Council established for that region. Rohan Edrisinha has however pointed out that the draft proposals do not adequately and effectively establish a supremacy of the constitution. There is reference in the preamble to the constitution that it is the supreme law of the land, but no substantive provision which emphasizes that all the organs of the government, all institutions and all citizens are subordinate to it (Tiruchelvam, 1996b).

Fourthly, an umpire to rule on disputes between the center and the region is also an important feature of these arrangements. The draft provides for an arbitral tribunal to be established in the case of a dispute between a regional administration and the central government. Each party to the dispute which is a regional administration and the central government shall be entitled to nominate a member and the members so appointed may nominate a chairman. Where there is no agreement between the members, the chairman shall be nominated by a Constitutional Council. An award or a determination made by a Tribunal shall be binding on the parties to the dispute. Critics however have contended that the arbitral arrangement is no substitute for the judicial resolution of disputes between the center and the region (ibid.). Rohan Edrisinha has argued that "what is tragic, but perhaps not surprising in Sri Lanka today is that no political party in the country is committed to what is the cornerstone of a constitutional democracy" (ibid. p. 20).

Fifthly, there are process and institutions to facilitate collaboration between the center and the region in respect of areas where governmental responsibilities are shared or overlapped. The Chief Minister's conference is an important innovation in this regard. It provides for the Chairman of the Conference to be elected by the Chief Ministers in rotation so that each Chief Minister will be able to hold office as Chairman for a period of 3 months. It is further provided that the Prime Minister must meet with the Conference and that a period of 3 months should not lapse between such meetings. The Conference has the authority to ensure full compliance with the constitutional provision relating to devolution in accordance with the spirit and intention of the constitution and to inquire into subject where more than one region have a common interest or to make recommendations on policy co-ordinations. The Conference can make representations to the Finance Commission and also address matters relating to financial administration and accountability. In addition to the arbitral arrangement referred to above, the Conference may also settle disputes by mediation or conciliation including disputes between the center and a region.

One of the significant shortcomings in the proposals relates to the absence of a second chamber of the regions which provides for the representation of distinct regional views. A proposal to establish such a chamber was made before the Select Committee but was subsequently withdrawn by the government.

In Sri Lanka, progress on political arrangements to secure minority rights has often been incremental. There has been in its recent history no dramatic leaps of faith which have resulted in fundamental transformation of constitutional arrangements. Nonetheless, we must conclude that the draft constitution in deviating and moving away from an entrenched unitary state has brought about a paradigm shift considered vital to a meaningful sharing of power between regions and communities.

Conclusion

The constitutional reform proposals undoubtedly represent the boldest efforts hitherto towards ethnic reconciliation, but are they adequate given the magnitude of the crisis facing Sri Lankan society. Critics have argued that they significantly fall short of the Thimpu principles advanced by all of the major Tamil formations at the political negotiations conducted in Thimphu, Bhutan. The four principles placed before the Sri Lankan Government were as follows:

1. The recognition of the Tamils of Sri Lanka as a distinct nationality.

2. The recognition of an identified Tamil homeland and guarantee of its territorial integrity.

3. Based on the above, recognition of the inalienable right of self-determination of the Tamil nation.

4. Recognition of the right to full citizenship, and other fundamental democratic rights of all Tamils who look upon the island as their country.

The principles further envisaged that the political structure envisaged for the resolution of the conflict should be based on a recognition of the above principles. It is an examination of these principles that has led some commentators to advocate the need for a new initiative based on 'the core aspirations of the Tamil People'. The Indo-Sri Lanka accord, by its emphasis on the need to nurture and protect distinct identities and by acknowledging that the northeast province constitutes the traditional habitation of Tamils and Muslims provides an implicit acknowledgement of some of the Thimpu concepts. However the mere symbolic acknowledgement of the definition of the national problem and the nature of Tamil national identity does not per se lead to a resolution. At the core of the Thimpu principles are substantive political arrangements for the redefinition of the nature of the state and the sharing of sovereign legislative and executive powers between the regions. The quest for a political resolution within a united Sri Lanka must therefore relate more to the substantive issues relating to the exercise of political power rather than the more abstract formulations of political identity.

REFERENCES

Bastian, S. 1983. "Political Economy of Ethnic Violence in Sri Lanka, the July 1983 Riots" in Das ed. *Mirrors of Violence*. pp. 286-304.

Edrisinha, R. 1998. "A Critical Overview: Constitutionalism, Conflict Resolution and the Limits of the Draft Constitution" in D. Panditaratre and P. Ratnam eds. *The Draft Constitution of Sri Lanka: Critical Aspects*, Colombo: Law and Society Trust.

Kanapathipillai, V. 1983. "The Survivor's Experience" in Das. Op. cit.. pp. 321-344.

Obeyesekere, G. 1984. "Political Violence and Democracy in Sri Lanka" in Committee for National Development, ed. *Sri Lanka: The Ethnic Conflict: Myths, Realities and Perceptions*. New Delhi: Perspectives.

Spencer, J.A. 1984. "Popular Perceptions of Violence: A Provincial View" in J. Manor, ed. *Change and Crisis*, London.

————. 1996. "Introduction: The Power of the Past" in J.A. Spencer, ed. *Sri Lanka: History and the Root of Conflict*, London.

Tambia, S. J. 1986. *Sri Lanka: Ethnic Fratricide and the Dismantling of Democracy*, Chicago.

Tiruchelvam, N. 1996a. "Devolution of Power: The Problems and Challenges" in *Sri Lanka: The Devolution Debate*. Colombo: International Centre for Ethnic Studies.

————. 1996b. "Sri Lanka's Ethnic Conflict and Preventative Action: The Role of NGOs" in R.I. Rothberg ed. *Vigilance and Vengeance: NGOs Preventing Ethnic Conflict in Divided Societies*. Cambridge, Massachusetts: World Peace.

NOTES ON CONTRIBUTORS

Pita Ogaba Agbese who was educated at the Ahmadu Bello University, Zaria, Northwestern University and the Keller Graduate School of Management is Professor of Political Science at the University of Northern Iowa. Most recently, he along with John Mukum Mbaku and Mwangi Kimenyi, edited *Ethnicity and Governance in the Third World*. He is also co-editor (with Kayode Fayemi) of *The Best is Yet to Come: Portrait of A Scholar Activist,* a volume on the life and work of Julius O. Ihonvbere. He has published extensively on the military, ethnicity, privatization and constitutionalism.

Etannibi Alemika holds a B.Sc. in Sociology from the University of Ibadan, an M.Sc. from Ahmadu Bello University, Zaria, and a Ph.D. in Criminology from Penn State University. A leading criminologist, Alemika has published extensively on crime and the police institution. He co-edited *Policing in Nigeria*, the most authoritative study of the Nigerian Police since the establishment of the colonial state in 1914. He is currently Professor of Criminology and the Head of the Department of Sociology, University of Jos, Nigeria.

Warisu Alli is a Professor of Political Science at the University of Jos, Nigeria. He studied at the University of Kiev in the former Soviet Union where he obtained an M.Sc. and Ph.D. in Political Economy. He has published widely in the area of International Political Economy and was until recently Head of the Department of Political Science and Dean of the Faculty of Social Sciences, University of Jos, Nigeria.

Awad Al Sid Alkassani is a Professor of Political Science and Head of the Department of Political Science, University of Khartoum, Sudan. He is the author of *Federalism in Sudan* and continues his research into the crises of federalism in Sudan.

Leo Dare was Professor of Political Science at the former University of Ife (now Obafemi Awolowo University), Nigeria. His extensive research and publications are in comparative political development. He served as President of the Nigerian Political Science Association before moving to Canada in 1994, where he continues his teaching career at Brock University, St. Catherines, Ontario. He is a consultant on African affairs in Ottawa, Canada.

Samuel Egwu has a B.Sc. from Ahmadu Bello University and an M.Sc. from the University of Jos, Nigeria where he is currently an Associate Professor of Political Science. Acclaimed as Nigeria's foremost authority on rural

rural ethnicity, with numerous publications to his credit, he has been visiting scholar at Northwestern University Program on African Studies; the Nordic African Institute, Upsala, Sweden, and the Port Harcourt-based Centre for Advanced Social Science. Author of the authoritative work on the impact of structural Adjustment and agrarian change on rural ethnicity, he is currently coordinating a study on ethno-religious conflict in Nigeria for the African Centre for Democratic Governance. His current research interests includes the citizen question in Africa, the Nigerian variant of which has received his incisive analysis.

J. Kayode Fayemi is the Director of the Centre for Democracy and Development. Dr Fayemi studied at the Universities of Lagos, Ife and London, where he received a doctorate degree in War Studies from king's College, London. Dr Fayemi's main research focus is peace and security. He has written on civil-military relations, constitutional reform, security sector reform and democratic development in Africa. His latest work, *Mercenaries: An African Security Dilemma* (with Abdel Fatau-Musah, Pluto Press, 1999) has received critical mention in scholarly reviews.

Aaron T. Gana who is Executive Director, African Centre for Democratic Governance—a research and advocacy organization based in Abuja, Nigeria—received his Ph.D. from Columbia University, New York. He taught at Ahmadu Bello University, Zaria, the City University of New York, the University of Oklahoma and the University of Jos where he was Chair of Political Science and Dean of Social Sciences before retiring in 1996. He was President of the Nigerian Political Science Association (1990-92), and President of the Social Science Academy of Nigeria (1992-94). His research and publications have focused on the state and the development process in Africa. He co-edited (with S. G. Tyoden) *Towards the Third Republic (1990)*.

Alex Gboyega is Professor and Head of the Department of Political Science, University of Ibadan. He is widely published in the area of Local Government. His *Political Values and Local Government in Nigeria* remains a classic in Local Government Studies in Nigeria. His current research focuses on the dynamics of local governance in Nigeria's centralized federalism.

Onje Gye-Wado is currently the Deputy Governor of Nigeria's Nasarawa state which was part of the old Plateau state until 1996. He studied Law at Ahmadu Bello University and the University of Nigeria, Nsukka where he received a Ph.D. in Law. He was a Research Fellow at the Nigerian Institute of International Affairs, Lagos, and Senior Lecturer in Law at the University of Jos before joining the political fray under the aegis of the ruling People's Democratic Party.

Jibrin Ibrahim is one of the few Nigerian bi-lingual scholars in the discipline of Political Science. A widely published scholar, Dr. Ibrahim received his Bachelors degree from Ahmadu Bello University, and a Ph.D. from the University of Bordeaux, France. He taught at Ahmadu Bello University rising to the rank of Associate Professor before resigning to join other colleagues to establish the Centre for Research and Development (CRD), Kano. He is currently the Country Director (Nigeria) for the Washington-based International Law Group working to strengthen democratic institutions around the world.

Julius Ihonvbere studied at then University of Ife, (now Obafemi Awolowo), Carleton University, Canada, and the University of Toronto, from where he received his Ph.D. Considered the most widely published African scholar of the last decade of the twentieth century, Professor Ihonvbere has authored, co-authored and edited over a dozen books and one hundred book chapters and articles in scholarly journals. He combines scholarship and political activism in a way few scholars do. He had taught at the University of Port Harcourt, the University of Toronto, Canada and the University of Texas, Austin, from where he resigned his tenured position as Professor of Political Science to join the Ford Foundation as Program Officer for Governance and Civil Society in 1997.

R. B. Jain was Professor and Chair of the Department of Political Science and former Dean of the Faculty of Social Sciences, University of Delhi. He was Professor and Chair of the Department of Public Administration at Punjabi University, and at the Indian Institute of Public Administration, New Delhi. He has held appointments as visiting Professor at various universities in Canada, Germany and the U.S.. A former Editor of the Indian Journal of Political Science, he has authored, co-authored and edited over twenty-five books, and published over 140 articles in scholarly journals. He is currently the Chair of the International Political Science Association's Research Committee 4 on Public Bureaucracies in Developing Societies and a member of the Advisory Panel of the Government of India's National Commission for the Review of the Constitution.

Mvendaga Jibo, a Commonwealth scholar, was educated at the University of Ibadan, Ibadan, Nigeria, and the University of Birmingham, England. He is Chair of the Department of Political Science, University of Jos, Nigeria. His current teaching and research interest includes the Media and Politics,

313

Ethnicity, Traditional Political Institutions, and Political Values. Dr. Jibo is author of *Tiv Politics Since 1959; Politics Mass Media and National Development; Chieftaincy and Politics* and *The Tor Tiv in the Politics and Administration of Tivland.* He has served as Commissioner in the government of Benue state in north-central Nigeria, and on a number of Federal Government Committees.

Asnake Kefale teaches Political Science at the Ethiopian National University, Addis Ababa. He has published extensively on the politics of the Horn of Africa, particularly on the national question in Ethiopia.

Mahmood Mamdani, one of Africa's most profound thinkers—received his Ph.D. in Government from Harvard University and is the current President of the Dakar-based Council for the Development of Social Science Research in Africa (CODESRIA). He was founding Director of the Centre for Basic Research, Kampala, Uganda and Director of the Centre of African Studies at the University of Cape Town before moving to Columbia University, New York, where he is Herbert Lehman Professor of Anthropology and Director, Institute of African Studies. He is author of several path-breaking works, including *Politics and Class Formation in Uganda* (Monthly Review, 1976), and the widely acclaimed *Citizen and Subject: Contemporary Africa and the Legacy of Late Colonialism* (Princeton University Press, 1996).

Bishnu N. Mohapatra is an Associate Professor at the Centre for Political Studies, Jawaharlal Nehru University, Delhi. He was educated at the University of Delhi, Jawaharlal Nehru University and Oxford University. He is currently coordinating a project on "Dialogue on Democracy and Pluralism in South Asia" and serves as a member of the steering committee on Afro-Asian Dialogue on Pluralism, Politics and Identity coordinated by CODESRIA (Dakar) and ICES (Colombo). Some of his current publications include *Democratic Citizenship and Minority Rights: A View from India,* Catarina Kinnvall et. al. (ed.), *Globalization and Democratization in Asia* (2002), London and New York: Routledge, *Social Connectedness and Fragility of Social Capital* (2001), Economic Political Weekly.

Abubakar Momoh belongs to the 'tribe' of social scientists—the political philosopher/theorist—who are an endangered specie in the scholarly community, especially in Africa and whose pre-occupation is the anchorage of social analysis on solid empirical/philosophical foundation, as his contribution in this volume demonstrates. He is currently Senior Lecturer and Chair of the Department of Political Science, Lagos State University. A widely published scholar-activist, Dr. Momoh has to his credit three books—one

314

co-authored (with Said Adejumobi,) and two co-edited (also with Said Adejumobi), the most recent being *The National Question in Nigeria* (London, Ashgate, 2002), and several articles in journals in books.

Tade O. Okediji is an Assistant Professor and the Director of Undergraduate Studies in the Department of Economics at the University of Oklahoma. His research interests are comparative international economic development, economic history and political economy. He is co-author of *Swings of the Pendulum: A Review of Theory and Practice in Development Economics* published in *The American Economist*. Dr. Okediji is currently a research scholar at the Hubert H. Humphrey Institute of Public Affairs at the University of Minnesota, Minneapolis.

Adebayo Olukoshi, currently the Executive Secretary of the Council for the Development of Social Science Research and Development in Africa (CODESRIA), was educated at Ahmadu Bello University, Zaria, where he graduated with a First Class degree in International Studies and proceeded to the University of Leeds for a Ph.D. in International Relations. He was Research Professor of International Relations at the Nigerian Institute for International Affairs from 1993 to 1998, and Senior Research Fellow at the Nordic Africa Institute from 1994–2001 when he assumed the leadership of CODESRIA. A prolific scholar, Olukoshi is a foremost authority on Structural Adjustment in Africa. Among his numerous works is *Challenges to the Nation-State* (with Laakso, Lisa ,1996, Uppsala, Nordiska Africa Institute).

Bade Onimode was Professor Of Economics, University of Ibadan. A one-time Deputy Vice-Chancellor of the University, Onimode was arguably Nigeria's most published economist. A passionate defender of the masses, he was a leading member of the Nigerian Left who succeeded where most other radical scholars had failed: exacting respect and academic 'space' for alternative economic and social visions for Africa from establishment Economics. Author of numerous works, Professor Onimode released his eighth book—*Africa in the World of the 21ˢᵗ Century* (University of Ibadan Press, 2000) and was working on another when death struck.

Eghosa Osaghae is author of the widely acclaimed and most authoritative work on the political development of Nigeria since independence in 1960—*Crippled Giant: Nigeria Since Independence* (London, Hurst & Company, 1998, Second Edition by Indiana University Press, 2002). An authority on the Ethnic Question, Professor Osaghae is Director of the Programme on Ethnic and Federal Studies of the University of Ibadan. He is Chair of the Democracy

Assessment Committee of the African Centre for Democratic Governance.

Charmaine Pereira is an independent scholar-activist living and working in Abuja, Nigeria. She is one of ten founding members of the independent Research Organization—The Centre for Research and Documentation, Kano. The Centre was established to promote the possibility of engaging in social research and policy dialogue at a time when the university system was in serious decline. Dr. Pereira has published extensively on women organizations and feminism, and is currently editing a collection of papers on globalization and democratization. She recently completed a major study on gender and the university system in Nigeria.

Wole Soyinka was 'the tree that made the forest' during the conference at which the papers in this collection were presented. Arguably Africa's most controversial literary guru and Nobel Laureate, Soyinka's literary ebullience is matched by his uncompromising detestation of dictatorship, whether of the Right or of the Left, whether in mufti or in flowing gown, as his keynote address, reproduced here in section one, unequivocally attests to.

Tiruchelvan Neelan was, until his violent death through an assassin's parcel bomb, Director of the International Centre for Ethnic Studies in Colombo, Sri Lanka. It is a pleasant twist of history that the position he took on the governance of his beleaguered country and for which he paid the supreme price is now the basis of the peace accord between the implacable advocates of self-determination and centralized despotism. An accomplished scholar, Professor Tiruchevan was author of several works.

Patricia Williams received her Ph.D. in Political Science from the University of Ibadan, Nigeria. She taught at Ogun State University, rising to the rank of Associate Professor before leaving in 1995 for York University in Toronto, Canada, where she served as Visiting Professor and Kathleen Ptolemy Fellow at the Centre for Refugee Studies. She was Coordinator of the West African Research Network at the Centre until 1997. Thereafter, she remained affiliated to the CRS and coordinated its Working Group on Nigeria between 1998 and 2000. A widely published scholar on the political economy of the African state, religion and violence against women, Dr. Williams' recent publications include *Religious Impact on the Nation-State* (1995) co-edited with Toyin Falola. She is currently completing another co-edited work, *Impact of Islam on Women in Hausaland and Northern Nigeria* with Adebayo Oyebade.

INDEX